50 WOMEN SCULPTORS

First published in the UK in 2020 by Supernova Books, an imprint of Aurora Metro Publications Ltd. 67 Grove Avenue, Twickenham, TW1 4HX

www.aurorametro.com info@aurorametro.com

twitter: @aurorametro F: facebook.com/AuroraMetroBooks

Editor: Cheryl Robson

Production Editors: Christian Müller and Cheryl Robson

Researchers: Anna Veprinska, Sam Spranger, Taylor Gill, Bella Taylor

Aurora Metro Books would like to thank Marina Tuffier, Ferroccio Viridiani, Saskia Calliste

Printed by T.J. International, UK on FSC grade paper

ISBNs: 978-0-9932207-7-7 (print)

978-1-913641-00-9 (ebook)

LOTTERY FUNDED

Supported using public funding by

ARTS COUNCIL ENGLAND

FOREWORD

Melissa Hamnett

Many twentieth-century women artists have fallen into obscurity. In part this has been a result of male dominance in the art world during the first half of the twentieth century and a prevailing assumption that women's creativity and skill as artists is not equal to men's. Linda Nochlin's seminal 1971 essay changed all that, shifting both the field of art history and the viewers' gaze. Since then, women have been an increasing focus of art-historical research and museums and galleries have responded actively to ensure the work of women artists, particularly of the late nineteenth and twentieth century, has been given its rightful place in the broader canon.

From the perspective of sculpture, however, the reappraisal of the role of women still has far to go. For too long sculptural histories have been solely dominated by men, upheld not least by the myth that, as a physically challenging medium, women artists could not or did not make ambitious sculpture due to "the strength and skill required to work traditional materials". Worse still, talented female sculptors such as Camille Claudel (1864–1943) or Malvina Hoffman (1887–1966) spent much of their careers – and indeed some of their art-history afterlife – in the full shadow of their male counterparts, such as Auguste Rodin. In recent years, the exposure of these extraordinary women's talents has been brought to the fore, alongside the increased promotion of better-known twentieth-century figures such as Barbara Hepworth and Louise Bourgeois. But in the main, female sculptors past and present remain almost as underrepresented in current scholarship as they once did in the artists' dictionaries of their day.

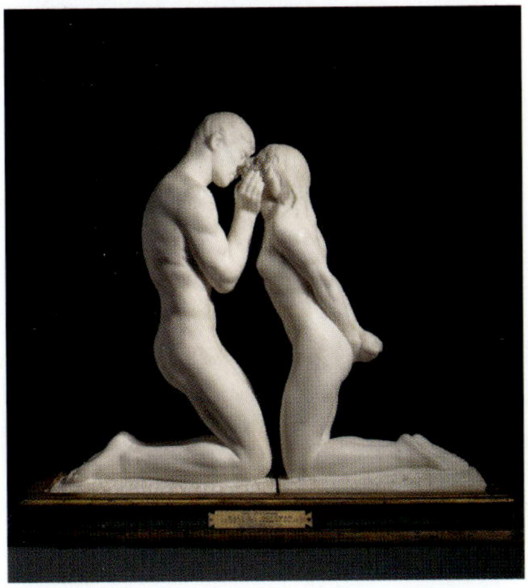

The Offering 1919 by Malvina Hoffman

Excellent inroads into the history of women sculptors have been made by scholars such as Marjan Sterckx writing on eighteenth-century artists such as Anne Damer (1748–1828), or by Melissa Dabakis writing on nineteenth-century American women, such as Harriet Hosmer (1830–1908). These lesser-known narratives remind us that within the broader context of patriarchal power structures, it was possible for a minority of women to exercise control and autonomy in aspects of their professional and personal lives and markedly contribute to the discipline of sculpture. In a similar vein, museum acquisitions such as a marble bust in the V&A dating to 1741 and attributed to Lady Henrietta Finch, present extraordinary instances of eighteenth-century women sculptors active long before they were admitted to art academies at the end of the following century. Although little known, these inspiring role models laid the foundation for an increasing number of women to enter the field of sculpture in the twentieth century and contribute to its creativity and ingenuity today.

With over a century since the Representation of the People Act (1918), (which gave women over 30 years of age the right to vote in Britain) this publication provides an important opportunity to re-examine the vital role of women artists across the globe, their spheres of influence and the cultural and political legacies that they have overcome. This political milestone was marked significantly by a sculpture commission of a woman by a woman: a bronze of the suffragist leader Millicent Fawcett by the Turner Prize-winning artist, Gillian Wearing. It is fitting therefore that this publication will focus on the lives and careers of fifty female sculptors, situating their practice within the wider context of modern and contemporary art. These women have not just altered the perception of sculpture today as a male-dominated art form, they have recalibrated it with themes and subjects drawn from their own, distinctly female, experience.

Melissa Hamnett

Melissa Hamnett is Head of Heritage Collections and Chief Curator at the Houses of Parliament responsible for the Parliamentary Art Collection, the Historic Furniture and Decorative Arts Collection and the Architectural Fabric Collection. Formerly Curator of Sculpture at the V&A.

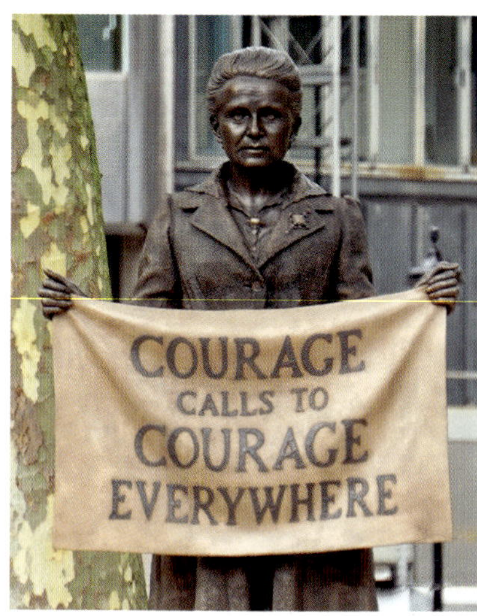

Millicent Fawcett – Courage calls 2018
by Gillian Wearing – Parliament Square
Photo: Garry Knight

50 WOMEN SCULPTORS

Dedicated to the memory of Dora Gordine,
a talented woman sculptor whose home, Dorich House,
is now a museum open to the public in Kingston, UK.

CONTENTS

2. CONTEMPORARY WOMEN SCULPTORS

INTRODUCTION

Joanna Sperryn-Jones

DOES IT MAKE A DIFFERENCE IF A MAN OR A WOMAN MAKES AN ARTWORK?

50 Women Sculptors does not seek to define a women's art by finding common threads, but instead, to highlight the huge diversity of practices in the use of materials, subject matter, scale and approaches to making. Women who come from a wealthy background will have a different experience of life from those from a poor background, older women different from younger, white women different from women of colour, a mother different from a daughter, a wife from those who are single. Along with this variety of life experiences and subject positions, there is also a diversity of approaches to dealing with the continuing dominance of the white western male in the canon of art history. In addition to raising the profile of women sculptors, this book raises questions around inequality, eliciting views on this from current female practitioners.

This book does not try and rank artists in any order. It seeks to celebrate female artistic heritage and to offer a broad range of contemporary artists working in a variety of media today. The juxtaposition of the section titled 'Pioneers and Legends' with the section on 'Contemporary Women Sculptors' enables the reader to consider the ways in which significant women sculptors have contributed to the context in which women sculptors work now. This influence is evident in many of the current sculptors' reflections on their practice. In the first section, the sculptors are listed in chronological order so that the reader can gain a historical overview of how the nature of sculpture has developed, whereas, in the contemporary section, the sculptors are listed in alphabetical order to avoid placing them in contrived categories and to enable the reader to make their own reflections on the questions raised in this introduction.

In creating a list of women sculptors, their almost complete absence from the canon prior to the twentieth century is immediately notable; this is even more marked than in the corresponding case of women painters. This can be partly explained by their exclusion from the canon of art history, but they faced additional adversity. Several waves of feminism have improved the situation, as have those women sculptors who have managed to establish recognition for their sculpture practice. However, as I discuss below and as is expressed unanimously through the current sculptors' views, the situation remains predictably unsatisfactory today.

DO THE BODILY, ECONOMIC AND SOCIAL EXPERIENCES OF WOMEN INFLUENCE THE MAKING OF ARTWORK?

Women did not gain the right to vote in the UK until 1918, and they only gained equal voting rights to men in 1928. This change in social status was driven by suffragists campaigning from the end of the nineteenth century. Women were not admitted to the Royal Academy Schools until 1860. Prior to this, women's options for instruction were from family or paid private tuition, often making this the preserve of those who could afford it. A majority of female artists in this earlier period engaged with painting, with only an exceptional few learning to sculpt. Stone carving was the most common form of sculpture while bronze casting only became popular again towards the end of the nineteenth century. It is easy to imagine the adversity faced by women wanting to pursue stone carving at this time as it involves more physical labour than painting, creates mess, so is less suitable for working at home, and the weight of stone makes it difficult to move without equipment. Stone is viewed as a resistant material that requires both physical and mental strength to shape, qualities which were viewed as masculine and not in keeping with feminine behaviour at that time.

Women who succeeded in learning to carve faced the difficulty of establishing themselves within the public realm of work, which was seen as a masculine arena. Those few who achieved this have mostly been left out of the canon of art history. A notable early Italian woman sculptor, Properzia de Rossi (c.1490–1530) developed a talent for carving fruit stones at home before expanding into the public realm and winning commissions to create large-scale stone carvings. Her career was cut short when she was persecuted by a male painter, resulting in damage to her reputation.[1] The American artist Harriet Hosmer (1830–1908) made her mark on the art world, and her reputation has been resurrected by feminists in the twentieth century seeking to reclaim women's art history. Hosmer's friend, Edmonia Lewis (1844–1907), the first African-American woman sculptor to work professionally, has also recently been given long overdue recognition.

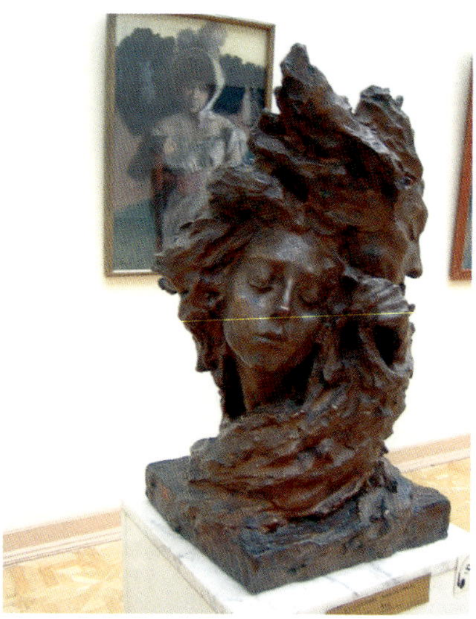

The Mist by Anna Golubkina

In France, Camille Claudel (1864–1943) is now one of the best-known women sculptors pre-1900, but she was overshadowed by Rodin during her lifetime. Taking Claudel's position after she left Rodin and working for three years as his assistant, Anna Golubkina (1864–1927), was the first notable Russian woman sculptor, [see *The Mist* left], followed a generation later by Vera Mukhina (1889–1953), who was nicknamed

1 Fine, E. H. (1978) *Women and Art*. New Jersey: Allanheld & Schram. p.8-9.

"the queen of Soviet sculpture" and now has a museum in her honour in Feodosia, Crimea.

DO WE READ THE ARTWORK DIFFERENTLY IF THE CREATOR IS A WOMAN RATHER THAN A MAN?

Male accomplishment in sculpture has been much invested in the study of the nude female body. The lack of access to the life room before the late nineteenth century made it difficult for women to study the female form. Rodin's sculptures evidence clear gender stereotypes in his portrayal of both men and women. Men are presented as thinkers, powerful and courageous, whereas women are dancers and muses. The female body is an object to be looked at by the male subject, whether artist or viewer. This notion continues to dominate in contemporary art and so the representation of the female body is an on-going area of debate for women artists today.

HOW DO WOMEN SCULPTORS DEAL WITH THE FEMALE FORM ONCE IT HAS BEEN SEXUALIZED AND OWNED BY MEN?

Camille Claudel offers glimpses of new portrayals of women in her work, especially in her choice of an ageing woman as a subject in *Clotho* (1893) and *Maturity* (1899). She portrays not a gracefully maturing woman but one that has been worn by the stresses of life and broken down to the point of insanity. This is not a female form to be desired by men but one that has been frustrated and obliterated by a patriarchal society. She gives presence to ageing women, but the hysteria expressed does not contribute to an empowering representation. As is often the case with oppression, the frustrated emotions expressed by the oppressed are used as further "evidence" of their inferiority by those in power. For the last thirty years of her life, Camille Claudel was committed to a psychiatric hospital by her brother Paul.[2] Ultimately, her exceptional sculptural talent, persistent energy and ability to express the human condition have proved impossible to erase. Not only has she become celebrated in sculpture, but she has informed and inspired many women sculptors following her, including many of those working now.

Alina Szapocznikow (1926-1973) made partial casts of her own body that emphasize the viscous nature of the human body but these are awkward and slightly repellent; a half-head filled with cigarette butts, or shrivelled rubbery skin with disjointed body parts. It's probable that the disturbing experience of being interned in Nazi concentration camps as a young person is expressed through her sculptures. Sarah Lucas (1968–) revels in the filthy and vulgar salaciousness of both male and female bodies; cigarette butts protrude from a variety of bodily openings and flesh is formed from lumpily stuffed tights with a prevalence of sexual body parts. She reveals the indignity of the desiring body.

During her lifetime, Niki de Saint Phalle (1930–2002) completed many public

2 Paris. R. M. (1988) *Camille: The Life of Camille Claudel, Rodin's Muse and Mistress.* London: Aurum Press. xxvii- xxviii.

Hon by Niki de Saint Phalle 1966 – Moderna Museet, Sweden.

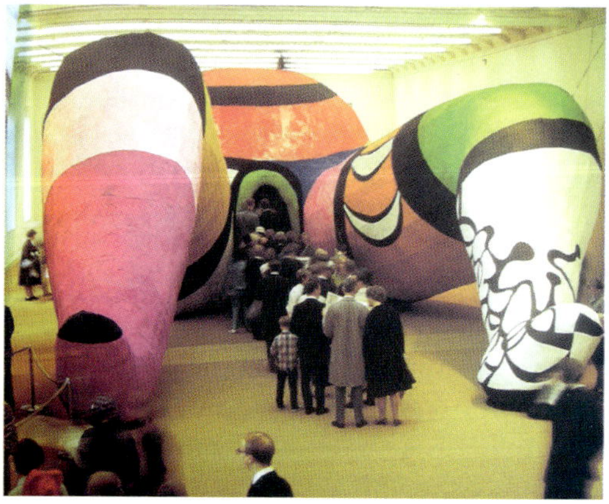

commissions for sculptures of women on a monumental scale including *Hon* (1966) (with Jean Tinguely and Per Olof Ultvel), which was 82 feet long and 30 feet wide and could be entered by visitors through the vagina [left]. Her work celebrates the female body as something to be lived in, rather than merely gazed upon. The scale emphasizes the power of these goddess sculptures.

Annie Attridge (1975–) works on a small scale in porcelain but also celebrates the female body as experienced in its lived sensuality. Her sculptures are not of a body to be desired but a desiring body with its own agency. The naughtiness of her desiring subjects subverts the conservativism associated with porcelain as ornamentation in the home.

HOW DO WOMEN SCULPTORS DEAL WITH THE MASCULINE OR FEMININE ASSOCIATIONS WITH MATERIALS?

Women sculptors have worked in a wide variety of materials from those associated with feminine crafts, such as soft fabrics and ceramics, to those considered masculine and industrial, such as large metal fabrications or new technology.

HOW DO WOMEN SCULPTORS CHOOSE WHICH MATERIALS TO WORK WITH AND WHY?

It might be thought that women have more chance of success by establishing themselves in using masculine "serious" sculpture materials, such as stone, metal and wood and many of the women sculptors in this book have chosen this route, often reclaiming those materials to their own ends. Others have chosen to raise the status of feminine crafts by working in textiles, ceramics or glass. More recently, female artists have combined performative elements, created installations or made use of digital technology to express their ideas, but there seems to be no general principle at work as to whether women choose to work with permanent or transient materials, or those which are resistant or easy to manipulate.

When Judy Chicago (1939–) first developed an interest in china plates, she was ambivalent: "Classically trained as a fine artist, I felt somewhat uneasy with my interest in decorative arts."[3] She attended classes to learn to paint china, and at first felt they were hobbyist rather than "serious", but then realized many of the women in the class had gone to art school and were looking to create something of value. Painting china meant they didn't have to choose between their work and family life.[4]

3 Chicago, J. (1979) 'The Dinner Party: A Symbol of Our Heritage'. In Stiles, K. & Selz, P. (1996) *Theories and Documents of Contemporary Art: a Sourcebook of Artists' Writings*. p.358.
4 ibid p.359.

She chose to work on china dinner plates for this very reason: "The china-painting world, and the household objects the women painted, seemed to be a perfect metaphor for women's domesticated and trivialised circumstances." In this instance, raising the status of the craft worked well, because it contained strong concepts and ambitions, and the many plates assembled on the dinner tables for *The Dinner Party* (1974–79) formed a significantly sized artwork. [5]

The first sculptural dress I saw by Susan Stockwell (1962–) was a wedding dress made from used coffee filters and cupcake cases. The romance of a wedding dress is subverted by the waste products of a household kitchen, stereotypically the place of the housewife, and this reminds us of everyday living and chores. Louise Bourgeois (1911–2010), on the other hand, says she can express herself best in marble because it requires "Persistence, repetition, the things that drive you towards tenacity, that force you to be tenacious. I am a tenacious person."[6] The material suits her personality. She has this in common with Claudel, and it is a good observation that carving needs tenacity and practise rather than physical strength as is often portrayed. Both Stockwell and Bourgeois work across a broad range of materials with both masculine and feminine connotations.

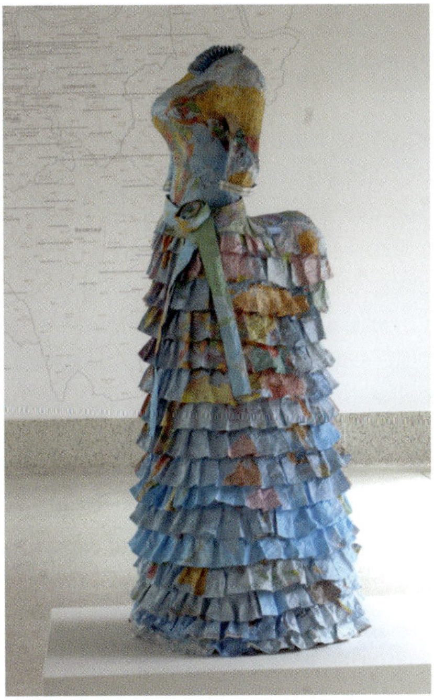

Colonial Dress by Susan Stockwell 2010
Photo: Colin Hampden-White

Rebecca Horn (1944–) created idiosyncratic machines to present a hybrid of manmade mechanics and the rhythms of nature through their unpredictable timing and movement. Horn deliberately mixes gendered associations in her machines: guns limply fire red liquid pumped from breast-like forms, a grand piano hung from the ceiling performs by spilling its guts, machine birds flap little paintbrush wings. The machines seem fragile, quirky, tentative.

Rachael Ara (1965–) trained as an artist, but then worked as a computer systems designer, and this has given her a strong foundation for the utilization of technology within her artwork. Ara's work frequently focuses on gender politics. *This Much I'm Worth* (2017) calculated its own worth! Ara wrote a programme to take into consideration the varying and changing factors that could alter its value, including the fact of it being made by a woman and that tweeting about the work increases its value. It raises questions about the value of art.

5 ibid p.360
6 Bourgeois, L. (1988) 'Interview with Donald Kuspit'. In Stiles, K. & Selz, P. (1996) *Theories and Documents of Contemporary Art: a Sourcebook of Artists' Writings.*

dock by Phyllida Barlow 2014 –Tate Britain Photo: © Tate

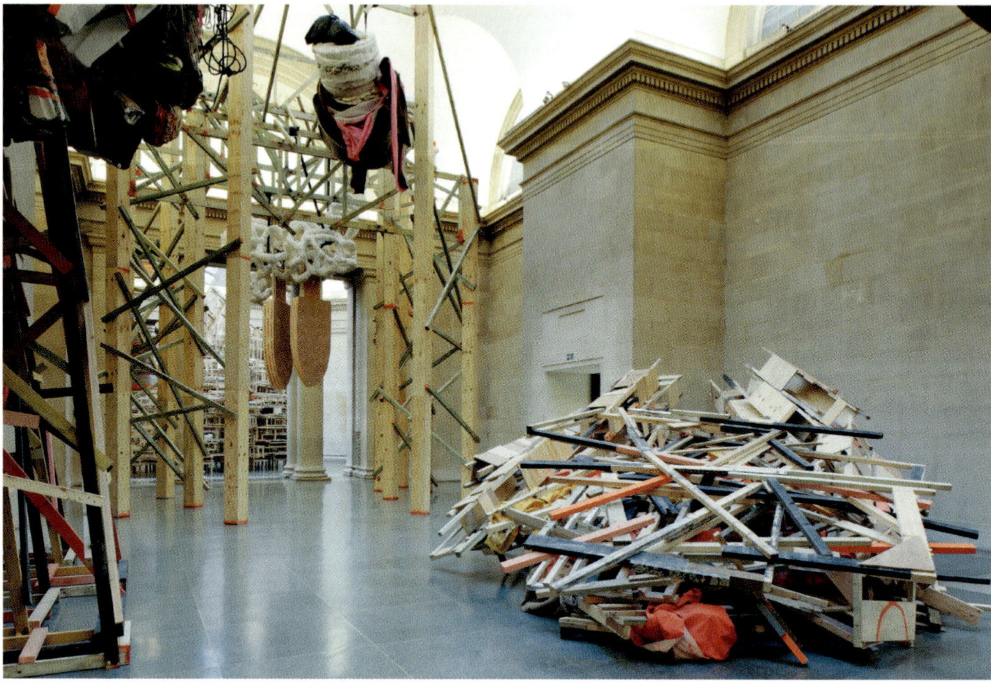

Phyllida Barlow (1944–) says, "*Tip* was made of cement, timber, steel mesh, and lots of different fabrics. I love the mixture: it's like really bad cooking, because the fabric and cement get all tangled."[7] The brightly coloured strips of fabric in *Tip* (2013) provide a strong contrast to the enormous grey cemented wood structure. Elsewhere, she uses giant fabric pompoms or large cement-covered polystyrene architectural pieces. She doesn't choose between traditionally masculine or feminine materials, she subverts both seamlessly. In *dock*, Barlow creates work on a monumental scale which seems to be collapsing and the antithesis of permanency. *Dock* obstructs the path of the spectator and their view of the grand Tate architecture with its rampant growth. Yet this dominance contrasts with its ramshackle appearance and use of degradable materials, such as cardboard. In talking about the subject of her work Phyllida Barlow says: "I've become fascinated by the fact that nothing is permanent. Nature constantly falls apart and rebuilds itself through huge events like tsunamis or volcanoes and small events like the change of seasons. Our mark on the planet is similar, and for me, sculpture is also about that, particularly in how I participate with materials that have their own way of being. Destruction and construction, or damage and repair, do meet in some way, however uncomfortably, and that's exactly what the sculptural process is about."[8]

In *The Creative Feminine and Her Discontents,* Juliet Miller observes that aggression

7. Cole, I. (2016) 'Simple actions: A Conversation with Phyllida Barlow' In *Sculpture Magazine*. May 2016.

8. ibid.

and destruction are often perceived as masculine traits and "forbidden" for women.[9] Miller proposes that in harnessing violence and destruction, a woman can temporarily be released from gendered restraints.[10]

DO GENDERED EXPECTATIONS OF BEHAVIOUR EFFECT THE PROCESSES BY WHICH WOMEN MAKE SCULPTURE?

During the last seven years of her working life, Claudel continued to sculpt intensively, but as a friend, Henry Asselin, recounts: "…each summer Camille would systematically destroy with hammer blows all her work of that year. Both her studios offered up a pathetic spectacle of ruin and devastation." [11]

By erasing her work, Claudel removed part of her legacy from the world and diminished her chance of professional success, a deliberately self-destructive act. In *Destruction of the Father* (1974), Bourgeois directs her destructive impulse straight towards her narrated cause – the father. She describes "the awful, terrifying family dinner table headed by the father who sits and gloats". The wife and children appear helpless in the face of his power until, "in exasperation, we grabbed the man, threw him on the table, dismembered him and proceeded to devour him".[12] Juliet Miller notes the attack is not just on Bourgeois's own father but on our phallocentric society. Bourgeois has moved from a position of restraint in the face of patriarchal authority to empowerment through taking control. Empowerment is determined both by what is destroyed and who is creating the destruction.

Niki de Saint Phalle used a gun to perform shooting paint on her sculptures. The important element here is not what is shot but that a woman is doing the shooting. Cornelia Parker (1956–) is best-known for her sculptural installation *Cold Dark Matter* (1991), where she employed the British army to blow up a shed. Parker retains a distance from the physical violence of the destruction, instead directing male-dominated professions to destroy the objects for her. However, she is the one in control. Regarding Cornelia Parker's sculptural installations Miller proposes: "By embracing her aggressive fantasies she breaks the link with culturally accepted forms of female creativity and finds instead a new creative path. The transgressive nature of this act is crucial in enabling the woman to temporarily release herself from gendered constraints." [13]

Doris Salcedo (1958–) created *Shibboleth* (2007), the crack through the Tate Modern Turbine Hall, which performs a visual threat to the patriarchal structure of the Tate galleries, which were being widely criticized for discriminatory practices in being almost entirely focused on the white western male. The timing of this work could not have been more appropriate, as the Tate galleries started a shift around this time

9 Miller, J. (2008) *The Creative Feminine and her Discontents*. London: Karnac Books p.122
10 ibid p.129
11 Paris. R.-M. (1988) *Camille: The Life of Camille Claudel, Rodin's Muse and Mistress*. London: Aurum Press. p.67.
12 Miller, J. (2008) *The Creative Feminine and her Discontents*. London: Karnac Books p.112.
13 ibid. p.113

in London to exhibit artwork that would better reflect the diversity of the audience in the city. The first woman Tate director, Maria Balshaw, was placed in post a decade later in 2017, shortly followed by Frances Morris at the Tate Modern. I'd like to think Salcedo's work had some influence.

HOW CAN THE DISCRIMINATION AGAINST WOMEN IN SCULPTURE BE REDRESSED?

The majority of current women sculptors in this book said they still felt it was more difficult for women artists to make a living than for men. The Freelands Foundation report for 2018 supports this perception. Although in many arenas women are equally represented – for example, in non-commercial galleries, as recipients of arts council grants and as nominees for the Turner Prize – in the business of selling art or employment in the arts industry, women continue to be under-represented: only 32% of artists represented by London's major commercial galleries are women and only 12% of Sotheby's Contemporary Art Evening Sales are by women artists. In academia, only 37% of the highest paid academic staff are female.[14] Overall, there has been a significant improvement over the last decade, but it would be good to see this trend continue.

For *The Dinner Party* (1979) [below detail], Judy Chicago researched significant women in history and chose to both reinstate them and emphasize how they had been "swallowed" by history by painting them onto dinner plates. During the process she reflected: "History has been written from the point of view of those who have been in power. It is not an objective record of the human race – we do not know the history of humankind. A true history would allow us to see the mingled efforts of people of all colours and sexes, all countries and races, all seeing the universe in their own diverse ways." [15]

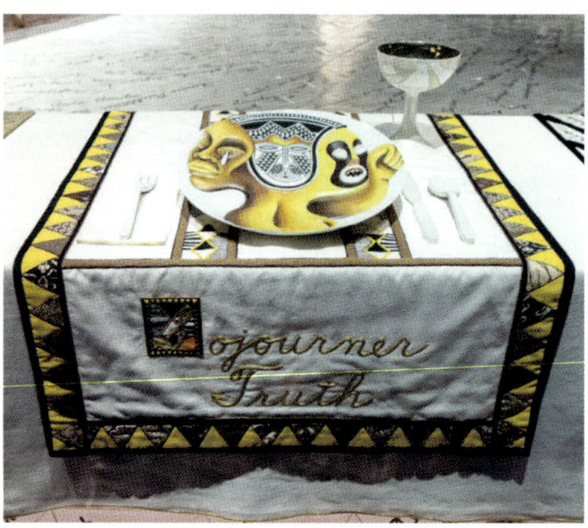

50 Women Sculptors attempts to show the diversity of practices, but this is difficult given on-going discrimination. Many of the artists in this book are from the UK or USA, showing the on-going cultural inequality. The situation is changing as institutions such as Tate make an effort to exhibit a more diverse range of artists.

I was also pleased to see that the Yorkshire Sculpture International 2019 had made a great effort to give significant

14. McMillan, K. (2019) *Representation of Female Artists in Britain During 2018*. London: The Freelands Foundation
15. Chicago, J. (1979) 'The Dinner Party: A Symbol of Our Heritage'. In Stiles, K. & Selz, P. (1996) *Theories and Documents of Contemporary Art: A Sourcebook of Artists' Writings*. p.362.
Above: Sojourner Truth *The Dinner Party* detail by Judy Chicago 1979 Photo: Jim Kuhn

space to women sculptors, and in particular, from different cultural backgrounds.

It has been a long and difficult process to select only 50 women sculptors to include here due to the numerous influential female practitioners who are now achieving success in various ways. Some of those not included are amongst my personal favourites having informed my own sculptural practice. I hope the reader sees this book as a starting point to explore more women sculptors. To name only a few: Nairy Baghramian, Lynda Benglis, Huma Bhabha, Christine Borland, Sylvie Fleury, Ann Hamilton, Nancy Holt, Cristina Iglesias, Cathy de Monchaux, Louise Nevelson, Chiharu Shiota, Kiki Smith, Sarah Sze, Tomoko Takahashi, Rosemarie Trockel, Ursula Von Rydingsvard, Pae White and Alison Wilding. As a practising sculptor myself, reading the journeys, thoughts and views of the current women sculptors, has given me much to reflect on in the choices I have made and can still make, in navigating what has been a male-dominated arena. I hope that other women sculptors will also find these contributions by artists in their own words as useful as I have.

It is not only artists, curators and historians who can influence the status of women sculptors. As museum visitors can vote with their feet, I hope this book will inspire the reader to seek out and visit exhibitions from the many ground-breaking women sculptors included here and beyond.

Dr. Joanna Sperryn-Jones

Joanna Sperryn-Jones is a Senior Lecturer in Fine Art Sculpture Practice at York St John University. As a sculptor she has had numerous exhibitions and has written many articles about art and sculpture notably: 'Cutting up conference papers: audience participation in breaking as making' in *Artistic Research: Strategies for Embodiment*, McGuirk, Tom & Fentz, Christine (eds.) Nordic Summer University Press (2015), 'Breaking as making: A methodology for visual work reflected in writing' in *Art and Destruction*, Walden, Jenny (ed.) Cambridge Scholars Press (2013).

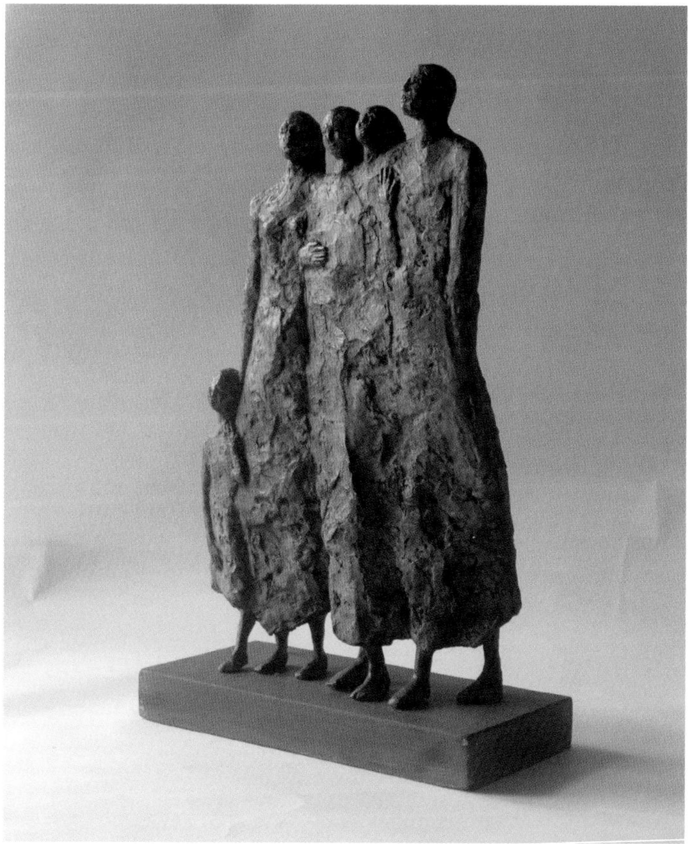

Family Group by Janis Ridley Photo: courtesy of the artist

50 WOMEN SCULPTORS

1. PIONEERS AND LEGENDS

"I honor every woman who has strength enough to step out of the beaten path when she feels that her walk lies in another."
– Harriet Hosmer

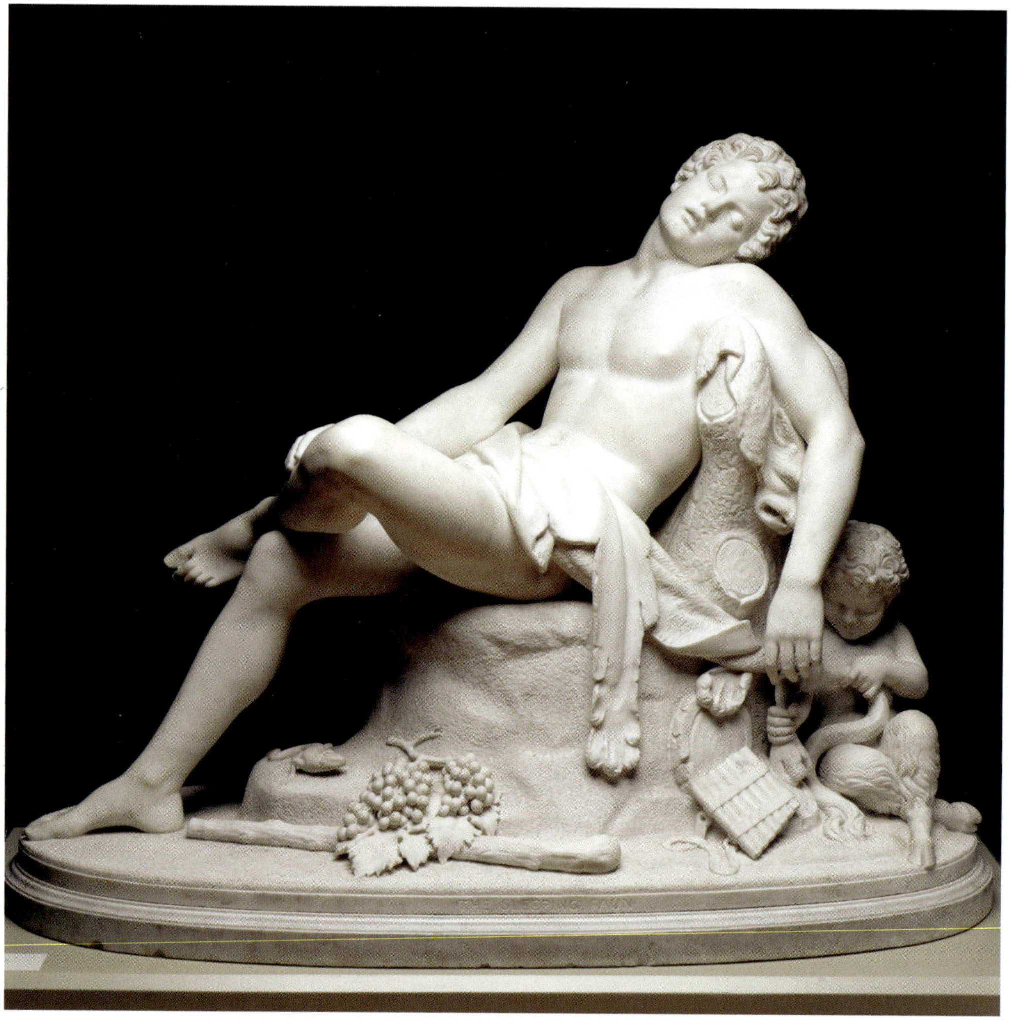

Above: *The Sleeping Faun* 1870 – Cleveland Museum of Art
Right: *The Clasped Hands of Elizabeth and Robert Browning* 1853 – Metropolitan Museum of Art

HARRIET HOSMER

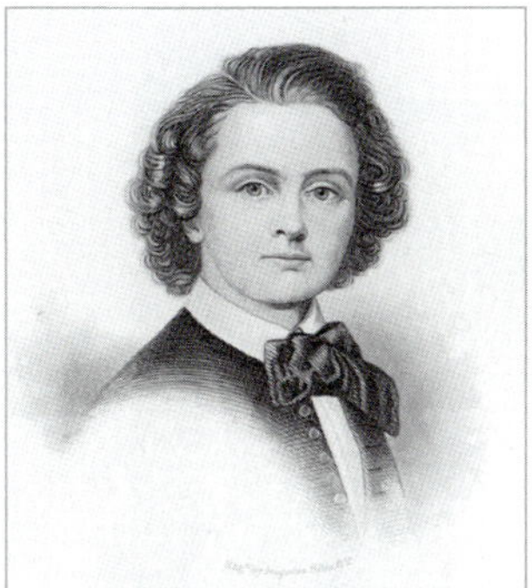

Harriet Hosmer (1830–1908) is widely considered to be the world's first successful woman sculptor. Born in Watertown, Massachusetts, her three siblings as well as her mother all succumbed to tuberculosis. In a bid to preserve the health of his surviving daughter, her father encouraged an active lifestyle. She became highly skilled in rowing, skating and riding at a time when active pursuits were generally considered the reserve of men alone. She attended the progressive Mrs Charles Sedgwick's School for Girls, where she was surrounded by many creative female role models.

Harriet wanted to study neoclassical sculpture, but in order to do this, she had to take an anatomy course. She applied to Boston Medical School but was denied admittance due to her gender. Her father managed to secure her instruction at Missouri Medical College and after passing the course, she sailed to Rome where she studied under the Welsh sculptor, John Gibson.

It was there that she was finally allowed to sculpt from live models and she became friends with other writers and artists including George Eliot, William Thackeray, Nathaniel Hawthorne and George Sand. When in Florence, she stayed at Casa Guidi, the home of Elizabeth Barrett and Robert Browning. When her father ran into financial trouble and was no longer able to support her, she sold fifty copies of her first notable work, *Puck* (1855) based on the character from *A Midsummer Night's Dream*. Her male contemporaries, perhaps out of jealousy, accused her of relying on others to create her work. Unperturbed, she went on to be commissioned by the State of Missouri to produce a monumental bronze of state senator Thomas Hart Benton. She had many more prominent and lucrative commissions throughout her life that surpassed many of her male contemporaries.

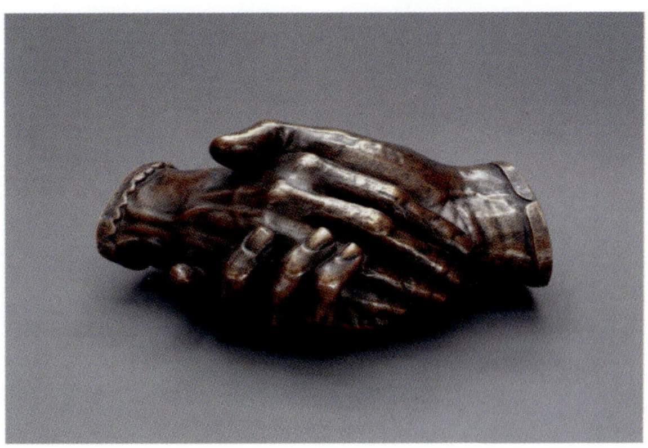

For twenty-five years she was romantically involved with Louisa, Lady Ashburton, a widowed Scottish art collector and philanthropist. Later in life, Hosmer also helped pioneer a process of turning limestone to marble. She died in 1908 in her hometown of Watertown.

"Until I was 12 years old I led this wandering life, fishing and swimming ... and making moccasins. I was then sent to school for three years but was declared to be wild – they could do nothing with me." – **Edmonia Lewis**

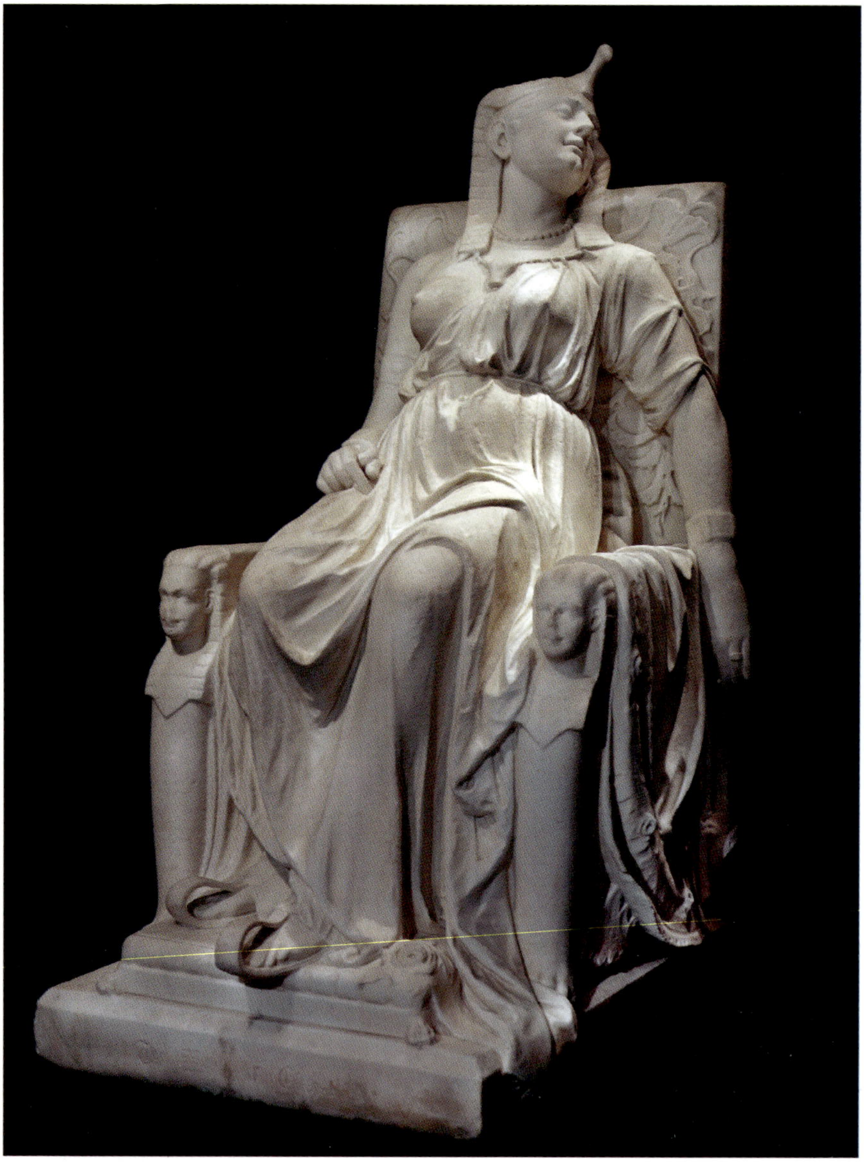

Above: *The Death of Cleopatra* 1876 – Smithsonian American Art Museum
Right: *Hiawatha* 1868 – Metropolitan Museum of Art

EDMONIA LEWIS

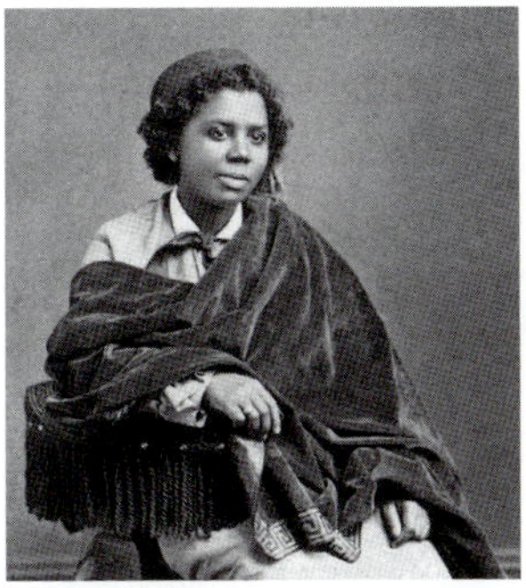

Edmonia Lewis (1844–1907) was the first African-American woman to become a professional sculptor. Born of Haitian and Native American Chippewa descent in the city of Rensselaer, her mother was a craftswoman who sold souvenirs to tourists, while her father was a gentleman's servant. Orphaned by the age of nine, she was adopted by her maternal aunts. Her half-brother Samuel went to California and made money in the gold rush and was able to pay for her to have an education. In 1856, Lewis enrolled at McGrawville, a Baptist abolitionist school in New York. There, she met many of the leading abolitionists who would help her in her artistic career. Her first success came from the sale of clay medallions with portraits of renowned abolitionists, including William Lloyd Garrison, John Brown and Wendell Phillips, an advocate for Native Americans. In 1864, she created a bust of deceased Civil War hero, Colonel Robert Shaw, who had commanded a troupe of African-American soldiers. The financial returns from this enabled her to travel to Europe. In Rome, fellow American, Harriet Hosmer, helped Lewis to pursue her art by finding her a studio that had once belonged to a famous Venetian sculptor, Antonio Canova. Although Hosmer could afford to employ local Italian carvers to make her sculptures, Lewis chiselled most of her own work herself.

During her time in Rome, Lewis created *The Death of Cleopatra,* a large and powerful work which took over four years and a great deal of money to complete. She had to return to the United States to sell some of her smaller sculptures to fund the project. In 1876, she finally completed the monolithic sculpture and had it shipped to Philadelphia for consideration by the committee selecting works for the Centennial Exhibition. Although many thought it too graphic in its portrayal of the dying moments of the famous Egyptian queen, the committee approved the sculpture and had it placed in Gallery K of the Memorial Hall, which had been designated as a space for the work of American artists.

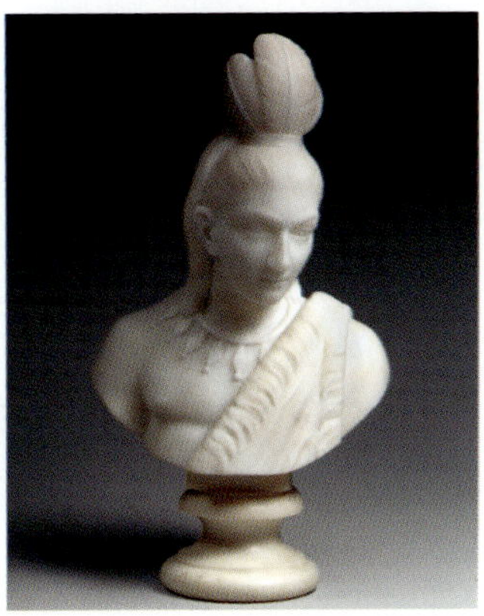

The popularity of Longfellow's 1855 epic poem, *The Song of Hiawatha*, enabled Lewis to make use of her Chippewa heritage and in 1868, she sculpted a pair of marble busts, depicting both the characters of Hiawatha and his Minnehaha, which are on display at the Metropolitan Museum of Art in New York. She died in Hammersmith, London in 1907.

"I am scared; I don't know what is going to happen to me. What was the point of working so hard and of being talented, to be rewarded like this? Never a penny, tormented all my life." **– Camille Claudel**

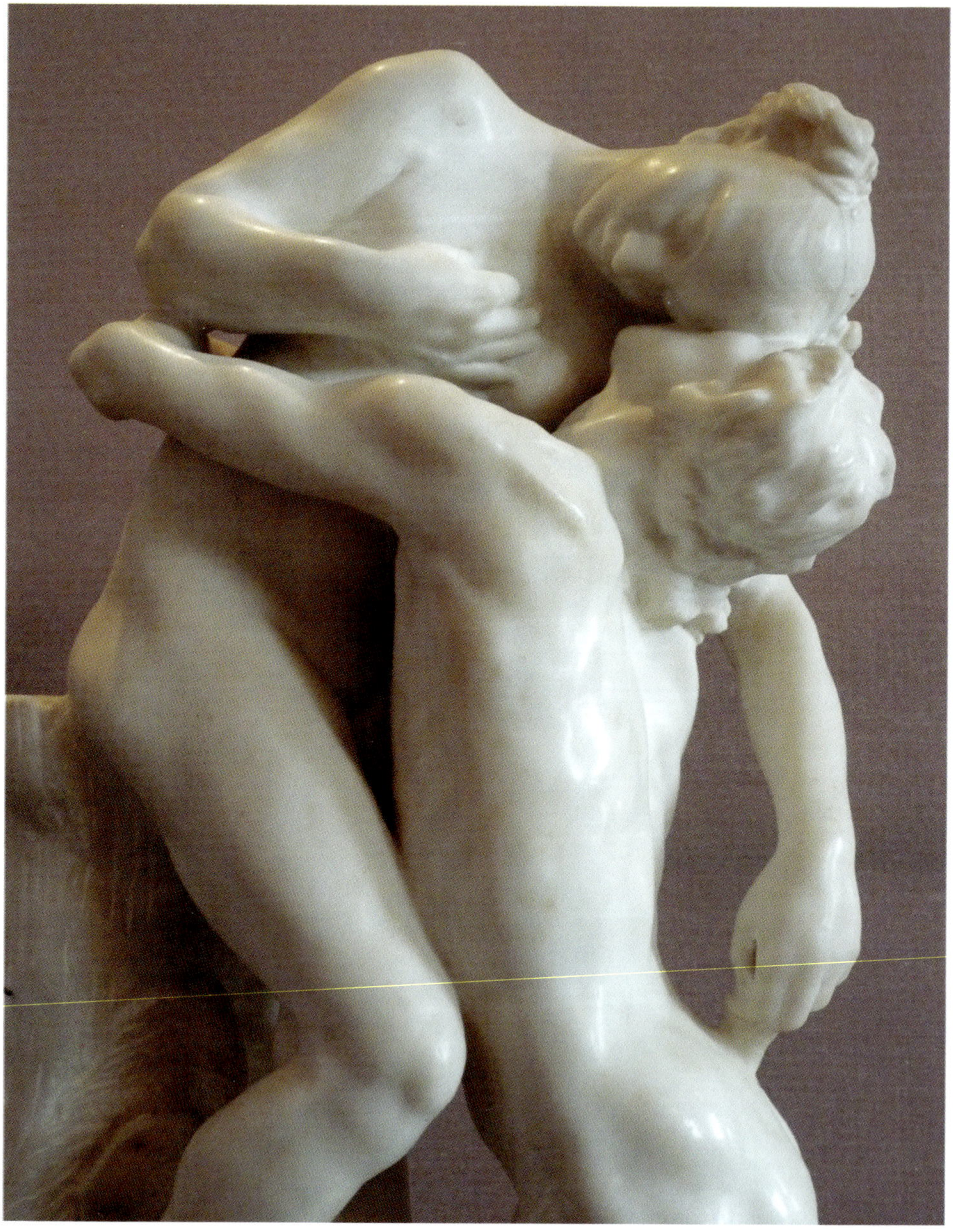

Above: *Sakuntala* or *Vertumnus and Pomona* 1905 – Musée Rodin, Paris.
Right: Camille Claudel in her studio with Jessie Lipscomb on the right. c.1887

CAMILLE CLAUDEL

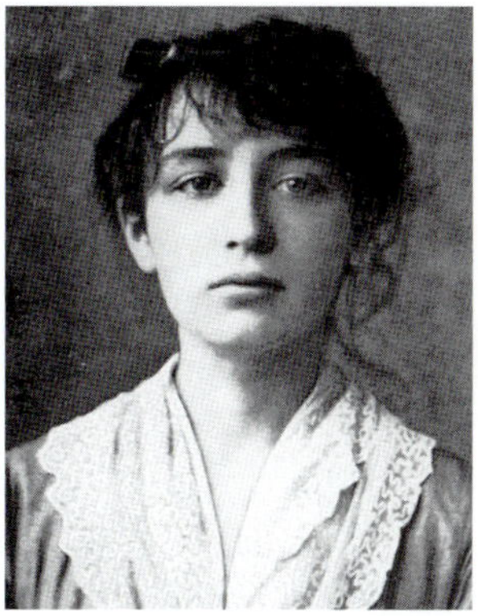

Camille Claudel (1864–1943) was born in Fère-en-Tardenois, France, into a wealthy family. Unable to study at the École des Beaux-Arts, she trained instead at one of the few places that did admit female students – the Académie Colarossi.

At the age of 18, she was being guided by the sculptor Alfred Boucher, who introduced Rodin to her as a replacement tutor. She rented a studio and worked with other artists such as Jessie Lipscomb. In 1884, she began to work in Rodin's workshop, and thus their turbulent and intense affair began. Due to social constraints and the often masculine nature of her work, she became reliant on Rodin to produce or put his name to her sculptures. It is uncertain how much of her work remains uncredited, but it is clear that the two artists influenced each other's work considerably.

Claudel's family disapproved of her lifestyle and following her father's death, her mother and brother, the influential French poet Paul Claudel, cut her off financially, leaving her almost entirely dependent on Rodin. After ten years, her relationship with Rodin broke down and she was able to free herself from his influence. However, Claudel continually suffered from financial troubles and mental illness, harbouring a deep resentment towards Rodin. An important government commission in 1905 was cancelled. Her paranoia led her to believe that Rodin, whom she nicknamed 'The Ferret', conspired to steal her ideas. By 1911, frustrated by the critics' negative response to her work, she destroyed many of her sculptures, with only around ninety remaining today.

In 1913, her family requested she be committed to the Ville-Évrard mental asylum near Paris. She ceased sculpting entirely and was later moved to a sanatorium where she remained until her death in 1943. Her family rarely visited her in this time, and she tragically ended up buried in a communal grave.

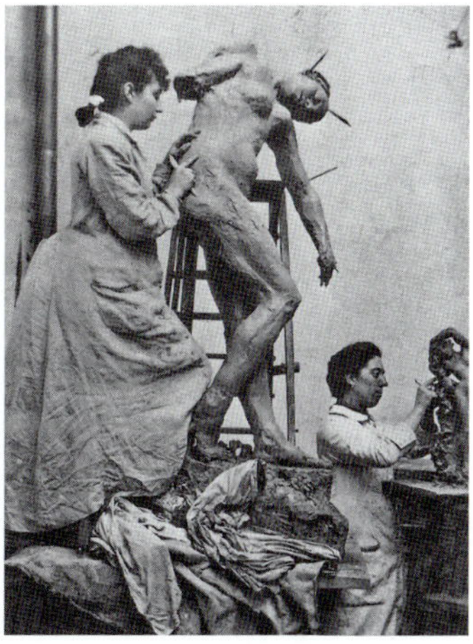

In 2017, the Musée Camille Claudel opened in Nogent-sur-Seine, Claudel's former home town. The museum honours her legacy and displays many of her works. On the 70th anniversary of her death, the Musée Rodin paid tribute to Claudel by presenting its collection of around twenty of the artist's works, many donated by her brother, Paul.

Many books and films have been made about the artist's life and her sculptures are now highly prized.

***"The development of self as a whole goes into your work. But it takes work. Work, work, work."* – Frances Loring**

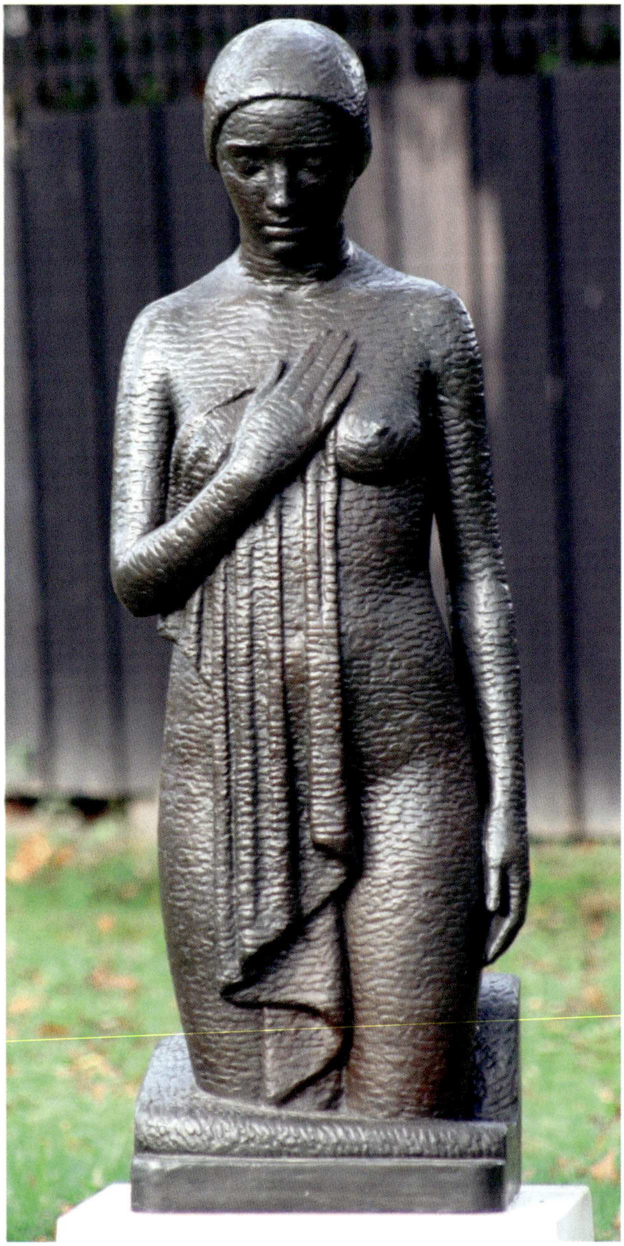

Above: *Young Girl* by Florence Wyle 1938
Right: Partial view of *Queen Elizabeth Way Monument* by Frances Loring 1939.

FRANCES LORING/ FLORENCE WYLE

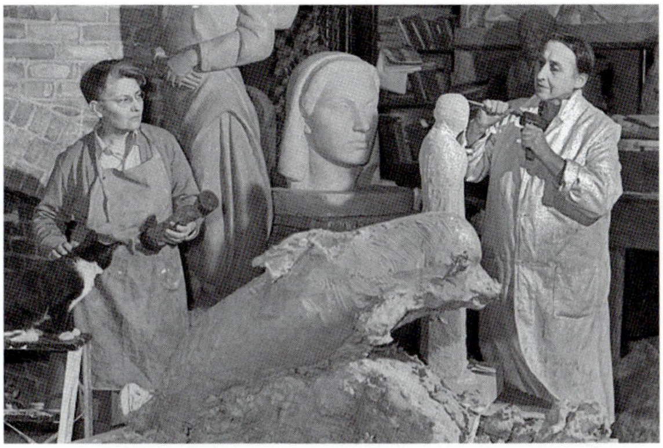

Frances Loring (1887–1968) was instrumental in expanding the role of women in art in Canada. Born in Wardner, Idaho, Loring showed an early interest for sculpture. She studied in Geneva, Munich and Paris before enrolling at the Art Institute of Chicago.

Florence Wyle (1881–1968) was born in Trenton, Illinois and in 1900 enrolled at the University of Illinois as a medical student where she studied anatomy. Three years later, she transferred to the Art Institute of Chicago where she began studying clay modelling with Lorado Taft and it was there that she met Frances Loring who became her lifelong partner and professional collaborator. Wyle shared a studio with Loring in New York's Greenwich Village in 1909 before they decided to move to Toronto in Canada around 1913. There, they became known as "The Girls".

Wyle excelled at portraits and was influenced by classical Greek sculpture. She worked as a sculptor in clay, stone and wood, carving her own works. Loring's 1918 statue *Grief* shows a woman slumped over, devastated by news from the war. At the end of the conflict, she went on to sculpt several large memorials. Wyle worked on a smaller scale, such as the bronze female nude called *Sun Worshipper* (1916), posing with one hand on her breast and the other extending toward the sun, that was considered to be mildly erotic. Her tribute to British nurse Edith Cavell in 1921 is a simple bronze relief depicting Cavell holding the hand of a wounded soldier.

Loring was the creator of the Queen Elizabeth Way Monument (1939), known as the Loring Lion, and a statue of Robert Borden (1957) located on Parliament Hill, Ottawa. In 1960, Loring represented Canada at the Venice Biennale.

Loring and Wyle both died in 1968, stipulating in their wills that the proceeds of the sale of their work should be donated to a fund, set up to purchase the works of young sculptors, which were to be exhibited in public galleries across Canada. This has led to a number of new and innovative sculptural movements in Canada.

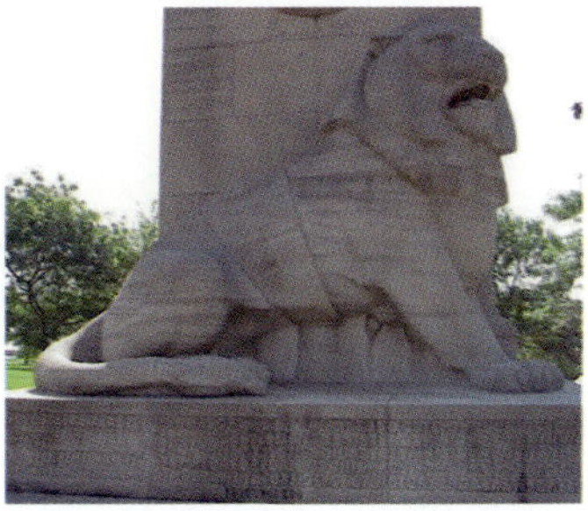

"I think every person looking at a sculpture should use his own body. You can't look at a sculpture if you are going to stand stiff as a ram rod and stare at it; with sculpture you must walk around it, bend toward it, touch it and walk away from it." **– Barbara Hepworth**

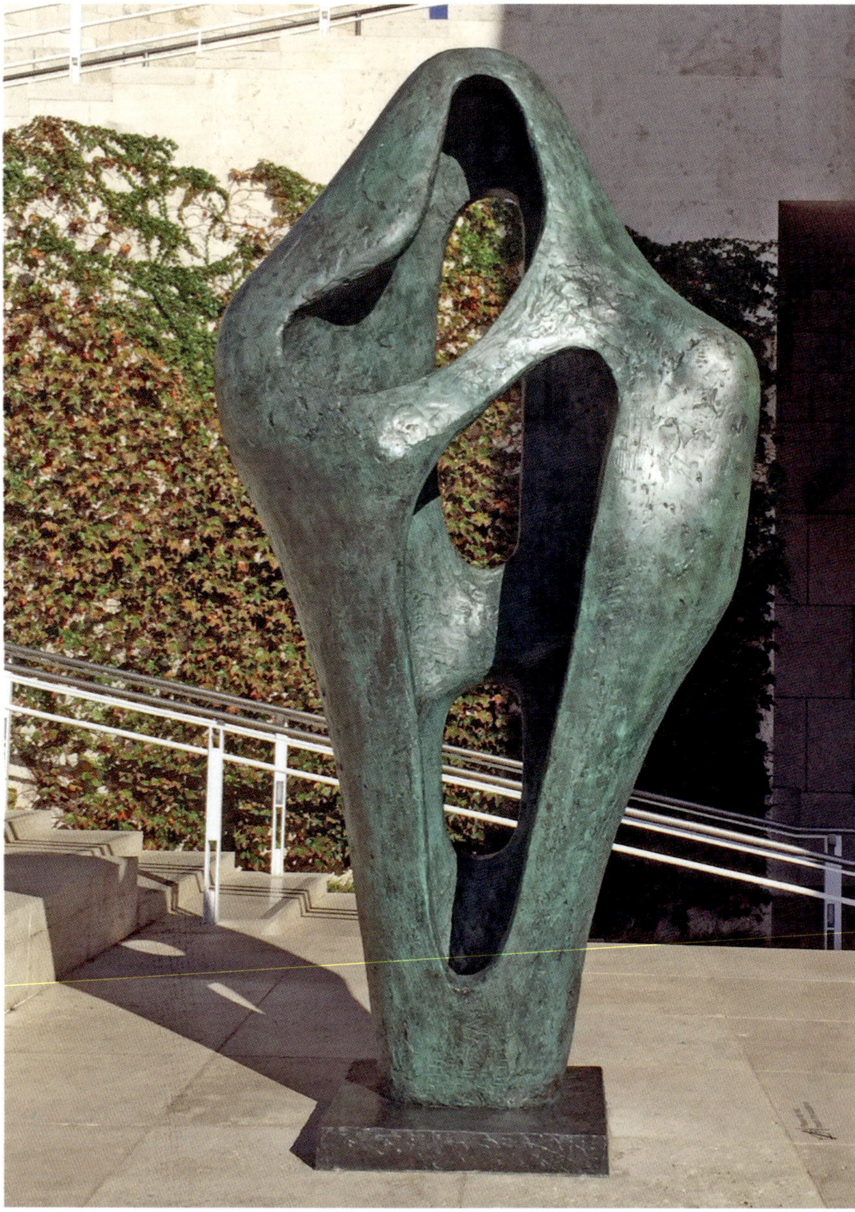

Above: *Figure For Landscape* 1960 – Getty Museum, Los Angeles
Right: *Figure Archaean* 1959, St. Catherine's, Oxford © Barbara Hepworth © Bowness.

BARBARA HEPWORTH

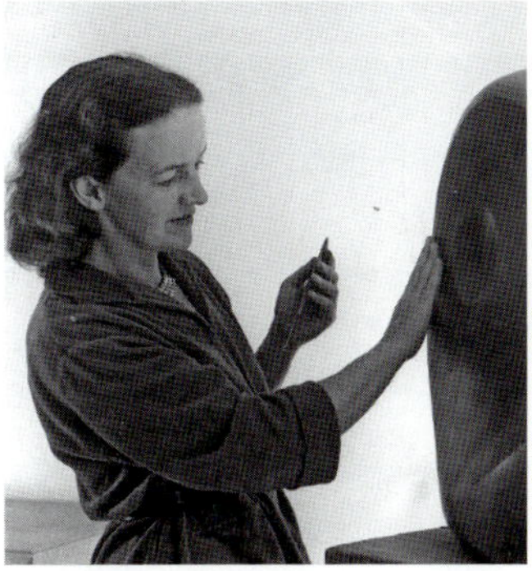

Barbara Hepworth (1903–1975) was born in Wakefield, Yorkshire and studied at Leeds School of Art (1920–21) alongside fellow artist Henry Moore. Both artists then continued their studies in sculpture at the Royal College of Art in London. They became proponents of Direct Carving, eschewing the traditional process of making a maquette which an artisan then uses to produce the finished work.

In 1924, Hepworth went to Italy on a scholarship where Giovanni Ardini taught her how to carve marble. She married fellow sculptor, John Skeaping, in Florence, returning to London in 1926 due to his ill-health, and setting up a studio in Hampstead. They had a son, Paul, in 1929 but separated a few years later. Hepworth carved her first pierced form in 1932 and formed a partnership with artist Ben Nicholson. The pair collaborated on many projects, as well as making short trips to Europe to visit the studios of abstract artists such as Brancusi and Picasso, and meeting Georges Braque and Piet Mondrian. In 1934, Hepworth gave birth to triplets, Simon, Rachel and Sarah.

Just before the outbreak of war in 1939, the family moved to St Ives. Hepworth's art became focused on the contrast between the chaos of the war and the beauty of the area. She created over six hundred sculptures that combine emotional force and a sense of tranquillity in their abstraction. After the war, she became involved in the local community and her studio became a hub for younger artists. She helped to rebuild and reinvigorate post-war St Ives with various public sculptures. Her style of carving holes and shapes in wood and stone pieces or casting bronze shapes with womb-like voids has been described as a particularly feminine aesthetic and her technique has influenced many artists including Peter Jensen and Rebecca Warren. Her son Paul died in an aircraft accident in 1953 and she went to Greece for a holiday to recover. On her return, she began carving sculptures from a large consignment of Nigerian guarea tree including *Corinthos* (1955) now in the Tate collection.

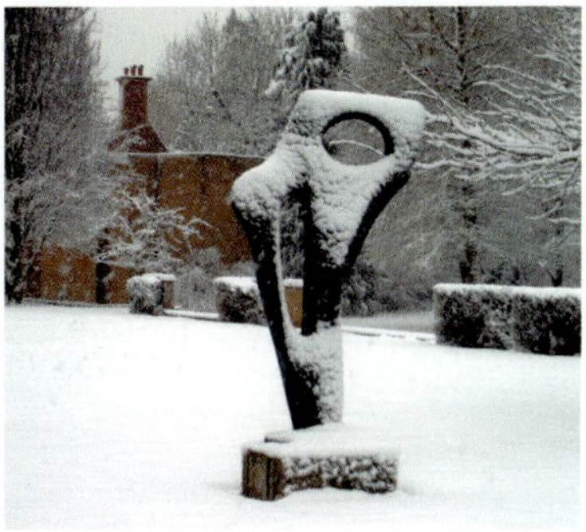

Hepworth became a major international figure, representing Britain at the 1950 Venice Biennale and winning first prize at the São Paulo Bienal in 1959. She died in an accidental fire at her studio in 1975, and later, the Barbara Hepworth Museum and Sculpture Garden was created in St. Ives on the studio site, as a way to preserve her legacy.

"The spider is a repairer. If you bash into the web of a spider, she doesn't get mad. She weaves and repairs it." – **Louise Bourgeois**

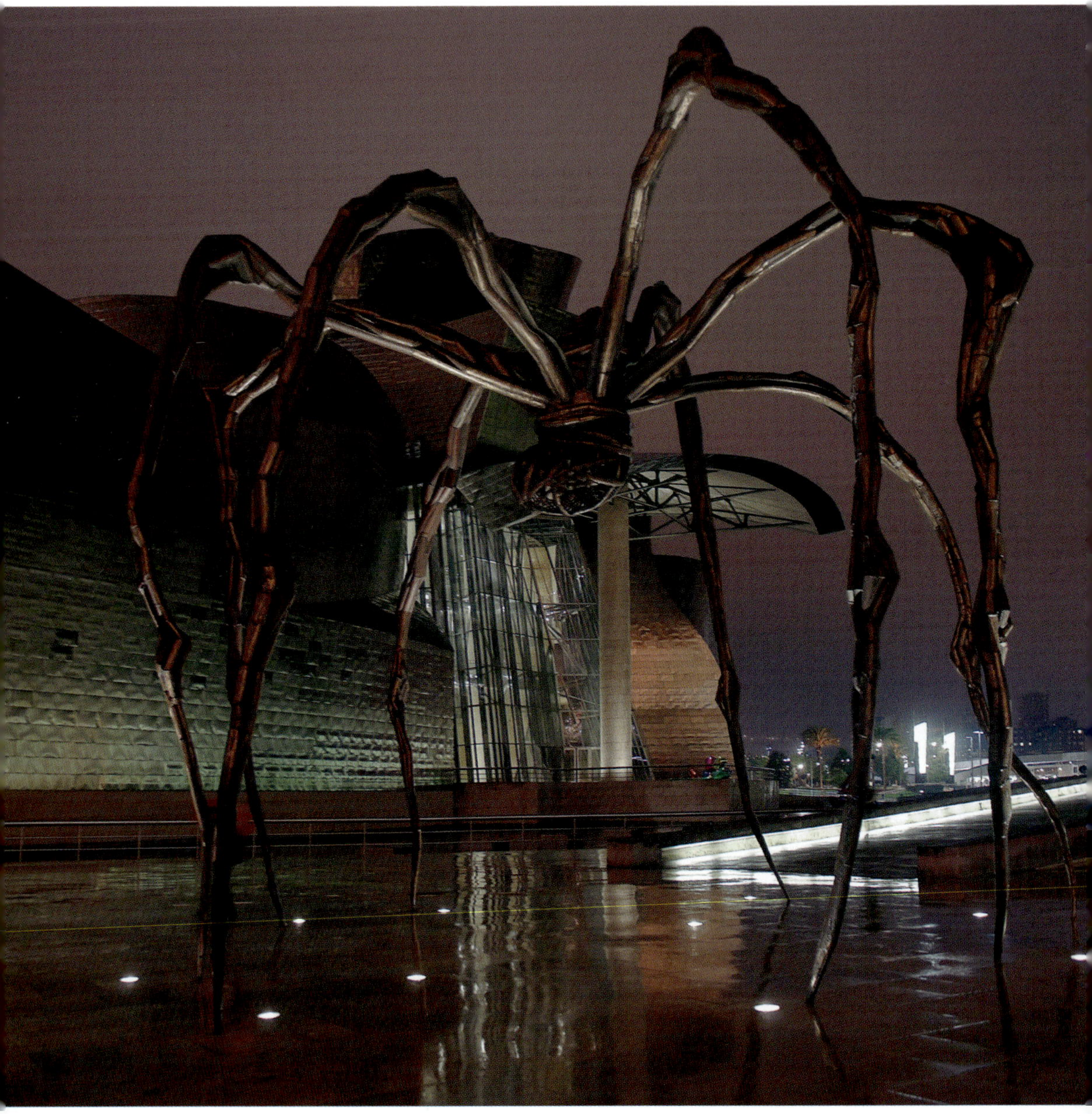

Maman 1999 – Collection Guggenheim Museum, Bilbao, Spain © The Easton Foundation
Photo: Didier Descouens

LOUISE BOURGEOIS

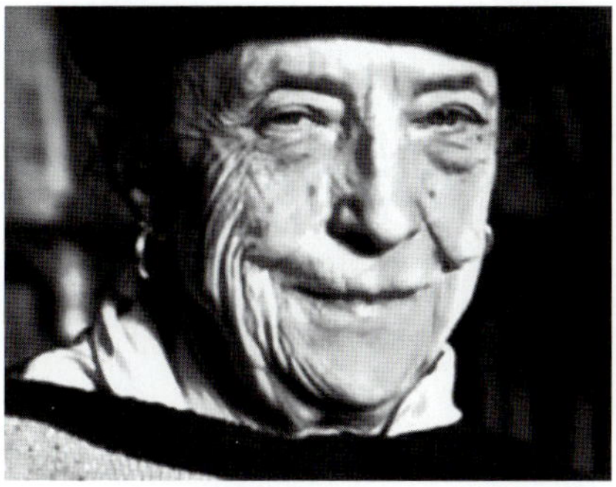

Louise Bourgeois (1911–2010) was born in Paris, the middle child of three children. The family lived on Boulevard Saint Germain, where they sold restored antique tapestries. Bourgeois's father was drafted to fight in World War I and was wounded in 1916. Her mother contracted the Spanish flu a few years later and died in 1932. This prompted Bourgeois to switch from studying maths to pursuing art instead. She studied in several academies and ateliers, including the studio of Fernand Leger. She married the American art historian Robert Goldwater in 1938 and they moved to New York, where she attended classes at the Art Students' League.

In 1945, by then a mother of three boys, she had her first solo show of her paintings at the Bertha Schaefer Gallery, New York. However, she soon turned to sculpture, producing her seminal series of *Personages* in the late 40s. Psychologically-charged, and symbolic of friends and family, these figures debuted at the Peridot Gallery in 1949. In 1951, Bourgeois's father died, leading to a period of depression and psychoanalysis.

In the 1960s, Bourgeois returned to the art scene with a new body of work, characterized by organic and biomorphic forms made of materials like plaster and latex. In 1966, she was included in the ground-breaking exhibition *Eccentric Abstraction* with the artists Eva Hesse and Bruce Nauman, among others. In 1980, several years after her husband's death, she acquired a spacious Brooklyn studio. This enabled her to create increasingly large-scale works, including her important series of *Cells.*

At the age of 71, Bourgeois became the first female sculptor to be honoured with a major retrospective at MoMA in New York (1982). She revealed at the time that her work was influenced by traumatic events from her childhood. From poetic drawings to room-sized installations, Bourgeois explored the psychological depths of human emotion. Memory, sexuality, love and abandonment are the core of her complex body of work. In 2000, London's Tate Modern commissioned her for their inaugural Turbine Hall installation. She presented three steel architectural towers (*I Do, I Undo and I Redo*) along with a monumental, thirty foot steel and marble spider, *Maman.*

Bourgeois hosted Sunday salons at her home in Manhattan in later years, where young artists would present their work for critique. She was renowned for being extremely honest with her criticism and once referred to these gatherings as "Sunday Bloody Sunday".

Above photo: Louise Bourgeois 1996 © Chris Felver

***"An artist is not special. An artist is an ordinary person who can take ordinary things and make them special."* – Ruth Asawa**

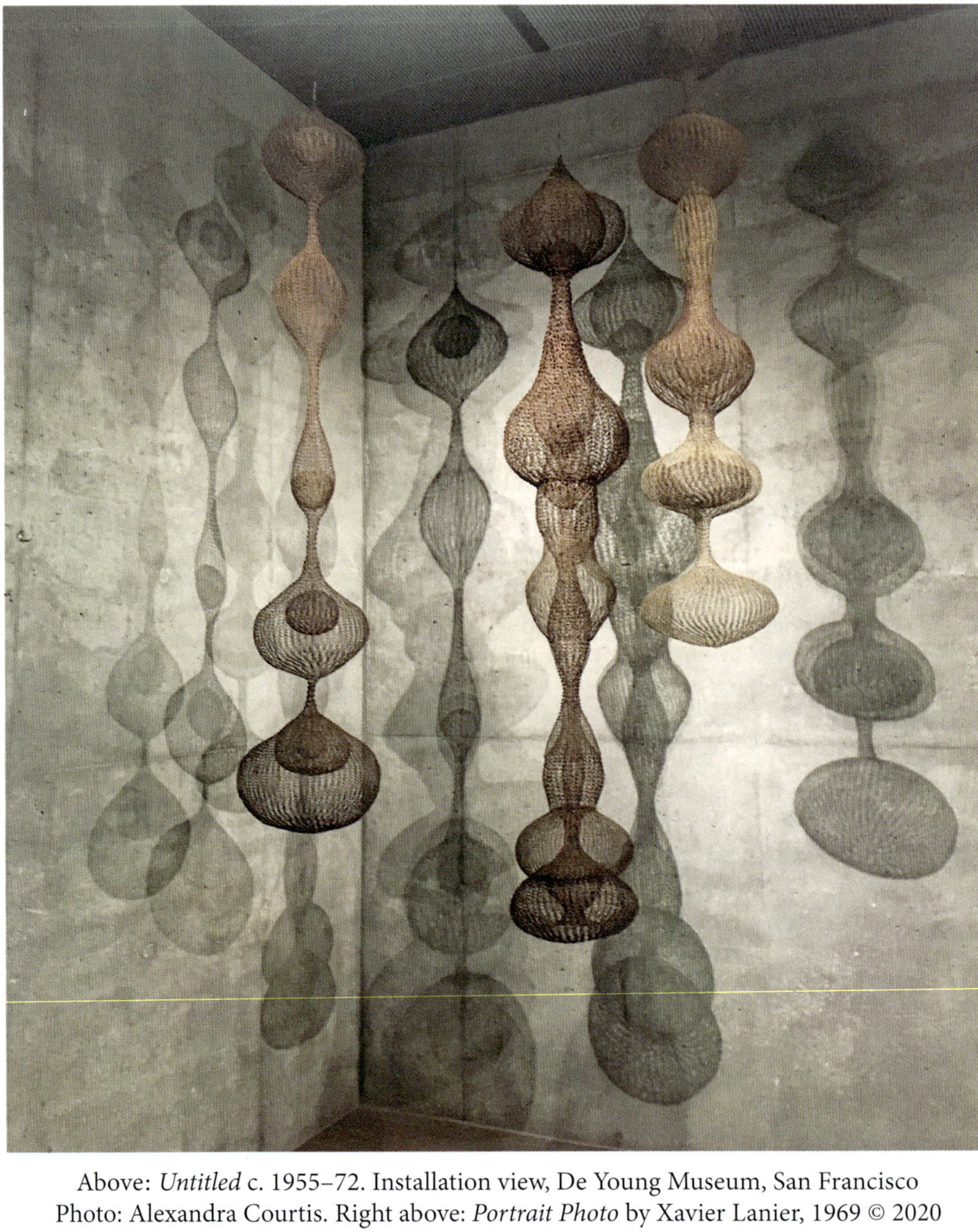

Above: *Untitled* c. 1955–72. Installation view, De Young Museum, San Francisco Photo: Alexandra Courtis. Right above: *Portrait Photo* by Xavier Lanier, 1969 © 2020 Right below: *Andrea* 1968 Ghirardelli Square, San Francisco. Photo: Nick Amoscato. © The Estate of Ruth Asawa / Artists Rights Society (ARS), New York. Courtesy The Estate of Ruth Asawa and David Zwirner

RUTH ASAWA

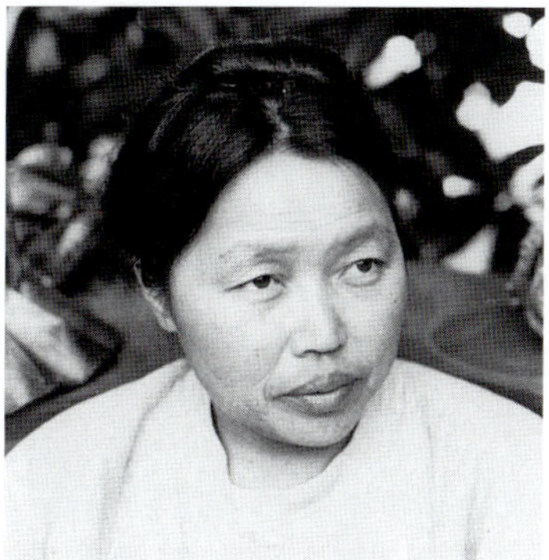

Ruth Aiko Asawa (1926–2013) was a Japanese-American artist who specialized in elaborate hanging forms using hand-looped wire. Born in Norwalk, California, the fourth of seven children to her Japanese-born parents who earned a living in the U.S. as farmers. After the bombing of Pearl Harbor, her father was imprisoned separately and she was sent to an internment camp with her family along with more than 100,000 West Coast Japanese. She lived for six months in the stables at Santa Anita Race Track in Los Angeles before transfer to a camp in Arkansas. She did not see her father again until 1948.

Asawa first studied art at high school then trained as a teacher at the Milwaukee State Teacher's College but wasn't able to complete her degree due to discrimination towards Japanese-Americans. Asawa then enrolled in the progressive Black Mountain College in North Carolina, where Josef Albers, a former teacher at the Bauhaus school in Germany, instructed her. She met her future husband, Albert Lanier at the college. They married in 1949, moved to San Francisco and raised six children.

Asawa began to experiment with wire, following a summer trip to Mexico in 1947, where she learned a basket-weaving technique. The hollow, transparent sculptural orbs that allowed light to permeate through the curved silhouettes proved popular in the 1950s. She had her first solo exhibit at New York's Peridot Gallery in 1954. In recent years, her work has been displayed regularly at the Whitney Museum of American Art and is in the collections at Solomon R. Guggenheim Museum, New York and at the De Young Museum in San Francisco.

Asawa was a guiding light for arts education too. She helped found the Ruth Asawa School of the Arts, a public art high school in San Francisco, which was renamed after her in tribute in 2010. She created several public commissions, such as the *Andrea* mermaid fountain (1968) in Ghirardelli Square and the *San Francisco Fountain* (1973) near Union Square. Her bronze bas-relief, *Japanese-American Internment Memorial* (1994), is on display at the Federal Building, San Jose.

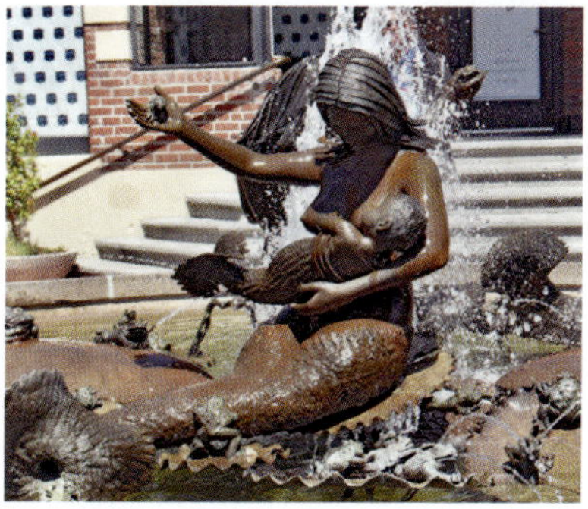

The Pulitzer Foundation in St. Louis, Missouri, honoured the artist with a survey titled "Ruth Asawa: Life's Work," in 2018–19 which presented her iconic work to a wider, national audience.

***"Fortunately we believe that in art everything has been done already, so nothing has been done yet."* – Alina Szapocznikow**

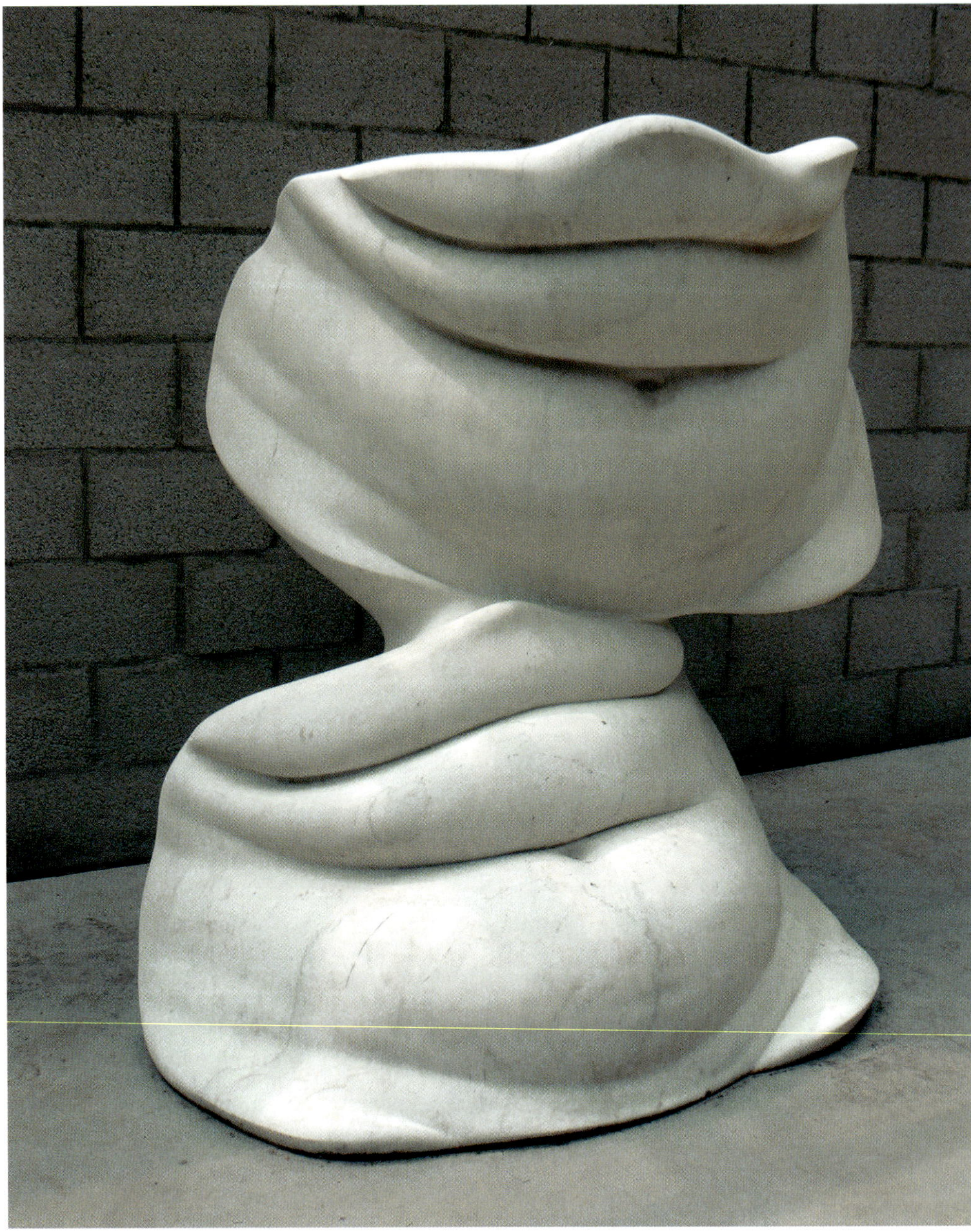

Above: *Big Bellies* 1968 in sculpturepark KMM/The Netherlands Photo: Gerardus
Right: *Woman with child* 1949 in Warsaw, next to the Comedy Theatre
Photo: Szczebrzeszynski

ALINA SZAPOCZNIKOW

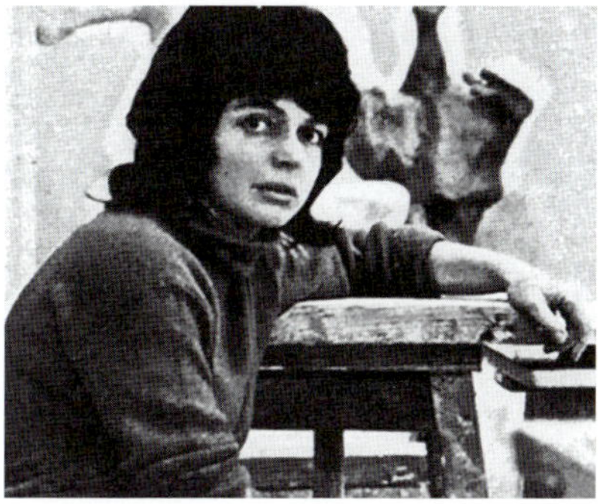

Born in Kalisz, Poland, to a Jewish family, Alina Szapocznikow (1926–1973) survived internment in a concentration camp as a teenager. Following World War II, she trained as a sculptor in Prague and the Ecole des Beaux-Arts in Paris. Plagued by illness for much of her life, Szapocznikow suffered from the then-untreatable disease tuberculosis and later breast cancer. The influence of pop art, surrealism and nouveau realism is prevalent throughout her works. Her sculptures explore the fragmentation of the human body, beginning with her early work in the 1960s, in which she produced casts of her own body in plaster, stone and bronze.

Later, in 1963, she was able to experiment with polyester resin and polyurethane, at the same time preserving some parts of her body casts whilst twisting and dissecting them in a way that evokes a sense of melancholy. Whilst she never publicly spoke about her experiences during the Holocaust, her art appears to express the deep trauma that comes from suffering so severely at a young age.

After her breast cancer diagnosis in 1969, she created works such as *Tumours Personified*, made from polyester resin, gauze and crumpled paper, as a way of confronting the way in which her illness was becoming part of her identity. In Szapocznikow's final works she explores a desire to engage with the infinite, and to mark the traces of what we, as humans, leave behind. Her art frames human existence as fleeting, drawing attention to the fragility and vulnerability of the human body.

One of her most instantly recognizable and popular sculptures is *Grands Ventres* (*Big Bellies*), which is considered to be less controversial and less distressing to look at than many of her other works, due to its realism and the absence of disfigurement.

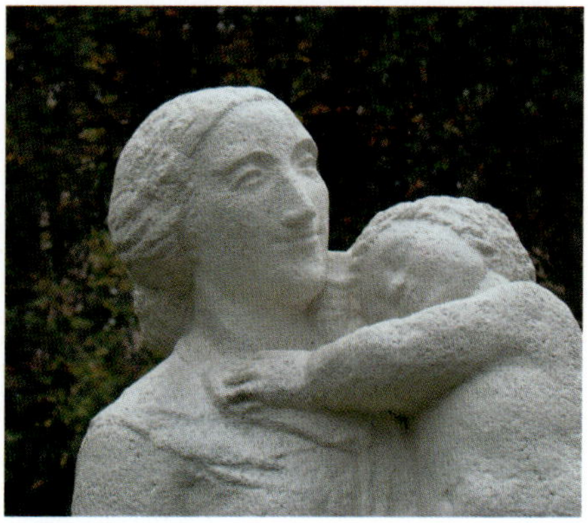

During her lifetime, Szapocznikow's work was largely ignored outside of Poland. However, following her death from cancer in 1973 at the age of just 47, her work has recaptured the public eye, with many major museums, such as the Museum of Modern Art in New York, celebrating her artistic achievements.

"I fight pain, anxiety, and fear every day, and the only method I have found that relieves my illness is to keep creating art. I followed the thread of art and somehow discovered a path that would allow me to live."
– Yayoi Kusama

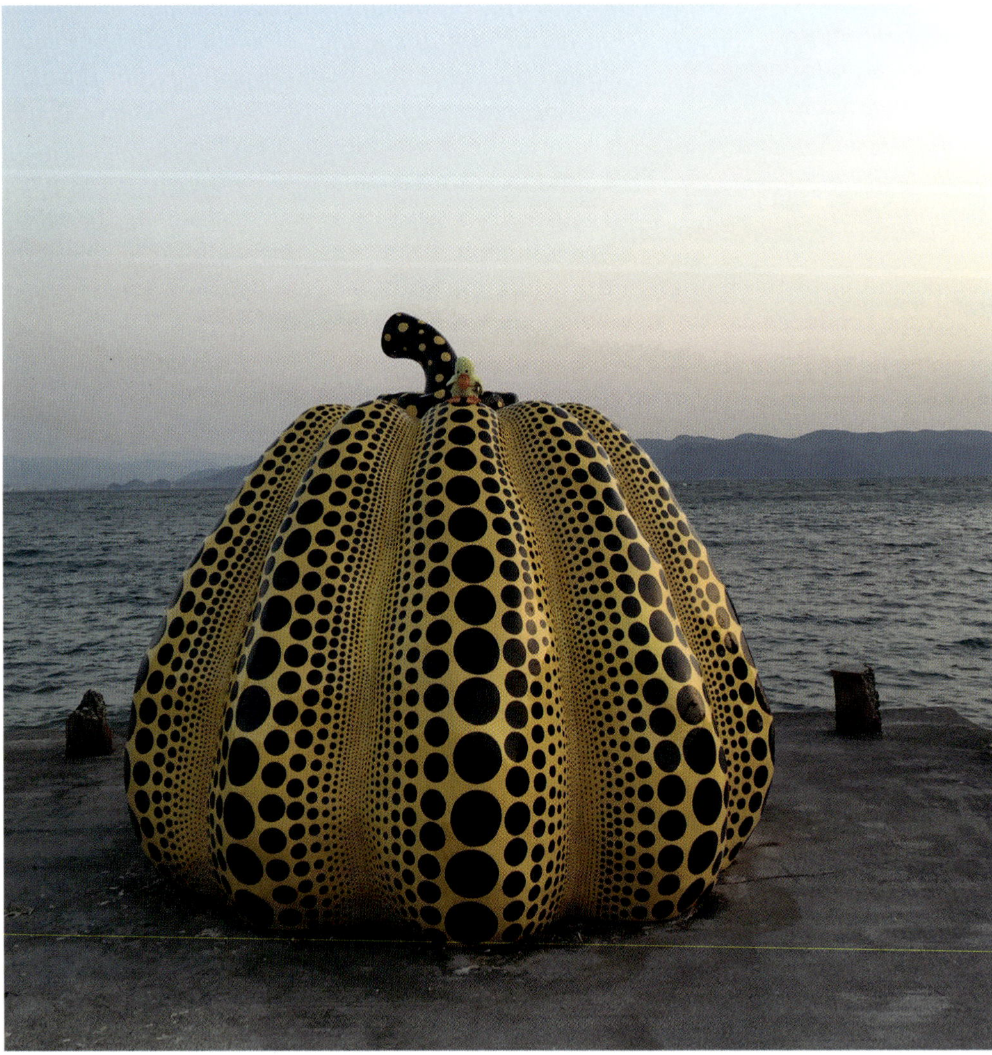

Above: *Pumpkin* 1994 – on Naoshima Island, Japan
Right: *Narcissus Garden* 1966/2009 – Installation view, Instituto Inhotim, Brumadinho, Brazil 2009

YAYOI KUSAMA

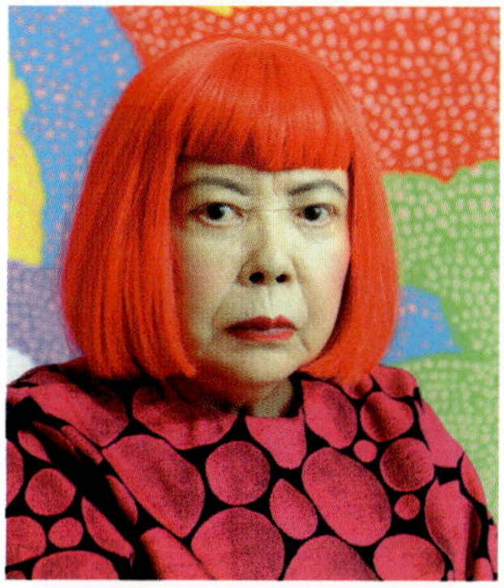

Yayoi Kusama (1929–) is a Japanese painter, sculptor and installation artist who is often referred to as "the princess of the polka dots" due to her obsession with spots. She was born in Matsumoto in Japan into a strict, traditional family. Kusama began painting at around the age of 10, after she repeatedly experienced a hallucination involving a field of dots. Her mother disapproved of her daughter's artistic interests wanting her to marry and become a housewife. Kusama has recounted how her mother would throw away her inks and paints. She moved to Kyoto to study Nihonga painting in 1948 but felt cramped by this traditional style and began developing a more avant-garde style of her own which led to her first solo exhibition in Japan in 1952.

She moved to New York in 1958, but the move was a shock for Kusama, due to her sheltered background in her hometown Matsumoto. She produced her trademark phallic sculptures; these were among her early creations, along with her characteristic net paintings, which featured thousands of tiny dots and seemed to extend beyond the limits of the canvas into infinity. In the 1960s she began to create her famous mirror rooms which were filled with lights, creating an illusion of never-ending space. She organised artistic protests over the Vietnam war and other political issues as well as happenings which often featured nude participants, gaining a reputation for being both brave and rebellious. Her works were reportedly copied by artists such as Andy Warhol, Claes Oldenburg and Lucas Samaras, who gained fame and success while she struggled.

She returned to Japan in 1973, and in 1977 checked herself into a psychiatric hospital, where she would eventually take up permanent residence. In 1989, she gained further recognition with a number of international solo exhibitions, including at the Center for International Contemporary Arts in New York, and in 1993, her exhibition for the Japanese Pavilion at the Venice Biennale helped establish Kusama as a world-renowned artist. She has created hundreds of influential works in her studio near to the hospital in Tokyo. Her work is now held worldwide in museum collections.

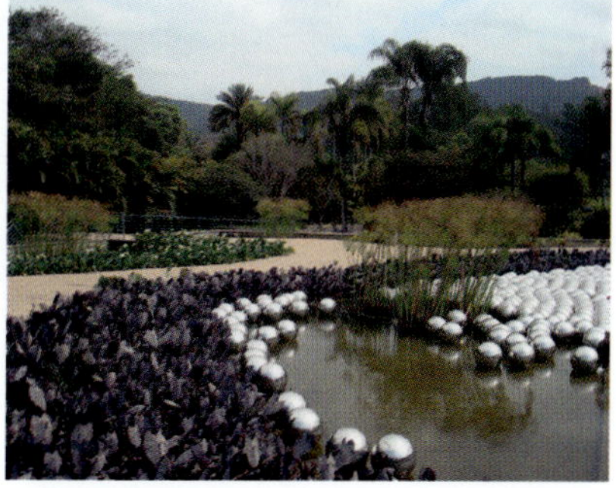

A museum dedicated to the artist's work, the Yayoi Kusama Museum, opened in Tokyo in 2017.

"I wanted to make some of the really important things of my generation and some of the biggest." – **Niki de Saint Phalle**

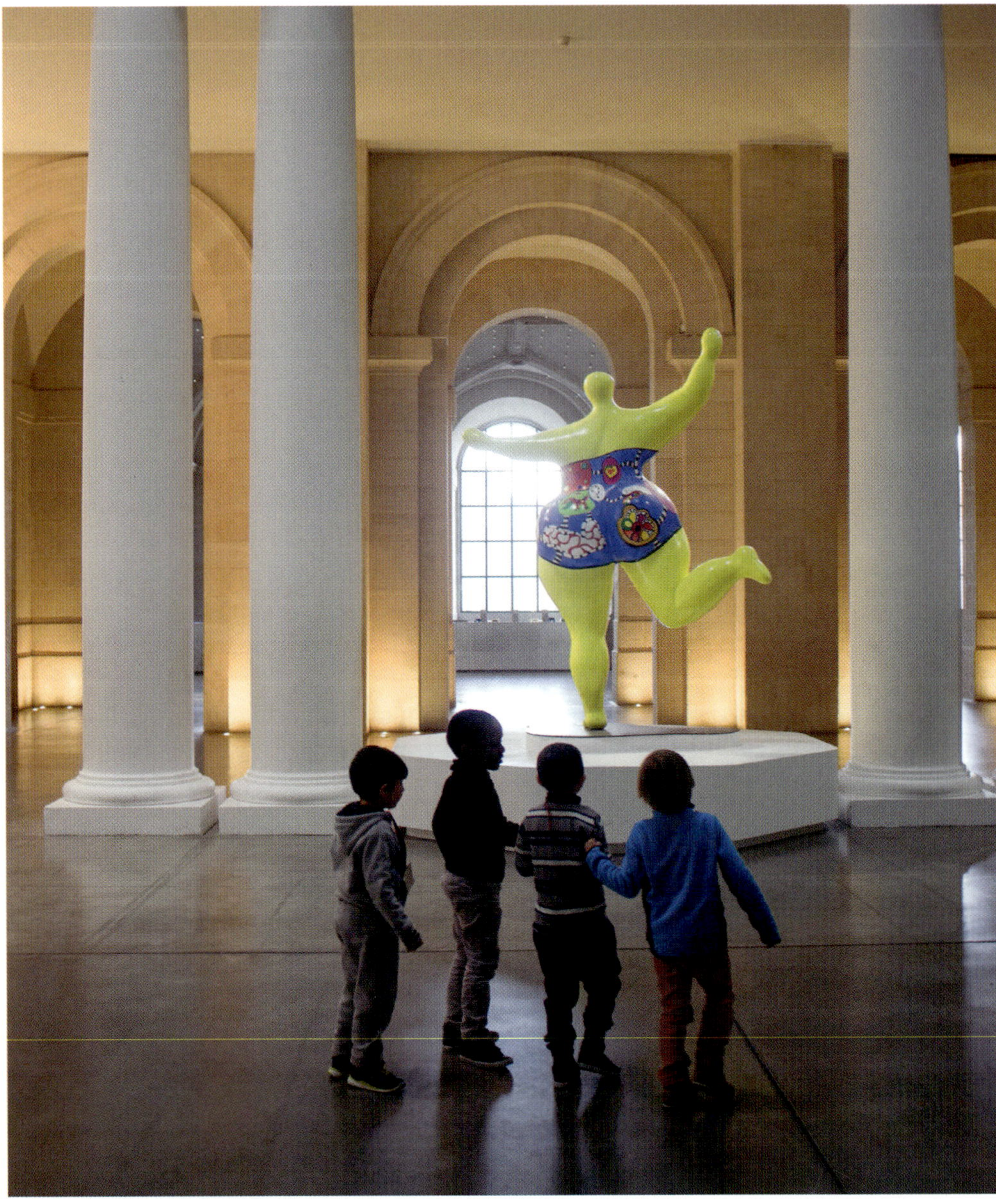

Above: *Dancing Nana* (yellow) 1995 Photo: Jean-Philippe Granger.
Right: *The Footballers* 1993 at the Olympic Museum, Lausanne Photo: Saliko

NIKI DE SAINT PHALLE

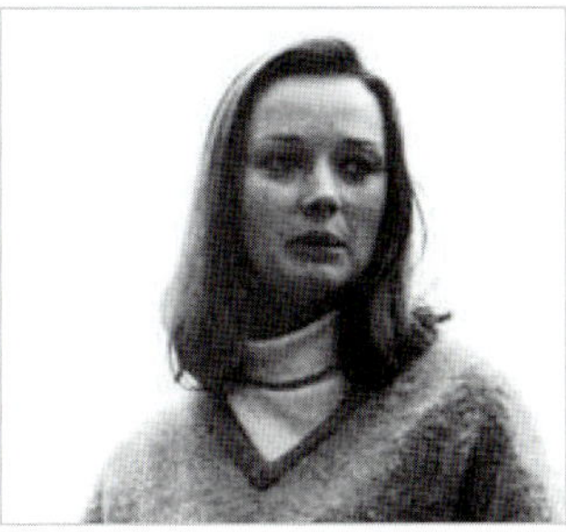

Born in Neuilly-sur-Seine, France, Catherine-Marie-Agnès Fal (1930–2002) known as Niki de Saint Phalle was a French-American sculptor who created large-scale, colourful statues of voluptuous women known as "Nanas" and fantasy creatures. She grew up in New York where her father's fortunes declined in the stock market collapse. She suffered sexual abuse by her father and turned to art to process her emotional turmoil. She was later expelled from school for painting the fig leaves on the school's classical statues red.

During her teens she became a fashion model, appearing on the cover of French *Vogue* and *Life* magazines. At 18, she married her childhood friend Harry Mathews. They had a daughter, Laura, and decided to leave the USA due to the tension caused by the McCarthy trials. They went travelling around Europe, but while living in Nice, Saint Phalle had a nervous breakdown. During her convalescence she had the time to develop her art. In 1954, the young family moved to Mallorca, Spain, where their second child, Philip, was born. She encountered the work of Gaudi, whose *Parc Güell* would later inspire her own garden exhibit, *The Tarot Garden.*

In 1956, she had her first exhibition of paintings and became aware of avant-garde artists like Jasper Johns, Jackson Pollock and Robert Rauschenberg. Experimental assemblages gave way to *Tirs,* or shooting paintings, bringing her international fame and association with the "New Realists", a group of artists which included Christo, Yves Klein, Arman and Jean Tinguely among others. Her many collaborations with Swiss kinetic sculptor Jean Tinguely included major projects like *Hon* in Stockholm (1966), *Paradis Fantastique* (1967), *Golem* in Jerusalem (1972), *Tarot Garden* in Italy (1980-1998) and *Stravinsky Fountain* in Paris (1983). Their close relationship led to marriage in 1971.

Later monumental projects include the UCSD *Sun God* (1983), *Noah's Ark* in Jerusalem (1998), the *Grotto* at the Royal Gardens of Hannover (1996–2003) and *Queen Califia's Magical Circle* in Escondido (1999–2003). Her Nana figures became plumper, more active and joyful figures, including *Black Venus* (1967) and several black Nanas in solidarity with the civil rights movement in America. Her work strongly influenced both feminist and conceptual art.

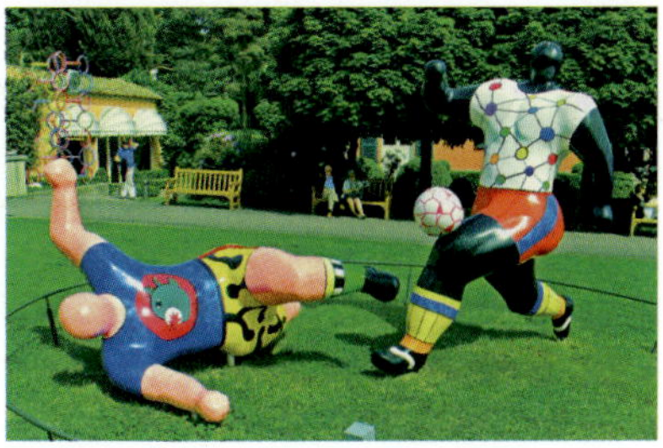

Saint Phalle died in 2002 in La Jolla, California from emphysema, a result of prolonged exposure to glass fibres and chemical fumes from her work.

"I have focused on the male because to me he is a subtle combination of sensuality and strength with vulnerability" – **Elisabeth Frink**

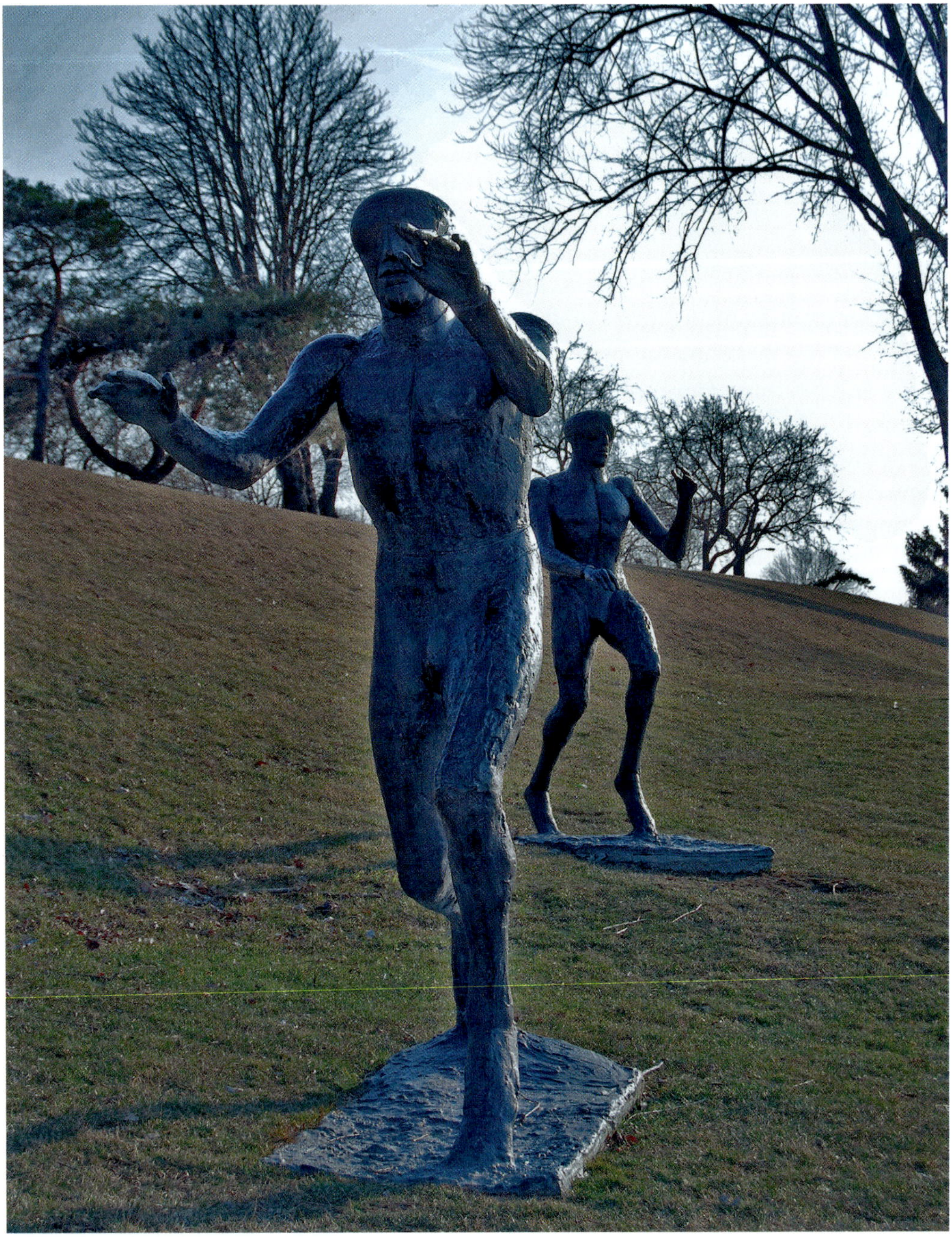

Above: *Flying Men* c. 1982 in Odette Sculpture Park, Windsor, Ontario, Canada.
Right: *Paternoster,* Paternoster Square, 1975

ELISABETH FRINK

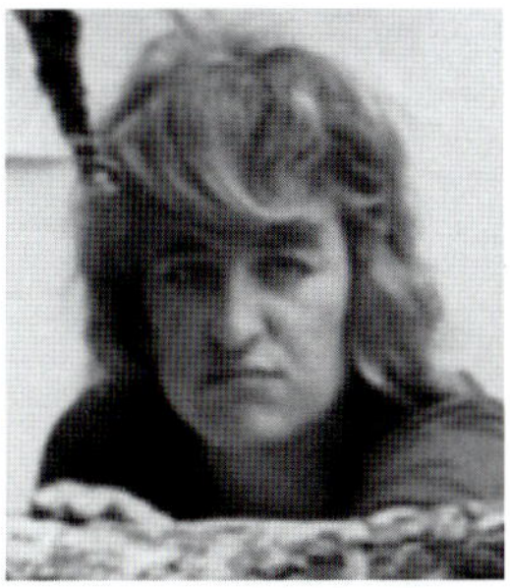

Elisabeth Frink (1930–1993) was born in the village of Great Thurlow, Suffolk. Her father was an officer in the Dragoon Guards and her childhood in the countryside influenced her choice of subjects such as dogs and horses. Living near an RAF base, Frink sometimes witnessed bombers returning battered or in flames during the war. Eventually, Frink and her brother were sent to lodge with a family friend in Exmouth, Devon.

After the war, Frink studied at the Guildford School of Art (now UCA) and at the Chelsea School of Art (1949-53). She was associated with an emerging group of British sculptors, nicknamed the Geometry of Fear school, which included Kenneth Armitage and Eduardo Paolozzi. She went on to teach at Chelsea (1953-60) and St Martin's School of Art (1955-7). Frink held her first major solo exhibition at the Beaux Arts Gallery in London in 1952 and the Tate Gallery purchased one work entitled *Bird*.

Frink is best known for her expressionistic animal and human figures. such as *Rolling Horse* (1982), *Flying Men* (1982) and *Running Man* (1976). Her technique involved the building up of layers of plaster placed on wire armature. Bits of wood and studio debris were often incorporated into the mass, which was then cast in bronze.

Frink married Michel Jammet in 1955 and had a son, Lin, in 1958 but the marriage was dissolved in 1963 a year before she married Edward Pool, a war hero. Feeling that her work was out of fashion in England, Frink and her husband moved to the Cevennes in France in 1967 where she was influenced by the work of Germaine Richier and the Algerian war. Here she began a series of sinister busts known as the Goggleheads.

On her return, she focused on male figures which became bulkier, smoother and larger in scale. The way of working with plaster changed and in the 1980s she began to experiment with carving rhythmic marks on dry plaster and creating coloured bronze surfaces. Frink married Alexander Csaky, a businessman, in 1974 and settled in Dorset. She was one of five women selected to be featured on British postage stamps in 1996 and in 1982 she was created a Dame of the British Empire.

Frink undertook several large commissions including *Eagle* (1962) for Coventry Cathedral, the *JFK Memorial* (1964) in Dallas, Texas and *Warhorse* (1991) on display at Chatsworth. She died of cancer in Blandford at the age of 62, one week after the installation of her statue *Risen Christ* at Liverpool Cathedral.

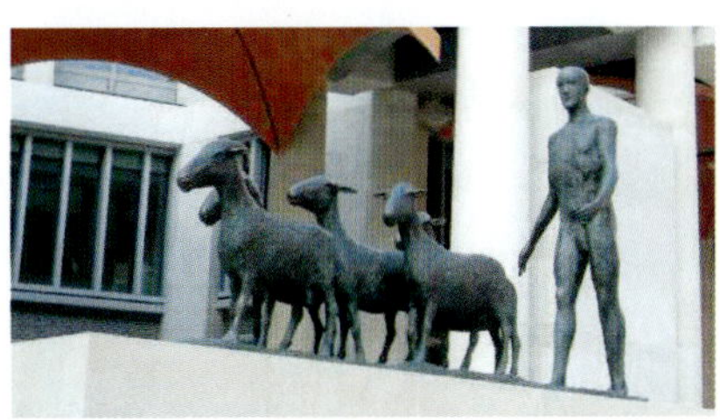

"Don't ask what the work is. Rather, see what the work does."
– Eva Hesse

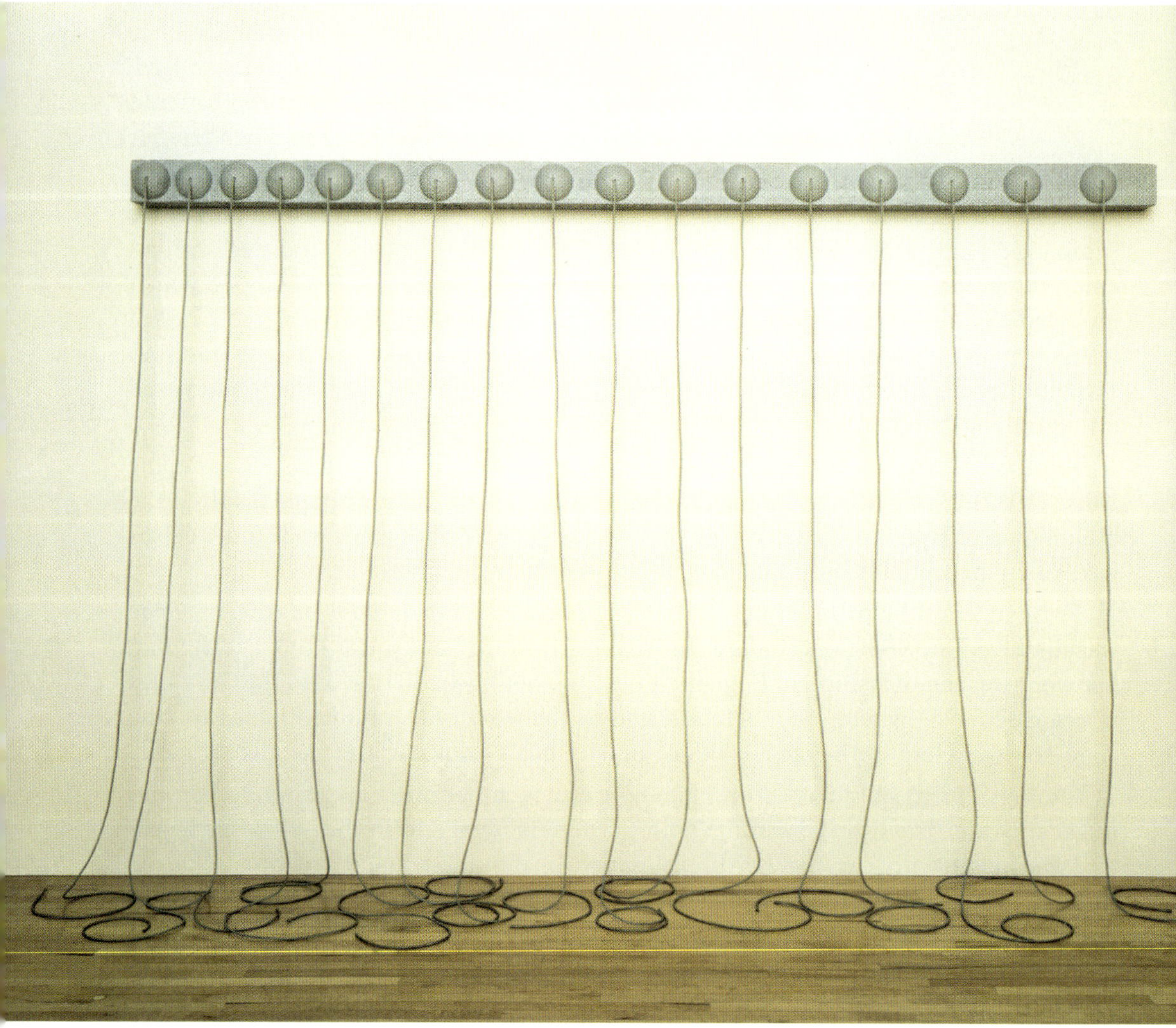

Above: *Addendum* 1967 – Tate, London 1979. Photo: © Tate
Right: *Hang Up* 1966 Art Institute of Chicago. Photo: Mark B. Schlemmer

EVA HESSE

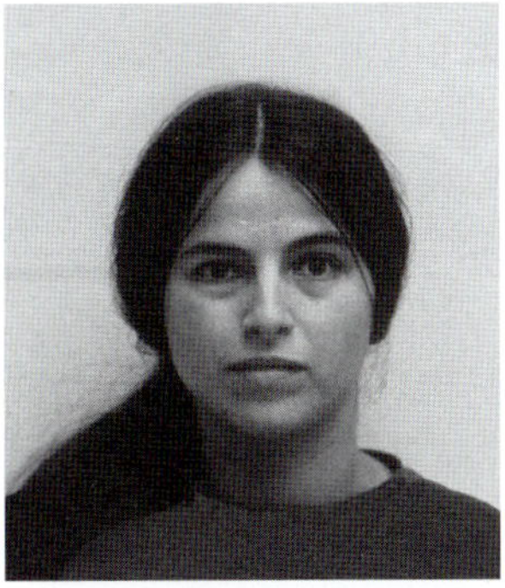

Eva Hesse (1936–1970) was a German-American artist who had a short but exceptional career. Born in Hamburg into a Jewish family, Hesse was forced to flee Germany during the rise of Nazism. Eva and her sister Helen travelled by Kinderstransport to Amsterdam, stayng at a children's home until their parents arrived three months later. Reunited, the family moved to New York in 1939 but Hesse's mother suffered from depression which led to her suicide in 1946. Hesse studied at New York's High School of Industrial Arts and the Art Students League graduating from The Yale School of Art andArchitecture in 1959. During this period she worked in an abstract impressionist style. In 1961, she exhibited a series of drawings and watercolours at the John Heller Gallery, the Brooklyn Museum and Wadsworth Athenaeum. She became friends with Sol Le Witt and Yayoi Kusama who were experimenting with minimalist and conceptual art and this influenced her style.

In 1961, Hesse married artist Tom Doyle, and in 1964, they moved to Kettwig an der Ruhr, Germany where Doyle had an artist's residency. Hesse worked in a studio in an abandoned textile mill, where she began to use found industrial objects in her work, transitioning from painting to sculpture. Her first solo show of sculptural reliefs was presented at the Kunstverein für die Rheinlande und Westfalen, Düsseldorf, in 1965. One of her most famous works, *Hang Up*, comprises a blank canvas with a cloth-wrapped frame and a steel rod extending from its surface *(below)*. Hesse said of it "It is the most ridiculous structure that I ever made and that is why it is really good." She described the relief *Ringaround Arosie* as looking like "a breast and a penis" but did not align her work with a feminist agenda. In an interview with the Women's Art Journal, she stated, "Excellence has no sex."

In 1968, she had a solo exhibition titled *Eva Hesse: Chain Polymers* at the Fischbach Gallery in New York. Her large sculpture *Expanded Expansion* showed at the Whitney Museum in the 1969 exhibition *Anti-Illusion: Procedures*. Hesse tragically died in 1970, following three failed operations to remove a brain tumour. In 1972, the Guggenheim Museum held a memorial retrospective of her work, the first time the museum had paid tribute to a female artist in this way. Since her death, her work has appeared in exhibitions around the world.

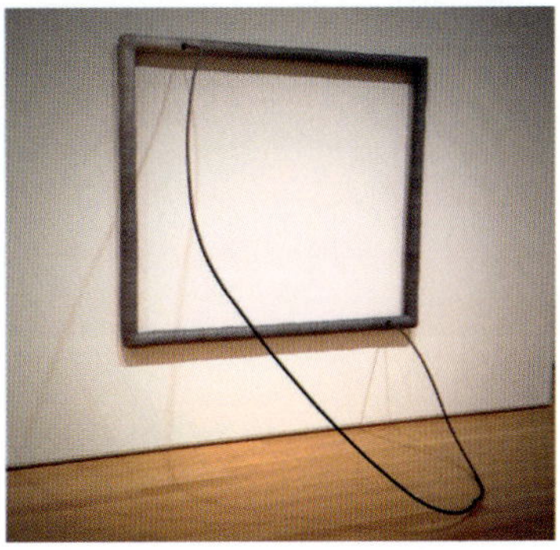

"Because men have a history, it is difficult for them to imagine what it is like to grow up without one, or the sense of personal expansion that comes from discovering that we women have a worthy heritage..."
– Judy Chicago

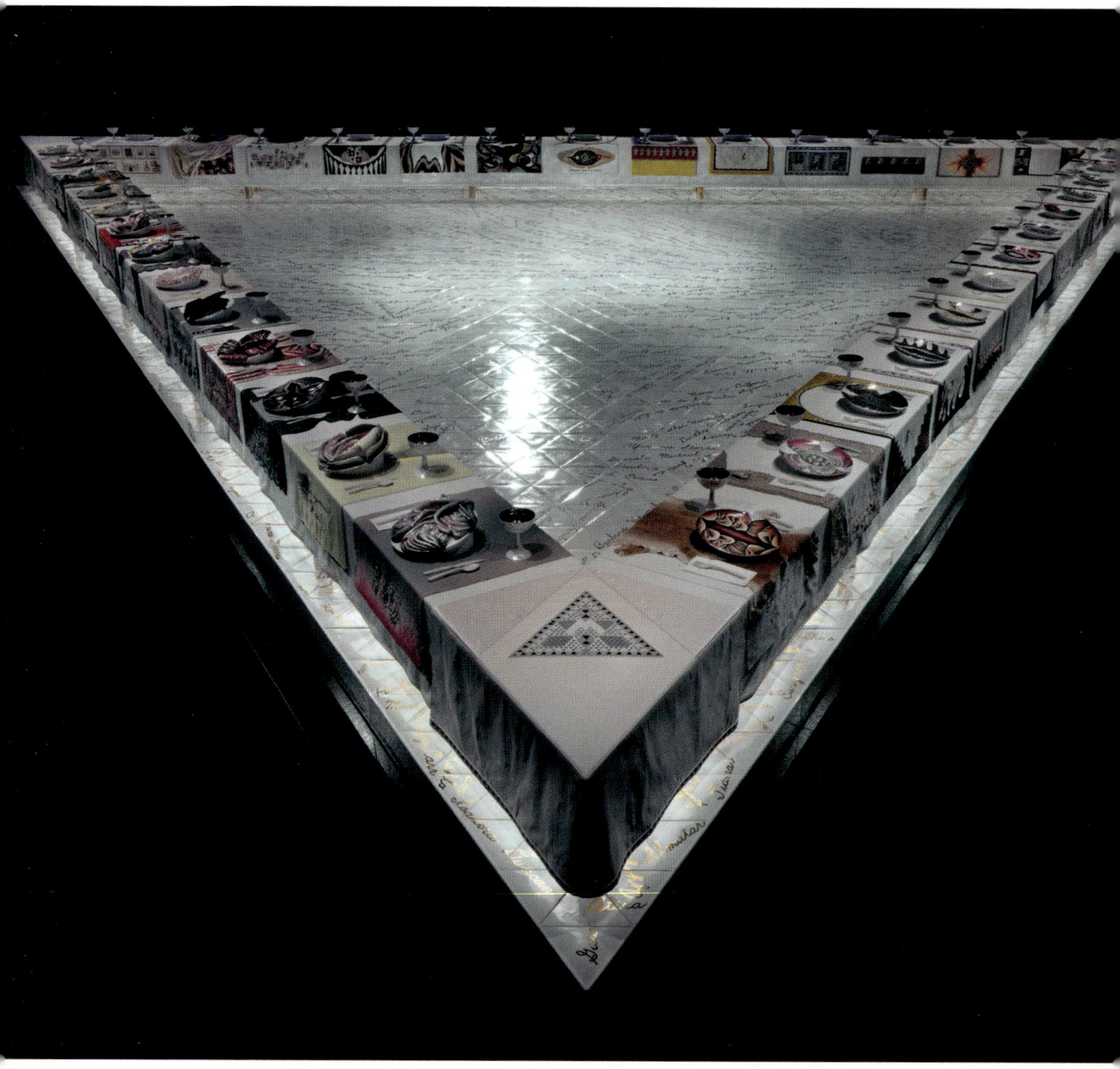

Above: *The Dinner Party* c. 1979 installation view © Judy Chicago ARS, NY and DACS, London 2020
– Elizabeth A Sackler Center for Feminist Art in the Brooklyn Museum, New York

JUDY CHICAGO

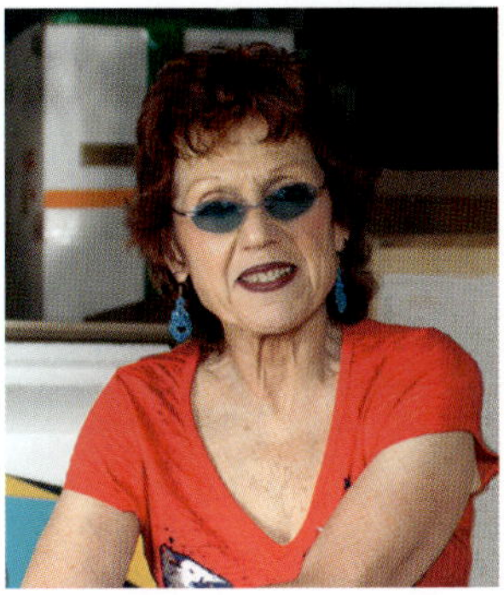

Judith Cohen (1939–) was born in Chicago, Illinois, to a family of Jewish socialists. She began drawing at the age of three. From 1947, she attended art classes at the Institute of Chicago but in 1948, her father left his union job during the height of the McCarthy era, fell sick and died two years later. She won a scholarship to train at UCLA, and married Jerry Gerowitz, but in 1961, he was killed in a car accident. She had her first solo exhibition in 1965 and in the 1970s her work took on more overtly feminist themes. She had remarried, to sculptor Lloyd Hamro, but invented a new surname – Chicago, rather than use her husband's surname.

In the early 70s, Chicago pioneered Feminist art and art education through a unique programme for women at California State University, Fresno, and has continued to develop educational initiatives such as the Feminist Studio workshop in Los Angeles where she began to run workshops for women artists. Chicago deliberately chose to work with traditionally female arts and crafts such as needlework, ceramics and glass, which were often seen as secondary to arts such as painting and sculpture.

The Dinner Party was created between 1974 and 1979 with the participation of hundreds of volunteers to celebrate the forgotten achievements of women in history. Its 16 exhibitions, which travelled to several countries, were seen by over a million viewers. Dismissed by male critics as "obscene" and "kitsch", today the iconic multimedia project stands as a symbol for the history of women in Western civilization.

In 1980, Chicago initiated a feminist art project called *The International Honor Quilt* (or the *International Quilting Bee*) as a companion piece to *The Dinner Party*. Comprising over 500 quilted triangles, the piece pays tribute to women globally. Next came a collective project about childbirth and then, after her third marriage to photographer Donald Woodman, Chicago began to explore her Jewish heritage.

The Holocaust Project: From Darkness into Light (1985–93) was an eight-year exploration of the holocaust, undertaken in collaboration with Donald Woodman. Chicago said it was "structured as a journey into the darkness of the Holocaust and out into the light of hope."

In 2014, in honour of her 75th birthday, numerous exhibitions of her work were held across the USA, culminating in *A Butterfly for Brooklyn*, a pyrotechnic work in Prospect Park, attended by 12,000 people.

"I like to use common objects ... plastic, masking tape, rocks, sand, water... I love to see them being transformed into something that's graceful, elegant, transformative, to the point where you see a poetry in the most simple material."
– Senga Nengudi

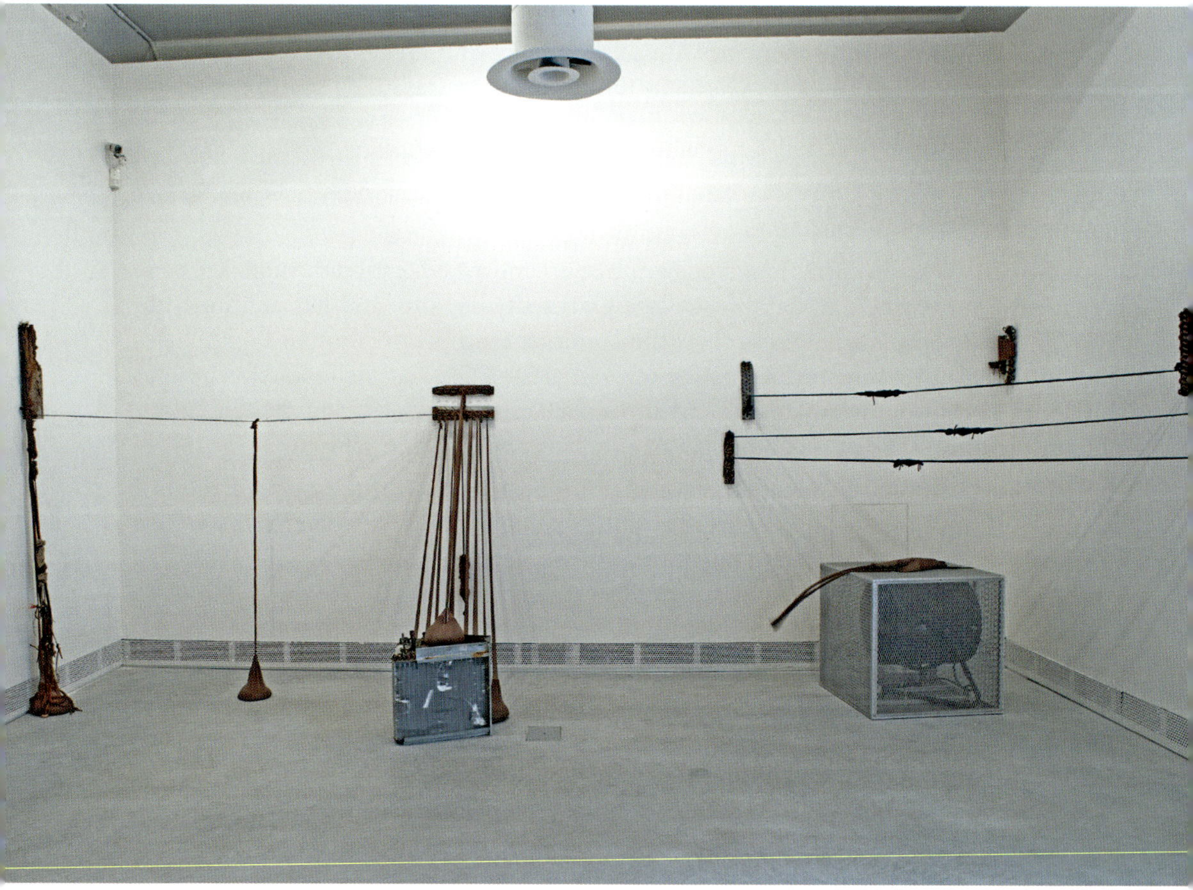

Above: *A.C.Q. (1)* 2016-17 –*Viva Arte Viva*, Venice Biennale 2017
Courtesy Thomas Erben Gallery, New York

Right: *Nuki Nuki: Across 118th St* c. 1981/2013, Installation view, Henry Moore Institute, Leeds, 2018–19. Courtesy the Henry Moore Foundation. Photo: John McKenzie

SENGA NENGUDI

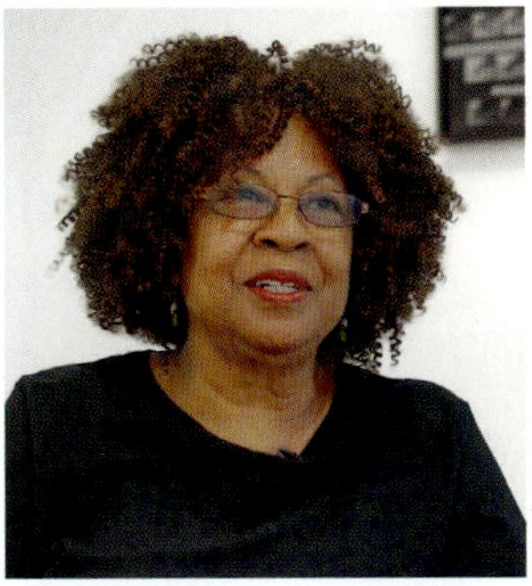

Senga Nengudi (1943–) adopted her name in 1974 to suit her politics of African-American empowerment. She was born in Chicago, Illinois as Sue Irons. Following the death of her father in 1949, she went to live with her mother in Pasadena, California, which disrupted her high school education due to the segregated school system. She went on to study art and dance at California State University, graduating in 1967. She loved dance but chose to be an artist as she felt it would offer her a longer career. Nengudi also studied Japanese Culture at Waseda University in Tokyo from 1966-67. She later completed an MA in sculpture at California State University in 1977.

Combining sculpture and performance art, Nengudi came to prominence in the late 60s and remains a vital figure on the avant-garde scene. One of her first trailblazing exhibitions was *R.S.V.P.* (1975–77) which incorporated stretched and deformed stockings and pantyhose to portray "abstracted reflections of used bodies" as well as to confront the changes in her own body following the birth of her son. *Untitled (Water Composition)* sculptures, made in the late 60s and 70s, resemble giant melting ice lollies, plastic tubes filled with coloured water, which the visitor can touch.

Nengudi's work explores themes of gender, race and ethnicity, drawing inspiration from African and Eastern philosophy and spiritualism. She was a leading figure in the Studio Z Collective, and works such as *Ceremony for Freeway Fets* (1978), which involved performance and photography, were carried out by members of Studio Z in the underpass of the freeway in Los Angeles.

Recent solo exhibitions include Henry Moore Institute, Yorkshire (2018-19), Institute of Contemporary Art, Miami (2017-18); USC Fisher Museum of Art, Los Angeles and Museum of Contemporary Art, Denver (2014). Nengudi's work was included in the 2017 Venice Biennale and has been featured in major group exhibitions, such as *Soul of a Nation: Art in the Age of Black Power,* Tate Modern (2017); *We Wanted a Revolution: Black Radical Women,* 1965-85, Brooklyn Museum, New York (2017); *Blues for Smoke,* Whitney Museum of American Art, New York (2013); *Radical Presence: Black Performance in Contemporary Art,* Contemporary Art Museum, Houston (2012). Nengudi currently lives and works in Colorado.

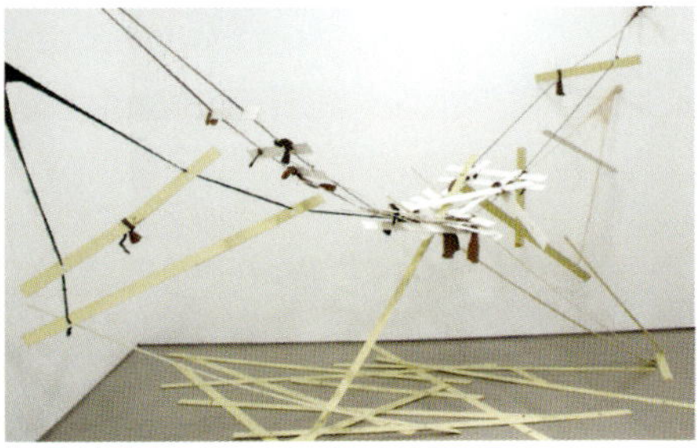

"Being an artist means forever healing your own wounds and at the same time endlessly exposing them."
– Annette Messager

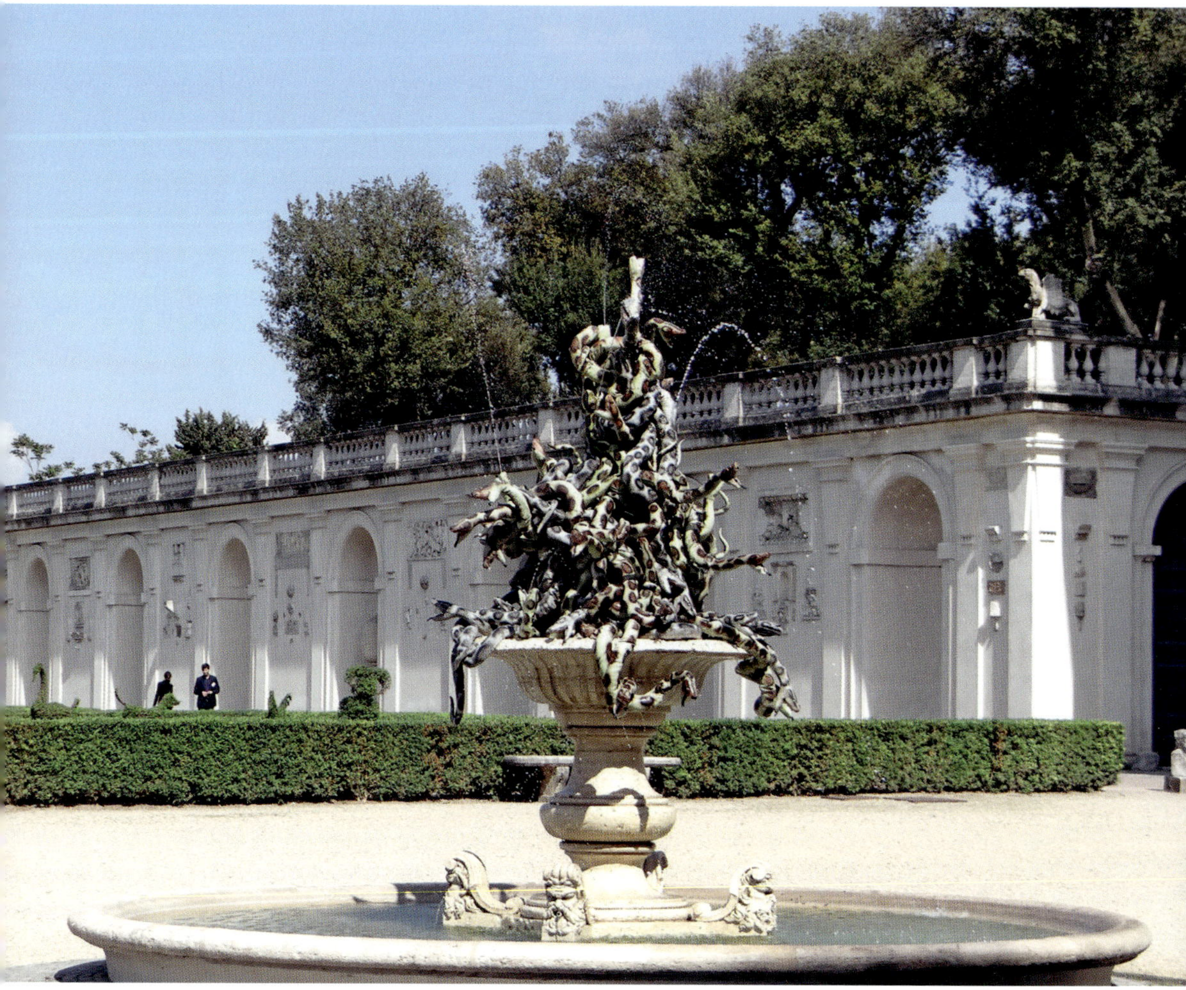

Above: *The Serpent Fountain* 2017 – Villa Medici, Rome. Photo: Jean-Pierre Dalbéra

ANNETTE MESSAGER

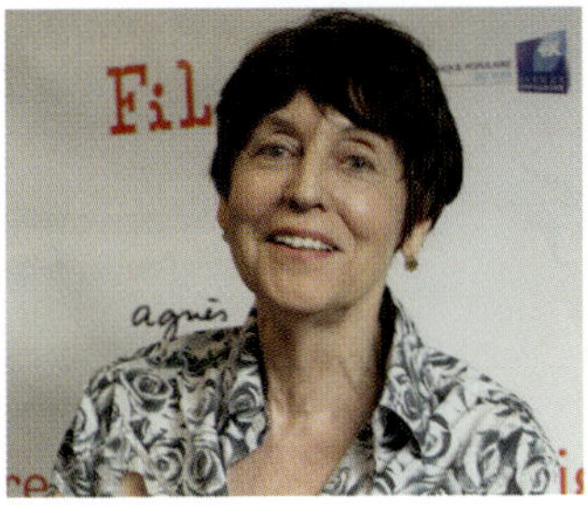

Annette Messager (1943–) was born in Berck-sur-Mer in northern France and was encouraged to pursue art from a young age by her father who was an architect and amateur painter. She went on to study at the École Nationale Supérieure des Arts Décoratifs in Paris where she produced several surrealist sculptures for her final exams. In 1961, Messager won the grand prize in an international competition sponsored by Kodak after her mother entered one of her early photographs. During her career she has made use of a range of materials such as photography, taxidermy, sculpture, domestic objects, toys, knitting and embroidery in her assemblage of her works.

In the 1970s several of her works were overtly feminist with exhibitions such as *The Approaches*, a series of photographs of men's crotches, and *Voluntary Tortures* (1972), a series of photographs of women submitting to beauty treatments. In the 80s she continued her exploration of identity and the human body in numerous exhibitions such as her installation *Them and Us, Us and Them* (2002), made up of hundreds of hooded stuffed birds suspended from the ceiling. Her use of embroidery in some of her works is ironic as she adopts traditional feminine crafts to highlight sexism and inequality.

In 2005, she was the first woman to represent France at the Venice Biennale and she won the Golden Lion Award for her installation *Casino*, a theatrical rendition of Pinocchio, which transformed the French pavilion with kinetic sculptures using red silk, rubber, fluorescent tubes and fans.

Perhaps her most notable exhibition is *The Messengers* (2009) which was displayed at both the Pompidou Centre in Paris and the Hayward Gallery in London. It offered a selection of her works over four decades from the intimate and conceptually driven pieces of the 70s to the large-scale sculptural installations and kinetic works of more recent years.

Messager was awarded the Praemium Imperiale for sculpture in 2016. Recently she has exhibited at the Institut Giacometti in Paris (2018), the Institut Valencià Art Modern (IVAM) in Spain (2018), the Villa Medici in Rome (2017).

She currently lives in Malakoff near Paris with her partner, the renowned artist Christian Boltanski.

"The transformation of the experience: that is pure art." – **Rebecca Horn**

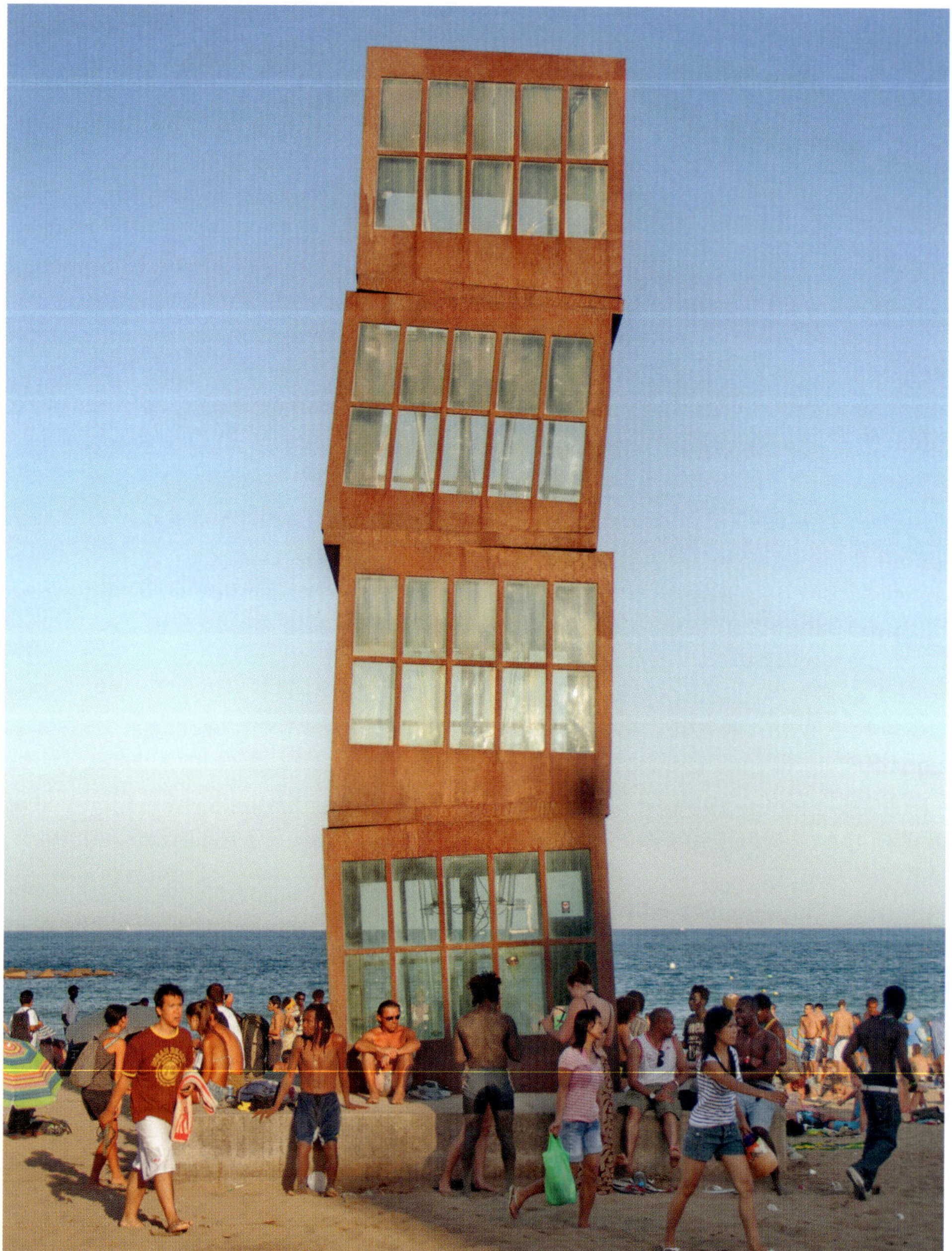

Above: *L'Estel Ferit [The Wounded Star]*, nicknamed *The Cubes* 1992, Barcelona

Right: *Glowing Core* 2015 – La Llotja de Palma, Mallorca

REBECCA HORN

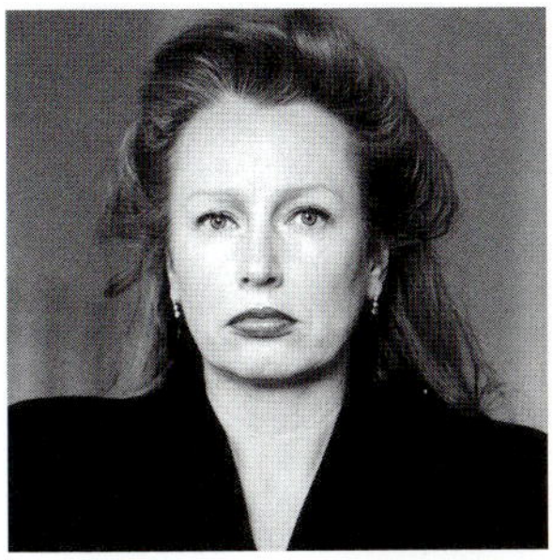

Rebecca Horn (1944–) is a multidisciplinary artist whose work encompasses sculpture, body art, paintings, films and poetry. Born in Michelstadt, Germany, she went to boarding school as a child. One of her memories of the cold severity of her schooldays is reflected in *The Moon, the Child and the River of Anarchy* (1992) which features school desks attached in rows to the ceiling with a series of tubes connecting them.

She originally began studying economics and philosophy at university, but began taking secret art classes on the side. She studied art full-time at Hamburg Academy of Fine Arts in 1963 much to the dismay of her parents. She began to make large-scale sculptures from polyester and fibreglass. Unfortunately, she did not wear a mask and so had to be hospitalized for lung poisoning in 1968. Tragically, during this same year, she lost both her parents. The young artist convalesced by making sculptures at her sanatorium from soft materials such as bandages. After a year recovering, she went back to art school and created body sculptures for performance art such as *Pencil Mask* (1972) enabling drawing with the face, and *Scratching Both Walls at Once* (1974–5) which allows the arms to reach across a room. She was invited to participate in Documenta 5 in Kassel in 1972 and the following year, Horn had her first solo exhibition at the Galerie René Block, West Berlin. In Berlin she began filmmaking with *Exercises: Dreaming Under Water,* and began using objects such as violins, suitcases, feather fans, hammers, funnels and pumps as the building blocks to make kinetic sculptures. She moved to New York in 1972 and by the 1980s she was producing large kinetic sculptures that surrounded the viewer in an immersive experience of sound and movement. These can be seen in films such as *The Gentle Prisoner* (1978) and *The Peacock Machine* (1979-82). In 1990 she made a feature film, *Buster's Bedroom*, starring Donald Sutherland. She returned to Berlin in 1981.

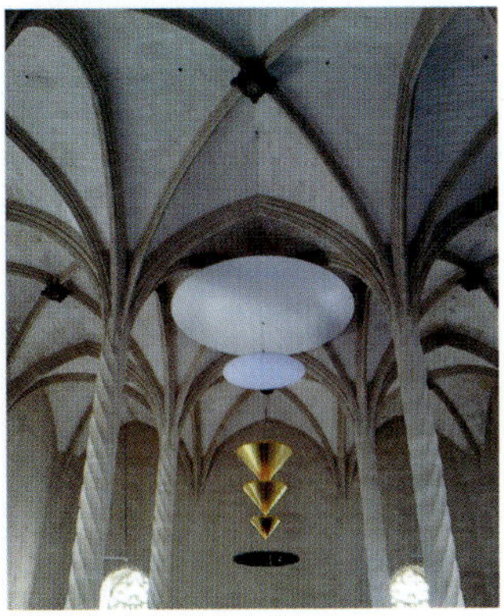

The *Tower of the Nameless* (1994) in Vienna, was an installation of mechanical violins for the refugees from the Balkans and in 1988, Horn won the Carnegie Prize for an installation work titled *The Hyra Forest/Performing: Oscar Wilde.* She was awarded the 2010 Praemium Imperiale in Sculpture and the Grande Médaille des Arts Plastiques 2011 from the Académie d'Architecture de Paris.

In 2012, Horn received the Austrian Decoration of Honour for Science and Art.

"With the other materials I began to discover – clay and plaster – there was a looseness, an approximation. You could maybe do something that was incredibly bad, but there was a way of approaching it that could be very exciting, like just pushing it over, or allowing things to break."
– Phyllida Barlow

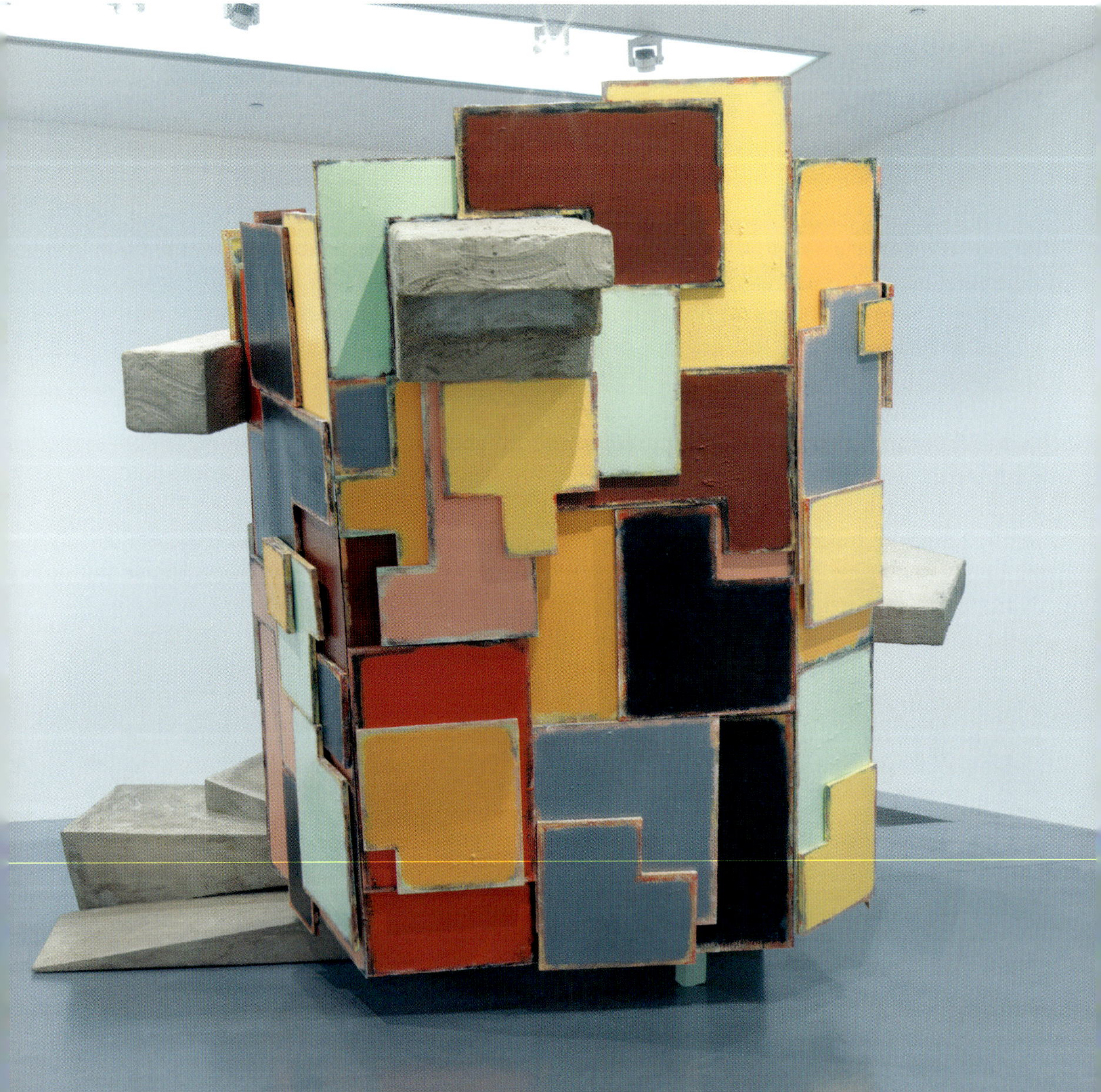

Above: *untitled: upturned house 2* – Installation view – The Tate Modern, 2012 Photo: © Tate
Right: *Rig* – Installation view, Hauser & Wirth, London 2011

PHYLLIDA BARLOW

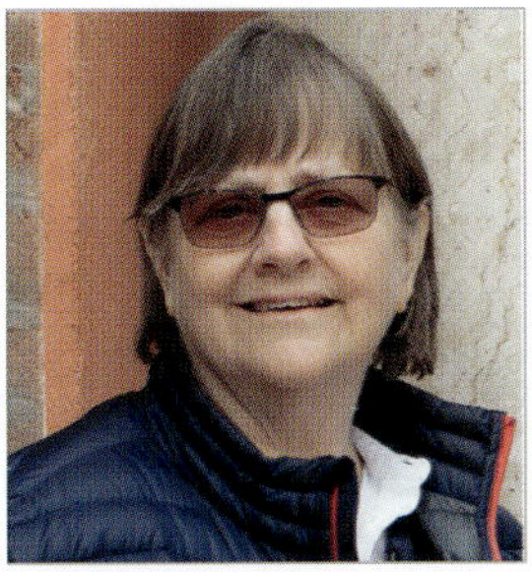

Phyllida Barlow (1944–) grew up in post-war Britain. Her father, the psychiatrist Erasmus Darwin Barlow, was the great-grandson of Charles Darwin. She graduated from Slade School of Fine Art in 1966 and began a forty-year long career as an art teacher at various institutions before she retired in 2009 to concentrate on her own art. During her teaching career she taught the celebrated artists Rachel Whiteread, Tacita Dean, Martin Creed and Ángela de la Cruz. Barlow and her husband, the artist and writer Fabian Benedict Peake, the son of Mervyn Peake, author of *Gormenghast*, have five children, two of whom are also successful artists – Eddie Peake and Florence Peake, leading the *Independent* to call them "a British art dynasty". In 2010, she had her first exhibition at the Serpentine Gallery in London. Her work such as *Rig* (2011) [below] is largely made up of objects she has scavenged, such as wood, plaster, fabric and cement. In 2011 she was elected as a Royal Academician.

Barlow's work is tactile, messy and precarious in appearance and imparts a sense of emotional intensity. Often painted in vibrant colours, her works deliberately leave the means of their construction visible. In contrast to the careful positioning of classical sculptures, her large-scale sculptural objects are generally placed in a way that disrupts the space around them, giving them an air of instability. Winning the Aachener Kunstpreis in 2012, Barlow was commissioned to do a solo exhibition for the Ludwig Forum für Internationale Kunst in Germany.

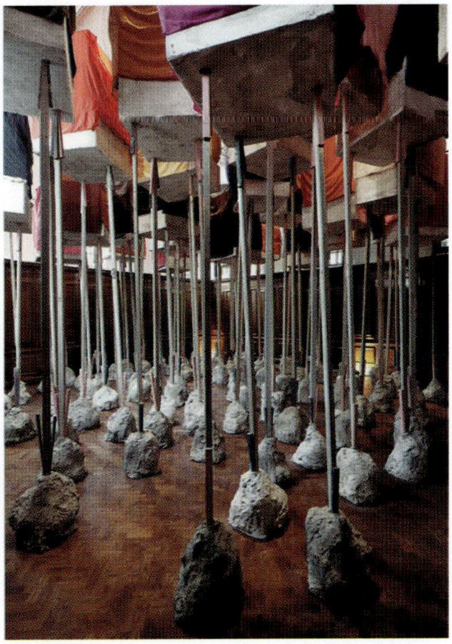

In 2014, commissioned to create new work for Tate Britain, she challenged the grandiose Duveen Galleries with an anti-monumental installation called *dock*.

In 2015 she was made a CBE for her services to the arts in the Queen's New Year Honours. The following year, Barlow presented a solo exhibition of new work at the Kunsthallerich. Nominated that year for the Hepworth prize, her work was displayed at the Hepworth Wakefield Gallery in West Yorkshire.

She was invited to represent Great Britain at the Venice Biennale in 2017 and produced a collection of popsicle pieces.

Above: Portrait photo by Ruth Clark
© Phyllida Barlow Courtesy the artist, Hauser & Wirth

"I'm often asked the same question: What in your work comes from your own culture? As if I have a recipe and I can actually isolate the Arab ingredient, the woman ingredient, the Palestinian ingredient. People often expect tidy definitions of otherness, as if identity is something fixed and easily definable." – **Mona Hatoum**

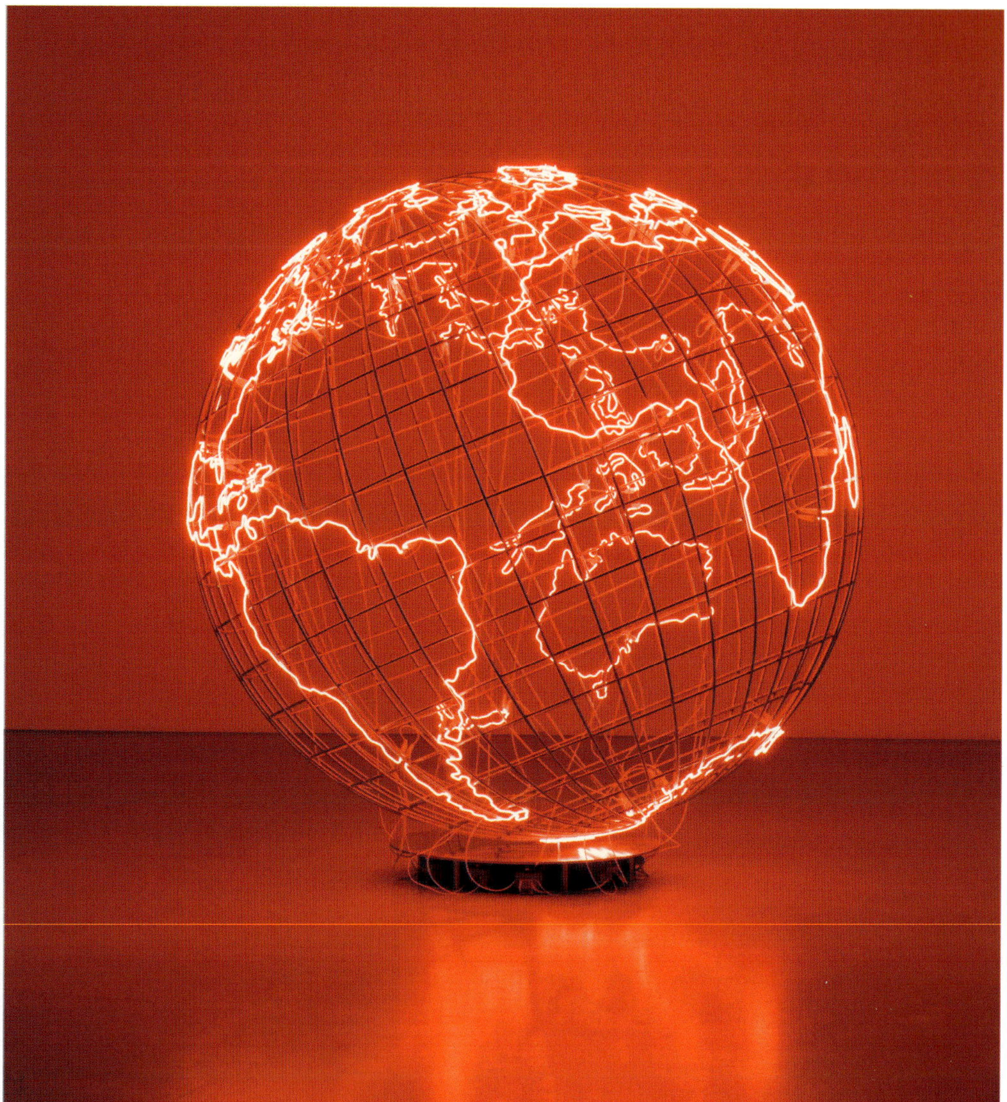

Above: *Hot Spot III* 2009 © Mona Hatoum. Courtesy the artist & MdbK Leipzig Photo: dotgain.info Right: *Impenetrable* 2009 – Installation view at Mathaf: Arab Museum of Modern Art, Doha © Mona Hatoum. Courtesy Mathaf: Arab Museum of Modern Art Photo: Markus Elblaus

MONA HATOUM

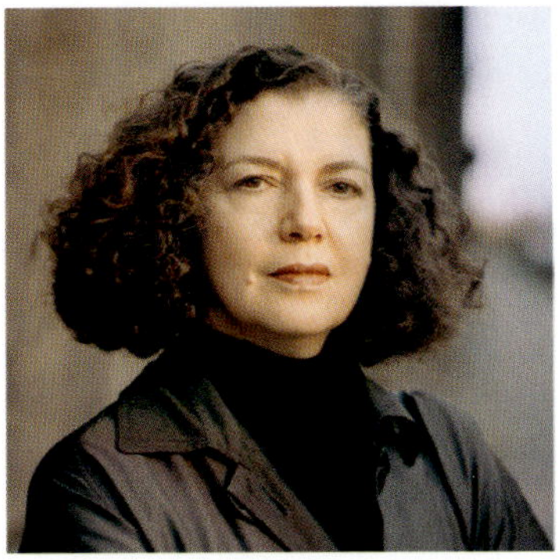

Mona Hatoum (1952–) is a sculptor and installation and performance artist who was born in Beirut into an exiled Palestinian family. As exiles, they were not able to obtain Lebanese identity cards, and so, despite growing up in Beirut, Hatoum always felt like an outsider. During a brief visit to London in 1975, civil war broke out in Lebanon, and she became stranded. Separated from her family, Hatoum continued her studies in London, attending first the Byam Shaw School of Art and later the Slade School of Art (1975–81). During this time she started to create videos and performances that focused on the body as a medium for making political statements about social discord and division. Her first successful work was a video called *Measures of Distance* (1988) featuring photographs of Hatoum's mother in the shower, overlaid with Arabic writing representing the mother's letters from Beirut to her daughter in London, which were also read aloud and recorded on the soundtrack by the artist. The piece shows the intimacy between mother and daughter, but also speaks of exile, displacement, separation and loss as a result of war.

In the 1990s Hatoum's work started to shift away from performance and videos to installation art and sculpture such as *Keffieh* (1999) depicting an Arab scarf with the distinct pattern embroidered in human hair. Her pieces are often concerned with the juxtaposition of opposites such as beauty and horror or desire and revulsion. In several of her works such as *Slicer* (1999), *Daybed* (2008) and *Paravent* (2008), Hatoum enlarged everyday kitchen tools. Presented on a giant scale, the objects lose their familiarity and become threatening. She has also created a number of works using metal grids that allude to exclusion and imprisonment.

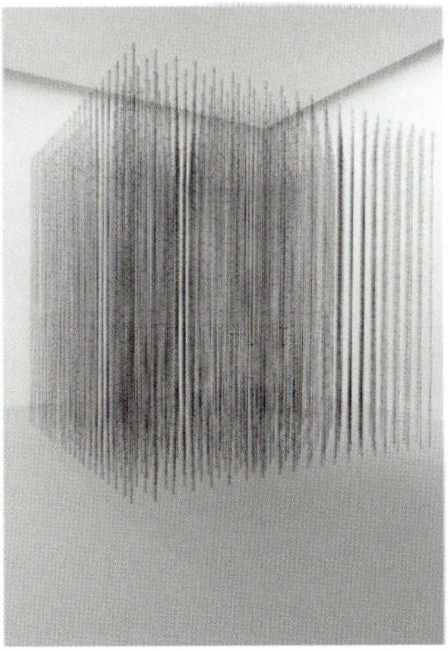

Throughout her career she has had a number of international solo exhibitions, and won many awards including: Nomination for Turner Prize (1995); Joan Miró Prize, Fundació Joan Miró (2011); 10th Hiroshima Art Prize, Hiroshima City Museum of Contemporary Art, Hiroshima (2017); Whitechapel Gallery Art Icon (2018); Nomination for Hepworth Prize for Sculpture (2018) and Praemium Imperiale lifetime achievement for the sculpture category (2019).

"I think everything can be a sculpture for me. From the beginning, I wanted to create a kind of middle world that took you behind the object again by yourself, a world that really surprises people like they haven't seen the object before." – **Katharina Fritsch**

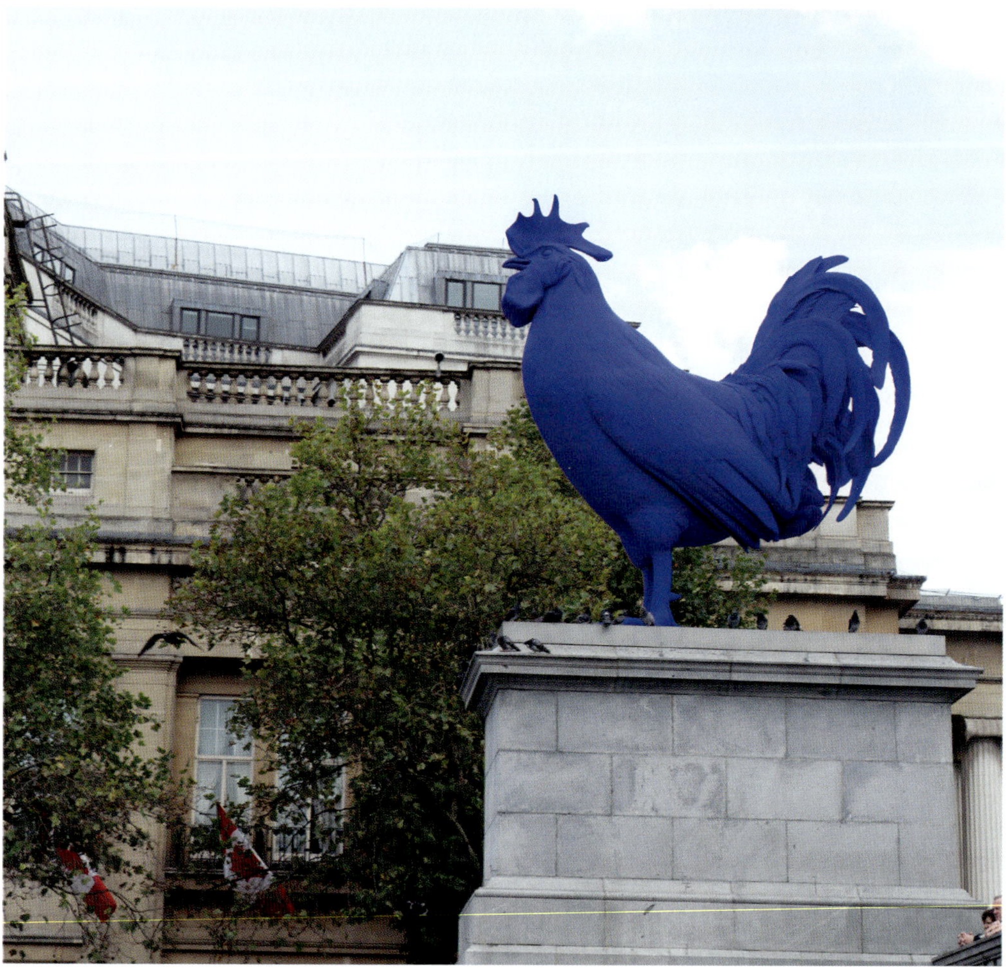

Above: *Hahn/Cock* c. 2013 – Fourth Plinth, Trafalgar Square, London
Right: *Rat King* c. 1993 – Schaulager, Basel, Switzerland

KATHARINA FRITSCH

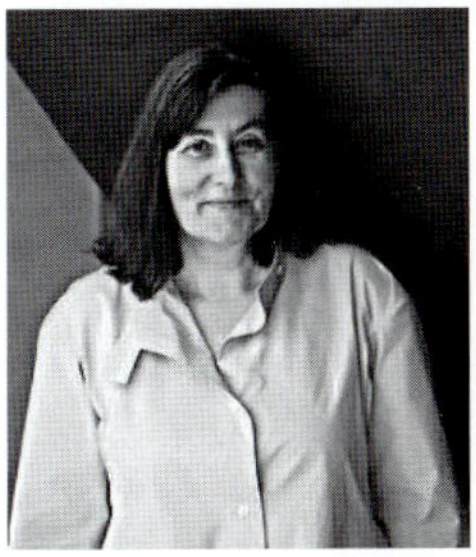

Katharina Fritsch (1956–) is a sculptor famous for her use of monochromatic colour and a precise, almost industrial standard, of sculpture. Born in Essen, West Germany, her grand-father was a salesman for the art supplier Faber-Castell, which may have influenced her use of colour in her work. She first studied art history at the University of Munster then transferred to the Arts Academy in Düsseldorf where she studied under Fritz Schwegler until 1984 and was influenced by Joseph Beuys. She is now a professor of sculpture at the Arts Academy of Düsseldorf.

She began by handcrafting her objects and now makes moulds or models which are used to produce them in her atelier aiding their universality. In this way, Fritsch can make any size or colour of the object, large or small, and can make several editions or copies to sell alongside the display of her sculptures at exhibitions. Fritsch's work replicates familiar objects, animals and human figures and transforms them into the surreal through a bold use of a single bright colour. She further unnerves her audience with the industrial precision with which she crafts her work.

Often compared to Magritte and Duchamp, *Black Table with Table Ware* (1985) was an early piece which sought to change perceptions of everyday objects, but it was her green lifesize *Elephant* that captured attention in the mid-80s. Fritsch came to prominence in 1993 with *Rat King* [below], which involves sixteen giant rats in a circle. Fritsch has collaborated with Frank Fenstermacher, a musician from Der Plan, who acted as her model, symbolizing Everyman. He has appeared in works such as *Tischgesellschaft* (1988), *Dealer* (2001) and *Monk* (2003). The Fourth Plinth Commissioning Group invited Fritsch to create the sculpture *Hahn/Cock*, which was unveiled in Trafalgar Square in summer of 2013. Then-mayor Boris Johnson commented on the irony of a French emblem taking roost in a place commemorating a British victory in the Napoleonic Wars.

She represented Germany at the 1995 Venice Biennale and has had solo exhibitions at Kunstmuseum Basel, the San Francisco Museum of Modern Art, the Art Institute of Chicago, Tate Modern, London and K21 in Düsseldorf. A retrospective exhibition of her work was held at Kunsthaus Zürich in 2009.

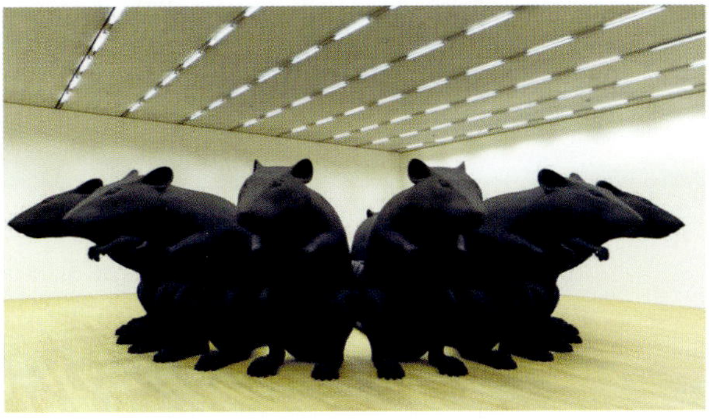

"I resurrect things that have been killed off... My work is all about the potential of materials – even when it looks like they've lost all possibilities."
– Cornelia Parker

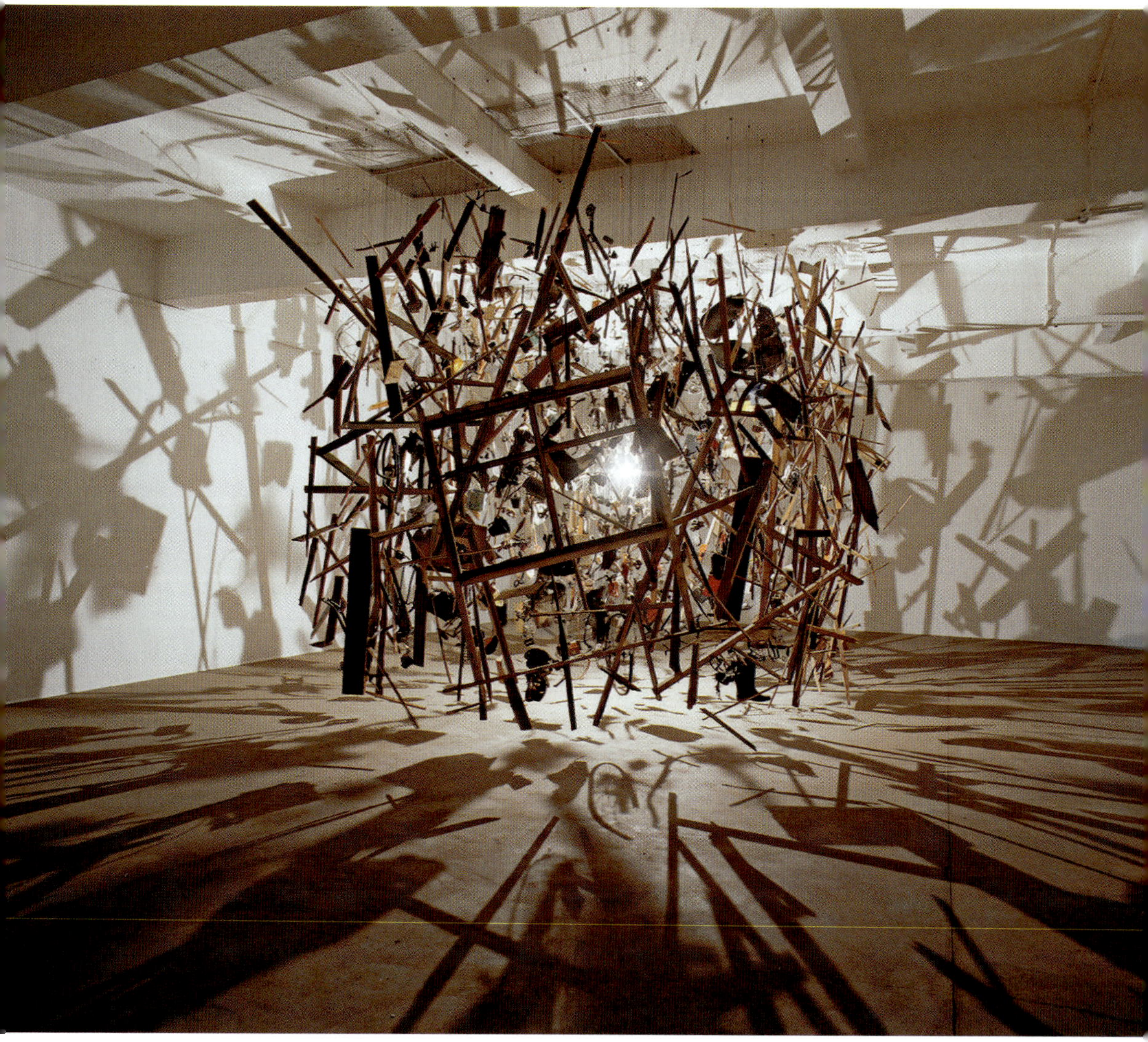

Above: *Cold Dark Matter: An Exploded View* 1991. Collection: Tate
Photo: Hugo Glendinning. Courtesy the artist and Frith Street Gallery, London

Right: *Embryo Firearms* 1995. Photo: Edward Woodman. Courtesy the artist and Frith Street Gallery, London

CORNELIA PARKER

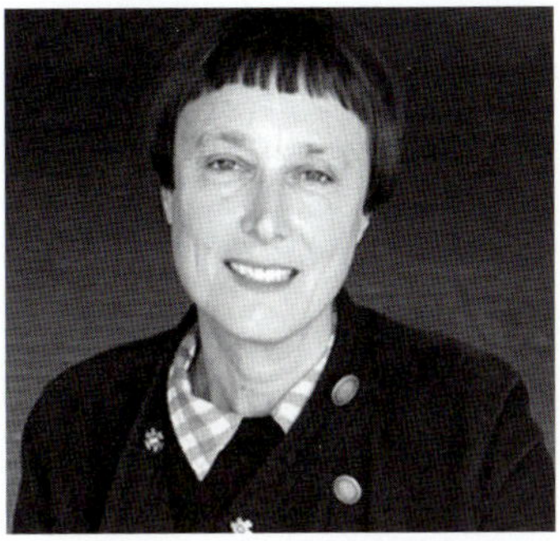

Cornelia Parker (1956–) is an English artist, best known for her bold sculptures and installation art. She was born in Cheshire to a German mother who was a nurse in the Luftwaffe during World War II. Her British grandfather fought in the Battle of the Somme in World War. I

Parker first studied at Gloucester College of Art in 1974, earned a Bachelor's degree at Wolverhampton Polytechnic, and then went on to study for a Master's degree at Reading University, graduating in 1982.

She focuses on the process of altering objects, exploding, cutting and twisting them until they are physically transformed. One of her most well-known works, *Cold Dark Matter: An Exploded View* (1991), first shown at the Chisenhale Gallery, East London, involved her contacting the British army to blow up a shed, taking the fragmented parts, suspending them from the ceiling and placing a single light source at the centre, which represented the centre of the explosion. In 1997 Parker was nominated for the Turner Prize for her series of small works *Avoided Objects*. Her entry titled *Mass (Colder Darker Matter)*, involved gathering the charred remains of a Texas church that had been struck by lightning and suspending them from the ceiling. In 2005, she made a companion piece, *Anti-Mass*, using the same process from a black congregation church destroyed by arson in Kentucky.

She collaborated with actor, Tilda Swinton, on *The Maybe* (1995) at the Serpentine Gallery, London, on a performance piece in which Swinton lay, apparently asleep, inside a vitrine. Parker surrounded the vitrine with other glass cases containing relics of famous historical figures. Her desire to engage with historical artworks saw Rodin's *The Kiss* sculpture in Tate Britain wrapped up with a mile of string, which she titled *The Distance (A Kiss With String Attached)* (2003). In 2009, she was elected to the Royal Academy of Arts and in 2010 she was appointed Officer of the Order of the British Empire (OBE). She also became the first woman to be chosen as the official election artist during the 2017 general election.

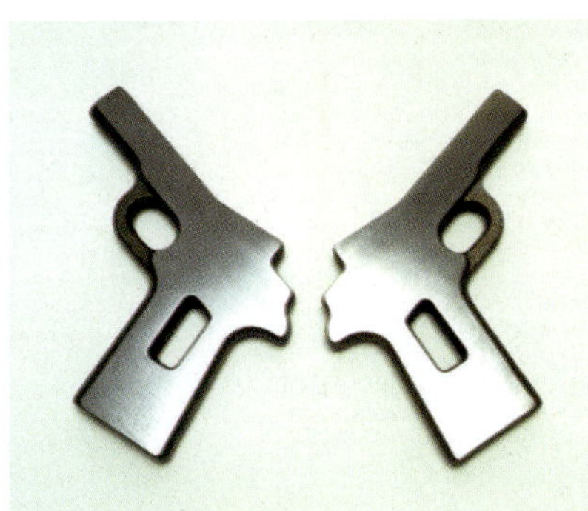

Parker had her first mid-career retrospective exhibition at the Museum of Contemporary Art, Sydney, Australia, in 2019. She is married, has one daughter, and lives and works in London.

***"Art names in order to bring into existence those aspects of reality that our society ignores and keeps in obscurity."* – Doris Salcedo**

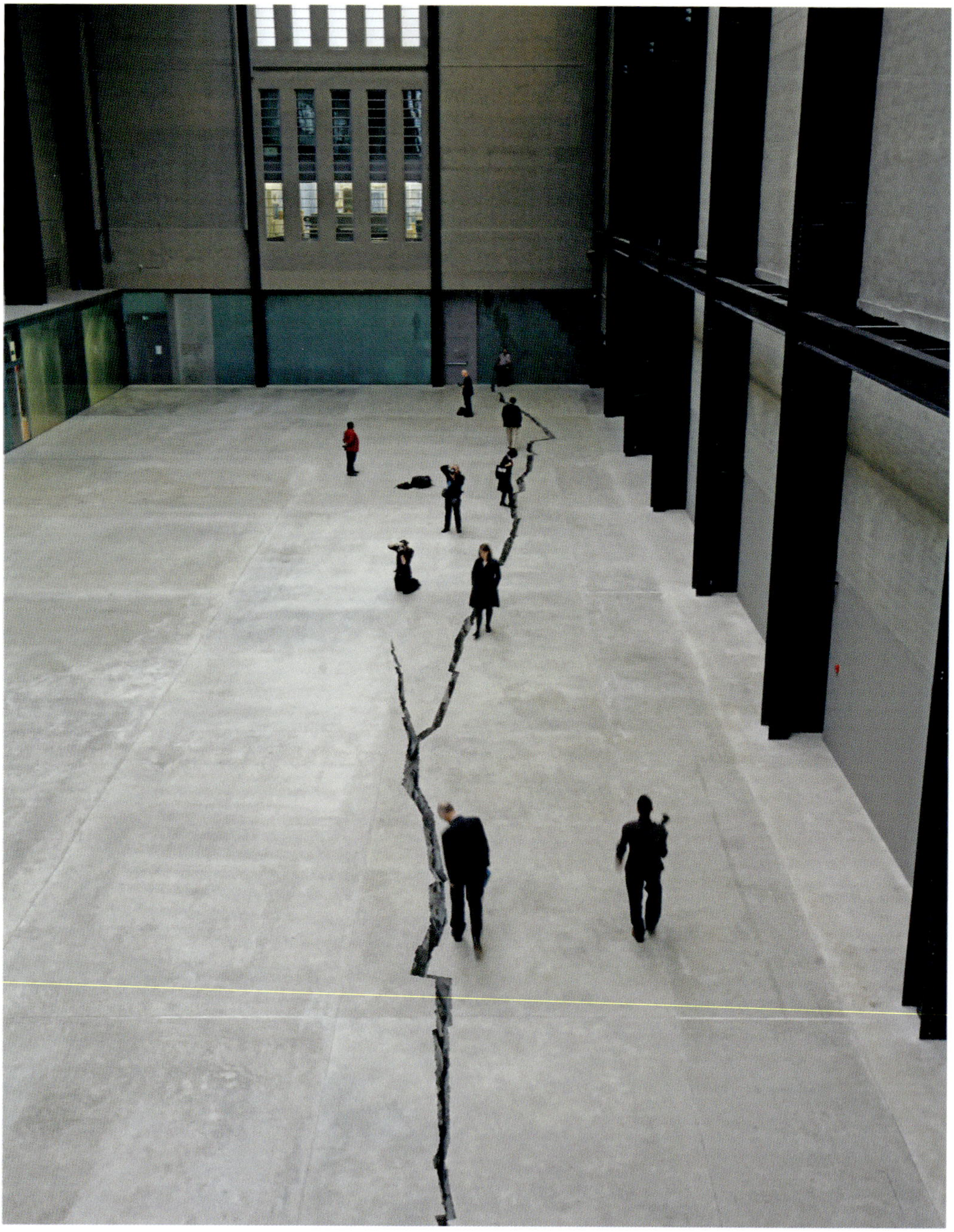

Above: *Shibboleth* 2007 – Turbine Hall, Tate Modern, London. Photo: David Levene

DORIS SALCEDO

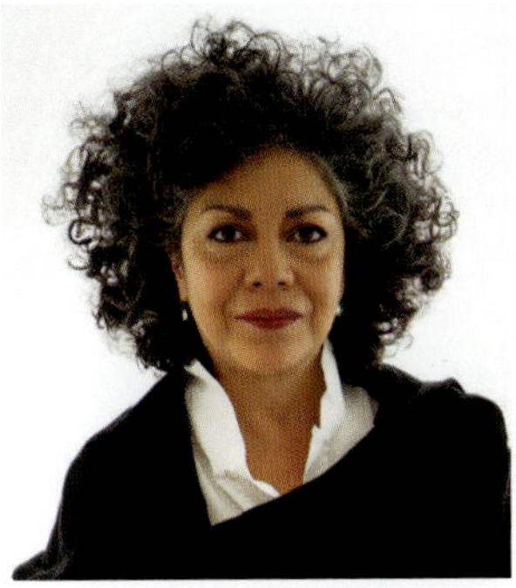

Doris Salcedo (1958–) is a sculptor, political activist, and visual artist. Born and raised in Bogotá, Colombia, her art is shaped by her life in Colombia and focuses largely on the ramifications of the country's political turmoil. She studied at the Universidad de Bogotá Jorge Tadeo Lozano, focusing on painting and then for a Master's degree at New York University, where she was influenced by the work of Joseph Beuys and his belief in the neccessity that an artist combines political awareness with art making.

In 1985, she returned to Bogotá. Her first solo exhibition was mounted at the Casa de Moneda, Banco de la República, Bogotá that same year. Interested in arts education, she worked as director of the Instituto de Bellas Artes, Cali (1987–88), and taught sculpture and art theory at the Universidad Nacional de Colombia (1988–91). Her first US solo show was held at Brooke Alexander Gallery, New York, in 1994.

Memory is central to her work, as well as the emptiness left behind by the disappearance of people, including the loss of her family members, in the Colombian political conflict of the past decades. Her installations are generally composed of commonplace items such as wooden furniture, shoes and clothing.

One of her most profound works *Noviembre 6 y 7* (2002) was to commemorate the 17th anniversary of the Palace of Justice Siege. The siege lasted fifty-three hours and so over a fifty-three-hour period wooden chairs were slowly lowered over the façade of the building to evoke the sense of absence left by those killed in the violence.

Salcedo became the eighth artist to have been commissioned to produce work for the Turbine Hall of the Tate Modern in London. She created *Shibboleth* (2007), a 167-metre-long crack running the length of the hall's floor that represents borders, immigration and racial hatred. *A Flor de Piel* (2013) is a large tapestry of thousands of preserved, hand-sewn red rose petals, intended to honour a nurse who was tortured to death in the Colombian war. It was gifted to the Harvard Art Museums in 2014.

Her awards include a Solomon R. Guggenheim Foundation Grant (1995), the Ordway Prize from the Penny McCall Foundation (2005), Premio Velázquez de las Artes Plásticas (2010) and the 9th Hiroshima Art Prize (2014).

"I think art should be amateur... it should be done for love. I've never seen art as a career and I still don't. If I wanted a career, or a fucking job, I would have gone into business." – **Sarah Lucas**

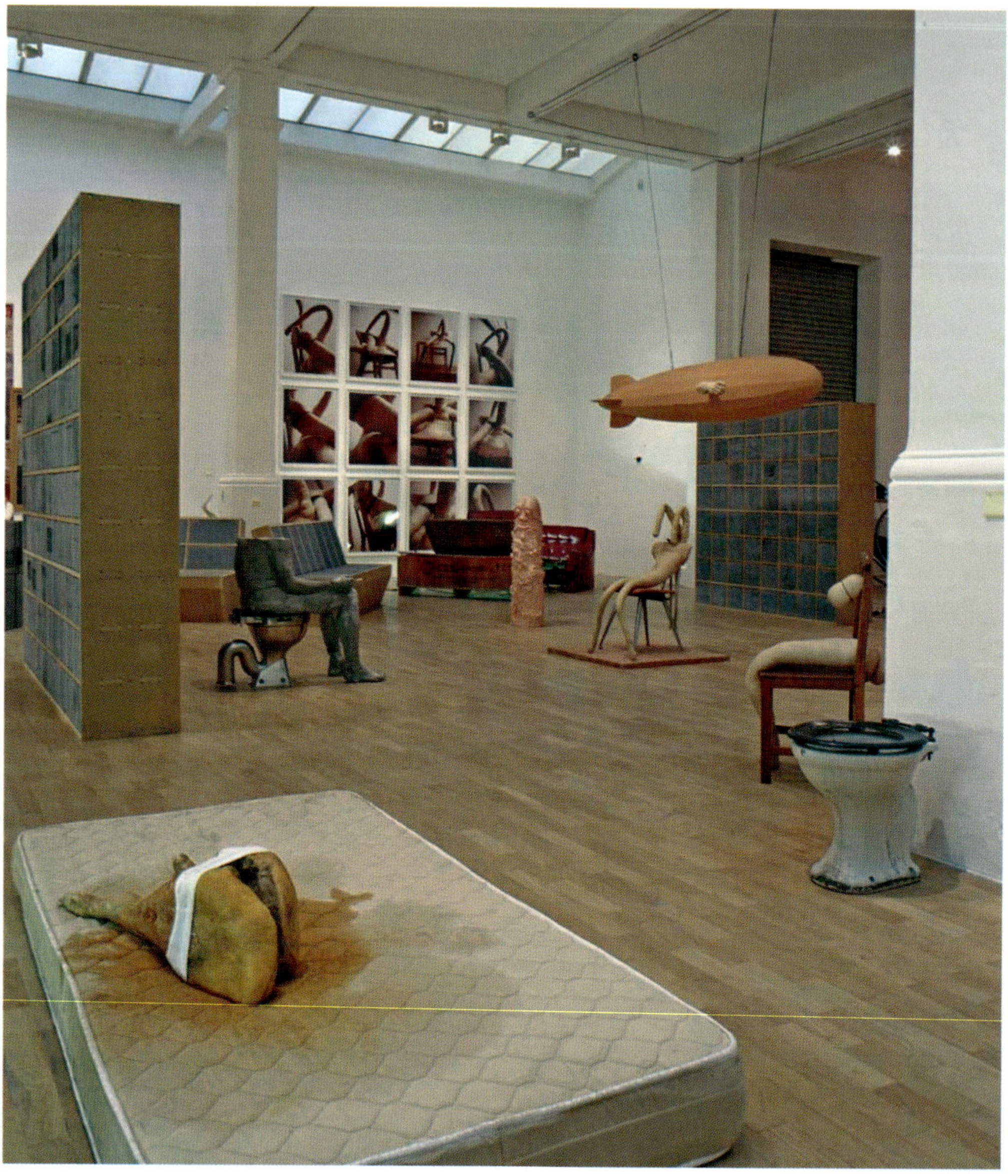

Above: *SITUATION Absolute Beach Man Rubble* 2013 – Whitechapel Gallery, London. Photo: Stephen White. Right: *Cigarette Tits (Idealized Smokers Chest II)* c. 1999. Photo: Andrew Russeth, *The Female Gaze* at Cheim and Read, New York.

SARAH LUCAS

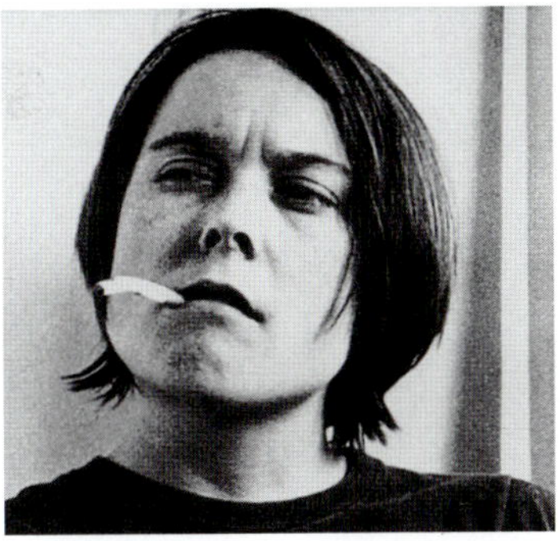

Sarah Lucas (1962–) is a multidisciplinary visual artist and sculptor known for her humour, visual puns and uncompromising exploration of gender, sexuality and language. She was born in North London to working class parents and grew up either playing on the street with boys, or making things to keep herself amused. At 16, she left school and hitchhiked around Europe before deciding to go to art school, enrolling at the London College of Printmaking in 1983. Studying at Goldsmiths College the following year, she met Damien Hirst, Angus Fairhurst and Gillian Wearing, forming part of the group who became known as the Young British Artists. The media attention they were able to attract, along with the support of collector Charles Saatchi, led to the growth of art galleries and art fairs in the capital. Lucas contributed to Hirst's seminal group exhibition, *Freeze*, in London's Docklands, and formed an early friendship with Sadie Coles who would later represent Lucas through her gallery Sadie Coles HQ. Lucas became increasingly dissatisfied with the focus on her male contemporaries, setting up a shop-cum-installation briefly with Tracey Emin to sell objects poking fun at male bias, inspired by Westwood and McLaren's shop selling punk clothing in Chelsea's King's Road.

Solo exhibitions such as *The Whole Joke* (1992) and *Bunny Gets Snookered* (1997) led to her inclusion in the *Sensation* exhibition at the Royal Academy in 1997. Damien Hirst has been a staunch collector of Lucas's work and while some of her YBA colleagues have become less popular over time, Lucas's work has gained in prestige. Her solo exhibition at the Whitechapel Gallery, *SITUATION Absolute Beach Man Rubble* (2013) brought together several of her iconic pieces from 1992 onwards such as *Where Does It All End?* (1994), *Unknown Soldier* (2003) and *Jubilee* (2012) and brought her new respect and a growing following.

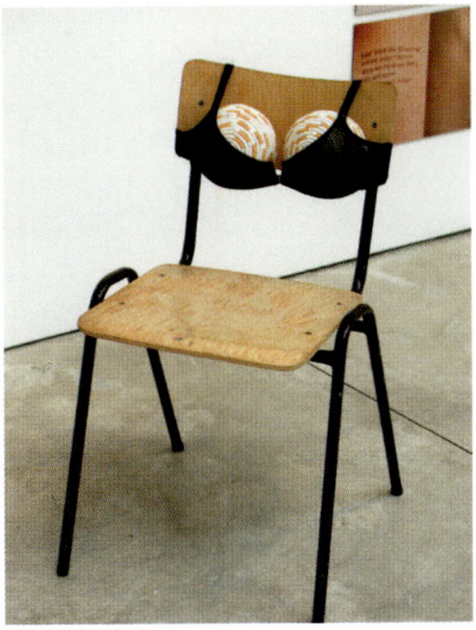

In 2015, *I Scream Daddio,* an installation of *Muses* comprising plaster half-nudes arranged in bawdy poses on modern furniture in a custard yellow room, startled in the British Pavilion at the Venice Biennale. In 2018, The New Museum in New York presented her first American retrospective, *Au Naturel,* which included *VOX POP DORIS*, a pair of four-metre-tall thigh-high platform boots cast in concrete.

Above Portrait: Sarah Lucas, *Fighting Fire with Fire,* 1996 © Sarah Lucas. Courtesy Sadie Coles HQ, London

"I make all this stuff in the studio, but I also work on these white elephants – like House or Untitled Monument – things that are incredibly ambitious, take an awful long time to do, involve a lot of controversy, an awful lot of people, and don't make any money particularly, but it's just because I need to make them."
– Rachel Whiteread

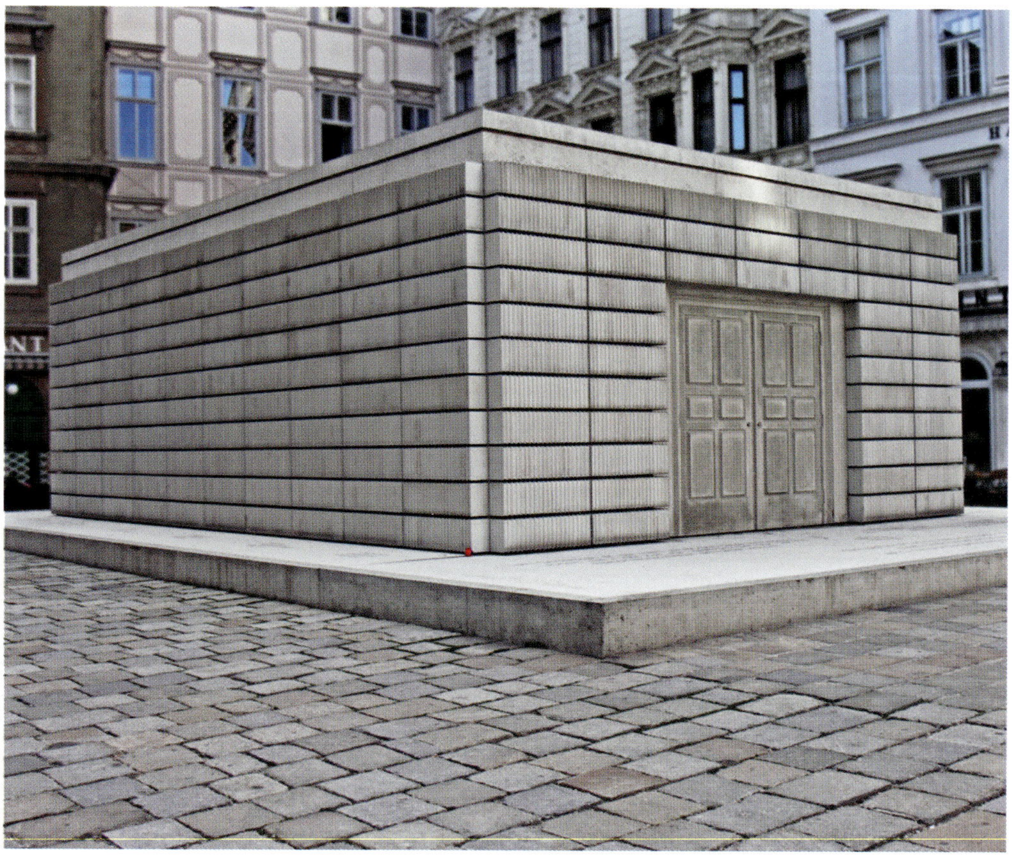

Above: *Holocaust Memorial* 1995-2000 – Judenplatz Vienna
Right: *House* 1993 – Grove Road, Mile End, East London, prior to demolition
© Rachel Whiteread/DACS 2020

RACHEL WHITEREAD

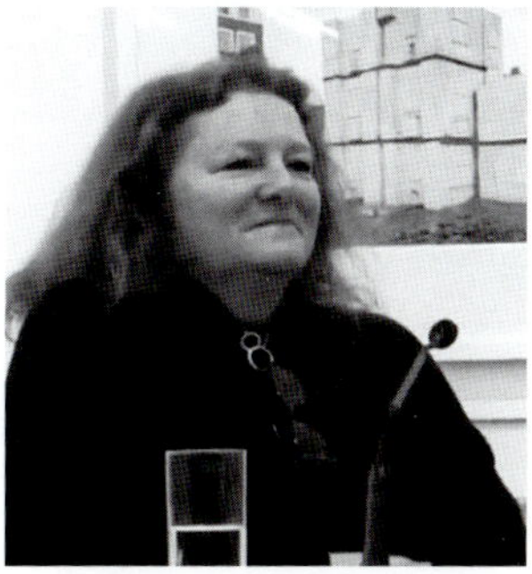

Rachel Whiteread (1963–) is a sculptor best-known for her work *House* which won the Turner Prize in 1993. Born in Ilford in Essex, her mother was an artist and her father a geography teacher. She studied painting initially at Brighton Polytechnic and then a Master's degree in sculpture at Slade School of Art, London (1985-87), where Alison Wilding and Phyllida Barlow were tutors. Whiteread's work is primarily concerned with the negative space around objects, which she says carries the "residue of years and years of use". In her first solo show in 1988 she exhibited two pieces: *Closet*, comprised the interior of a closet cast in plaster, based on comforting childhood memories of playing hide-and-seek; the other one was *Shallow Breath*, the underside of a bed, made in response to the death of her father. *Ghost* (1990) was first shown at the Chisenhale Gallery and was picked up by Charles Saatchi for inclusion in his first Young British Artists show in 1992. *Ghost* had the good fortune to be sent to the Gagosian Gallery in London, just prior to a fire in the storage warehouse which destroyed many works in the Saatchi collection. In 2004, it was sold to the National Gallery of Art in Washington, D.C.

House [below], a concrete cast of the interior of a Victorian house, caused controversy when it won the Turner Prize in 1993, and brought Whiteread to public attention as the first woman to win the prize. *House* was sited in Mile End, East London and was demolished by Tower Hamlets council a few months later.

Whiteread won the commission to make a Holocaust memorial in the Judenplatz, Vienna. Also known as *The Nameless Library* it features cement books in a library with the spines of the books facing inwards so that the titles are unable to be read. It speaks of the cultural absence, memory and loss left by the 65,000 Austrian Jews who were murdered by the Nazis.

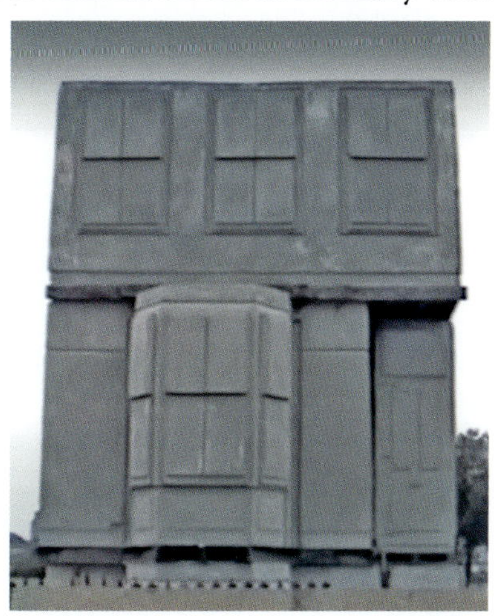

Invited to fill the Turbine Hall at Tate Modern in 2005, her installation, *Embankment,* resembled ice cubes stacked to varying heights and a maze for visitors to enjoy.

Whiteread was appointed a CBE in 2006 and a Dame in 2019. She lives with partner, fellow sculptor Marcus Taylor. The couple have two sons.

"It's pretty hard to do anything that's not a cliché now."
– Anya Gallaccio

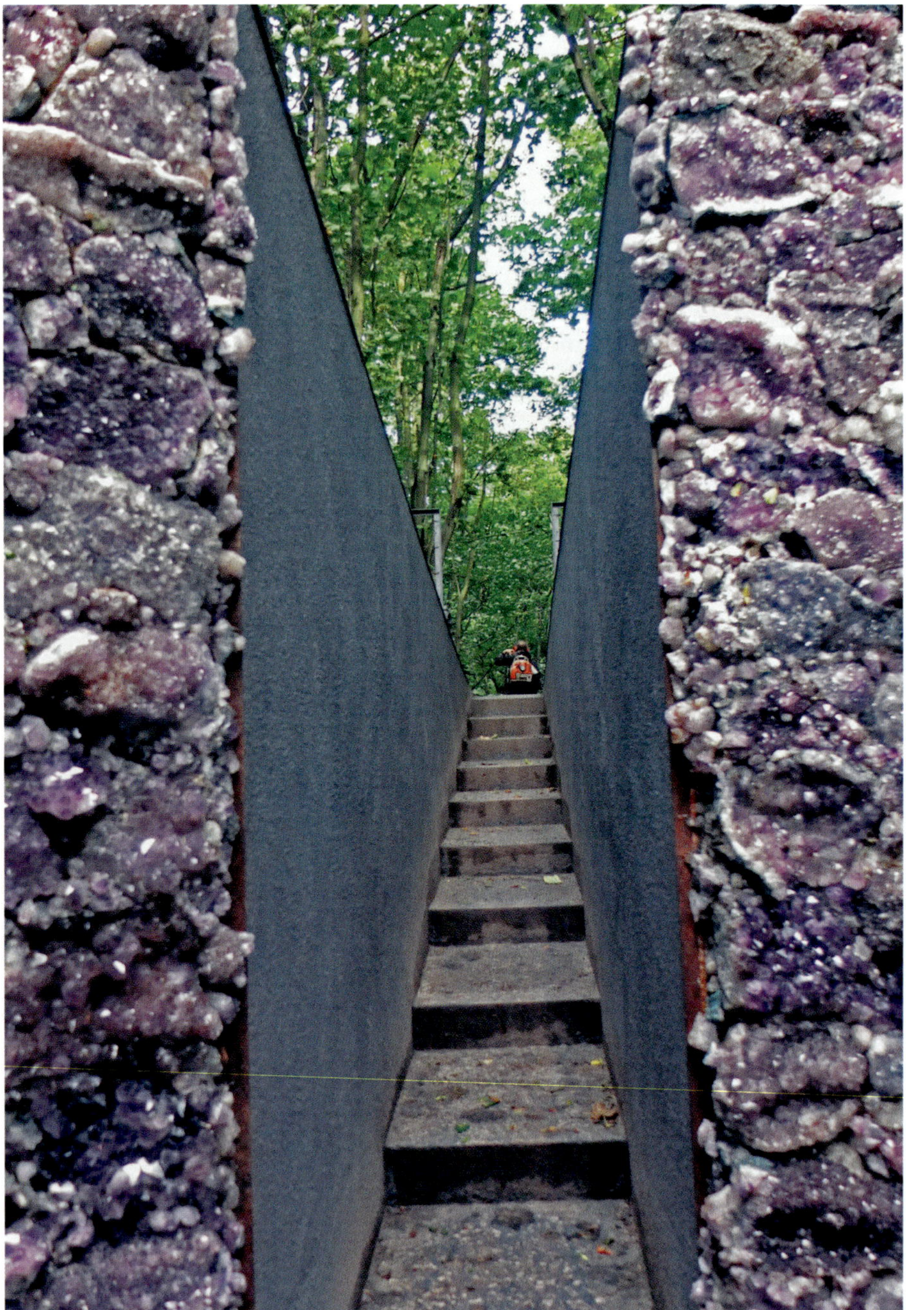

Above: *The Light Pours Out of Me* 2012 – Jupiter Artland, Wilkieston, West Lothian. Photo: Jim Barton © Anya Gallaccio.

ANYA GALLACCIO

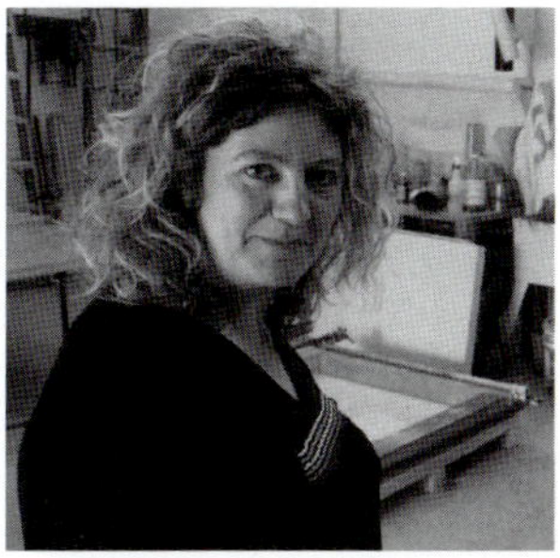

Anya Gallaccio (1963–) is an installation artist. She was born in the Scottish town of Paisley, and grew up in south-west London. She attended Kingston Polytechnic in the mid-80s then Goldsmiths College (1985–88), where she was a contemporary of Damien Hirst. Gallaccio rose to prominence early in her career after participating in Hirst's *Freeze* exhibition in 1988, in which she poured a ton of molten lead onto the floor of a building in the Surrey Docks.

Gallaccio often works with organic substances such as flowers, chocolate, sugar or ice, valuing the unpredictability and transient nature of these materials. In her work *Intensities and Surfaces* (1996), Gallaccio built a thirty-two ton stack of ice, which then melted over a period of three months. There is an inevitable impermanence about her work; it transforms throughout her exhibitions as natural materials change: fruit rots, flowers wilt and ice melts. In some of her works this transformation is halted for example when bean pods or whole trees are cast in metal, freezing a moment in time.

Gallaccio's solo show at the Icon Gallery, which included a bronze apple tree, was nominated for the Turner Prize (2003), *because I could not stop* displayed at the Lehmann Maupin Gallery New York. The work features an apple tree cast in bronze adorned with red apples. The apples slowly decayed through the months of the exhibition, filling the gallery with the smell of rotting.

Her work has been influential in the way it explores the language of sculpture and challenges the traditional notion that a sculpture should be an eternally fixed monument. Instead, her works endure through the memories of those who experienced them. In *Red on Green* (1992) she gathered 10,000 red roses at the ICA, London and allowed them to decay, providing a visible emblem of death and the passing of love.

In 2016, she utilized digital technology to create a stainless steel tree to replace a plane tree which had died for the Whitworth Gallery in Manchester. Also working with digital technology, she made a huge 3D printer to extrude a clay mountain, for her show *Beautiful Minds*, at the MCASD, San Diego in 2015.

Gallaccio has had over fifteen solo exhibitions of her work presented internationally and her work was also included in the Walker Art Center's *Brilliant!* show. She is a Professor in the Department of Visual Arts at the University of California, San Diego.

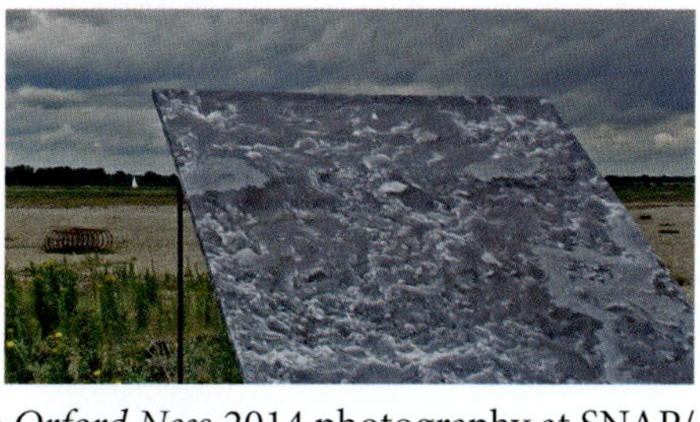

Above: *Orford Ness* 2014 photography at SNAP/ Aldeburgh Festival Photo:Amanda Slater

"There is something about working big that I find really exciting. It's more physical and you get a much better feeling of the space that the sculpture occupies. When a piece is complete and I stand back and look at it, I hope to get that tingly feeling you get when you hear a beautiful piece of music. It's then that I know I'm getting somewhere." – **Sophie Ryder**

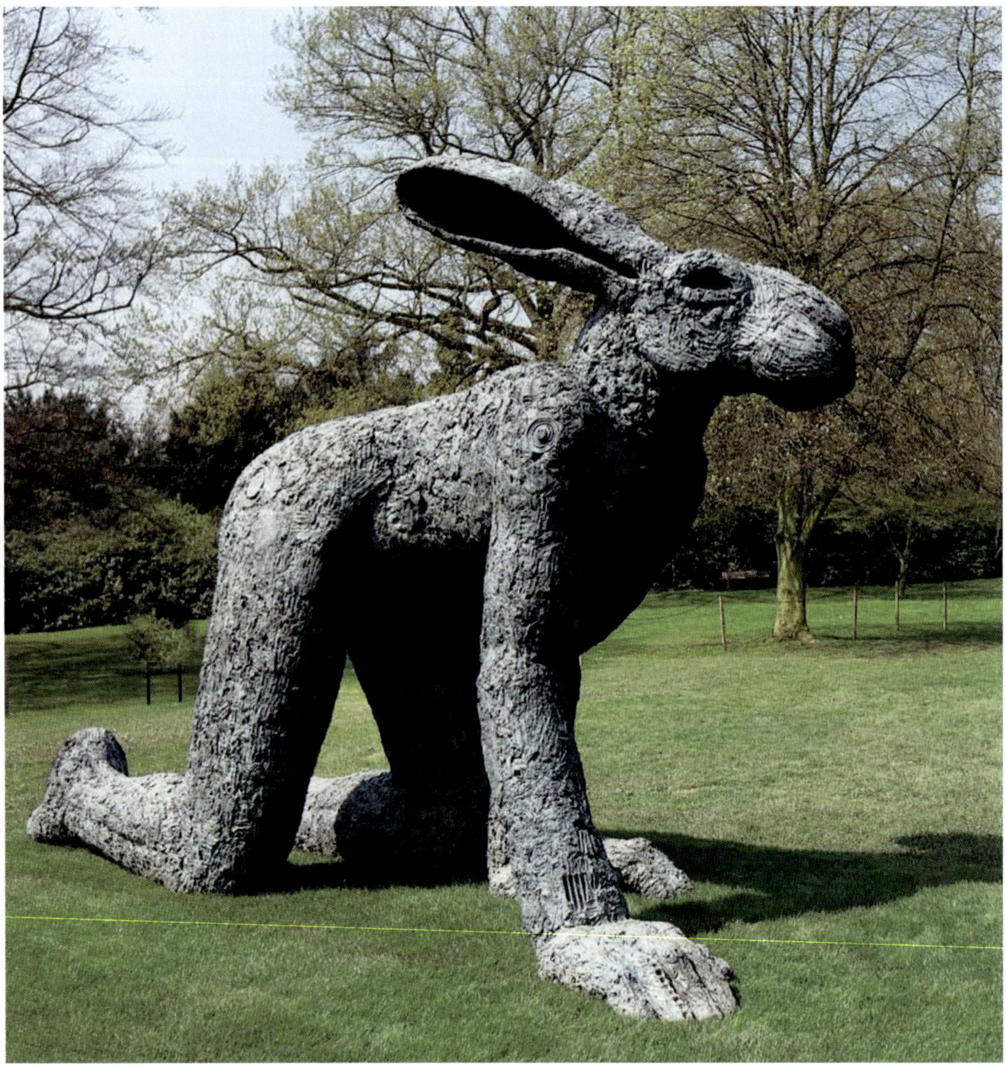

Above: *Crawling* c. 2000. Photo: Jonty Wild. Courtesy Yorkshire Sculpture Park
Right: *Pink Lady Hare and Big Brown Dog* c. 1999. Photo: Tania Dolvers
Portrait photo right above: Gabriel Kenny-Ryder

SOPHIE RYDER

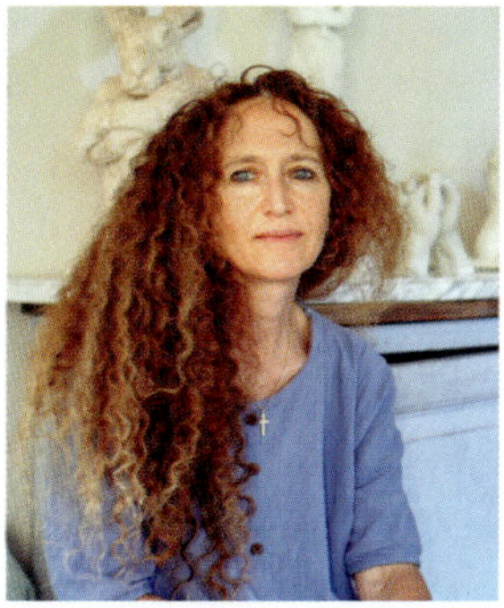

Sophie Ryder is a sculptor who infuses playfulness in her works using wire-framed sculpture, sometimes on a monumental scale. Born in London to a French mother, as a child, she spent her summers in France and loved Picasso's work. His image of the minotaur influenced her own work.

Ryder first studied at Kingston Polytechnic (1980-81) and then Combined Arts at the Royal Academy of Art (1981-84) but was encouraged to pursue sculpture by Sir Hugh Casson, the then director of the Royal Academy. She was appointed artist-in-residence at Yorkshire Sculpture Park on leaving the Royal Academy.

Combined with her animalistic subject matter, her major works are often situated outdoors where they draw upon nature to reflect the character of her subjects, such as the giant *Crawling* Lady Hare, recently installed in Berkeley Square, London. She decided to use the figure of a hare, with its feminine and fertility associations, as a counterpart to her minotaur figure. Ryder modelled the hare's body on her own. Her giant hybrid creatures, part human, part animal explore human sexuality and emotion, often inspiring awe in the viewer who chances upon them in a public place. She is not concerned with simple representation, seeking to work on a mystical level. Ryder makes an initial maquette and then scales this up to full size. Her treatment of the bronze surface is unique. At the initial plaster stage, she gouges out sections of her work and adds in elements to give texture, such as old machine parts, wire, paper and plaster.

Ryder enjoys working on a large scale, despite the construction challenges. She says she tries to: "make sure that the wire is not too dense and that the light can still shine through, so that when they are walked around they give a feeling of movement that helps to bring them to life." In 1994 a sculpture of five minotaurs fell foul of church censors and was banned from an exhibition at Winchester Cathedral because of the prominence of their genitalia. In 1996 she created an installation called *Temple to 200 Rabbits* which has been shown all over the world prior to arriving at the Hignell Gallery in London in 2017.

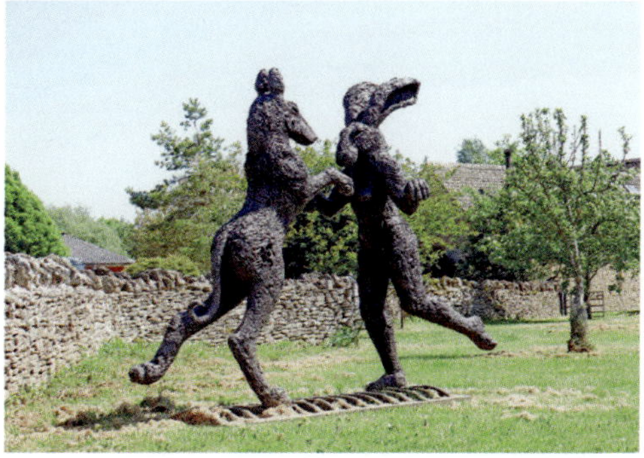

She lives on a farm in the Cotswolds with her partner and four dogs and has a studio in Provence, France.

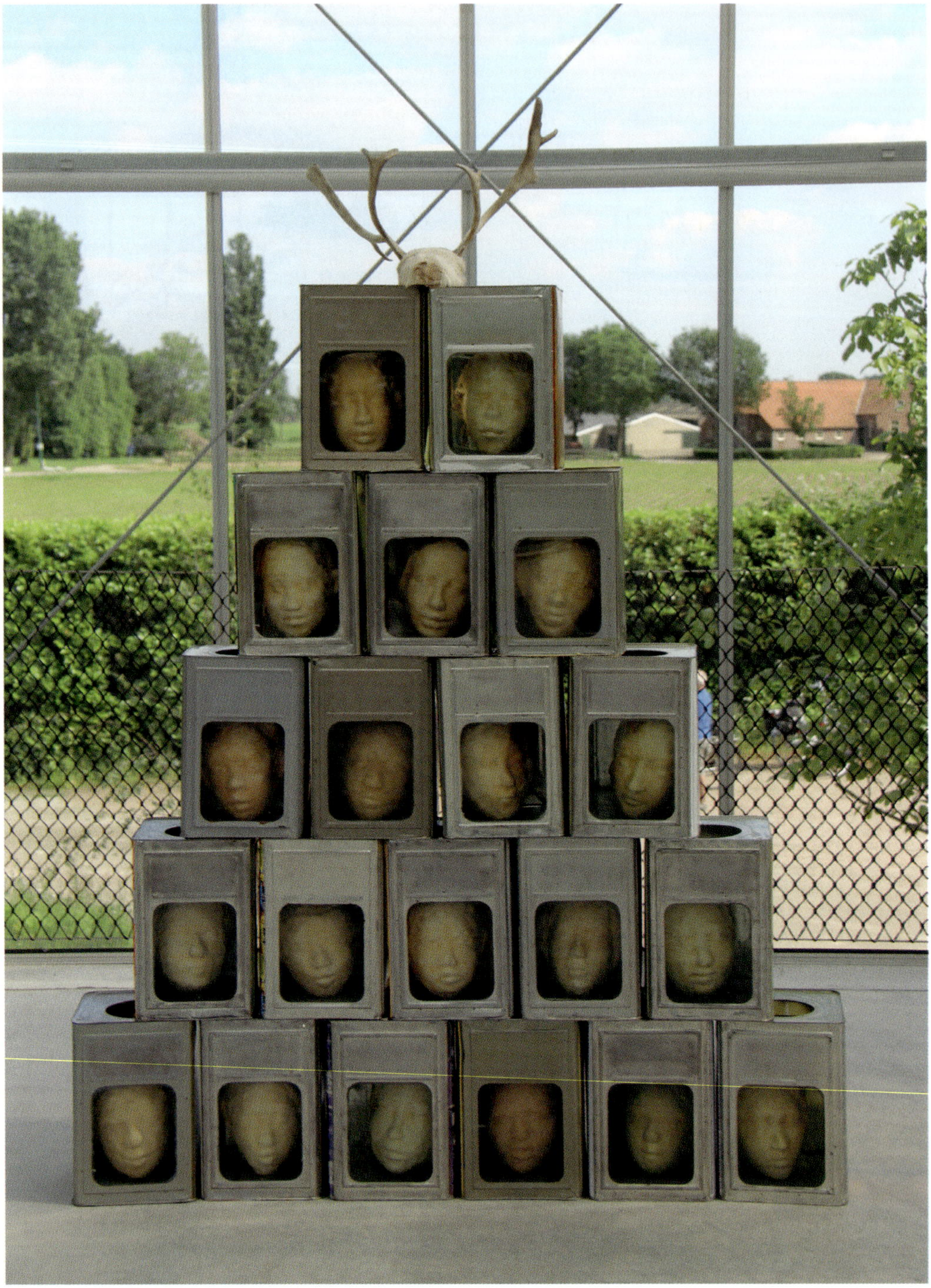

A Day in the Woods © Caroline Kampfraath 2015

50 WOMEN SCULPTORS

2. CONTEMPORARY WOMEN SCULPTORS

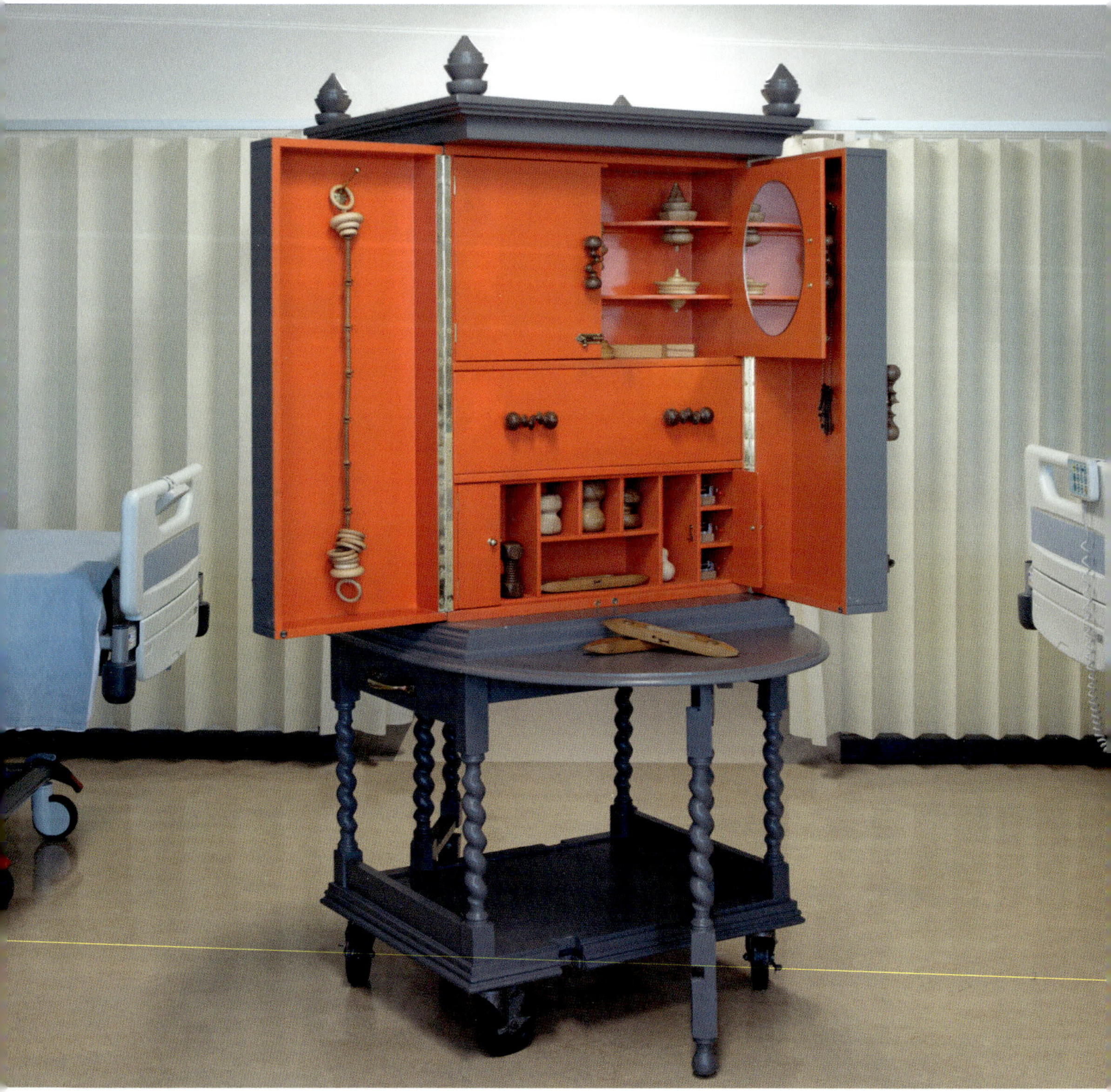

The Dispensary 2016. Private collection.
Photo: Anne Purkiss/RSS

TABATHA ANDREWS

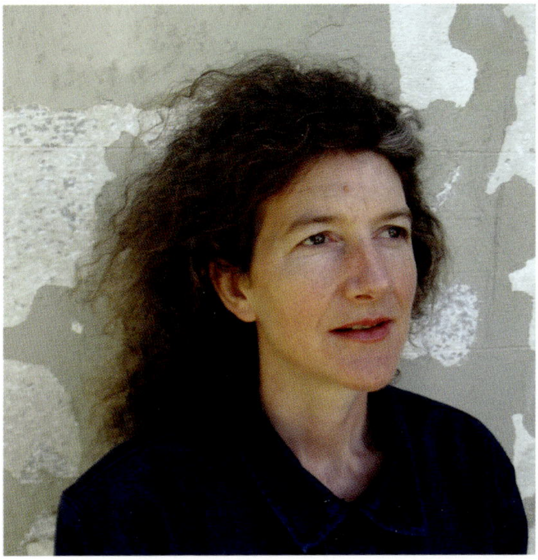

Tabatha Andrews makes sculpture, performance and installation exploring how materials and sound embody memory. She works across disciplines and in a wide variety of communities and contexts, often working collaboratively. Commissions include work for the Monument to the Fire of London, the Forest of Dean Sculpture Trust, Plymouth Art Weekender, Science Gallery London and Chelsea and Westminster Hospital. In 2015 she made *Among Remote Lost Objects* for ROOMartspace London and KARST Plymouth, a sound installation involving composer John Matthias and blind opera singer Victoria Oruwari. She won the First@108 Public Art Award to make sculpture for the Dementia wards of Chelsea and Westminster Hospital, resulting in *The Dispensary*, a 'haptic cabinet of curiosities' made with local woodturners, which won the Building Better Healthcare Award in 2017. She was shortlisted for the Mark Tanner Sculpture Award, 2018 and was granted a Kings College London Innovation Funding Award to explore communication and listening with the neurobiologist Andrea Streit. The resulting performance *Stillpoint* took place at Somerset House in 2019. Andrews collaborated with composer Charlotte Harding on the vocal work *Antiphon*, a commission for Science Gallery London (2019). She was Artist in Residence at Gloucester Cathedral in 2002–3 and studied at Edinburgh University, Glasgow School of Art, Skowhegan School of Art and The Slade. Andrews teaches at Falmouth School of Art and the University of Plymouth.

HOW DID YOU COME TO MAKE SCULPTURE?

In the 70s, I lived in a rambling Victorian house which had unused spaces and places to dream: a large dressing up chest, old chicken houses you could crawl into, wardrobes with cut glass handles to peer through and a basement with a long dark corridor full of unlikely objects. I remember my mother making ludicrous deserts – giant apple strudels with pastry stretched across the dining room table, huge crenellations of sponge fingers. My grandmother was a total eccentric who lived in a house piled high with junk and would go through our rubbish bins to see what we had thrown out, and my grandfather, who was a psychiatrist, collected extraordinary artefacts we played with – a shadow puppet theatre from Indonesia and a polyphon, which is a giant Edwardian music box. My father was a brilliant caricaturist and teacher. My earliest installations were houses built out of hay bales that progressed to clay and straw structures built around climbing frames. I also remember a children's serial *The Changes* – there was an underground, totemic stone that spoke unintelligibly and affected the electrical energy in all things. I had some nasty electric shocks as a child and started to feel this energy was in everything – this sense has permeated my work.

WHO WERE YOUR INFLUENCES AND OR ROLE MODELS?

Phyllida Barlow was a crucial influence during my time at the Slade – she bored straight into the back of my head, and called my work "thunderous". I'm particularly fond of her *Touchpiece* series, which she made in the dark when her children were asleep.

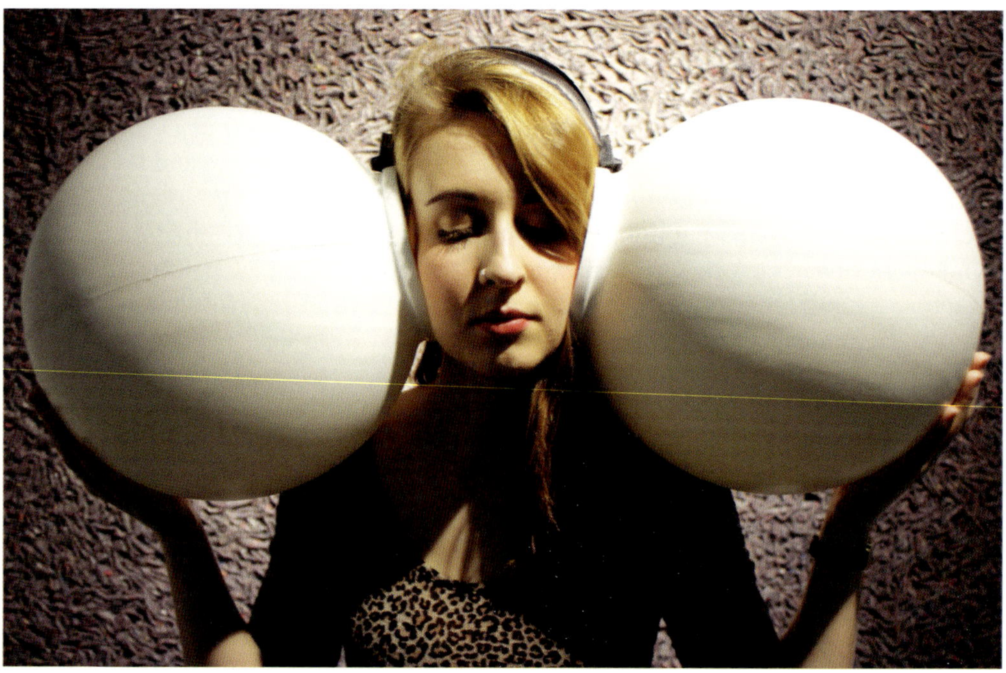

Listening Objects 2014–2019

The way Alice Oswald talks about her poetry is close to the way I feel about making work – the word becoming alive as a thing or energy in space, rather than just telling a story. The plays of Samuel Beckett excite me too – that uncanny power of the inner voice, the starkness of his stage direction, the way he uses light, darkness and restricted, repetitive movements in *Not I* and *Quad*.

Going to experience James Turrell's *Gasworks* installation at the Henry Moore in Halifax in 1993 was incredible – you were pushed lying on a stretcher into this gas sphere, as if having an MRI scan, and then subjected to an incredible variety of coloured light changes in a ganzfeld-type psychology experiment. This work, combined with visiting him in Arizona a year later, was an important influence on my later work with sensory perception and light.

The Paraorchestra with Charles Hazlewood have been doing extraordinary work recently. *The Nature of Why* (2019) mixed disabled and non-disabled dancers and musicians with the audience – incredible, transformative work that broke boundaries at every level and left people feeling lost for words but deeply connected.

WHO ENCOURAGED YOU?

Many encounters, some short, others over time, with Liz Ogilvie, Suzanne Treister, Guy Brett, Shirin Neshat, Susan Derges, Jim Harold, Sandie Macrae – and most of all, friends and family.

DID YOU HAVE ANY FORMAL TRAINING?

I've always been happiest between disciplines. While studying Art History at Edinburgh University (1987-1991), I acted in James Joyce's *Ulysses* and then a one-woman show, *Medea*, at the Bedlam Theatre. My director had studied at Le Coq – putting gesture and emotion before language was a powerful influence on me. In 1992 I began a degree in Environmental Art at Glasgow School of Art. This was a raw and ground-breaking course about art responding to context. We had to make public art projects out in the city, beyond the gallery. Then to develop my studio practice, I moved into Painting, where I graduated making an architectural installation. This was difficult at the time as the Painting department was very male dominated and old school and I was awarded my degree because the Sculpture department fought for me!

My time at the Slade (1999-2001) was challenging but absolutely crucial. The art world at the time was market-driven, revolving around image-based work as commodity. I chose the Slade because its teaching bucked this trend – we were encouraged to really get immersed in the process, to hold onto the integrity of the work above all else, whether it was easily documentable or not. There I made works about voice, language, emotion and authority. UCL was great as you could work across disciplines – I would go into Phonetics to work with speech, or into Physics to borrow waveform oscillators. I

Stair 2001 Photo: Cliff Haynes

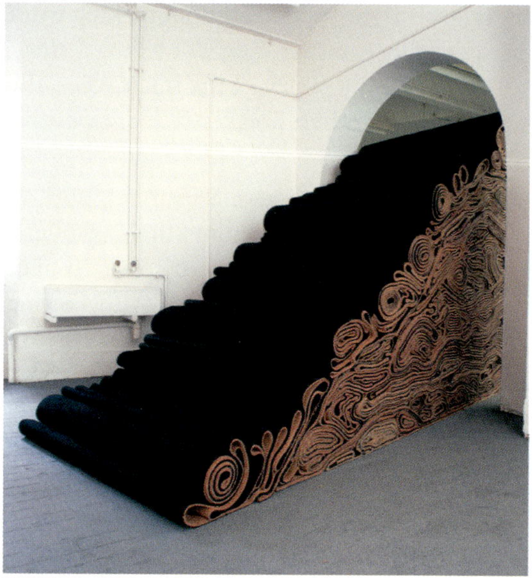

made the bronze casts *Forbitten Words* and the felt installation *Stair* at that time. I was also part of a strong peer group (including Nathaniel Rackowe, Amanda Francis, Conrad Shawcross) and we made some great group shows in disused warehouses across London.

IS THE ENVIRONMENT IMPORTANT?

In 1994, while at Glasgow, I won an award to visit James Turrell and the Roden Crater in Arizona. The Painted Desert was deeply affecting – there is very little light pollution there so the stars are extraordinary, while the lack of oxygen (due to its altitude) means you get nosebleeds and static shocks – you can't help but feel really alive and connected to the cosmos. This infiltrates the work. So living on Dartmoor is constantly inspiring to me - it is a bleak, primordial, craggy expanse and the way light rakes across it changes the landscape constantly.

EPHEMERAL OR LONG-LASTING?

The work usually becomes a transitory event rather than a monument, surviving as a photograph once a project is over. This is a paradox – the installations are often controlled and immersive situations, yet the photographs go on to tell a new kind of story and can be treacherous.

I like to combine a powerful material presence with the more fugitive energies of light, sound or physical movement. I've made several works that use the human voice as material and metaphor, including *Among Remote Lost Objects* (2015) a performance installation which explored resonance as presence and absence. Victoria Oruwari, an opera singer who is blind, sang to a small audience in a pitch-black, sound-deadening chamber made of felt, which smelt strongly of wool and soaked up light and sound. Singers usually use their body and architecture as resonators, but here you could hear the body producing sound in a new and intimate way that some people found difficult and others loved.

A lot of my work is collaborative, interdisciplinary and participatory – I love being challenged by different ways of knowing the world and often work with musicians and scientists. I made the performance *Antiphon* (2019) with composer Charlotte Harding at Science Gallery London. *Antiphon* was inspired by otoacoustic emissions, those tiny sounds our ears make in response to external sounds, almost as if we are bats trying to locate ourselves in space. Oruwari sang this in a call and response sequence with Harding playing cajon, sounding out a vast stairwell.

IS THERE A PARTICULAR THEME OR THEMES WHICH ARE CENTRAL TO YOUR WORK?

I use the stuff of the world to make sculpture and installations that translate the energy around us into material – whether that's sound, light, memory or thought. These works are usually visual but at the same time they are trying to involve the other senses at a heightened level; to experience the world as a tiny child, before the senses split apart.

I am a matterist in the sense that, like Carl Andre, who coined this term, I want to free matter from depiction, to assert a world of haptic experience beyond the visual. The world I experience is so often a flat skin of images – I want to break through this skin and make it three-dimensional. Or rather I think I am trying to climb inside matter, to reach a space that can't be depicted or described or possessed, a space of physical experience that reminds me I am alive. This space is a grey area between thingness and nothingness. I think of it as the membranes through which we perceive the world; the skin, the eardrum, the retina, the tongue. The place where thought becomes thing.

Sculpture occupies an awkward position in the real world. It inhabits our physical space, but it speaks of a world of mental images beyond the material. For me, sculpture is a way of bypassing language – and vision, our dominant sense – to get to a state of suspension of judgement, or latency. This can be disorientating or unsettling for the viewer as it often involves the removal of the structures that make us feel safe, but I'm interested in how this heightened awareness can trigger memory and the unconscious.

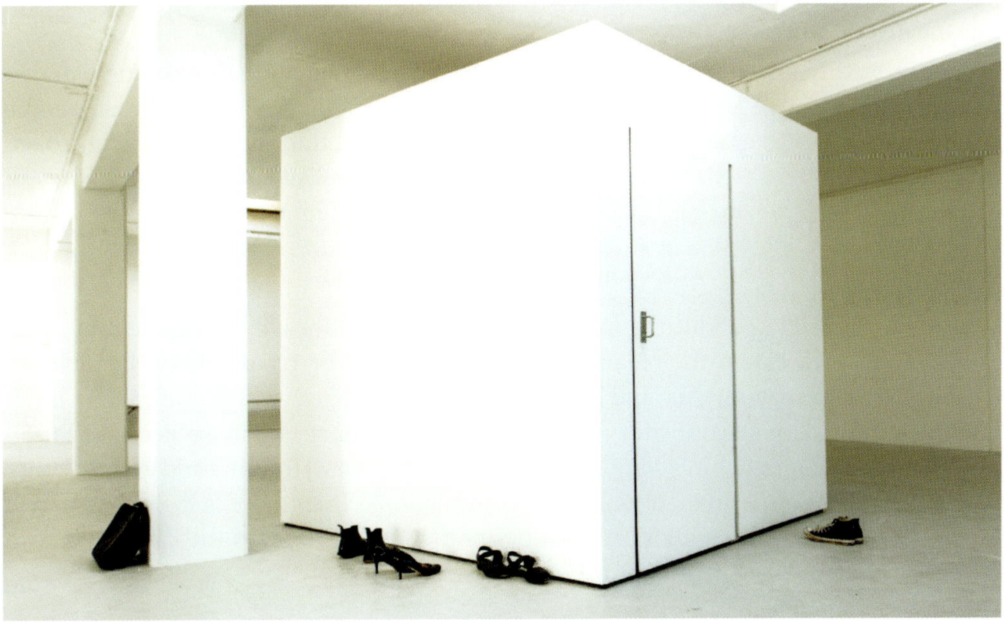

Among Remote Lost Objects, 2015 Photo: Dom Moore/ACE

I'm fascinated by materials that have low status, like underlay, made to lie buried or unseen. The shoddy felt used in *Among Remote Lost Objects* was made of old carpets and clothes: full of memories and mashed up forms. To me, these materials also refer to marginalization and unwritten histories – I'm taking something ignored and making it highly visible and physically affecting.

I do feel uneasy about the loss of industry in Britain and a certain lack of confidence in making things, not helped by the terrible limitations on school curriculums. We are a very screen and image-based culture and I think this is becoming a problem – this flatness, the way it limits the movements of the body and compels the eyes in one direction. We need a more physical engagement with the world.

HOW DO YOU GET YOUR IDEAS FOR AN ARTWORK?

I immerse myself in new situations and experiences – and often go on ridiculous wild goose chases before finding the work was waiting there all along. I once made a video installation for ROOM in Bristol (*Descent*, 2005) that transformed its white modernist gallery into a dark cave – and to research this I went caving which was pretty terrifying, especially when I was told we were so far underground that the magnetic poles of the earth were reversed.

TELL US HOW YOU HAVE DEVELOPED AS AN ARTIST.

I'm less frightened of trusting my instincts and working with doubt. Some work has moved people to tears, or creates really positive reactions, but I've also been told my work can be claustrophobic, aggressive, even terrible. I often get mixed reactions but this means the work is active.

I've moved from an emphasis on studio-based practice and site-specific work to a more participatory approach – working with marginalized communities, people with dementia, local craft groups, special needs artists. I find Lygia Clark's approach really inspiring here – there are aspects of her work that are ritualistic, healing and grounding. I love her *Bichos* that were always meant to be moved by people.

IS IT MORE DIFFICULT FOR WOMEN ARTISTS TO MAKE A LIVING THAN MEN?

Yes, if you are talking about the art market, which is still heavily dominated by male artists. To a small extent the balance is being readjusted by recent efforts by galleries to show more female artists and artists from marginalized backgrounds. I'm more interested in work that is transitory rather than self-contained, sellable objects, so I fund my practice through teaching, temporary commissions, award funding and grants, rather than gallery sales or permanent public art commissions. Then there is the practical and economic question of being an artist and a mother and who takes the career break to raise the children – it's tough.

TELL US ABOUT YOUR FAVOURITE SCULPTURES – YOUR OWN OR BY SOMEONE ELSE.

Recently I have been interested in works made to be held – that exist somewhere between fetish and talisman, or that act as a mediator between object and body, self and the world. The *Handheld Objects* Moholy-Nagy made with his students at Bauhaus do this brilliantly. I'm passionate about the weavings of Anni Albers – fields of digital communication that look like they are vibrating or speaking to you, and Laurie Anderson's *Handphone Table*, which explores the primal quality of sound and how we hear through the bones in our body via an everyday object.

WHAT'S NEXT?

I'm currently engaged on a project about listening with the neurobiologist Andrea Streit, who works with regenerating the tiny hair cells in our inner ear. With choreographer Katrina Brown we have devised *Stillpoint,* a performance for one person at a time, which uses paper to construct 'sound objects' in space. It's a very synaesthetic piece – the 'audience' experiences the work with their eyes closed. We've made a short film about the work with Liberty Smith which explores where the 'eye of the ear' is, asking how film can delve into non-visual territory.

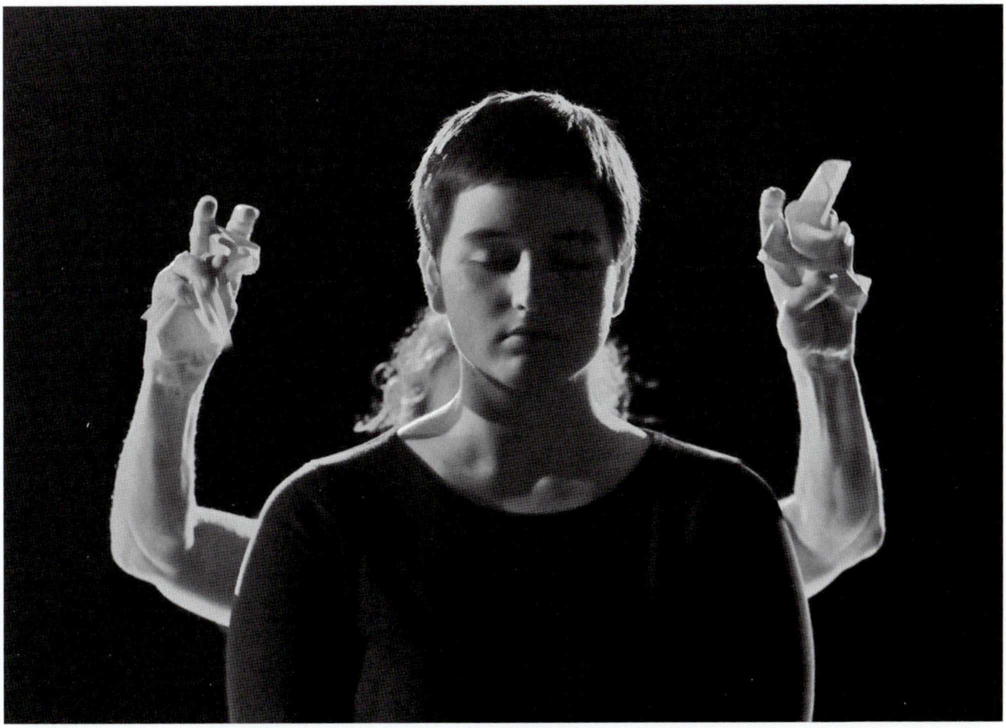

*Stillpoin*t 2019 Still: Liberty Smith/Rich Davies

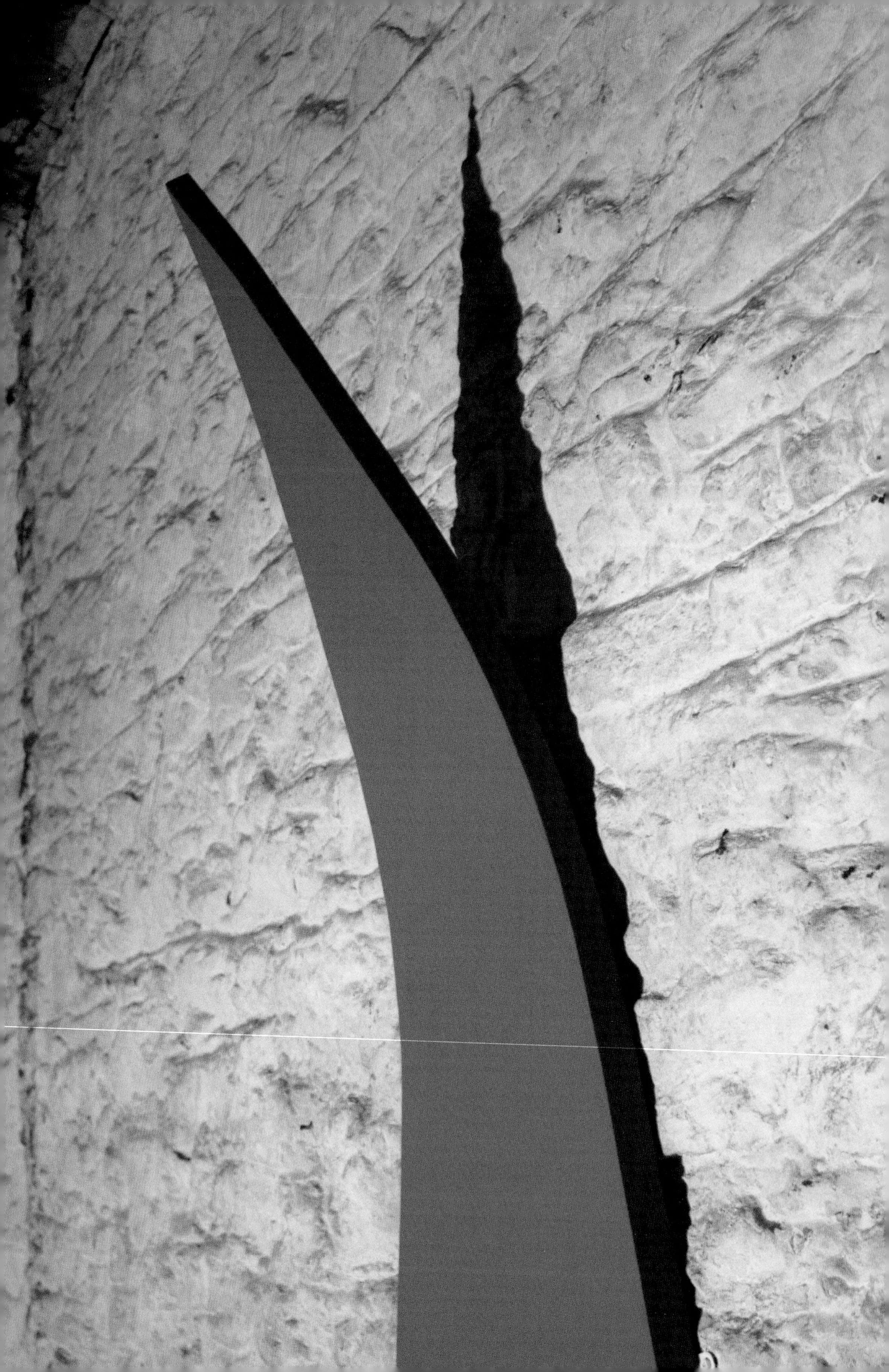

RACHEL ARA

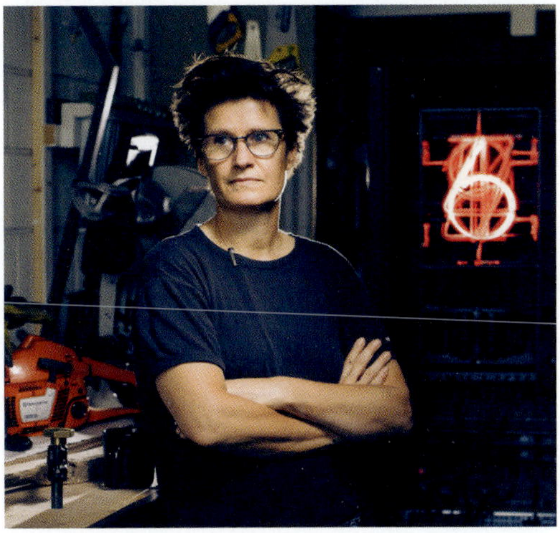

Rachel Ara worked for almost thirty years in Computing, also studying for a Foundation in Art and Design at the City Lit and then a BA Fine Art (Hons), Goldsmiths College, London where she won the Neville Burston Award. She uses her background in programming and cabinet-making to create complex works that interrogate their own function and raise questions around gender, technology and systems of power. Her many other awards include: 2016 Winner of the International Aesthetica Art Prize, finalist for the Lumen Prize. 2017 Barbican G Floor Commission, finalist Arte Laguna Prize, Venice, Italy, Near Now Fellowship for pioneering artists, RWA Academician. In 2018 she was selected for the London Open Triennial at the Whitechapel Gallery and became Artist in Residence at the V&A London. 2019 saw her large-scale work shown at the London Design Festival, V&A, Vienna Biennial and MMCA, Seoul. She recently won the CoLAB commission for sculpture that was completed and installed at the Slade / UCL in 2020. Her technical drawings have recently been acquired by the V&A Museum for the national collection.

HOW DID YOU COME TO MAKE SCULPTURE?

I've always made things since I was very young. Generally I'm a very hands-on, practical person. At home I do the renovations, electrics, plumbing… it's very natural for me to work with my hands so I guess this has carried through into the artwork.

The outcome of my work is driven by my ideas so it could be 2D or 3D. So if a concept has to manifest in 3D then it becomes a sculpture.

Left: *Fraught (Because Life Isn't Pure, Simple, Silent, Honest and Absolute)* 2015
Above Portrait photo: Andy Porter

This Much I'm Worth (the self-evaluating artwork) 2017 – Anise Gallery

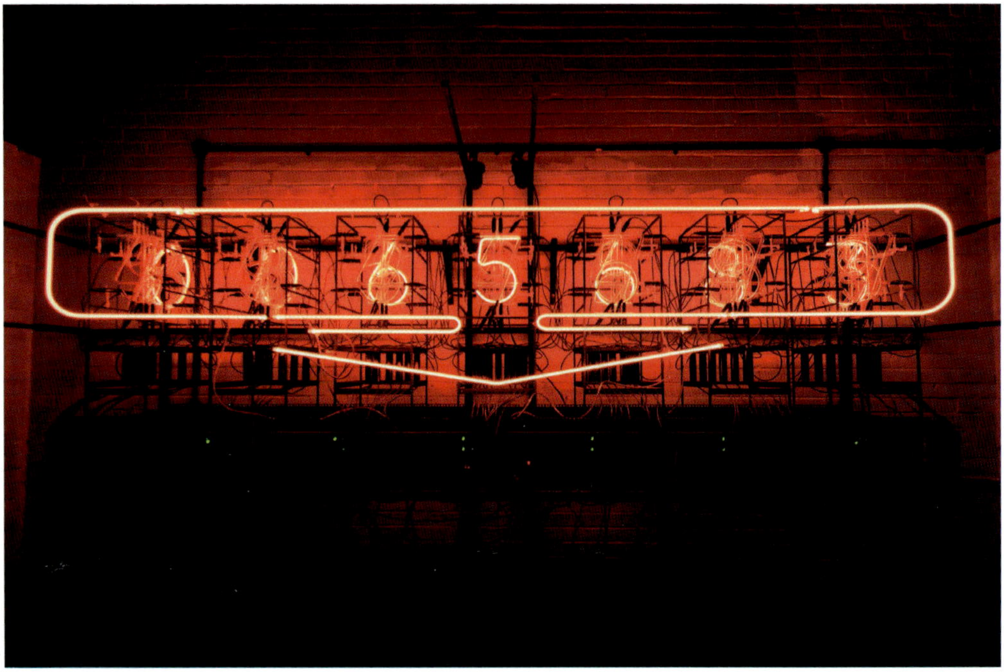

WHO WERE YOUR INFLUENCES AND OR ROLE MODELS?

I don't really see anyone as an influence or role model. I'm quite self-motivated and driven. I do admire people with a very hard work ethic.

WHO ENCOURAGED YOU?

In terms of art, no one in particular…does that sound sad? My grandmother was always incredibly supportive and interested in what I was doing.

DID YOU HAVE ANY FORMAL TRAINING?

I studied Fine Art at Goldsmiths. The training there is very conceptual/ideas-based. In terms of learning skills – I've had formal training for cabinet-making and attended various workshops over the years if I need to acquire skills. Nowadays I tend to use YouTube as a training resource.

DO YOU USE THE HUMAN FIGURE IN YOUR WORK?

Occasionally, but whatever I do I'm always aware of the relationship of the body to the work.

DO YOU USE FOUND OBJECTS?

Yes, I do – for various reasons. In terms of my digital work, as it's too expensive to buy the equipment, I source second-hand equipment on eBay or from server room refurbishments. I also use the freecycle at our studio, and am always finding various old equipment that I can strip useful bits out of. I also find it hard to pass a skip without diving in, especially if I'm in the van.

DO YOU USE THE NATURAL WORLD?

Not specifically in my artwork. But I do have some ideas for future projects that might. I lived for ten years in France on a farm where we looked after the land, and had a coppiced chestnut forest. I did a lot of drystone walling and green woodwork – so I'm quite in touch with nature and I'm sure it will appear in my work at some point.

FREE-STANDING OR ATTACHED?

I always feel more conformable if something is bolted down!

IS THE SCALE IMPORTANT?

The scale of a work is important in terms of how it relates to you physically. It should not be important in terms of judging its worth. But sadly the world likes big – likes bling – so big generally has a higher value regardless of the quality.

The reason I built the sculpture *This Much I'm Worth* so large was specifically to play up to the machismo in the artworld of building "big". People notice you when you make large work and I wanted to comment on this. Specifically as a woman, where there are many factors that prevent you from doing so.

IS THE ENVIRONMENT IMPORTANT?

The environment of the artwork is crucial. It places it in context. If it's a commission it has to be built for the environment. The artwork and environment are inseparable.

EPHEMERAL OR LONG-LASTING?

In between … when I make a work it has to be robust and showable. I don't like the idea of works lasting for an eternity. We have to make room for the next generation of artists, and I have no desire to be remembered. I like the idea of the work being recycled back into other works.

MULTIMEDIA OR ONE MEDIUM?

The concept dictates the medium – so I never know what I'm going to work with next. So far it's been an incredibly diverse mix. One day I may be doing a lot of programming, the next day welding.

IS THERE A PARTICULAR THEME OR THEMES WHICH ARE CENTRAL TO YOUR WORK?

Feminism, gender, technology and systems of power.

HOW DO YOU GET YOUR IDEAS FOR AN ARTWORK?

Ideas flow the whole time. It's a case of living with them until you have time to act on them. Inspiration comes from the world around me – the work is just trying to make sense of it. I find in terms of inspiration – misogyny is the gift that keeps giving.

DO YOU LIKE TO DO COMMISSIONED WORK OR NOT?

I like the challenge of a commission. The few I've had, I've had total creative freedom and that's been great. I don't mind physical restrictions and difficult spaces to work in – I usually rise to that challenge – but I wouldn't like creative restrictions as in restrictions on the concept.

TELL US HOW YOU HAVE DEVELOPED AS AN ARTIST.

I had a career in the tech industry for nearly thirty years so I was a late starter. I couldn't see a way to survive in the art world and I could not work and do art part-time – whatever I do I have to throw myself in 100% – and the job earned money, so there was not a choice. After decades working, I was in a position to take five years off and focus on my artwork, I feel I've got no time to waste, so have been working incredibly hard the last five years creating works.

WHERE IS YOUR SCULPTURE EXHIBITED?

More recently I've been lucky enough to show large works in major museums internationally. In 2018, I showed at the V&A, Whitechapel Gallery and Barbican Centre, London. In 2019, at the MMCA (Museum of Modern and Contemporary Art) in Seoul, South Korea, the Vienna Biennial at the MAK and the V&A. Currently I have a sculpture installed at the Slade / UCL in Central London for UCL Year of Sculpture.

IS IT MORE DIFFICULT FOR WOMEN ARTISTS TO MAKE A LIVING THAN MEN?

Generally women don't get taken as seriously in sculpture (or most things) – I think that's changing more in painting. There are many women practising but they tend to thin out when you get to the high-end galleries where the money is.

Financially, women tend to have fewer resources – you can see it at the studios where I'm based. The larger studios are generally occupied by men, and women make do with smaller and shared spaces – that obviously has an effect on the scale of the work.

Also with sculpture there are a lot of practical issues. When your work is going into directions that have typically been defined as male – such as technology, cabinet-making, welding, etc. – men tend to help each other, and are less willing to help women and when you work in these areas that are predominately male – you need this knowledge to learn.

TELL US ABOUT YOUR FAVOURITE SCULPTURES – YOUR OWN OR BY SOMEONE ELSE.

I remember seeing Mona Hatoum's work at the Pompidou Centre in the 1990s. She was showing *Light Sentence* and some other works. I just remember being incredibly moved by the work – it's hard to describe – but that's what I want to give and get from art.

WHAT'S NEXT?

In 2019 I won the CoLAB commission for women who make sculpture. I have just completed this work and installed it at the Slade / UCL in London. The day I finished install, the virus pandemic took hold in the UK and the university closed. The sculpture is called *Dissent Module (Escape from Semiramis)* and takes the form of a large metallic space descent module that appears to have crash landed at UCL (from a female utopia in the future). It's a very complex engineered piece, and is controlled by feminist AI. I am currently adapting the AI so that she can interact with the audience over the web as people are in isolation and the physical sculpture cannot currently be seen or entered.

"What next?" is probably the most pertinent question for 2020.

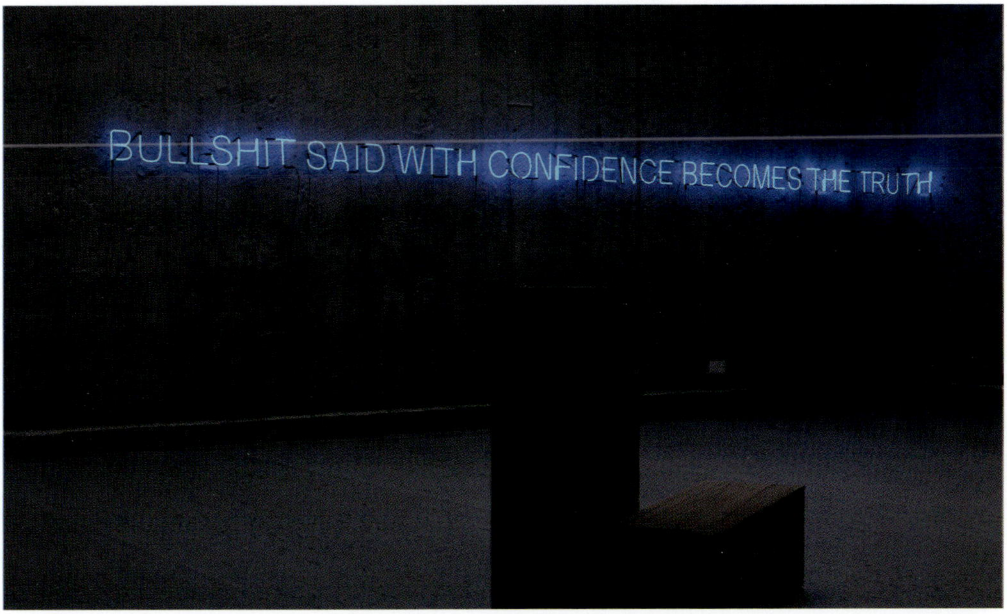

Cocksure (is anything ever what it seems?) Working image 2016

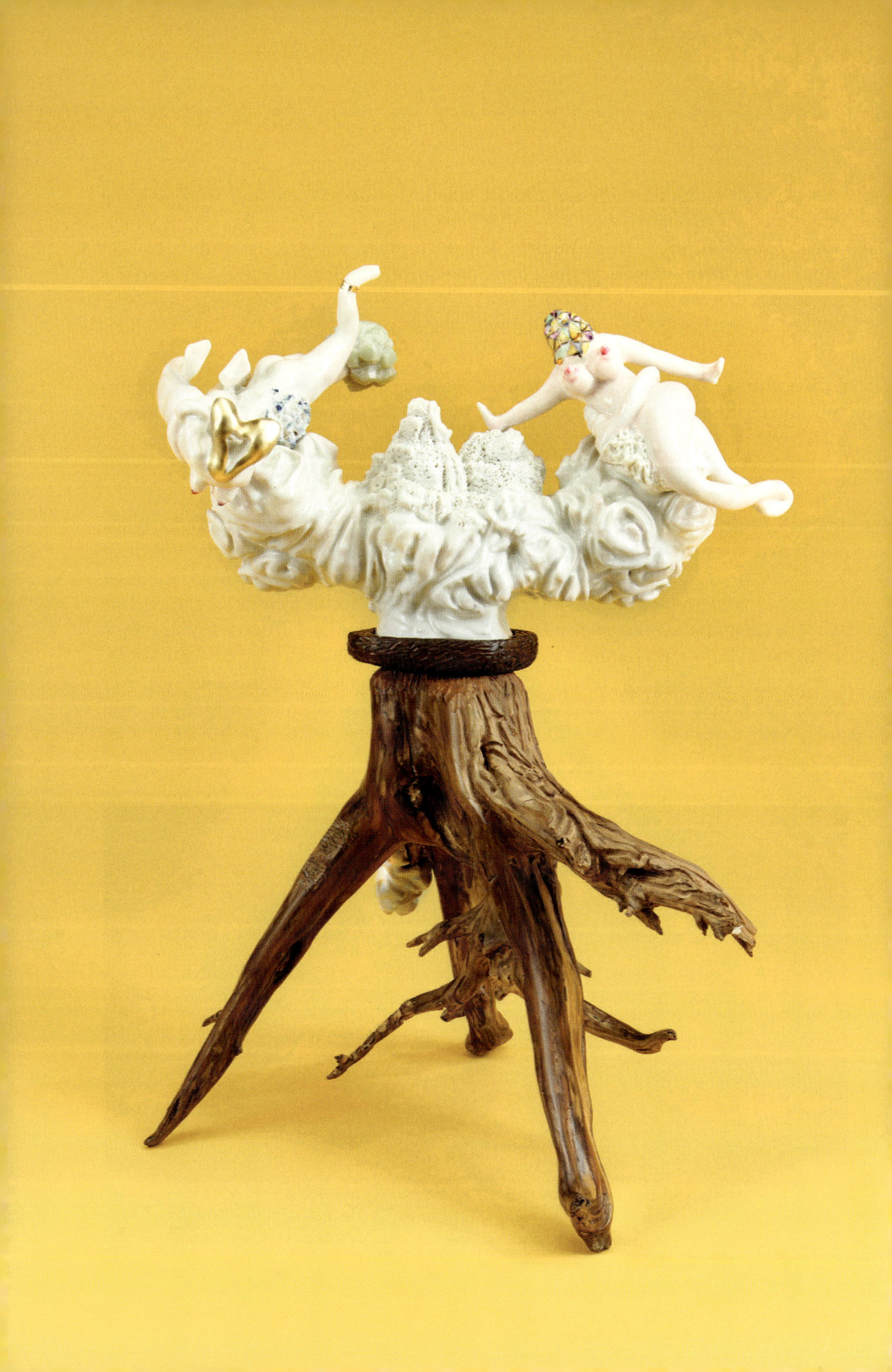

ANNIE ATTRIDGE

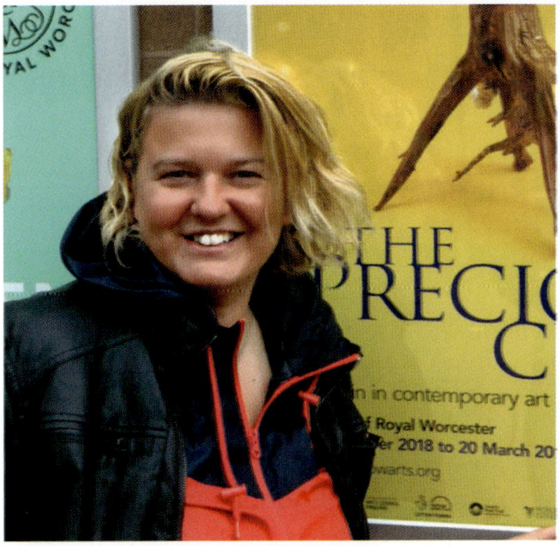

Annie Attridge studied at the Royal Academy Schools, for her MA Fine Art, London and a BA in Fine Art Painting at University of Brighton. Since graduating in 2002, Attridge's work has received reviews from *The New York Times*, Channel 4 News, *ArtReview*, the *Evening Standard*, and *L Magazine*. Publications include *Design Behind Desire* by Lisa Morgan (2011) and *Nature Morte,* Thames & Hudson (2013). Solo shows (2012-2013): *Hearts of Oak*, Asya Geisberg Gallery, New York (2011).

Group exhibitions include: *Nature Morte*, Guildhall Museum, London (2017–18), *In Your Face,* Salisbury Art Centre, UK (2017), *Creekside Open*, The Art in Perpetuity Trust, selected by Jordan Baseman & Alison Wilding, UK (2017), Body Kristin Hjellegjerde Gallery (2018), *If You Can't Stand the Heat, Roaming Projects*, Camden Arts Centre, London (2018), Artquest: *PEER FORUM* (2017-18), *Precious Clay* Museum of Royal Worcester (2019-2019), *The Loft* Alan Servais Family Collection, Brussels March 2020 Wellington Club, *Tutti Fruitti* London April 2020. www.annieattridge.com

Interview by Vanessa Murrell, DATEAGLE ART, 2018

YOUR PORCELAIN WORKS ARE MADE IN THE BASIS OF BEING CONSTANTLY NURTURED AND CARESSED. WHAT CAN YOU TELL US ABOUT THIS DELICATE PROCESS?

Porcelain tends to be treated in three processes, each particular and delicate in their own ways. You need to plan your treatment of the material to some degree, but each

Left: *The Divine and the Mortal* 2018 Photo: Matthew Booth

stage presents an opportunity to work into the material and caress sensual shapes and forms from its form. The first phase is wet and sloppy. It's easily malleable. In this state, you create your skeleton, the structure on which to build your story. The second phase is a leather state. The time when you assert your choices, you cut and carve things, create holes, you poke this fledging form, you subtract and add. The last dry phase allows you to nurse the naturally formed cracks, like Victorians creasing their orchids; embracing imperfections and making better upon them.

It's a sensitive material, it has a memory, whereby it wants to return to its original form, the first caress. It needs to be handled gently with the knowledge that this memory will always exist within the form.

THERE IS A PERFORMATIVE ELEMENT IN YOUR PROCESS, OFTEN INVOLVED IN PRAYING TO THE KILN GODS AND GODDESS WHEN MAKING SCULPTURE; ONLY DRINKING RED HERBAL TEA WHEN PAINTING; AND STANDING ON WOOD WHEN MAKING YOUR TEXT-BASED WORKS. WHAT CAN YOU TELL US ABOUT THESE RITUALS?

I didn't intend for these strange habits to be rituals, but after a practice of 17 years, these habits have become ritualistic. Like a meditation, it sets the mood. Of course, I could function without them, but these simple pleasures tend to calm the mind.

WHEN I VISITED YOUR STUDIO, YOU SHOWED ME YOUR NEVER-SEEN BEFORE TEXT PIECES. IN WHAT WAYS ARE YOU INCORPORATING LANGUAGE INTO YOUR PRACTICE? IS THIS AN EXTENSION OF TITLING YOUR WORKS? WHY HAVE YOU CHOSEN TO USE A TYPEWRITER AS A SELECTED MEDIUM FOR THIS?

Language and prose has always played a part in my work; through the titling but also through my inspiration. I love poetry and song lyrics. Poetry is a law unto itself, it doesn't adhere to the normal prescriptive notions of the English language, and being dyslexic, this really appeals to me. There's a freedom in using language in associative ways, and allows the viewer to make their own connections. The use of the vintage typewriter is part of my interest in old forms of printmaking. I collect and research modes and machines used for printing from different eras – the typewriter is unique and distinctive.

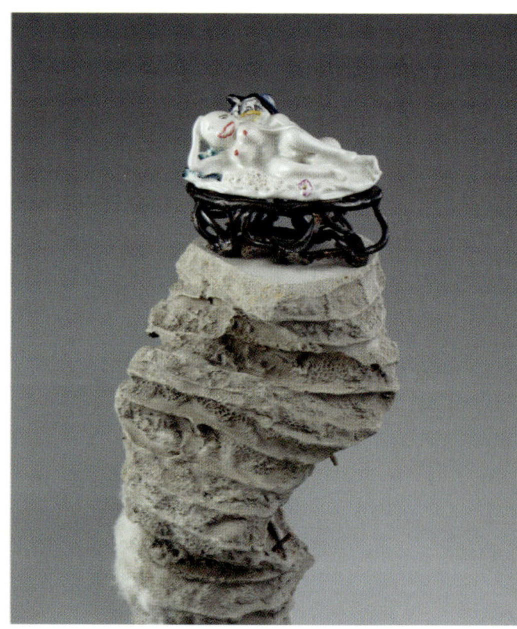

Should of, could of, would of, no. 10 2016
Photo: Matthew Booth

Your Borders, Your Rivers, Your Tiny Villages 2013

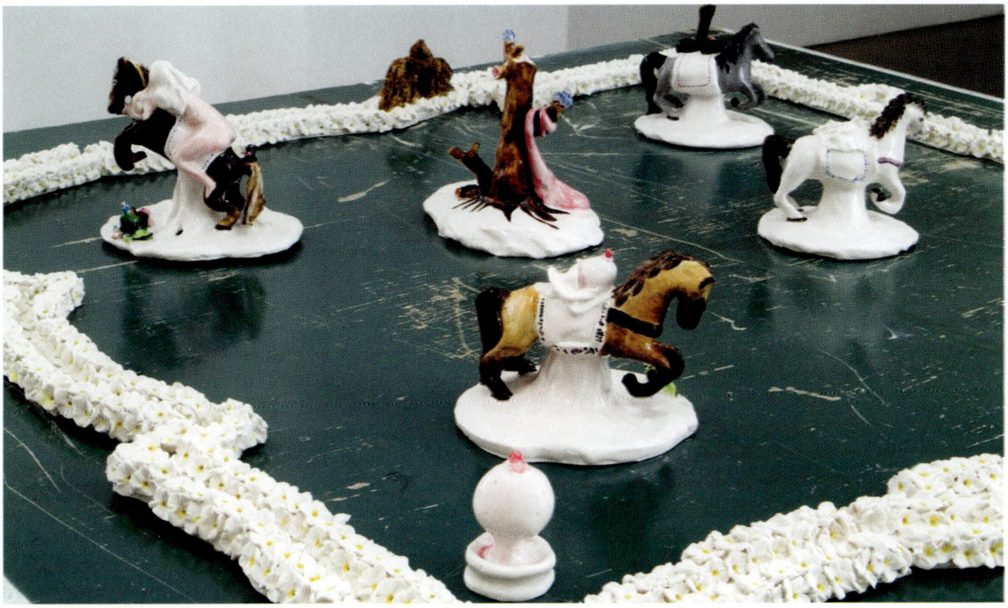

YOU WORK WITH RECOGNIZABLE SYMBOLS VARYING FROM HAMMERS TO LOVE BIRDS. IS THIS SYMBOLISM A NEW ADDITION TO YOUR PRACTICE?

The repetition of certain motifs in my work is a conscious decision. They may have secret meanings to me but often they are quite obviously romantic or gender icons. My work has always featured abstracted bodily forms and as a collection you see there are lots of more recognizable fictional characters also.

FROM MAKING MONOPRINTS, TO WELDING, CARVING, MAKING TILES OR EXPERIMENTING WITH CYANOTYPE, WHAT DRAWS YOU TO A CERTAIN TECHNIQUE OR MEDIUM?

I don't really think that my approach is medium-specific. As an artist, I am constantly learning new techniques, and the ones that excite me usually find their way into my work. In recent years I've enjoyed juxtaposing different techniques and approaches and I'm pretty happy with the outcomes. My choice of medium may be led by the quality and texture of its finish, colour and the process, but ultimately I treat my use of materials in the same way. Similarly to how I've described working with the porcelain, their treaments are phased. Obviously some materials are less forgiving and harder to work and you have to be more considered – but everything is a journey.

YOU MENTIONED AT YOUR STUDIO THAT SOMEONE ONCE TOLD YOU TO MAKE WORKS THAT "TURNED YOU ON"... IN THIS SENSE, ARE YOU LITERALLY MAKING WORKS IN THIS MANNER?

Yes, to a degree. You have to love what you're making. Of course, we are often creatively challenged but it's important to stay grounded and make work that excites you as an artist and not overly worry about how future audiences are going to react to it.

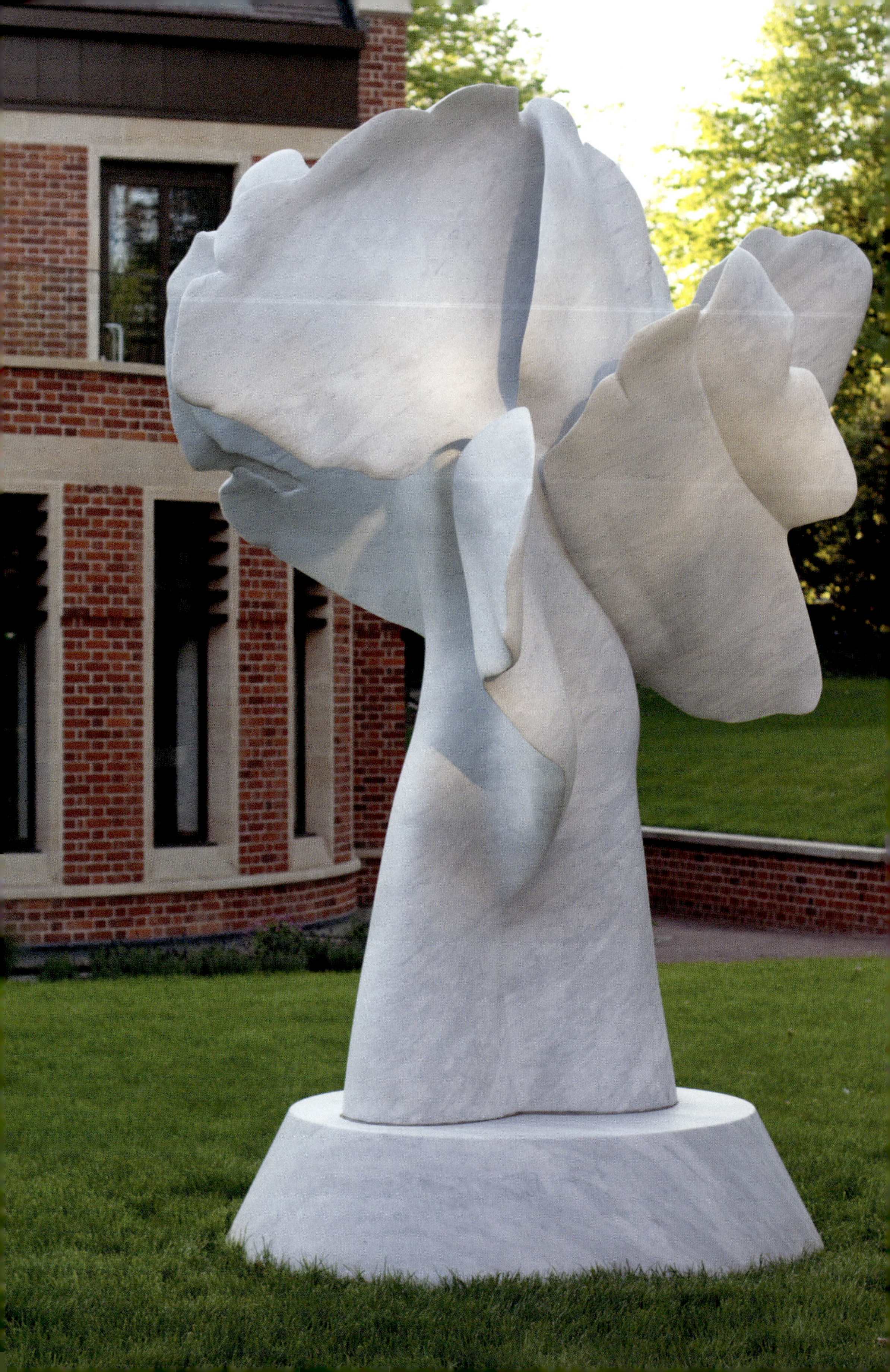

HELAINE BLUMENFELD

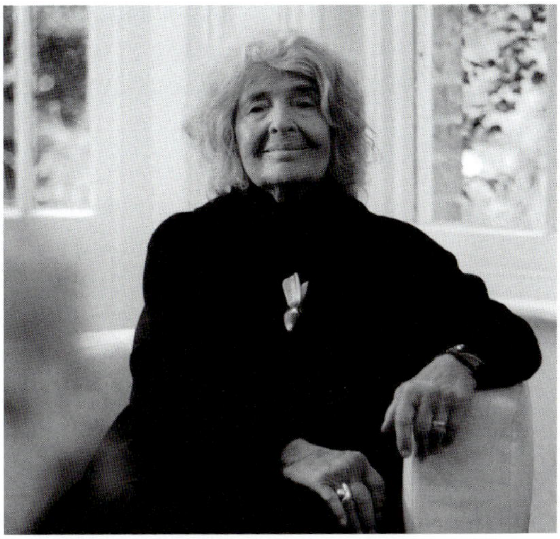

Helaine Blumenfeld OBE grew up in New York and graduated from the University of Michigan. She studied Moral Philosophy at Columbia University, receiving a PhD in 1964. She married her husband Yorick in 1963 and moved to Paris where she studied sculpture with Ossip Zadkine. She had her first solo exhibition in 1966 in Palais Palfy, Vienna. There follows an impressively long list of exhibitions in Britain, Europe, Scandinavia, China, Korea, Singapore and the United States. Most notable recent exhibitions include: Ely Cathedral, Pilane Sculpture Park, Huygens' Hofwijck Museum in the Netherlands and the largest show of her work to date at Canary Wharf (2020).

Best-known for her monumental public commissions, Blumenfeld is passionate about bringing sculpture into the public domain, creating works that have become integral to the cultural landscape of the UK. Most notably, *Tempesta,* overlooking Hyde Park in London, installed in 2012, as well as *Fortuna* (2016) and *Metamorphosis* (2019) in Canary Wharf and *Tree of Life: Encounter* installed at the Woolf Institute, Cambridge (2018). Blumenfeld spends her time working in her studios in Pietrasanta (Italy) and in Grantchester, on the outskirts of Cambridge.

Blumenfeld is a Fellow of the Royal Society of Sculptors and has served on its council and as its Vice President. In 2007, she was the first woman to win the International Sculpture prize Il Premio Pietrasanta e la Versilia nel Mondo. Blumenfeld was awarded an Honorary OBE for services to the arts in 2011. She is the subject of the recent Sky Arts film *Hard Beauty: The Sculpture of Helaine Blumenfeld.* Three monographs have been written about her work. Blumenfeld is represented by the Hignell Gallery.

Left: *Tree Of Life: Encounter* 2017. Photo left and above Portrait photo: Bo Lutoslawksi

IN HER OWN WORDS

As a child, I frequently had visionary dreams that were overwhelming. I'd wake up and want to express what I had dreamt to my family. I realized that the words I was using were inadequate. I thought it was that I just didn't have the right words. For many years I pursued a search for language. But I gradually began to understand that I would need an extraordinary means of expression to be able to communicate my dreams. It was only when many years later my hands discovered clay, that I began to develop that extraordinary language through sculpture.

I came to this breakthrough at the time I was finishing my doctorate in philosophy. During a visit to the National Museum in Naples I was captivated by the small, early Cycladic terracotta figures. They seemed to communicate on so many levels. Shortly thereafter, fate brought me to Paris. There I studied at the Académie de la Grande Chaumière where Ossip Zadkine had been teaching. He discovered my exploratory clay work and encouraged me. During that time I began to make all my models in clay and have continued to do so ever since. I think that's my "drawing."

During the initial stages of my process I am working almost irrationally through my unconscious. I never use an armature. I never look at what I'm doing until it has reached a stage where I "know" what it is. At that point I must stand back and see rationally whether or not the model has potential. To know how to alter it requires

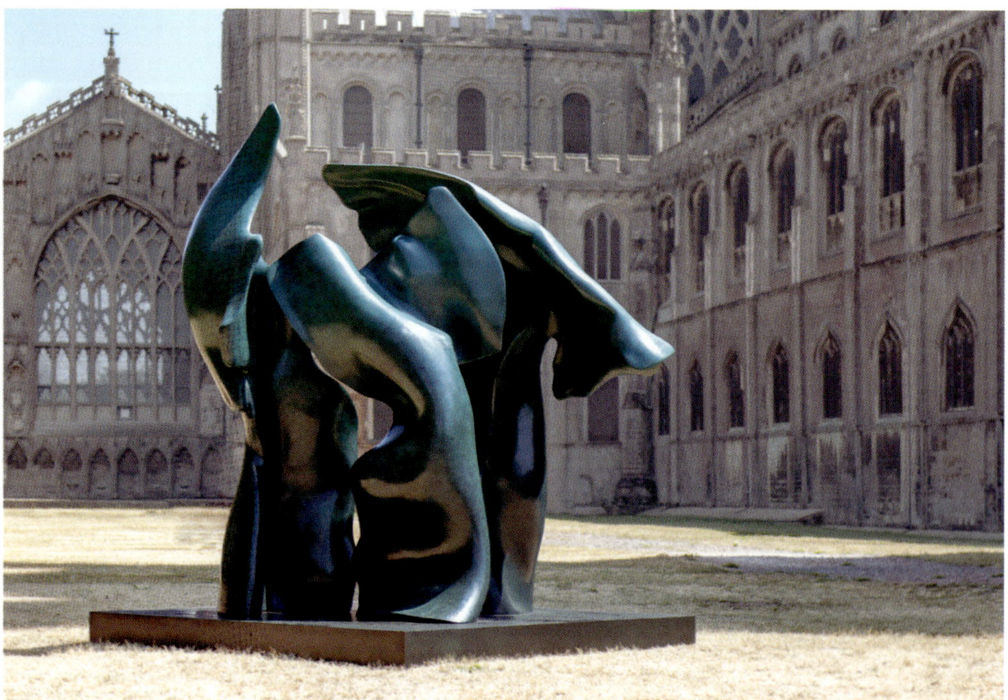

Illusion 2018 Photo: Henryk Hetflaisz

Taking Risks 2019 Photo: Sean Pollock

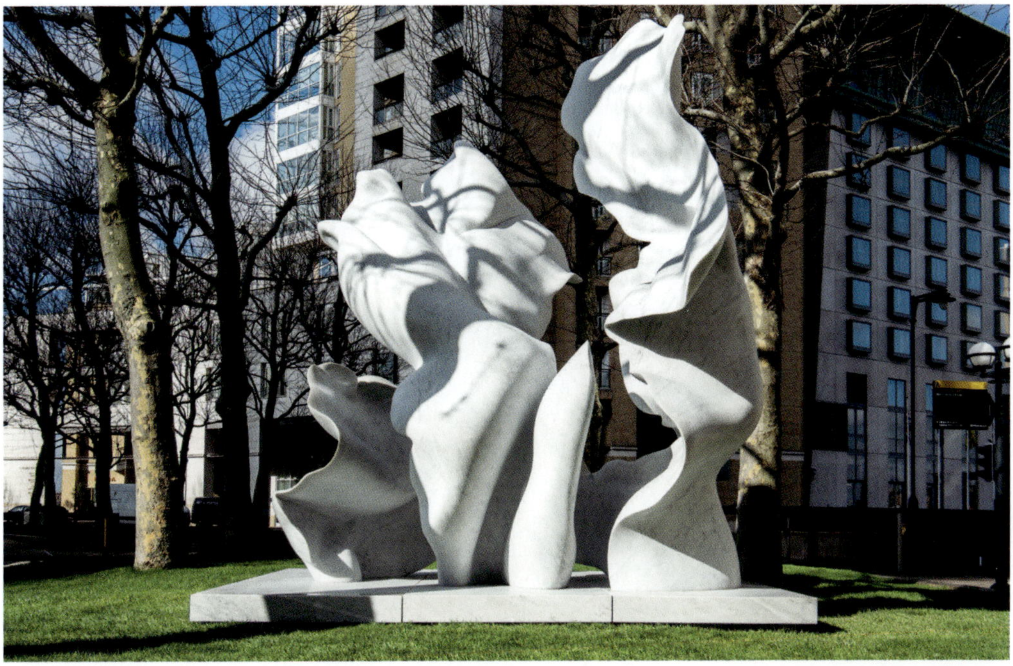

an intellectual appraisal. I will judge the piece critically. This is very important. The sculpture moves from being a subject, which depends on me for its existence, to an object that can stand alone without any explanation.

In trying to represent human feelings and dreams, as well as "the mysteries of the human soul," I began by depending on the human figure and gestures. The search for this led me away from conventional forms of representation. I discovered that abstracted fragments could convey intense emotion, combining physical elements could suggest movement. The further I was able to abstract gestures and figurative references, the closer I was to developing my own language of form.

My earliest sculptures were realized in bronze and I enjoyed being in the foundry, learning how to work with wax and create patinas. On a trip to Pietrasanta to visit a friend, I fell in love both with the town (where sculptors have gone since the time of Michelangelo) and the marble. Its translucence offered the possibility of allowing light to enter my forms.

It was very hard for me to break into the male-dominated culture of the studios in Pietrasanta. Women were not respected there in the early 1970s. The struggle was not only learning to carve, but keeping to a strict discipline and overcoming the reputation of women who had come before me and had not been perceived as being serious. Respect came through the sculptures I made as I learned to carve. The decision to work in marble was life-changing.

Toward The Precipice 2019. Photo: Erio Forli

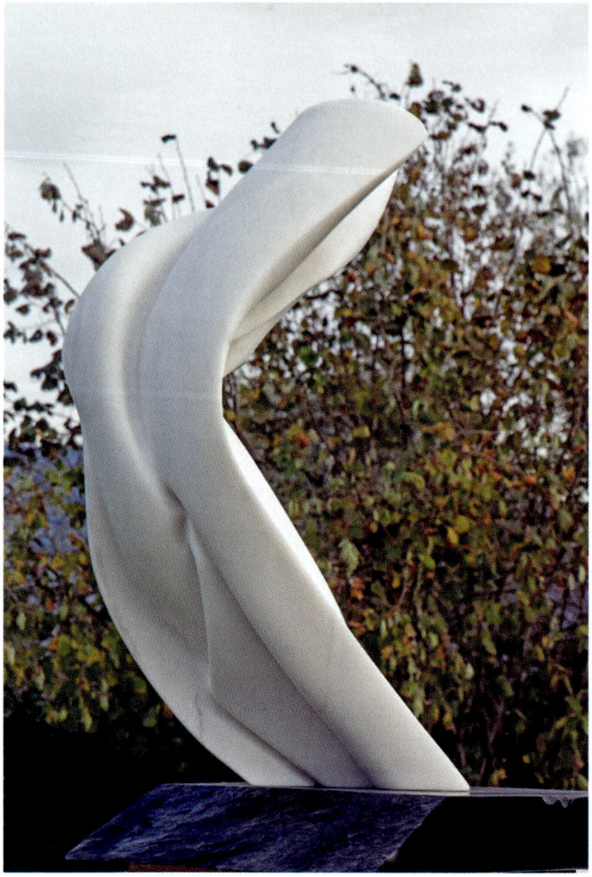

Over the years I have continued to develop my skills working with marble, granite, wood, terracotta and casting in bronze, but the real inspiration always comes when I am creating with clay. I am only able to express who I am by searching within my psyche and drawing upon my inner vision and experience. Those are my true raw materials and clay is my transmitter.

For me, creativity is about expressing something beyond the self. The question is: How do we get from what is a very personal experience to something which is going to touch all people and bypass the personal? Every aspect of creativity involves and requires risk. The struggle between chaos and order is continuous in the process of creating a "work of art." I never know what to expect. Without drawings, an inner structure, or references, I am creating the very conditions of uncertainty.

I was described in *The Independent* as being "fearless" because I have not been afraid to create work which is unapologetically beautiful. I feel that now, living in a turbulent world, it is more necessary than ever to create beauty that will be transformative. I have never felt that there was a contradiction between beauty and pain.

On the contrary, only by revealing a profound emotional reality which recognizes the upheaval and disruption in our lives can we ever hope to transcend it. Beauty is not a denial of pain, but an acceptance of it.

For me, the precondition of being an artist has always been a radical confrontation with reality and an effort to achieve a distance from it.

In my journey as an artist, I have moved from the expression of intensely personal themes to addressing the moral and physical upheaval of the wider world. I hope in the next years to continue commissions focusing on the creation of public sculpture. I have been involved with projects that were sited in parks, hospitals, universities, city centres, community plazas, libraries, theatres and ships. Each project has had different parameters, but I have always been concerned with creating something that will provide a reference point to the viewers who experience it and that will connect the physical with the conceptual space.

Beauty is the reason that public art exists. My objective has been to create things of the spirit, which will add another dimension to the daily lives of people that experience them. The most successful sculptures create a sense of place. There is a feeling of civic ownership for the work. People interact with it and the sculpture adds life and personality to the landscape. I recently completed a commission to create a monumental sculpture that celebrated the strength and potential that can be achieved by the much needed global cooperation of Muslims, Christians and Jews – *Tree of Life: Encounter* at Cambridge's Woolf Institute. This four meter white marble sculpture has been one of my favourite and most memorable commissions.

What's next is the opening at long last of my enormous show at Canary Wharf. It is the largest exhibit of my life with more than forty pieces from the past four decades. This reveals my development as a sculptor in marble, bronze, wood and terracotta.

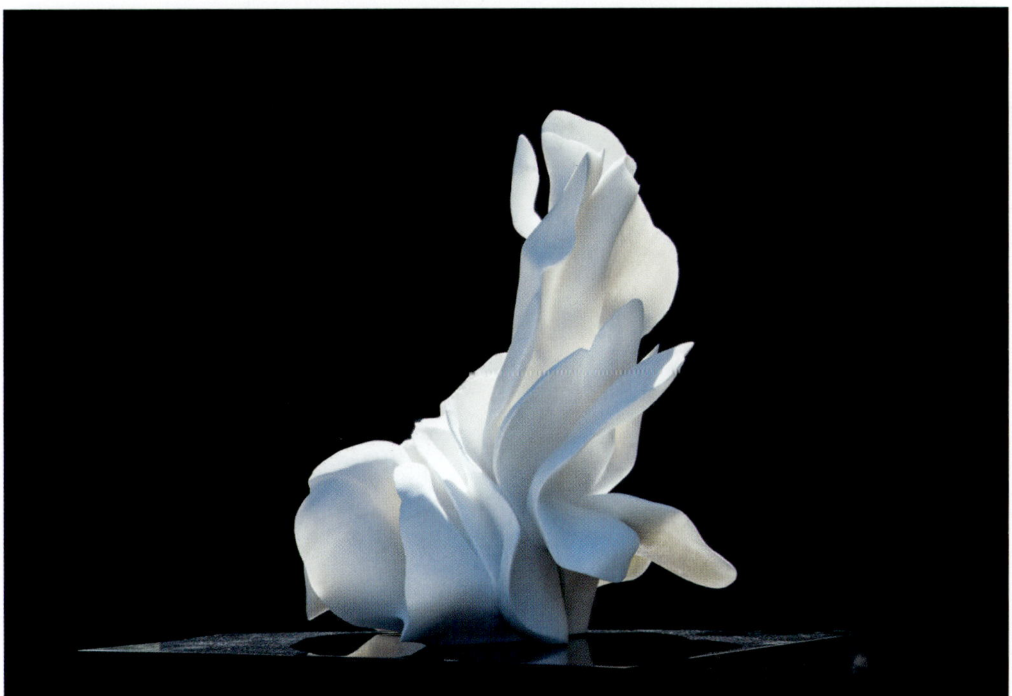

Exodus III 2019 Photo: Erio Forli

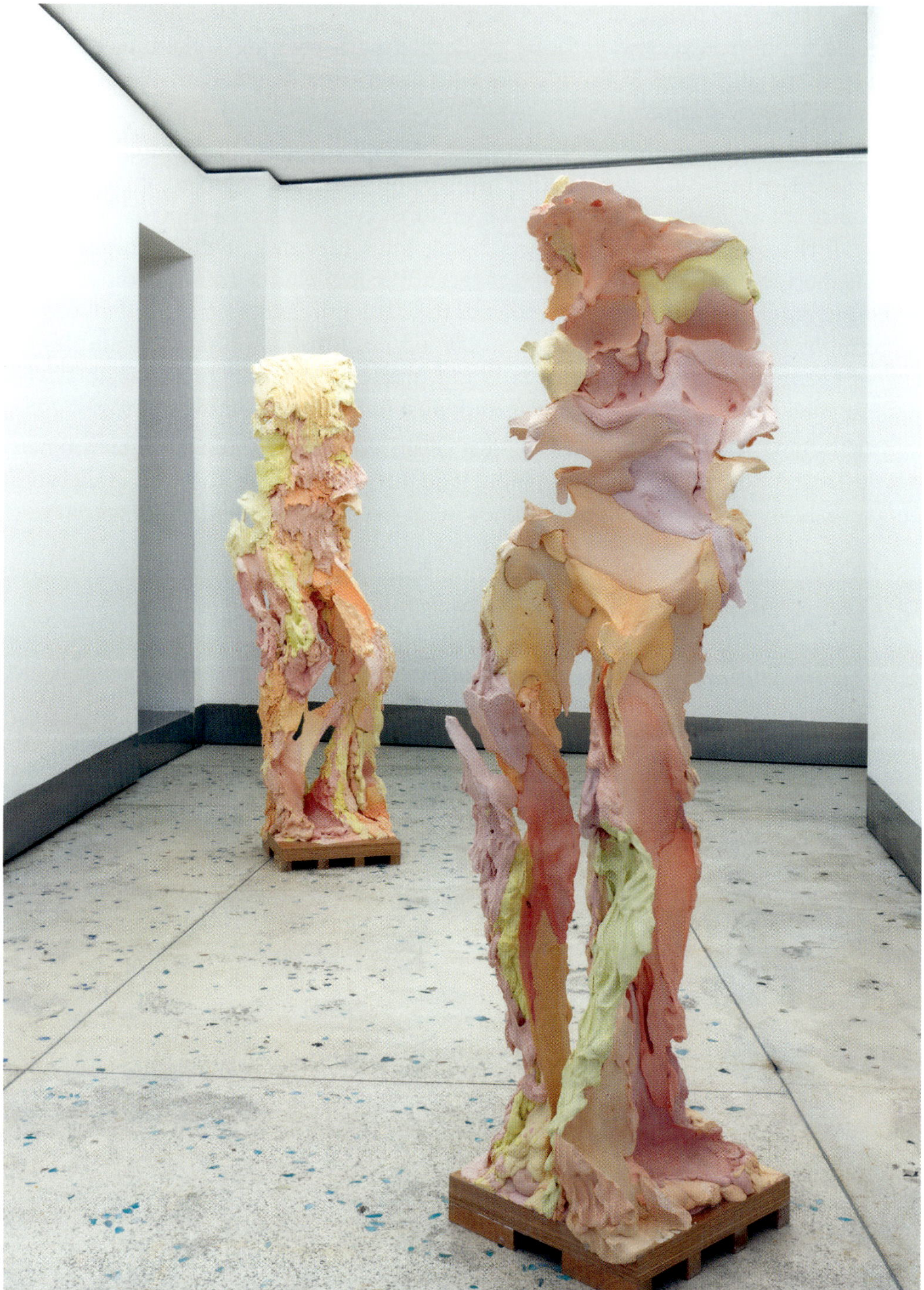

Solaris installation view, Alma Zevi Gallery, 2017. Photo: Enrico Fiorese

JULIANA CERQUEIRA LEITE

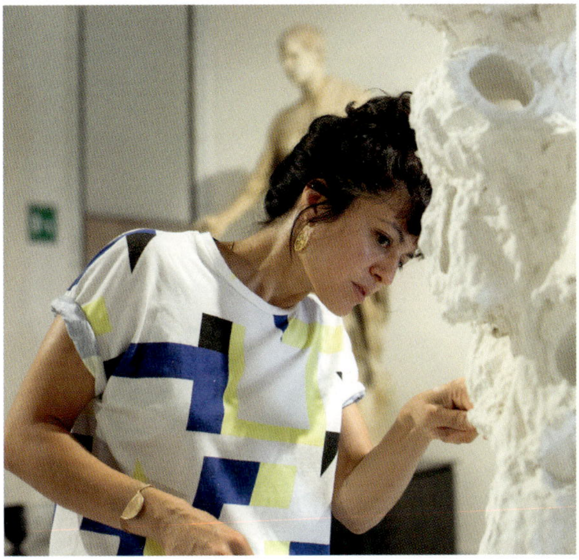

Juliana Cerqueira Leite is a Brazilian sculptor based in New York and São Paulo. Her artworks in sculpture, photography and video navigate the history, contexts and possible futures of representing the human form. She was awarded a Pollock-Krasner Foundation Grant in 2019 in support of her solo exhibition *Orogenesis* at the National Archaeological Museum in Naples, Italy. In 2016, she was awarded the Furla Art Prize for her contribution to the 5th Moscow Young Art Biennale.

Leite has exhibited her work in group shows internationally, including the Sculpture Center (New York, USA), Saatchi Gallery (London, UK), the Venice Biennale Antarctic Pavilion, the Vancouver Sculpture Biennale, Kunsthaus Erfurt (Erfurt, DE), Marres House for Contemporary Culture (Maastricht, NL) and Hordaland Kunstsenter for the 2019 Bergen Assembly. She has exhibited her work in solo shows including Instituto Tomie Ohtake (São Paulo), T.J. Boulting Gallery (London), Alma Zevi (Venice), Galeria Casa Triângulo (São Paulo), Regina Rex and Arsenal Contemporary (New York). Cerqueira Leite graduated from the Slade School of Fine Art MFA in London in 2006, as recipient of the Kenneth Armitage Sculpture Prize. She is represented by Alma Zevi, TJ Boulting and Casa Triângulo galleries.

Above: Portrait photo by Federico Cavazzutti

Orogenesis, installation view at National Archaeological Museum in Naples, Italy, 2019. Photo: Enrico Fiorese

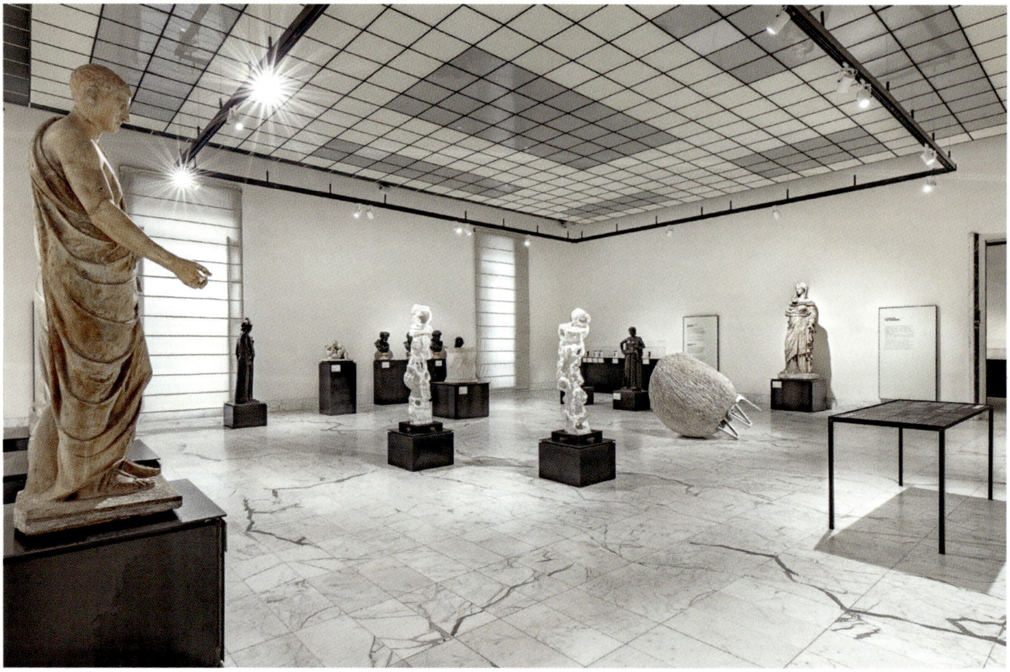

HOW DID YOU COME TO MAKE SCULPTURE?

I started making sculpture in earnest after I moved to London in 2000. I applied and got into Chelsea College of Art on a painting portfolio and had every intention of being a painter. But because of the Foundation year I had to try out sculpture, which I already knew I liked anyway, but had never taken too seriously. That year I found myself running around Wandsworth with a stolen supermarket trolley full of other people's discarded furniture and making these weird installations with trash, make-up and bits of chairs…

WHO WERE YOUR INFLUENCES AND OR ROLE MODELS?

I naturally gravitated towards other female sculptors. Louise Bourgeois and Lygia Clark were probably the artists that most captured my imagination as a teenager, and then of course this changed with time and I started to appreciate the work of people like Eva Hesse, Rivane Neuenschwander and Goshka Macuga. My tutorials with Phyllida Barlow and Eva Rothschild at the Slade still come to mind as important moments.

WHO ENCOURAGED YOU?

I was lucky to have a sensitive primary school art teacher called Claudette Castro, who felt I had a talent for art. She pulled my mother aside one day and convinced her to allow me to stay after school and have some extra art lessons. My mother then always encouraged me to make art, but was then suddenly shocked and against it all when I decided to make it a profession. It's something we both laugh at now, but there was resistance at first from my family, because they felt I'd be settling for a difficult life and with little money.

DID YOU HAVE ANY FORMAL TRAINING?

I graduated from the Slade School of Fine Art MFA programme in 2006.

IS THERE A PARTICULAR THEME OR THEMES WHICH ARE CENTRAL TO YOUR WORK?

The way I work today has its origin in a sort of existential crisis. I stopped making work for a while and nearly failed my MFA because of it. I felt suddenly that the world was so full of crap, why would I ever add anything to the pile of stuff? I also felt a serious problem with how I perceive us, as human beings, how we relate to what we call the natural or given world as somehow inferior, not possessing agency. I'm talking about how we handle materials, other living creatures – or even other humans depending on whether you're a racist or sexist person – as if they were only ever "resources" to be used in our transcendental projects.

The way out of this came one day when I mixed up a huge tub of cheap plaster and poured it all on the floor. I started to pull the wet plaster back together, trying to keep it from running outwards into a thin puddle. This action of dancing with the quality

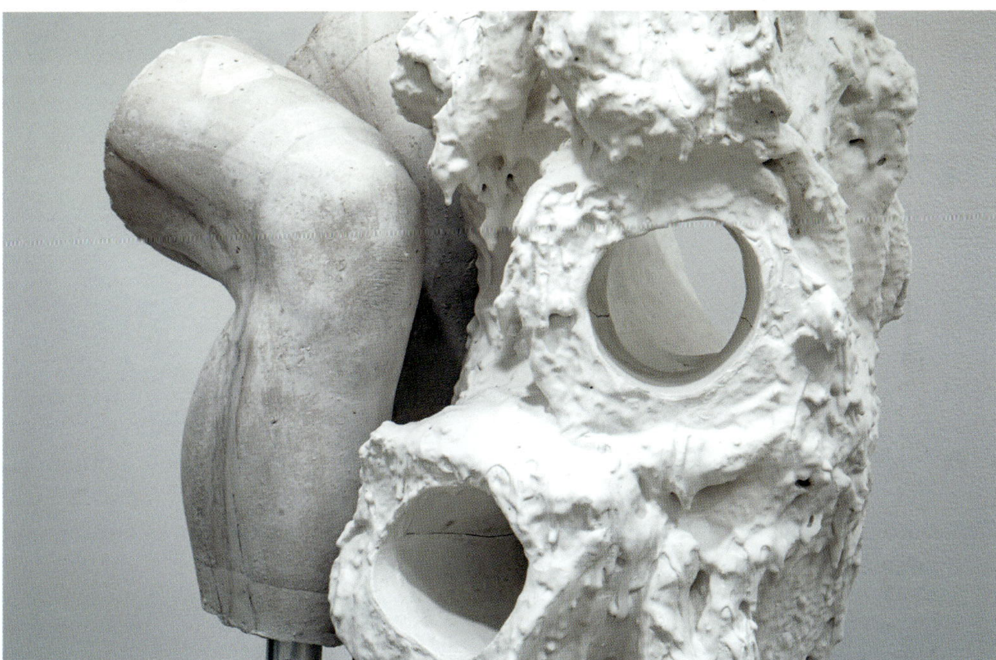

Contraction 3, 2019 courtesy Alma Zevi Gallery. Photo: Enrico Fiorese

Blind Spot 2, 2015. Installation view at Luswarande, Tilburg, Netherlands.

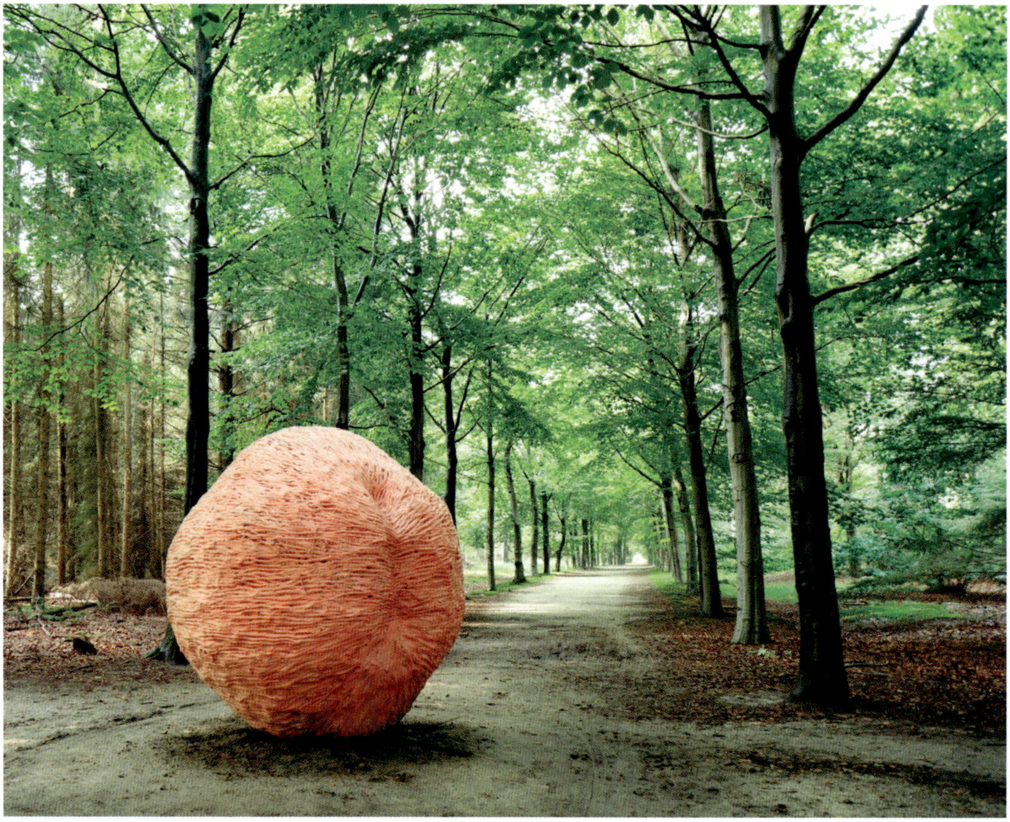

of the material is probably what led to everything I make today. My body is always involved, and I think of it as an actor or dancer thinks of their body. None of the work is autobiographical; I'm a human body for my own work, just as anyone else could be for their own activities. The work is therefore maybe figurative, but the body is often so abstracted by its own movements and activity. I don't really care to represent visually recognizable bodies – why should I bother with that? It's much more interesting to me how the body distorts itself by actualizing itself in the world.

HOW DO YOU GET YOUR IDEAS FOR AN ARTWORK?

My works often start with small movements. I move around in the studio a lot, as if I was about to choreograph something. Or sometimes a historical representation of a body will catch my attention for being weird or having an unusual quality to it. I can then fall into a hole of research, where I'll go to archives, end up at museum storage facilities, or travel to look at things. If I draw at this stage it's often to map movements: I never draw the sculptures before I make them, they aren't illustrations of ideas or pre-planned that way. I want to learn from the making.

WHAT'S NEXT?

After a few years in the field you might get to a point where you realize that you're inside an opaque topography that makes your activity viable, integrated into various social, economic and political structures. While these forms facilitate your agency, they also become its moulding force.

I find that I don't want to finish where my materials finish, but I want to keep pulling, pushing, subtracting and adding elements of the realities that form the possibility of doing things. The gallery, the institution, the collector, the art fair and the commission, the museum, the book, the world at large.

The white box world of contemporary art is anachronistic, and in being so it is like a slippery hole. If we are trapped in an eternal now, then nothing can effectuate the future. Still defining what we do as contemporary, is that an assumption of the end of history? The white box, like the black box of the theatre, creates a frame where the art object can exist in some sort of purity, separate and bracketed from the contaminated relationships we've established with other objects. The sculpture is a single type of bacterium cultivated in a Petri dish, ready for analysis. What biologists are finding now is that these types of studies provide a deceptively simplistic perspective, since the behaviour of bacteria is highly relational, embedded in systems of exchange and adaptation. The eternally contemporary artwork suspended in the frozen time/space agar of the white cube is given permission to pull out of the here and now and it takes our minds with it.

I don't have the solution to this yet, but I think moving into a messier space is an important thing to do at this moment.

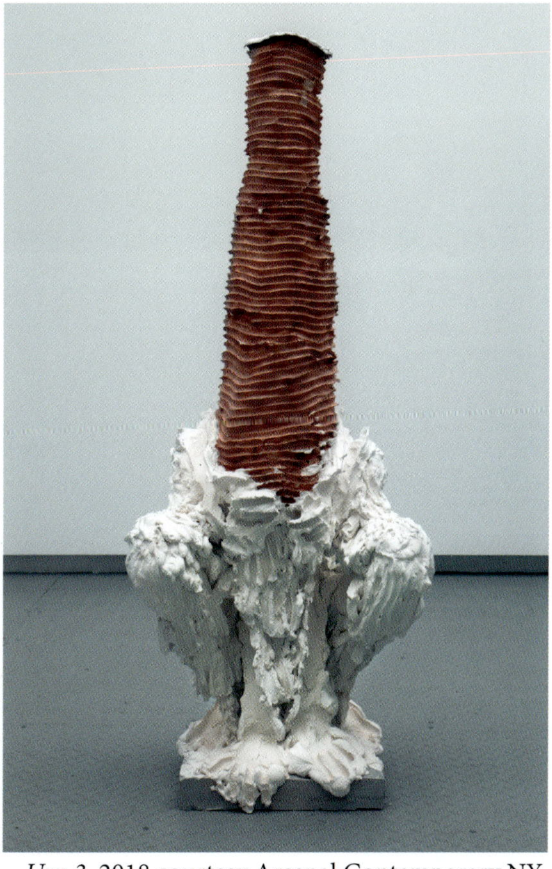

Urn 3, 2018 courtesy Arsenal Contemporary NY.
Photo: Greg Carideo

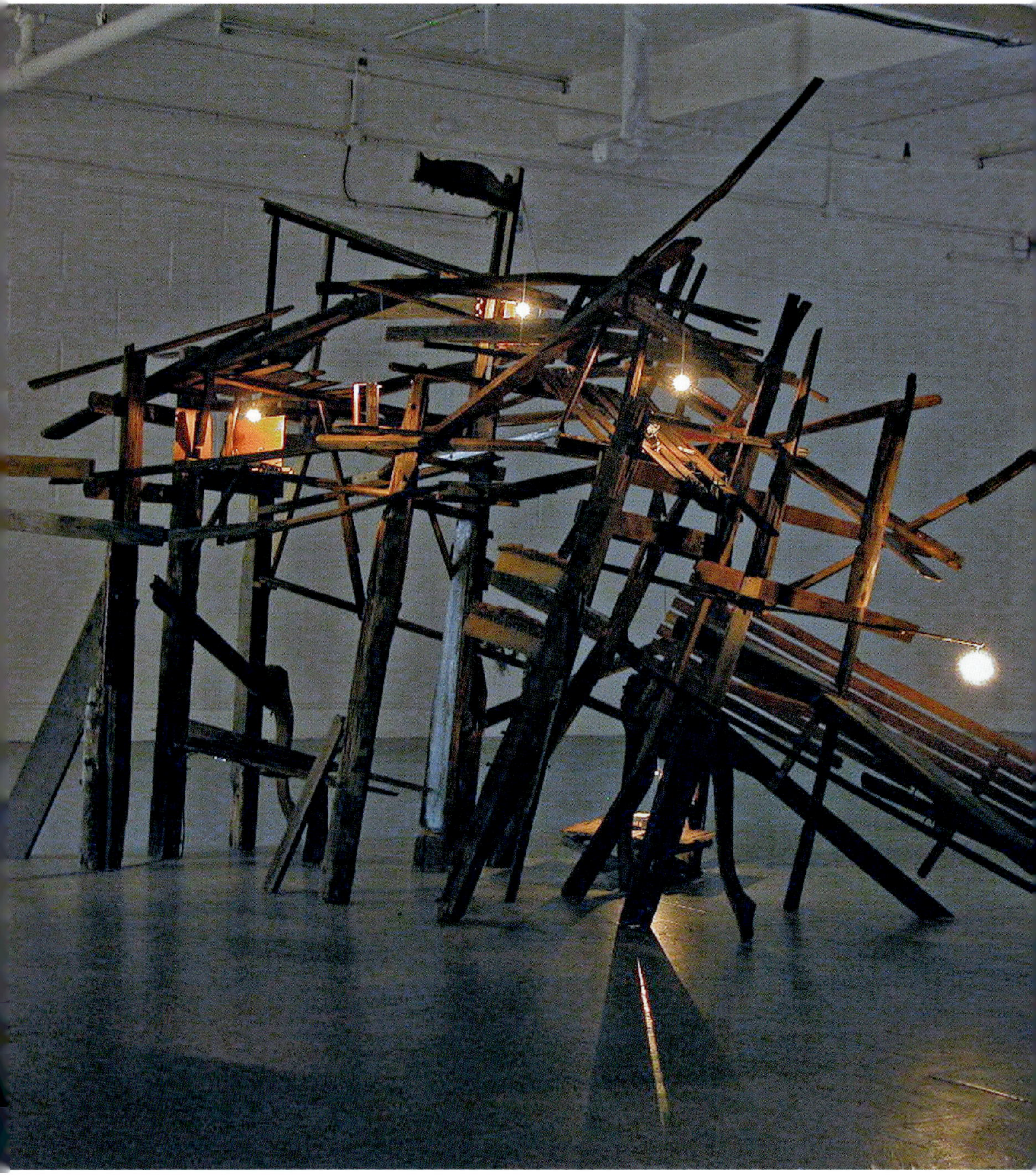

Richter, 2006.

SILKE DETTMERS

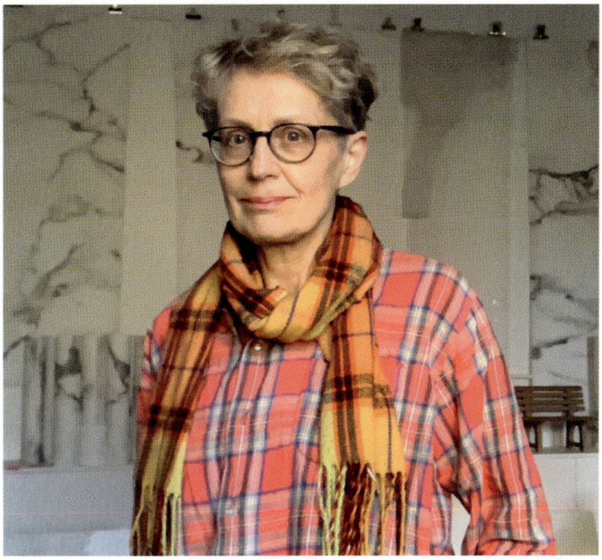

Silke Dettmers was born in Germany and trained at St. Martin's School of Art and the Royal College of Art, London and Braunschweig University of Art, Germany. Her artistic practice comprises of sculptures, drawing and photography. She exhibits regularly, and in 2017 she was the resident artist at the Nunnery Gallery, London, for *RAW Materials: Wood.* Dettmers' work was included in 2014 in the group exhibition *Mark Wallinger Presents...* (Bermondsey Project, London) and *Territories* (Windkracht Gallery, Den Helder, NL) in 2012. In 2008 her work was selected for 'art projects' (London Artfair) and *Concrete Dreams* (APT Gallery, London). She has been part of Bow Arts Studios since 2007.

HOW DID YOU COME TO MAKE SCULPTURE?

Looking back, I have always been a "maker" – from childhood onwards. (I built a very wobbly chair when I was about eleven years old). But it has been quite a long journey. Initially, I moved from graphic design to illustration, then to painting and printmaking. I found painting overwhelming, however – colour in particular. More importantly, I realized that the metaphors I was using in my work needed another type of presence: rather than describing them in paint I wanted to make them.

Means of Travel 2, 2016

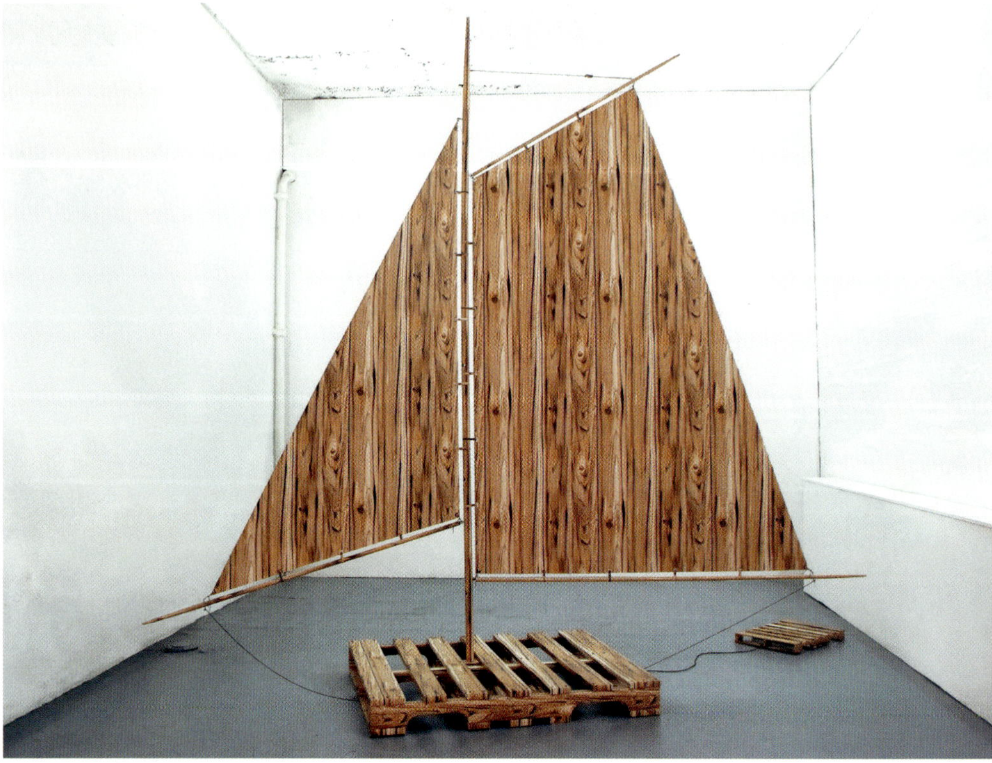

WHO WERE YOUR INFLUENCES AND OR ROLE MODELS?

If I had to name the art movements that had the biggest influence on my work, it would be Conceptual Art and Surrealism.

WHO ENCOURAGED YOU?

Nobody. I wish I had had the opportunity to do a foundation course after A-levels – it would have made a tremendous difference.

DID YOU HAVE ANY FORMAL TRAINING?

Yes, I went to art college. But I did not study sculpture. I studied Visual Communication.

DO YOU USE THE HUMAN FIGURE IN YOUR WORK?

No. But I have sometimes alluded to human presence in my work.

DO YOU USE FOUND OBJECTS?

Yes, very often. They are triggers for my imagination (always have been). Found objects tell stories. They can make me laugh, they open doors to memories – collective as well as private memories. Mostly, I feel an instant need to change the objects that so intrigue me. Through appropriation, found objects reveal a poetic mutability: what once was a violin is now also a mountain, and the suitcase becomes a bed of carrots.

DO YOU USE THE NATURAL WORLD?

No. I am a city girl.

FREE-STANDING OR ATTACHED?

My early sculptures were still "hugging" the wall, but for many years now you can walk around my work.

IS THE SCALE IMPORTANT?

Yes, absolutely, scale is so potent! Consideration of scale has been one of my main occupations as a sculptor throughout the years. A millimetre in a small work, or a centimetre in a large work, can make all the difference in terms of visual dynamics. But changing the scale of a familiar object altogether – from miniature to gigantic, or vice versa – can be utterly puzzling and can evoke the uncanny.

IS THE ENVIRONMENT IMPORTANT?

The built and manufactured environment is important for me.

EPHEMERAL OR LONG-LASTING?

My work is often physically fragile and "endangered", but not necessarily ephemeral.

MULTIMEDIA OR ONE MEDIUM?

At the moment I am working exclusively with cardboard and paper. This is quite unusual – I normally incorporate a diverse range of media in a single work. On a few occasions, I have used sound in my sculptures and once I did include two live goldfish in a piece.

IS THERE A PARTICULAT THEME OR THEMES IN YOUR WORK?

I work in series – each body of work, in my eyes, is quite different. Maybe one could say that I like to puncture the given, the assumed "state of affairs". Beyond that, I do not have a signature style, or a single central theme that occupies me. But there are a few ideas that re-emerge: the precariousness of living, paradoxes (visual or conceptual), wonder (as in the *Wunderkammer*), the possible and impossible, faking it (truth and lies). The one thing that all my work has in common is that it is visually quite restrained and meticulously produced. Leaving expressive traces of the process of making would be a distraction.

HOW DO YOU GET YOUR IDEAS FOR AN ARTWORK?

I get ideas from the "real" world, sometimes from architecture, very often from mass-produced, discarded objects. More recently, also from evocative manufactured materials, such as wallpaper.

DO YOU LIKE TO DO COMMISSIONED WORK OR NOT?

I have certain reservations when it comes to being commissioned and have not really sought out this kind of work. I fear, and, in the past, have experienced "closing down" creatively in the face of someone else's expectations. In 2017 however, I was proven wrong – I had a most enjoyable and energizing experience when I was chosen to be the resident artist on a local history project.

TELL US HOW YOU HAVE DEVELOPED AS AN ARTIST.

Not having studied sculpture at art college gives you advantages and disadvantages. The advantage is a kind of liberating naivety – I never had any preconceived ideas what sculpture "should" be – e.g. it never crossed my mind that sculpture in the twentieth century would concern itself with mimetic representation – instead, anything was possible. The 70s – which were my formative years – reinforced this perception: artists were using mud and margarine, Charlotte Moorman "played" Nam June Paik as a *Human Cello*, Panamarenko's flying machines did not take off, there were many half-empty rooms that forced me to think and/ or imagine the work. The disadvantage of not having had a formal education in sculpture is not the lack of technique, but the absence

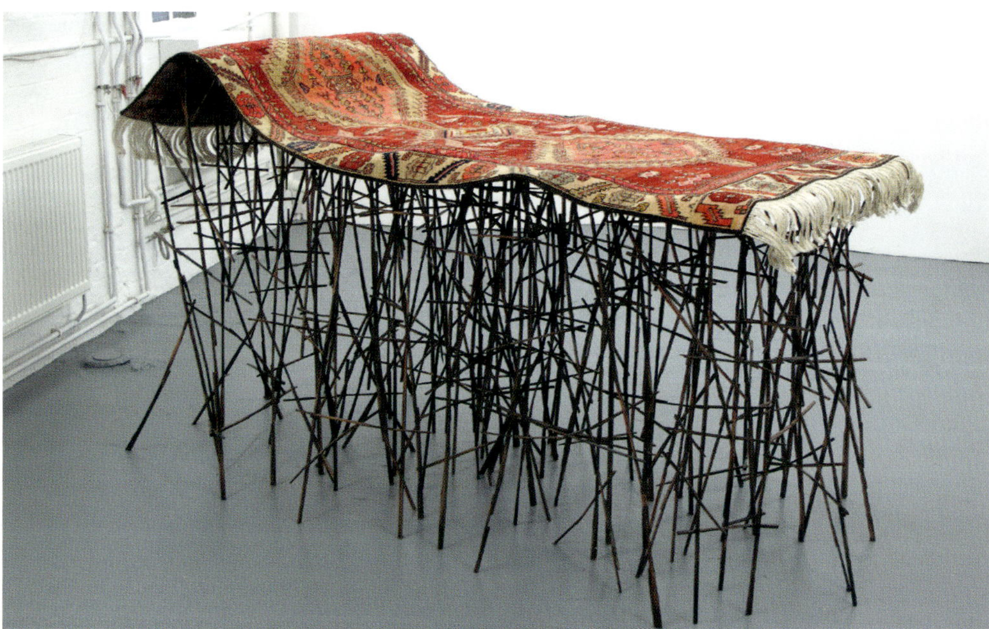

Untitled (Carpet), 2014

of the sustained debate around emerging work that art school provides. That, and not having anything to rebel against, means that you find yourself out in the wide, open sea, and it just takes a very long time to find the course that you want to navigate.

WHERE IS YOUR SCULPTURE EXHIBITED?

Normally in group shows in the UK and, occasionally, abroad. Sometimes I am approached by a curator, at other times I enter Open Submission shows.

IS IT MORE DIFFICULT FOR WOMEN ARTISTS TO MAKE A LIVING THAN MEN?

Yes, parity in the art world is still an issue. Just look at the statistics (see the Guerrilla Girls). I myself have never assumed that I would financially survive as an artist, which was the main reason for me starting to teach.

TELL US ABOUT YOUR FAVOURITE SCULPTURES – YOUR OWN OR BY SOMEONE ELSE.

There are many, many "favourites" (and they keep on changing), but top of the list for a number of years now is Veija Celmins's *To Fix The Image in Memory* (1977–82). If I had a few million pounds… I would be a very happy person to live with this work! And that is because its spell does not dissipate. Rationally, I fully understand how *To Fix The Image in Memory* came about. I have read up on it. When not in the actual presence of Celmins's eleven pairs of identical pebble stones, I can still bring them up in my mind most clearly. It is not a work that, on first encounter, entrances with any overt visual flourish. It is an extremely "quiet" work. There is no "noise" around it, actually the opposite is the case, an absence of any palpable action. Celmins says that she had wanted "to create a challenge for [the] eyes", but this work is as much a perceptual provocation as it is a conceptual one – looking and thinking are intricately and elegantly entwined here. It is an "impossible" work, really, which raises elemental questions about art and art-making.

I have seen Celmins's twin stones in two separate exhibitions, and I was transfixed to the same degree each time. Nothing can explain away the pull and push between eye and brain. This is where its persistent energy resides. It is an extremely infuriating piece of art, yet I am happily trapped in this work.

WHAT'S NEXT?

At the moment I am working with abandoned polystyrene forms, found by the roadside. I am attracted by their often very beautiful negative shapes (created by unknown designers), which speak of the absent objects once contained by them. I am scaling these shapes up, to make them monolithic and, hopefully, turn the mundane and functional into something strange yet beautiful. I invest the obsolete with value and the materials I am using – corrugated card and marble trompe l'oeil wallpaper – add another twist to the perceived reality of these works.

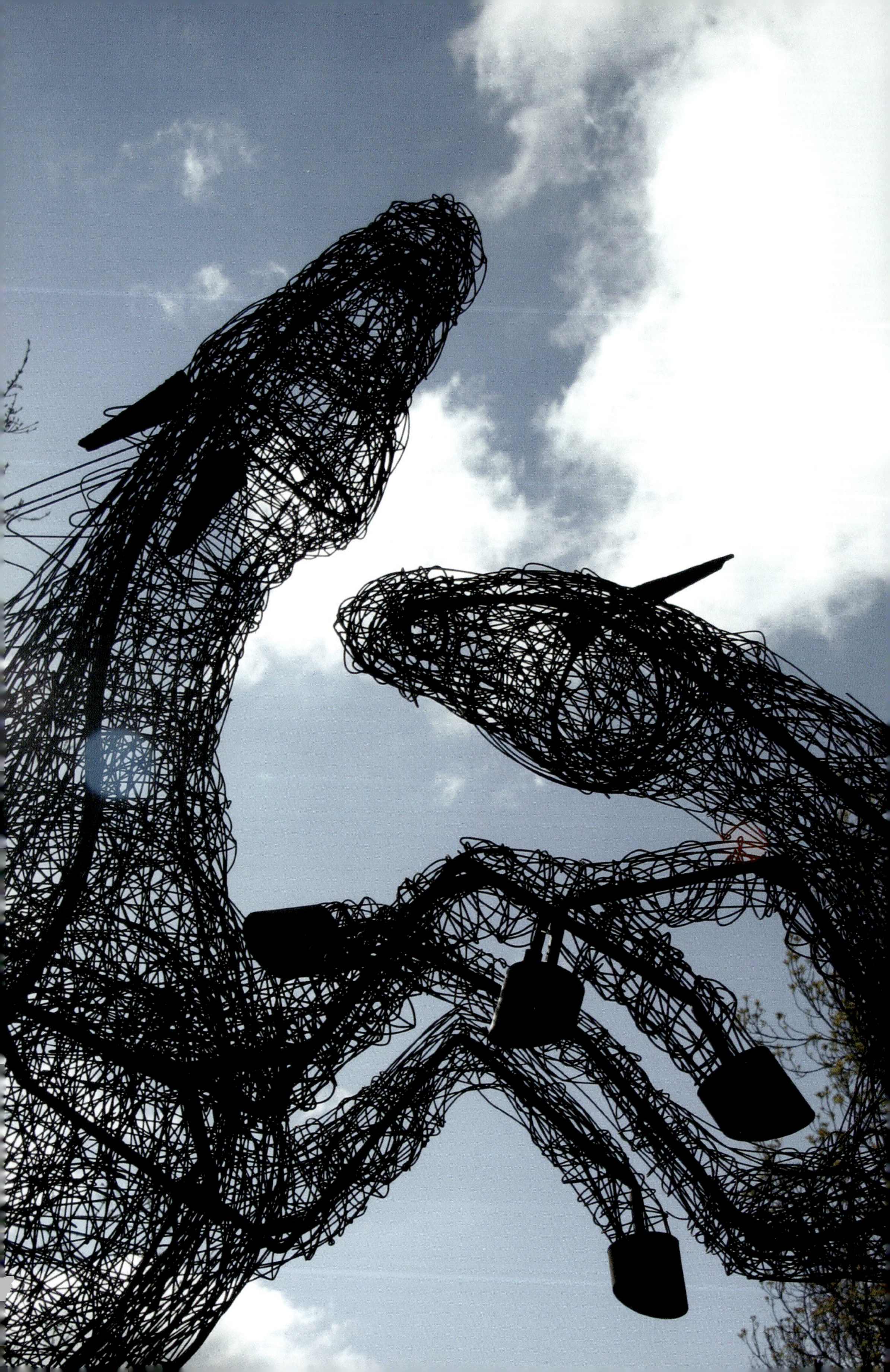

LAURY DIZENGREMEL

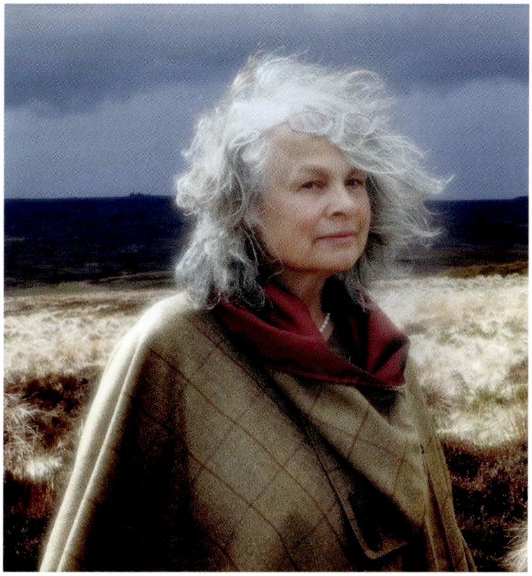

Born in France, Laury Dizengremel is an award-winning sculptor with public works located in Honduras, Vietnam, South Korea and China, as well as France, Canada, Ireland, Wales and England. Her lifesize portrayal of Lancelot 'Capability' Brown was installed on the Thames Walk in Hammersmith in 2017. She has been Artist-in-Residence for the Belvoir Castle estate in Leicestershire for over nine years, conducting workshops in schools as well as creating a number of artworks for the Duchess of Rutland. An obelisk she created was featured on More 4 TV in a programme hosted by Alan Titchmarsh. Dizengremel exhibits personal works in exhibitions such as biennales at Doddington Hall in Lincolnshire, and several of her monumental works are permanently exhibited at Broomhill Sculpture Gardens in North Devon. One current project is the first ever full figure portrayal of the writer Virginia Woolf for Richmond Upon Thames.

HOW DID YOU COME TO MAKE SCULPTURE?

As a child I walked the streets of Paris, deeply intrigued and touched by the vast quantity and diversity of sculpture on offer. Public statuary, museum sculpture, architectural elements such as reliefs and caryatids, they were all there for me to absorb, admire, or be awed, even humbled, but inspired by.

Left: *Rearing Horses* 2017, Chalabre, France.

WHO WERE YOUR INFLUENCES AND OR ROLE MODELS?

I was greatly influenced by the book *This Proud Heart* by Pearl Buck (written in 1938), which I read in 1968. It portrays a woman's journey as a passionate sculptor. Role models include Rodin and his pupils Camille Claudel and Malvina Hoffman, as well as countless other sculptors too numerous to mention. My taste in art is so eclectic that identifying all influences would end up long and boring rather than reflecting the exciting adventure of developing – and continuing to develop – as an artist.

WHO ENCOURAGED YOU?

Seeking encouragement is a losing game. My motto is that one has to self-motivate, kick oneself in the butt and keep going despite all obstacles. Having said that, fellow artists (painters, sculptors, dancers, poets) and some family members and friends have greatly encouraged me at various times of my life. If you are still alive and read this – you know who you are!

DID YOU HAVE ANY FORMAL TRAINING?

I had a very small amount of initial training in my early twenties, from two sculptors, Martine Vaugel (French-American) and Jan Valentin Sæther (Norwegian), back in the late 1970s at the Venice Sculpture Studio in California. Later I learned bits and pieces of technique at the Beaux-Arts in Paris from Jacques Perrin, who took me on as an unregistered student for a year in 1985, then, starting in 2001, while taking part in various international sculpture symposia, I sought tips from a number of Chinese sculptors such as Zhang Yaxi, and Chen Lian Fu. I finally decided to get a degree when I was aged 50, completing a two-year Master's of Fine Art International Practice degree at the University of the Creative Arts in Canterbury, Kent, England, in 2006.

DO YOU USE THE HUMAN FIGURE IN YOUR WORK?

Mostly yes. I have experimented with abstract and conceptual only to return again and again to the use of the human (or animal or geographical) body.

DO YOU USE FOUND OBJECTS?

I have often played with found objects and have also discovered, when conducting workshops with small or large groups, that creating with natural world "stuff" was one of the easiest ways to introduce notions of scale and form.

DO YOU USE THE NATURAL WORLD?

It is a constant inspiration. Almost nothing that is natural is truly flat. Almost everything has some degree of planes that are either concave or convex… Look at a human face. Look at an animal. Look at the landscape of our world… The abundance of inspiring

Artists of the Silk Road 2004, Broomhill Sculpture Gardens, England

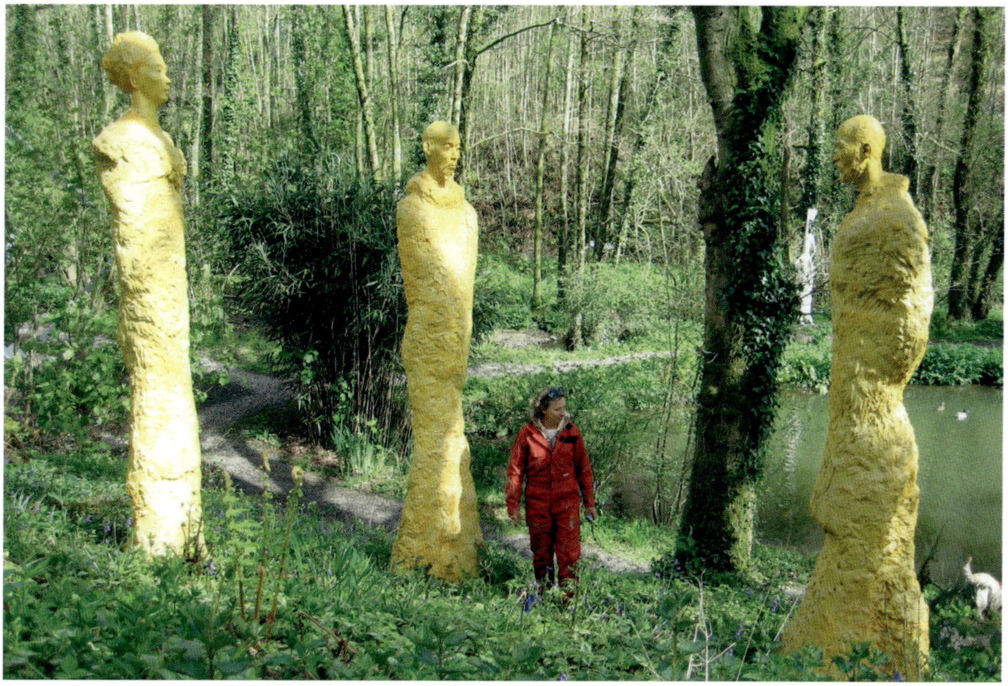

natural shapes, volumes, textures and media is brilliant to behold.

FREE-STANDING OR ATTACHED?

Either. Each has its place!

IS THE SCALE IMPORTANT?

Scale is very important. Lifesize can look very small in an outdoor environment, and a room can be overwhelmed by too large an artwork. A sculptor who truly understands scale is halfway there…

IS THE ENVIRONMENT IMPORTANT?

Hugely. It determines scale, use of materials; the environment should dictate many other aspects of a sculptor's engagement with an artwork.

EPHEMERAL OR LONG-LASTING?

I get a real kick out of thinking that if you tipped one of my smaller bronze pieces (a bust or some such) from a great height it would only get slightly damaged – and from the thought that I have had permanent pieces installed all around the world in public spaces for generations to come to enjoy (unless future generations melt them down for new-style canons). But I also got a great buzz creating a monumental snow sculpture

Lancelot 'Capability' Brown 2017 prior to location on Distillery Wharf, Hammersmith, UK.

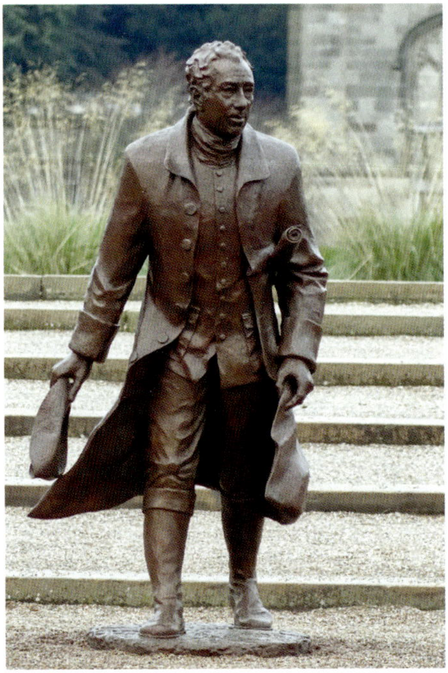

on a frozen lake in northern China which melted in the spring, or from crafting lifesize willow horses which lasted only a few years.

MULTIMEDIA OR ONE MEDIUM?

For sure lots of different media (from clay to lost-wax bronze busts and figures, willow experiments of small to large pieces, woven and welded steel artworks, monumental snow sculpture, plaster, etc.) and quite a few artworks have been multimedia (i.e. concrete and bronze, steel and fabric).

IS THERE A PARTICULAR THEME OR THEMES WHICH ARE CENTRAL TO YOUR WORK?

Own works: redressing the imbalance in under-representation of females in public statuary worldwide, site-specific/context-specific responses to given cultural parameters, explorations into the recycling of fragments of my old work into new pieces and playing with various concepts concerning the role of artists in society throughout the ages. Commissioned work: memorialization (capturing the essence and personality of a given animal or person who is alive today or was once alive).

HOW DO YOU GET YOUR IDEAS FOR AN ARTWORK?

It's a tiny spark that develops further as I make, and even further as time passes when the work is finished and people start to interact with it and comment and ask questions, and then (and only then) am I forced to properly formulate the idea into words. Unlike many of my fellow artists I don't engage in much rumination or what I like to call "mental masturbation" before starting on a piece. Nothing against the former but it just ain't my thing.

DO YOU LIKE TO DO COMMISSIONED WORK OR NOT?

I think there are three main categories of sculptors when it comes to the subject of enjoying commissioned work: those who eschew commissions and concentrate solely on developing a single voice, those who love and thrive only on commission work, and those who navigate a balanced or unbalanced path between the two approaches. Personally, I have a passion for commissioned work, yet have also enjoyed creating a bunch of "own" works, but never, ever, ever with a single voice, as I am way too busy exploring different materials and styles.

TELL US HOW YOU HAVE DEVELOPED AS AN ARTIST.

Aged three I think it was already obvious I was into the creative band of activity. Whether performance, writing poetry or a fine art form was going to be prime for me was just a matter of time. I have woven aesthetics into every part of my life, from arranging flowers to decorating a room to throwing a tasty dish together, creating a sculpture or writing a poem – it's all part and parcel of a continuing adventure, a passionate exploration of the creative realm.

WHERE IS YOUR SCULPTURE EXHIBITED?

In an eclectic bunch of places, from the inner wood-panelled boardroom of Berry Bros. & Rudd on St James Street to the very public bank of the River Thames, from the United Nations El Picacho Park in Honduras to the Mekong Delta in Vietnam, from the World Sculpture Park of Changchun in China to the banks of the Boyne River in the town of Drogheda just north of Dublin in Ireland.

IS IT MORE DIFFICULT FOR WOMEN ARTISTS TO MAKE A LIVING THAN MEN?

Sure – it is still no different in the field of art than it is in any other sphere. Equality is not yet a reality. However, I am not sure it will ever be, for even if all of society comes to recognize equal worth, as long as a female artist chooses to also be a parent and takes on the role of the main carer, she's going to need to divide her attention between her work and her kids while they are in need of nurturing.

TELL US ABOUT YOUR FAVOURITE SCULPTURES – YOUR OWN OR BY SOMEONE ELSE.

Too many to describe. I love all of my work (even flawed pieces – or if too flawed I destroy them), and I love a good fifty percent of everything I have ever seen. That's a hell of a lot of good "favourite" work. Again a very eclectic taste means I have had the good fortune to have appreciated a vast amount of works ranging from representational to conceptual.

WHAT'S NEXT?

Ever more development. Ever more experimentation. Hopefully ever more commissions as well. I have to keep putting food on the table and always will. I can never afford to – nor do I ever want to "retire".

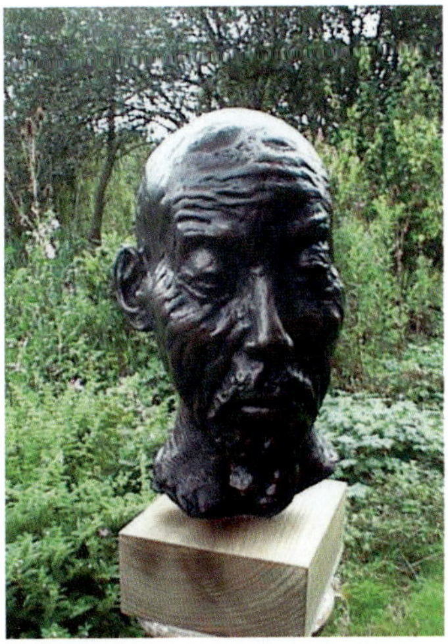

Feng Shui Master

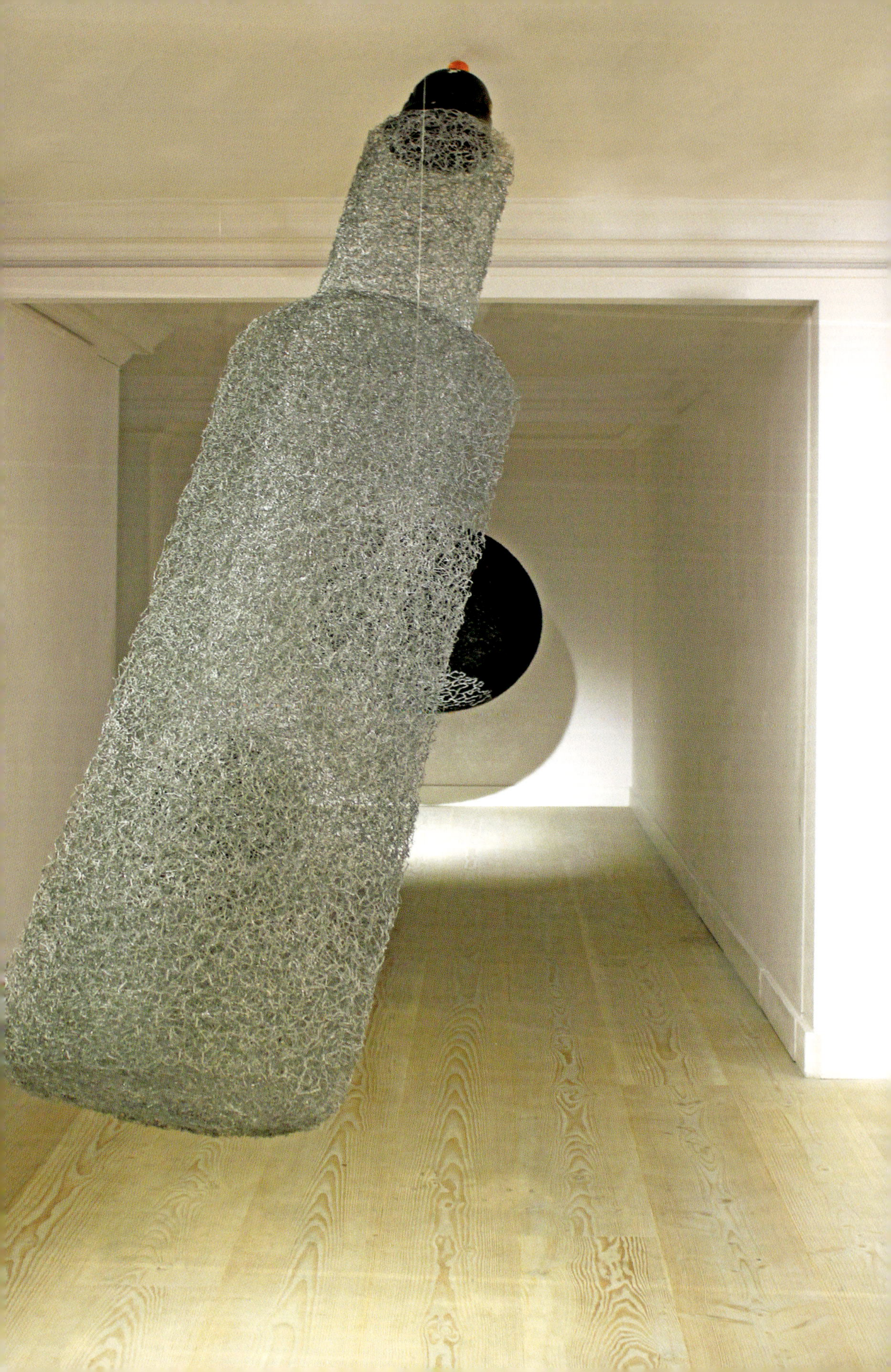

JANE McADAM FREUD

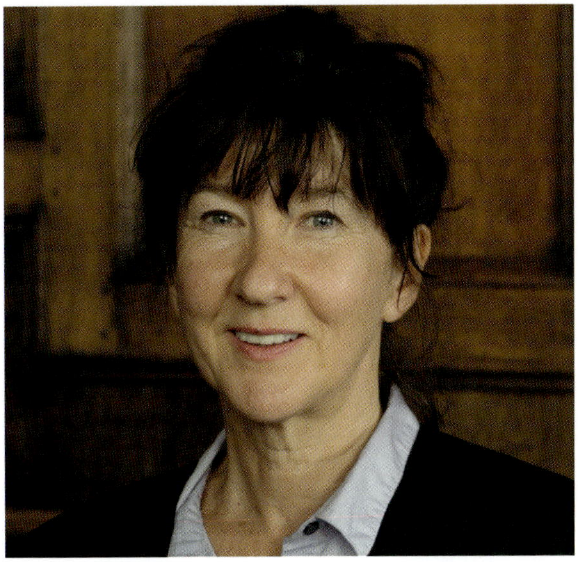

Jane McAdam Freud MA-RCA, FRSS studied at Wimbledon, Central, Royal College of Art in London and was awarded the British Art Medal Scholarship in Rome. She was granted the Freedom of the City in 1991 due to her work being represented in major public collections at home and abroad and has since mounted 58 solo exhibitions, the most recent at the Palazzo Ducale, Genoa in 2019. Retrospectives include the Wooyang Contemporary Art Museum, Gyeongju-si, South Korea in 2015 and the Freud Museum, London in 2006. In 2014, along with Annie Leibovitz, McAdam Freud won the European Trebbia Award for achievement in the arts. Jane lectures at the University of the Arts, London.

Represented by Gazelli Art House, London and CE Contemporary, Milan.

HOW DID YOU COME TO MAKE SCULPTURE?

I always wanted to make sculpture – it started at around 7 years old when I fantasized about making heads of the people I knew. I knew I would be an artist from the start as both my parents went to art school and our family friends were all artists, so I really didn't learn that it might be a choice, not that it would have made any difference. Sculpture was something all of my own – not painting, which was my father's domain, nor design, which was my mother's (she did fashion at St Martin's).

Left: *EdensNede* 2015 Photo: Gazelli Arts House. Above: Portrait photo: Rachel Marchant

Love and Myth reverse 2013

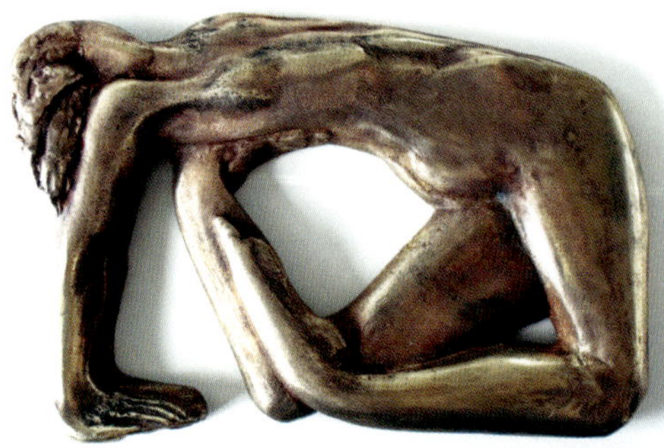

WHO WERE YOUR INFLUENCES AND OR ROLE MODELS?

I trained at the Royal College and in Rome. My supervisors at the RCA were Eduardo Paolozzi, Michael Roe and John Stezaker, so my influences were quite eclectic.

WHO ENCOURAGED YOU?

They all encouraged me, along with Gino Marotta, a highly acclaimed Italian sculptor who taught me at the Academy in Rome. John Mills, the then president of the Royal Society of Sculptors, under whom I received Fellowship in 1994, also encouraged me.

DID YOU HAVE ANY FORMAL TRAINING?

I trained up until the age of 31, first at the Central, then in Ravenna, Italy, followed by a year at Goldsmiths and a sculpture scholarship in Rome for three years, followed by a research Master's at the RCA.

DO YOU USE THE HUMAN FIGURE IN YOUR WORK?

I do use the human figure in my work even though less so as I proceed. I allude to it and more recently work directly with the figure as an actual object, drawing around the sitter to create an eerie outline picking up on the 'uncanny' of being.

DO YOU USE FOUND OBJECTS?

More and more so. Objects "speak" too, I find.

FREE-STANDING OR ATTACHED?

Free standing if possible or carefully selected "holding" devices are what I prefer (to plinths).

IS THE SCALE IMPORTANT?

Life size is important, even though some of my life-size objects are small – like Coke cans. I enjoy something I can work on in the hand so have made many "pups" – i.e. pick-up pieces. I call them the "small dog of sculpture".

MULTIMEDIA OR ONE MEDIUM?

Definitely multimedia – even an artist is not an island!

IS THERE A PARTICULAR THEME OR THEMES WHICH ARE CENTRAL TO YOUR WORK?

Underlying themes are Freud, Family and Feminism, and I can trace these three aspects through the trajectory of my sculptural practice.

HOW DO YOU GET YOUR IDEAS FOR AN ARTWORK?

Unconsciously, through unknown impulses coming together with evocative objects.

DO YOU LIKE TO DO COMMISSIONED WORK OR NOT?

Not particularly, I prefer to have the ideas myself.

WHERE IS YOUR SCULPTURE EXHIBITED?

I exhibit internationally, mainly in museums and public galleries. The V&A, the British Museum and Freud Museum have my works on show in their public collections and I am represented in the Tate Gallery Audio archives and National Gallery archives. Abroad, I have works which were purchased and shown by museums and institutions in USA, Asia and Europe including the Pushkin Museum, Moscow, National Arts Club, NYC, Berlin State Museum and Rijksmuseum, Leiden NL, National Gallery of Greece and National Museum of Copenhagen.

IS IT MORE DIFFICULT FOR WOMEN ARTISTS TO MAKE A LIVING THAN MEN?

Definitely, however this holds true in all areas not just the arts, although sculpture is of course predominantly a male "stronghold".

TELL US ABOUT YOUR FAVOURITE SCULPTURES – YOUR OWN OR BY SOMEONE ELSE.

Always the Italians. I love Piero Manzoni, who did the first set of poos in tins – right up to Claudio Costa, who is Italy's Marcel Duchamp in my opinion. I am an Italophile, and although Italy is a traditional society, it is extremely cultured, with an established disseminated (through the media) understanding and appreciation of contemporary art and sculpture, which is becoming rarer in Northern European institutions.

WHAT'S NEXT?

Colour (avoided for a lifetime) – painted Sculpture, and that is not as literal as it sounds, but watch this space!

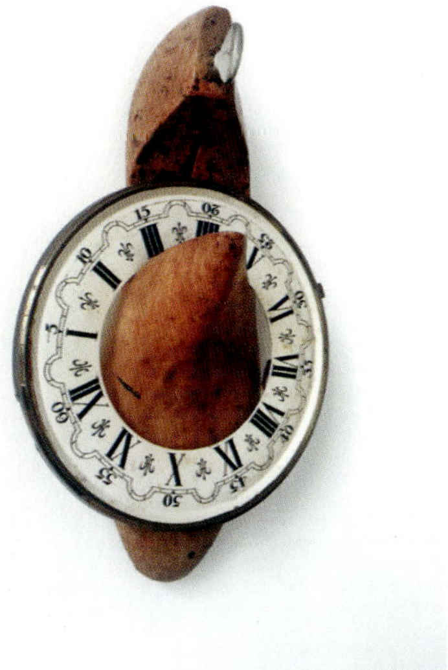

Time for She 2018
Photo: Armando Pastorino

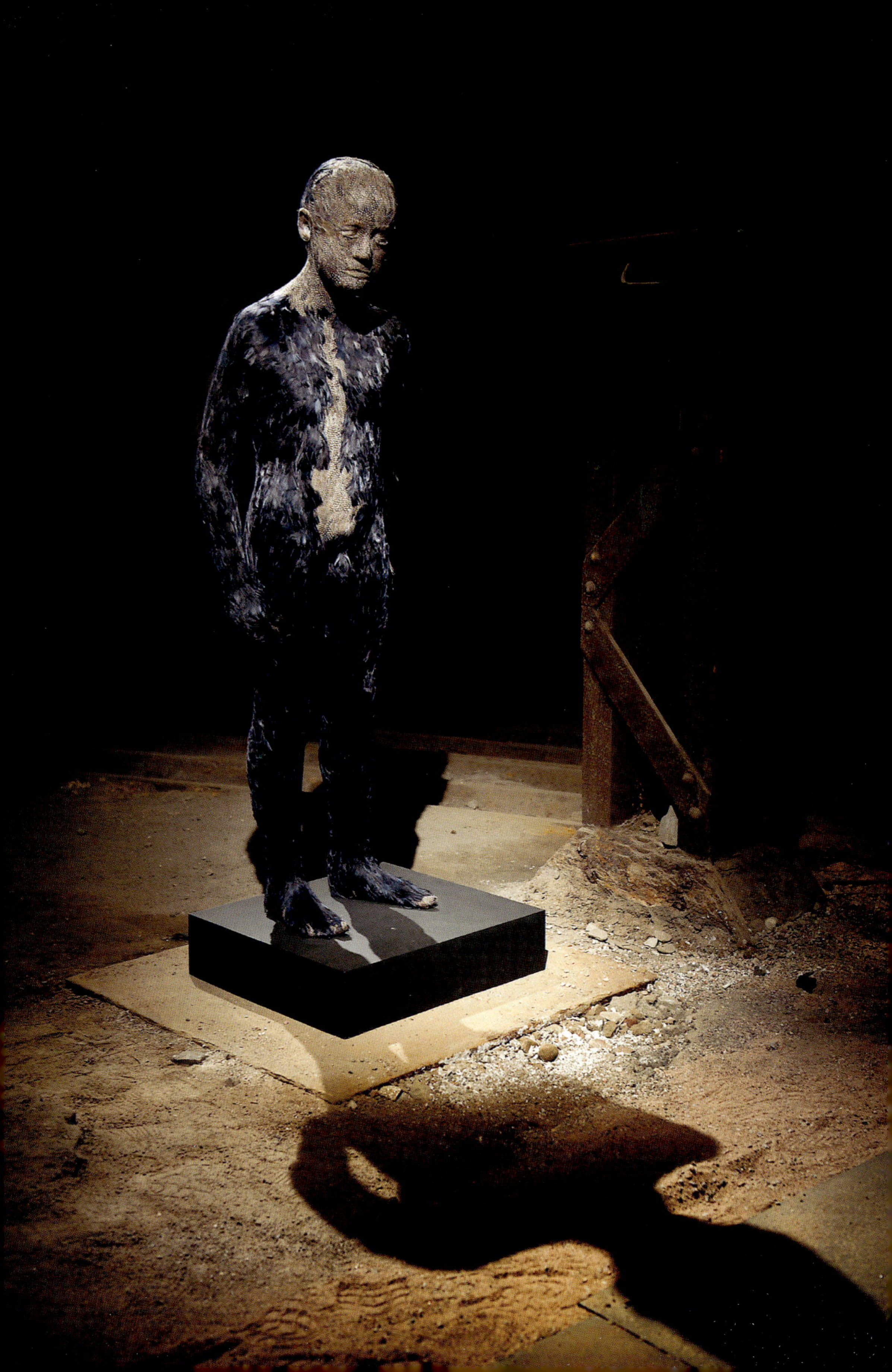

LUCY GLENDINNING

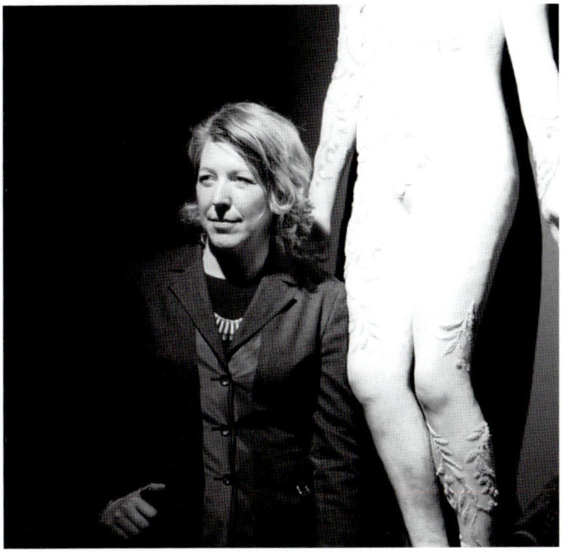

Lucy Glendinning was born in 1964 and lives and works in Somerset. She studied Fine Art Sculpture at University of the West of England, Bristol. After leaving college, she worked for Elizabeth Frink in a bronze foundry, learning how to do casting. She has exhibited extensively including at the Ashmolean Museum, Royal Academy London, Grand Rapids Art Museum, USA, Abbaye Saint-Riquier, La Halle Saint Pierre Museum, Paris, Halle14, Leipzig, Centre d'Art Contemporian, France, Boras Museum of Modern Art, Sweden, Meijer Sculpture Gardens, USA and the Saatchi Gallery London. Glendinning has completed 11 public commissions throughout the UK, which have won several awards including the Civic Trust Award in 2009, and 2011, the Landscape Institute Award in 2010 and 2011, and a 'Red Rose Award' in 2011. Most recently, she has had a solo exhibition at Da-End Gallery in Paris and a large exhibition at Villa Tamaris Museum of Contemporary Art in Toulon.

HOW DID YOU COME TO MAKE SCULPTURE?

I have made things as long as I can remember. As a child I found education quite challenging, as I am dyslexic. I was drawn to building and making things. Somehow it was a less linear thought process and I found it more comfortable, and people responded when I made things.

Left: *The Unknown Boy* 2012 Photo: Therese Asplund, Atelje Linslusen

WHO WERE YOUR INFLUENCES AND OR ROLE MODELS?

My husband who is a sculptor /land artist has been the biggest influence on my work; we met at art college, and have worked closely together ever since. His work is very different from mine, but we work easily alongside each other. His discerning eye and love of sculpture and architecture have a huge influence on my work. The role models I keep returning to are Louise Bourgeois and Kiki Smith for their freedom of thought and honesty.

WHO ENCOURAGED YOU?

I am lucky, lots of people have encouraged me, my family, and friends, who often did not understand what I was doing or trying to do. My in-laws, who are a family of architects, but most of all Mark Merer, my husband has been my biggest support.

DID YOU HAVE ANY FORMAL TRAINING?

Yes, I did art foundation and then a BA at University of the West of England in Fine Art Sculpture.

DO YOU USE THE HUMAN FIGURE IN YOUR WORK?

I use the human figure as a tool, I find it a fascinating subject. I am fascinated by how they work and how our mental state affects our physical posture and movement.

DO YOU USE FOUND OBJECTS?

Yes, I do sometimes, usually as surface materials.

DO YOU USE THE NATURAL WORLD?

Yes, I am very influenced by the natural world and use natural materials as mediums in my work such as feathers and leaves. I have recently worked on a series of drawings called animal drawings, which are images made from the marks made by animals and insects in the landscape. We live very rurally in Somerset, and this is a big influence on my work.

FREE-STANDING OR ATTACHED?

Mainly freestanding, but some wall pieces like the skins which are in relief.

IS THE SCALE IMPORTANT?

Scale is really important. I think every work has its perfect scale, and the scale of a work can completely change it.

IS THE ENVIRONMENT IMPORTANT?

Absolutely, we are really running out of time and it's hard to know what to do. It's as if we are on a sinking ship and the captain and crew are arguing about the destination.

EPHEMERAL OR LONG-LASTING?

Both but as I get older I become more interested in making ephemeral works.

MULTIMEDIA OR ONE MEDIUM?

Multimedia. I usually use casting as a process, and the materials I use are, more often than not, part of the concept for the piece. I love using wax as it has such a skin-like transparency. I use feathers a lot, which are extraordinary things. I use rubber as I love the transformation from liquid to solid. Most recently, I have started to use ground-up recycled plastic as part of a casting material. The materials I use for a piece are part of the works concept, and I often experiment with new materials.

IS THERE A PARTICULAR THEME OR THEMES WHICH ARE CENTRAL TO YOUR WORK?

Yes, I work on themes which run through my work in series, but always concerned with possible futures. For individuals as well as for society, which I explore through research and investigation, a bit like a very bad scientific research project.

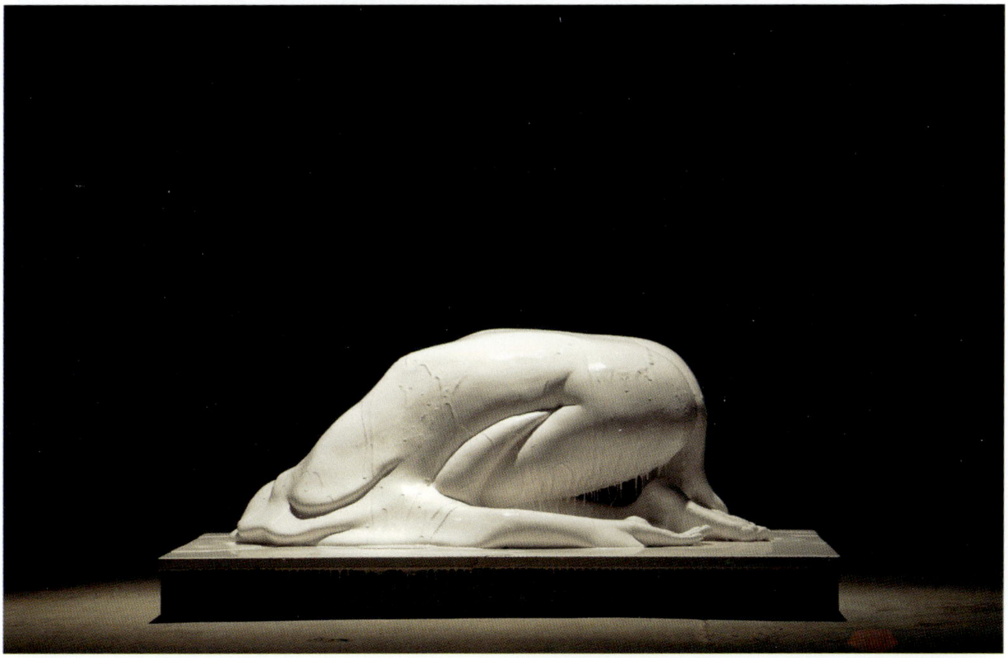

Folding Girl 2011 Photo: Claus Bach, Halle14

Distortions 2011 Photo: Lucy Glendinning, Galleri Andersson Sandström.

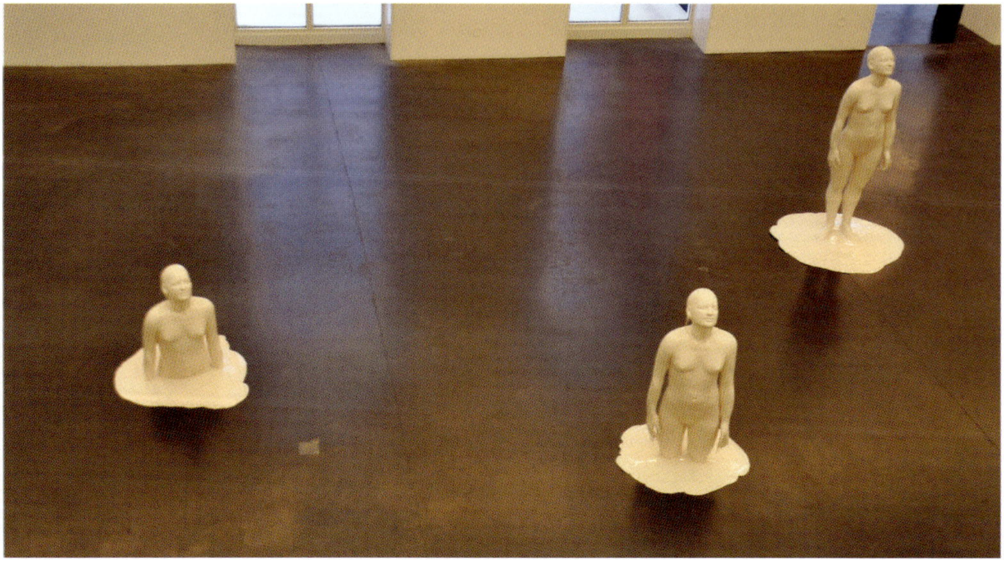

The two recurring themes are: will we be able to resist the genetic manipulation of the human? And the ghost in the machine: the physical effects of mental states.

HOW DO YOU GET YOUR IDEAS FOR AN ARTWORK?

I research ideas and concepts. They often start as poems, which are like notes, which then develop into pieces. Sometimes they move quickly, and the idea becomes a piece quite fast, but more often than not I like to test them for whether it is a strong idea. If it is, it will bother me to be made.

DO YOU LIKE TO DO COMMISSIONED WORK OR NOT?

I love doing commissions if they are not restrictive and I am not being asked to make someone else's idea.

TELL US HOW YOU HAVE DEVELOPED AS AN ARTIST.

I think I have become braver as I get older; there is less time, and it is more important to be making work which is challenging me.

WHERE IS YOUR SCULPTURE EXHIBITED?

I exhibit work mainly in Sweden, France, Germany, Belgium, Netherlands and UK.

IS IT MORE DIFFICULT FOR WOMEN ARTISTS TO MAKE A LIVING THAN MEN?

It's better than it was and better than a lot of professions. It's really hard to make a living as an artist, man or woman. The statistics are better but not great for women, so sadly, still yes, but less.

TELL US ABOUT YOUR FAVOURITE SCULPTURES – YOUR OWN OR BY SOMEONE ELSE.

I love Louise Bourgeois, particularly her fabric heads, Berlinde de Bruyckere's work, particularly her horses. My favourite work at the moment is Kohei Nawa's deer, extraordinary and beautiful. I love Kiki Smith's work, and also Udo Rondinone and Erwin Wurm.

WHAT'S NEXT?

I am working on new works, on different series, such as *The Ghost in the Machine*, exploring further the physicality of a mental state, and the effect of technology on this. Alongside new works about our relationship with animals, our internal animal and the animals around us, which doesn't have a title yet.

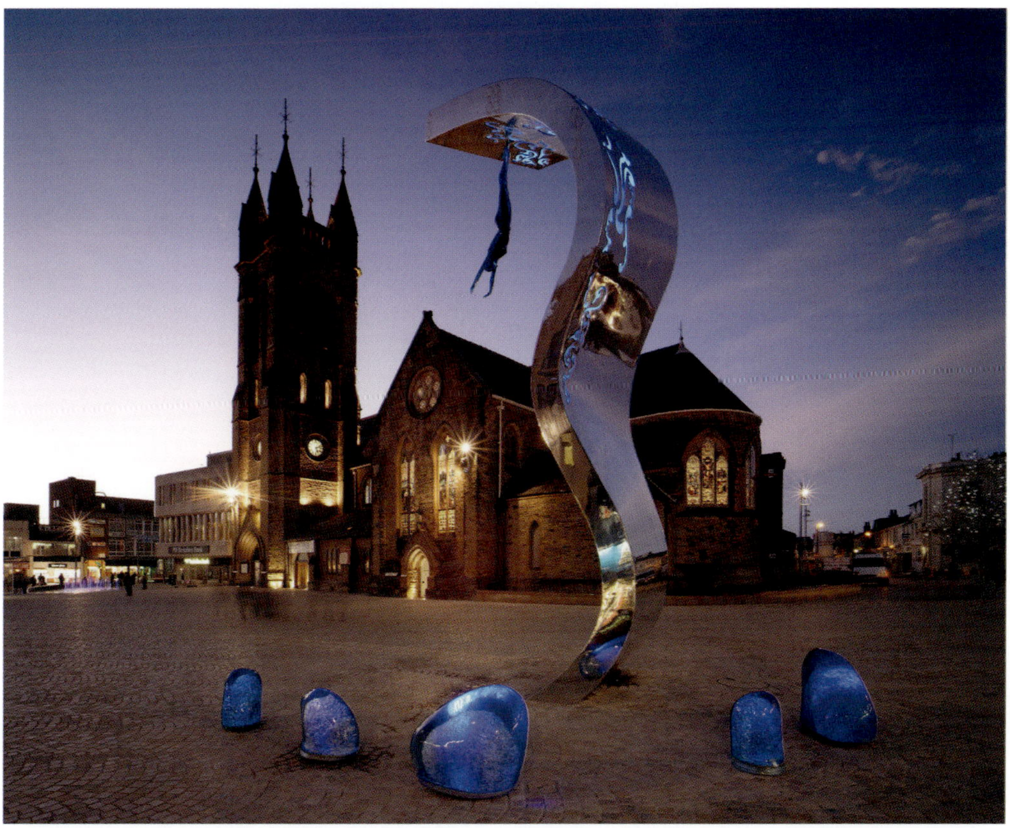

The Wave 2009 Blackpool. Photo: Sean Conboy

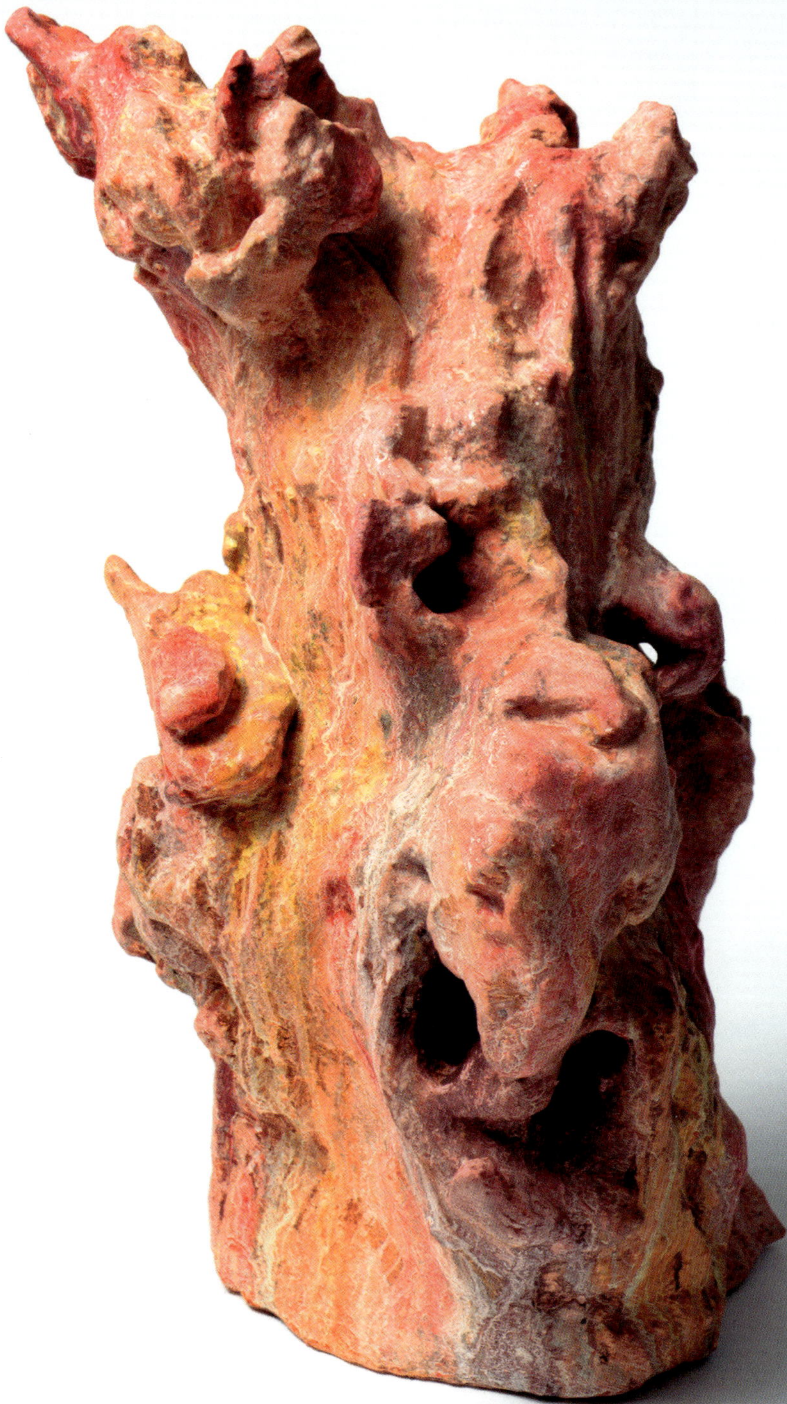

MAGGI HAMBLING

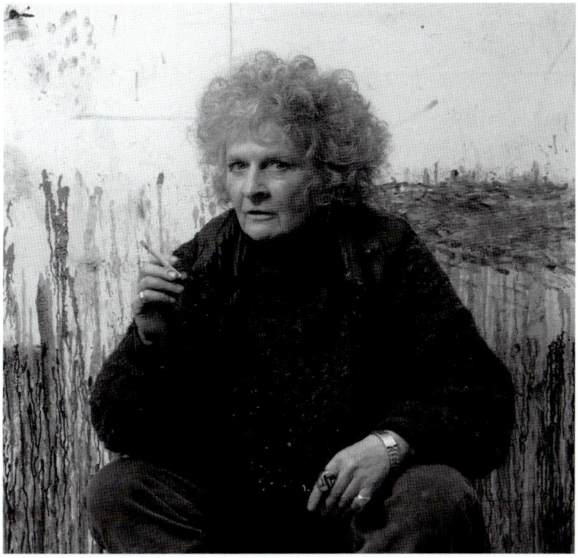

Maggi Hambling CBE (born 1945) lives and works in London and Suffolk. Hambling studied with Lett Haines and Cedric Morris, and then at Ipswich, Camberwell and the Slade Schools of Art. In 1980, she became the first Artist in Residence at the National Gallery, London, and in 1995 won the Jerwood Painting Prize (with Patrick Caulfield). In 1998 her sculpture *A Conversation with Oscar Wilde* was unveiled at Adelaide Street, London, facing Charing Cross Station. In 2003, a sculpture to celebrate Benjamin Britten was unveiled at Aldeburgh, Suffolk titled *Scallop* and in 2005 Maggi was awarded the Marsh Award for Excellence in Public Sculpture for *Scallop*.

Her work is represented in major collections internationally, and in the UK these include the British Museum, Tate, Victoria and Albert Museum, National Portrait Gallery and National Gallery. Recent museum shows include: *Maggi Hambling: Walls of Water* at the Hermitage Museum, St Petersburg, Russia (2013) and the National Gallery, London (2014), *War Requiem & Aftermath* at Somerset House (2015), *Maggi Hambling: Touch*, a retrospective of works on paper at the British Museum (2016), *The Quick and the Dead: Hambling, Horsley, Lucas, Simmons, Teller* at Hastings Contemporary (2018), *Maggi Hambling: For Beauty Is Nothing but the Beginning of Terror* at both CAFA Museum, Beijing and Guangdong Museum of Art, Guangzhou, China (2019).

Left: *Aftermath (Politician),* 2015. Photos left and Portrait above: Douglas Atfield

IN HER OWN WORDS

Sculpture numbered among the disciplines at Ipswich Art School, where I studied (1962–64) before the Camberwell and Slade Schools of Art. My portrait of the sculptor Bernard Reynolds (1963) was first modelled from life in clay, and a bronze cast is now in the collection of Christchurch Museum, Ipswich. Sculpture did not re-enter my practice until late 1992, when I worked at the RCA in thinly rolled clay, which was then fired, painted with engobe and fired again – *Hermaphrodite* (self-portrait) (1993) was acquired by the V&A. Later that year I began to work with the lost wax process, and my first exhibition of bronze sculpture was held at Marlborough Fine Art in 1996 – *War Coffin* (1994) is held by Tate.

Scallop, my tribute to Benjamin Britten, was fabricated in steel with J.T. Pegg & Sons, Aldeburgh, Suffolk, and installed on Aldeburgh beach in 2003. While *A Conversation with Oscar Wilde*, as with most public sculpture, was commissioned, *Scallop* is the result of my own initiative. Both were controversial when unveiled. While a painting hangs safely on a wall, and may be easily passed by, a public sculpture confronts people in real space.

Scallop, 2003 on Aldeburgh Beach

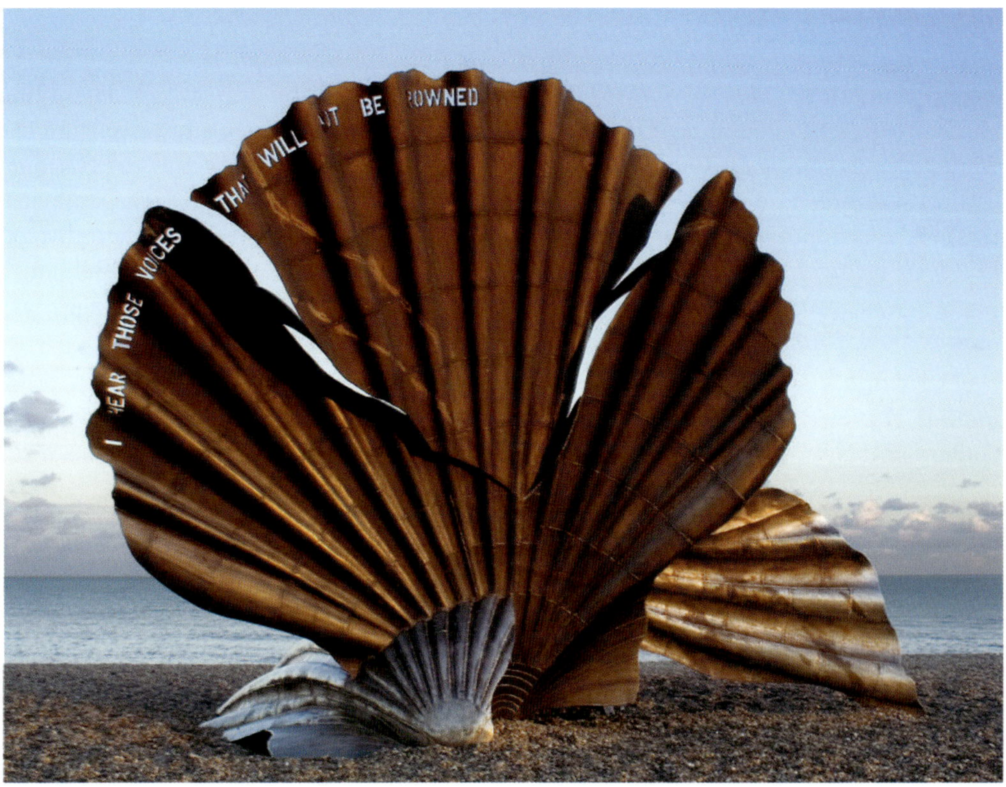

Whereas painting is a solitary activity, for me, sculpture involves other people in its execution. *A Conversation with Oscar Wilde* (1998) is situated in Adelaide Street, near Trafalgar Square in the heart of London. It was made with Arch Bronze Foundry, Putney, with whom I always work with bronze.

The sculpture is engraved with a quotation from Oscar Wilde's play *Lady Windermere's Fan:*

"We are all in the gutter but some of us are looking at the stars".

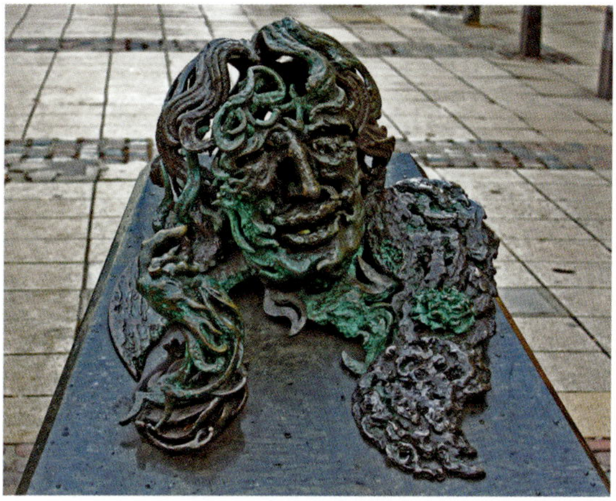

Above: *A Conversation with Oscar Wilde,* 1998
Photo: Gareth Williams

More recently I have made work which originates in found pieces of dead wood, which are then carved, modelled and, when complete, cast in bronze and then painted. These formed part of my *War Requiem & Aftermath* exhibition at Somerset House in 2015.

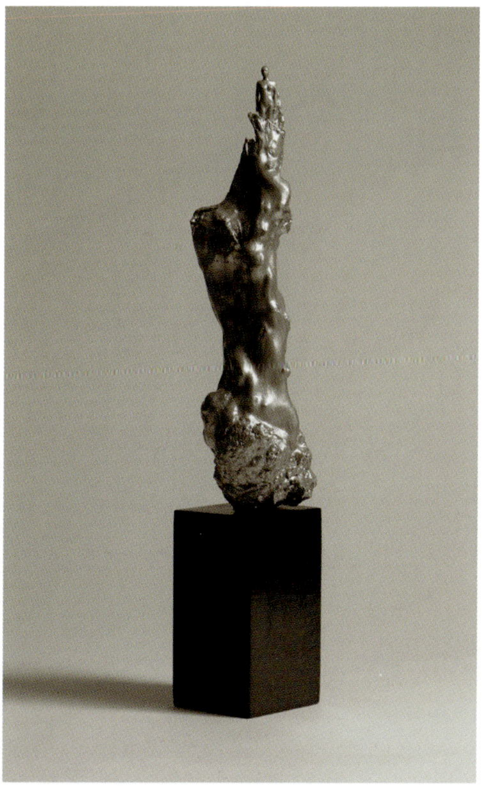

At present I am working on two commissions for public sculpture: one to commemorate Mary Wollstonecraft in London – widely deemed the "foremother of feminism" – which will feature Wollstonecraft's inspiring words: "I do not wish women to have power over men but over themselves," and to be situated on Newington Green in Islington.

The other for Edward Carpenter in Sheffield, who was a socialist writer and poet, and an early activist for gay rights and animal rights.

Left: Sculpture maquette for Mary Wollstonecraft. Photo: Douglas Atfield

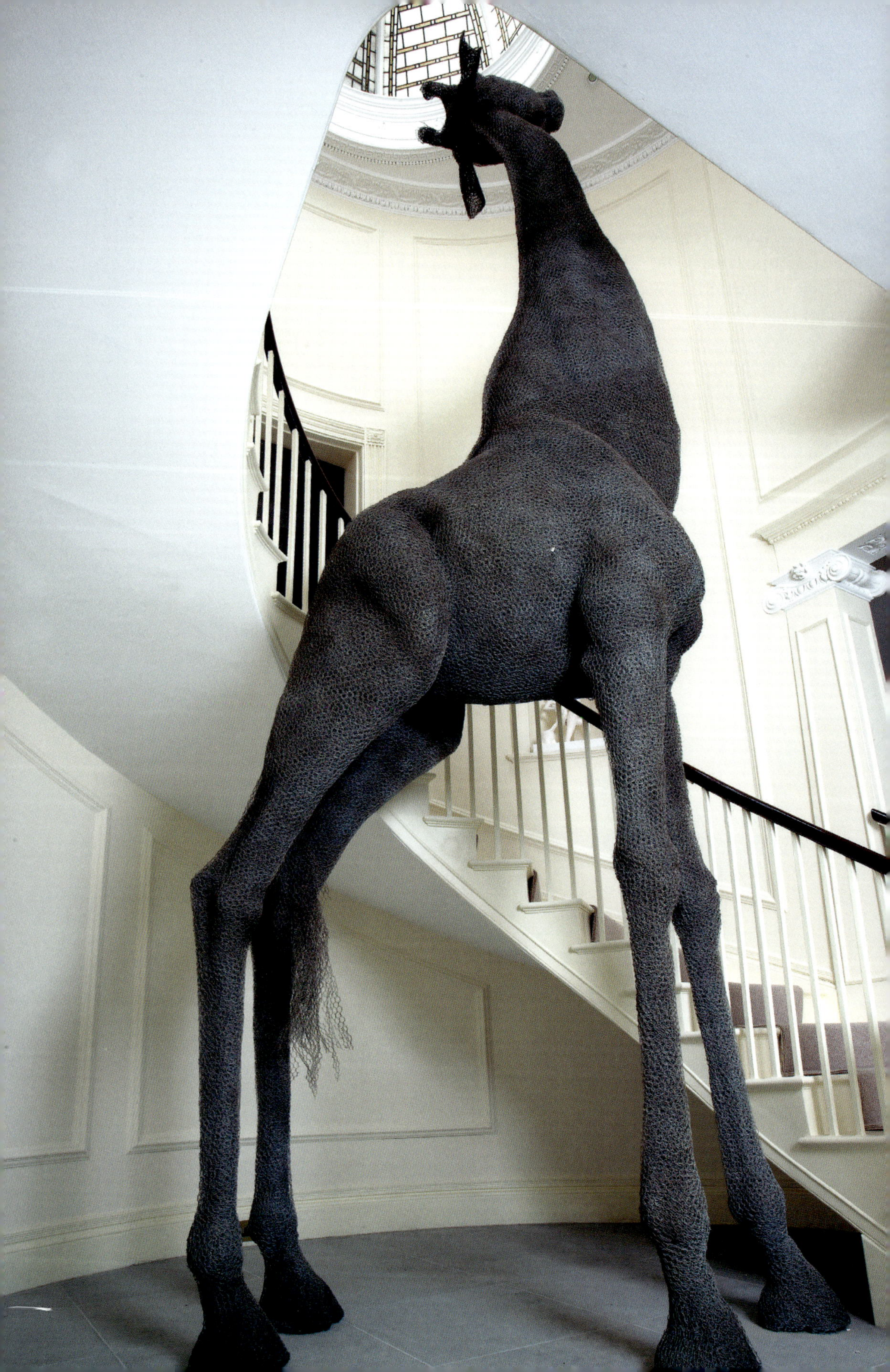

KENDRA HASTE

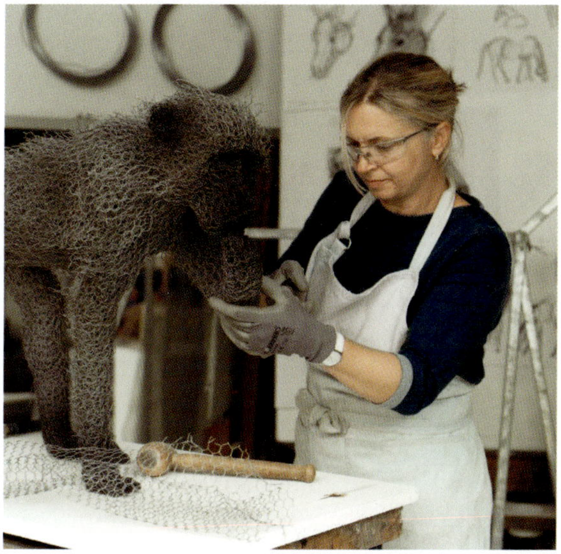

Kendra Haste MRSS grew up in Putney and graduated from Wimbledon College of Art (1990), achieved a B.A. Honours in Illustration from Camberwell College of Arts (1993) before studying for her Master's degree at the Royal College of Art where she became interested in wire mesh sculpture. In 1999, she won the BBC Wildlife Art Award with her sculpture of a baboon. She has since established a considerable reputation in her field with work included in collections worldwide. She is an elected member of the Royal Society of Sculptors, the Society of Wildlife Artists (UK) and a signature member of the Society of Animal Artists (USA). Public sculptures in the UK include an elephant at Waterloo Station, London, 13 works at the Tower of London, commissioned by Historic Royal Palaces in 2010 and a rhinoceros at Cannon Hall Museum, Barnsley. Her work is also in the collection of the National Museum of Wildlife Art, Jackson, Wyoming.

HOW DID YOU COME TO MAKE SCULPTURE?

As a child I always enjoyed drawing and making models, and this constant pleasure and love of drawing eventually led me to study illustration at college. At art college I was encouraged to work three-dimensionally, and this has developed over the years into the sculpture I make today.

Left: *Giraffe* 2004, private collection, UK

WHO ENCOURAGED YOU? DID YOU HAVE ANY FORMAL TRAINING?

My father, David Haste – a practising artist and writer who was head of Fine Art at the Kent Institute of Art and Design, now the University for the Creative Arts – has been a big artistic influence throughout my life. My sister, who studied painting at art college, is now a senior teacher in art and design, and my brother is a master craftsman in antiques restoration. We all grew up with art, fully participated in art and were encouraged to make things, so we understood that creativity was vital to life.

I took my Illustration B.A. Hons degree at Camberwell College of Arts, and my M.A. at the Royal College of Art where I studied Natural History Illustration. Natural History Illustration at the RCA was led by the late artist and conservationist, Professor John Norris Wood. He was a wonderful tutor, passionate environmentalist and campaigner for animal welfare and wildlife preservation, hugely influential in inspiring us all to understand the importance and seriousness of the subject we studied. He reinforced our shared sense of responsibility to the natural world and for the survival of flora and fauna.

DO YOU USE THE HUMAN FIGURE IN YOUR WORK?

I enjoy life drawing and studying anatomy and musculature, but my interest in the human figure is in the comparative anatomy of animals. Animals, in all their variety, are the sole subject for my sculpture, and it is the exploration of how much we share and how differently each species has evolved that makes the study of animals so fascinating.

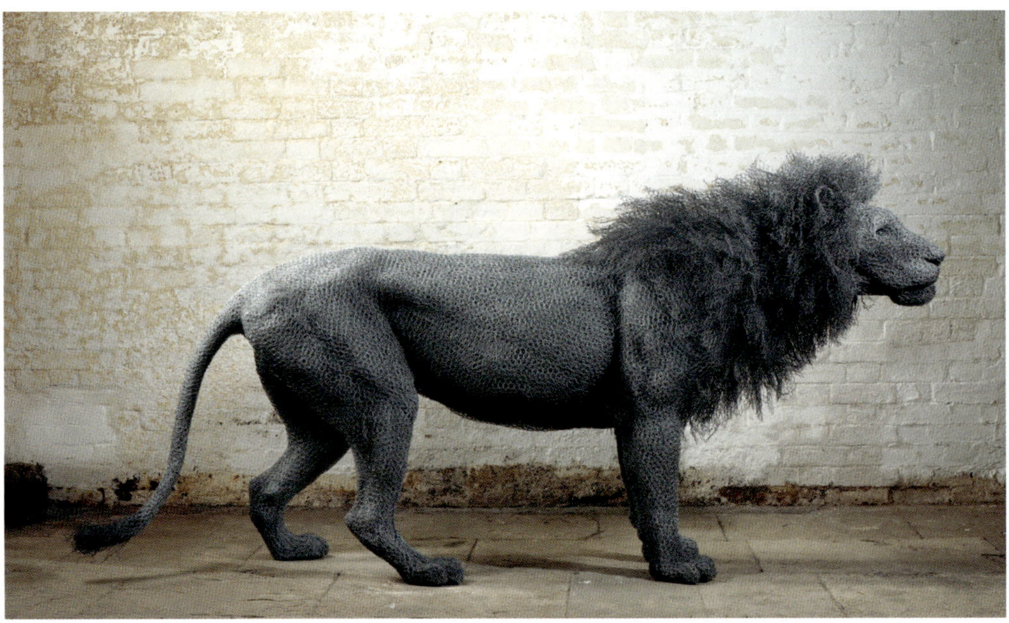

Male Lion 2013 at the Tower of London

DO YOU USE FOUND OBJECTS?

I work in mild steel, binding wire and wire mesh. I have recycled wire, but as my sculptures are often made for outdoor display, the wire has to be of the best quality to avoid any rust or deterioration that might threaten the longevity of the pieces.

DO YOU USE THE NATURAL WORLD?

Animals, and in particular wildlife, are my exclusive subject. I am inspired by the natural world, and animals have been a passionate fascination throughout my life. I have been fortunate to travel abroad to study animals in their natural habitats, on field trips to Asia, America, Africa and Australia, and of course I also observe, study and enjoy wildlife closer to home too, in the natural environment as well as in zoological collections.

FREE-STANDING OR ATTACHED?

I make both free-standing and wall-fixed pieces. The appeal of wire and wire mesh as my chosen medium is its linear aesthetic and being akin to drawing in space. The wall-reliefs lend themselves particularly well to this as they correspond directly to drawing. My free-standing pieces are far more dense and robust and often have an internal steel armature but still retain certain qualities of graphite drawing.

IS THE SCALE IMPORTANT? IS THE ENVIRONMENT IMPORTANT?

Scale is very important to my work. Unless the environment where the sculpture will be placed in determines a larger scale, I generally work in large-life scale. Naturalism is key to the work I produce, and it is important that my animal depictions are well observed and understood. Sometimes, for commissions, I make smaller maquettes, often in plasticine, with wooden architectural models of the site to work out the exact scale and how the sculpture will relate to the space. I rarely make smaller than life-scale pieces, as I feel it diminishes the presence and authenticity of the subject. Nature itself provides all the power and majesty required.

EPHEMERAL OR LONG-LASTING?

The wire I use can have an ephemeral, delicate quality to it, but ultimately I want my pieces to be long-lasting, especially as many pieces are sited outside, so the wire mesh is built up in multiple layers to create solidity and strength.

MULTIMEDIA OR ONE MEDIUM?

Wire and wire mesh are my sculpture medium of choice. I love the linear qualities of wire and the close assimilation to drawing three-dimensionally. I find cast metals and bronze sculptures too cold and heavy to realize animal forms and can have a deadening effect. The fact that mesh has holes and no solid surface, even when worked more densely, adds a sense of vitality and life to the sculptures. The layers of wire depicting the bone and muscle can be sensed through the different layers and beneath the final skin, hair and surface detail. For such a heavily processed material, the mesh is sympathetic and works well in creating organic forms. Drawing is also key to my sculpture, and I spend much time drawing and sketching my animal subjects before I begin to sculpt. I also draw out large charcoals whilst creating a sculpture, which helps with the understanding of the form, not only helping to resolve my sculpture but for drawing's sake as a different creative medium.

IS THERE A PARTICULAR THEME OR THEMES WHICH ARE CENTRAL TO YOUR WORK?

Animals are the central subjects of my sculpture. I am interested in the different forms, behaviours and energies of our fellow creatures. The depth of subject is so rich for visual artists, and considering the fragility of survival for so many species there is no greater time to celebrate as well as highlight the vulnerability of wildlife.

HOW DO YOU GET YOUR IDEAS FOR AN ARTWORK?

Inspiration for sculptures often comes from a direct experience of observing animals, ideally in the wild or in zoos. They are very much portraits of individual animals observed and studied. I want to avoid sentimental anthropomorphism that can be detrimental to honest depictions of wild animals and detracts from the seriousness of wildlife as a subject. My objective is to ultimately create naturalistic, authentically observed portraits of animals and to capture something of the essence, energy and majesty of our fellow creatures.

DO YOU LIKE TO DO COMMISSIONED WORK OR NOT?

I enjoy working to commission with all the challenges this provides, which can stretch creativity and exploration of new ideas. I have been very fortunate to have had some very stimulating commissions, a good example being the Tower of London commission for thirteen sculptures for the *Royal Beasts* Exhibition of 2013; these pieces remain there on permanent display.

TELL US HOW YOU HAVE DEVELOPED AS AN ARTIST.

My work has developed over the years from illustrative renditions of animals into the more robust, powerful sculptures I make today. My subject knowledge has evolved through extensive and greater depth of study and research that directly feeds back into the production of my sculpture.

WHERE IS YOUR SCULPTURE EXHIBITED?

I have many pieces in private collections in Europe, USA and in the UK, and in various

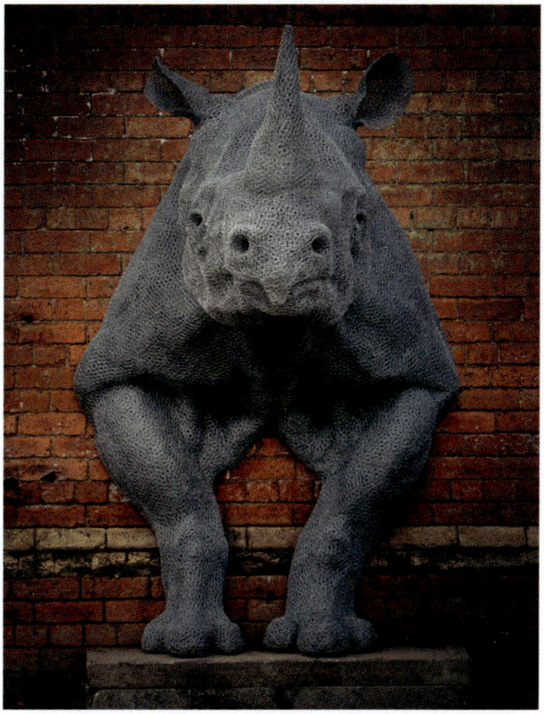
Rhinoceros 2000 Cannon Hall Park, Barnsley

public group exhibitions such as Glasgow Museums and Kew Gardens in London. I have also had work exhibited in public group shows across Europe, India, United States and Taiwan. My sculpture on permanent public display includes a baboon and rhino at Cannon Hall Park, in Yorkshire, an elephant at Waterloo Station and thirteen animals at the *Royal Beasts* exhibition on permanent display at the Tower of London.

IS IT MORE DIFFICULT FOR WOMEN ARTISTS TO MAKE A LIVING THAN MEN?

I feel very fortunate to have making sculpture as my profession. There is undoubtedly a sense that in the past male artists were taken far more seriously than women. Raising a young family has impacted on travel and time, but being a mum has been incredibly gratifying and given me a deeper empathy with maternal instinct shared with animals.

TELL US ABOUT YOUR FAVOURITE SCULPTURES – YOUR OWN OR BY SOMEONE ELSE.

I love looking at the ancient Assyrian wall reliefs in the British Museum. The animals are so beautifully observed and exquisitely executed. The animal studies of Auguste Rodin and Rembrandt Bugatti are also inspiring and are some of the best examples of naturalism in sculpture. More contemporary artists I admire include Elisabeth Frink and Nicola Hicks. Frink's sculpture has a strength and powerful physicality to it, in particular the Goggle Heads series and her horses, and Hicks manages to breathe life into her bronze work through her expressive, captivating plaster and straw sculptures.

WHAT'S NEXT?

I have recently visited Australia and am beginning to research wildlife I observed there. I find the different evolutionary paths fascinating, and the marsupials are an intriguing fresh field of study and discovery. I am currently completing a life-size wild mustang horse, inspired by a recent trip to the Arizonan desert.

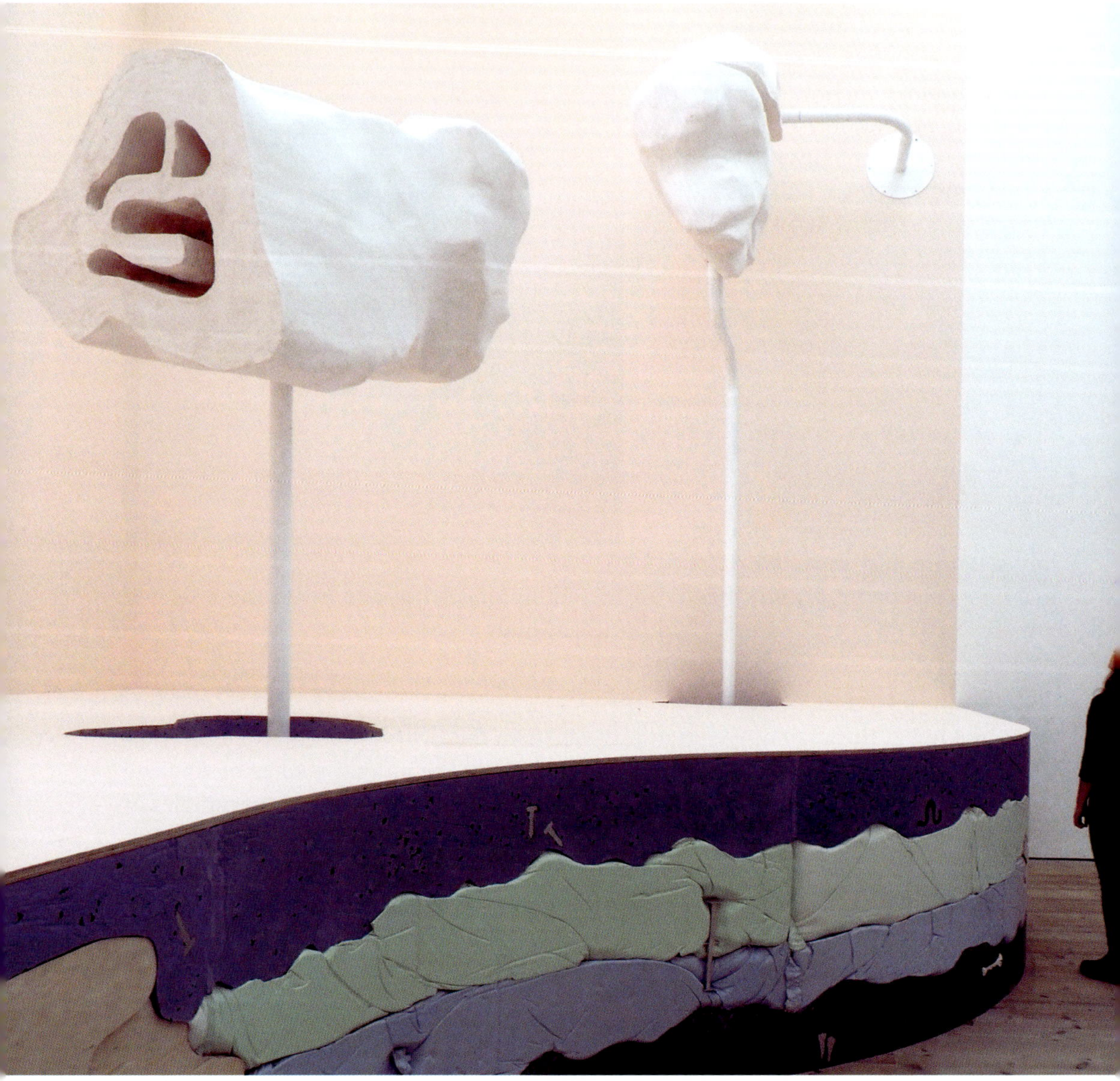

Wrot 2017, Baltic Centre for Contemporary Art
Photo: Mark Pinder

HOLLY HENDRY

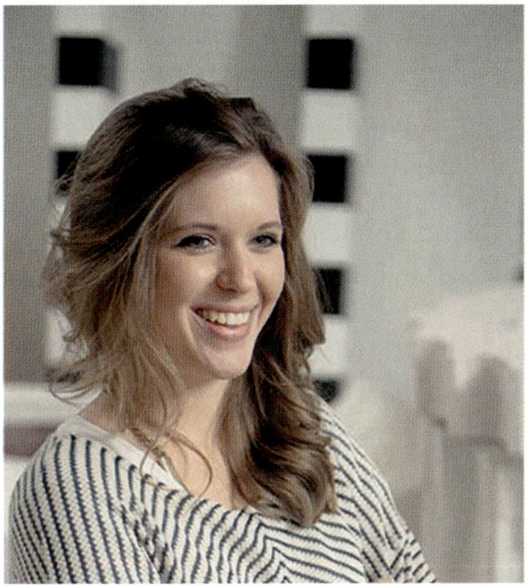

Holly Hendry (born 1990 in the UK) lives and works in London. She studied at the Slade School of Art (2009–2013) and Royal College of Art (2015–16). She has exhibited internationally at institutions such as: Yorkshire Sculpture Park, Wakefield, UK (2019–20), Baltic Centre for Contemporary Art, Gateshead, UK (2017), Sharjah Art Foundation (2014) and was part of the Liverpool Biennial (2018) and La Biennale De Lyon (2019). Hendry was the Rome Fellow in Contemporary Art at the British School at Rome in 2018 and was awarded the Arts Foundation Award for Experimental Architecture in 2019.

Represented by the Stephen Friedman Gallery, London.

IN HER OWN WORDS

My sculptures look at the back of things, open cracks where you see the gooey insides. The works deal with internal and external in terms of the body, display and production – architectural rear spaces and hidden bodily activities or situations that are brought into view through specific objects, textures or forms. Through scale and material manipulation, I try to address concerns of permeability and morbidity through a visual language that speaks of comic insignificance.

My work employs and sometimes exploits the language of architecture, where the physical edges and the function of a space become a starting point for me. I like to

Above: Portrait photo: Simon Veit-Wilson

combine the idea of function with something more ridiculous which draws attention to the formal aspects of the spaces that we use all the time, and how these walls that we build then become a physical script that conditions the way we move and live. By physically interacting and intervening with these places, I aim to draw attention to the sites themselves – the building as a framework that grapples with the succulence or absurdity of the work.

Often beginning with research undertaken from archives or collections (such as the Mutter Museum's 'Collection of Swallowed Objects' and 'The London Crossrail Archaeology Archives'), I draw on various objects and our own bodily or architectural relationship with them, as well as how these final forms have come to be. My current research addresses the idea of the hole (wholes, body holes, potholes, black holes) as a marker of both absence and presence. Large-scale casting and moulding methods within my sculpture-making has led to a focus on the idea of the mould as a sculptural form – an absence which highlights the presence of its sculptural counterpart – and its relationship to the replication or the copy. I have been focusing on historic methods of fossil formation and casting, and parallels with future uses of similar processes within medicine and the link this has to the idea of a copy. This research looks at these fakes and forgeries (from fossils and bones to body parts and replications of such objects as educational models, toys and scientific components) in parallel to sculptural moulds – as both a precious original and a cheap reproduction.

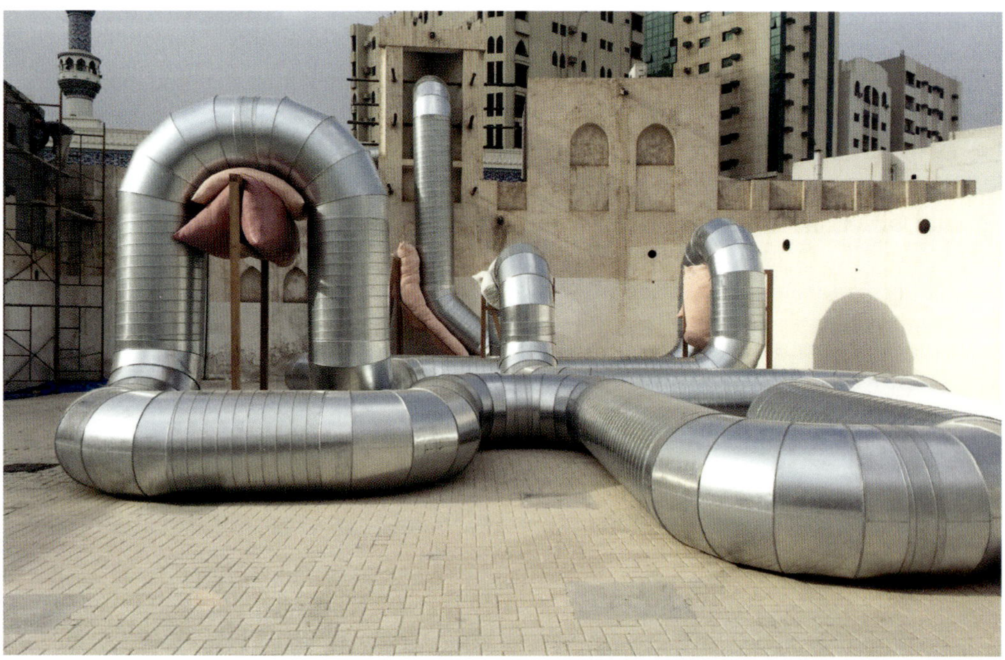

Homeostasis, 2014 – Sharjah Art Foundation

Step Through Please 2019 – Frutta Gallery

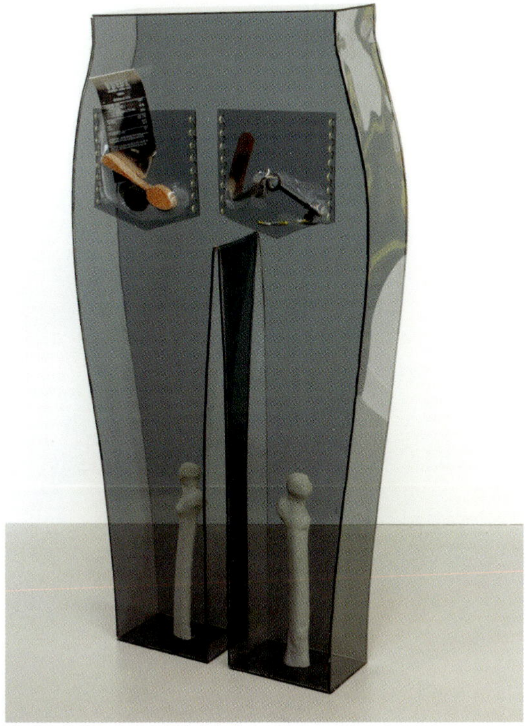

Harriet Smith Hughes wrote of my latest exhibition at the Yorkshire Sculpture Park: "*Slacker*, [below] which dominates the sunlit Weston Gallery, should feel intimidating: it's a monster machine of revolving cylinders and silicone, on which a body is splayed, cartoonish guts and innards spliced into its fabric. But instead, its presence is oddly comforting. That speaks to the dualities that Hendry's work engages: *Slacker*, like her 2017 exhibition *Wrot*, is made up mainly of pastel pinks, greens, and blues, which slip smoothly past the eye, carrying with them hard-to-place associations of splints and medical scrubs. The silicone on which the body is printed has been made by coating a cotton fibre band – like a supermarket checkout belt – with liquid silicone, which moves in one great, seamless continuum around the structure." – *this is tomorrow* Contemporary Art Magazine

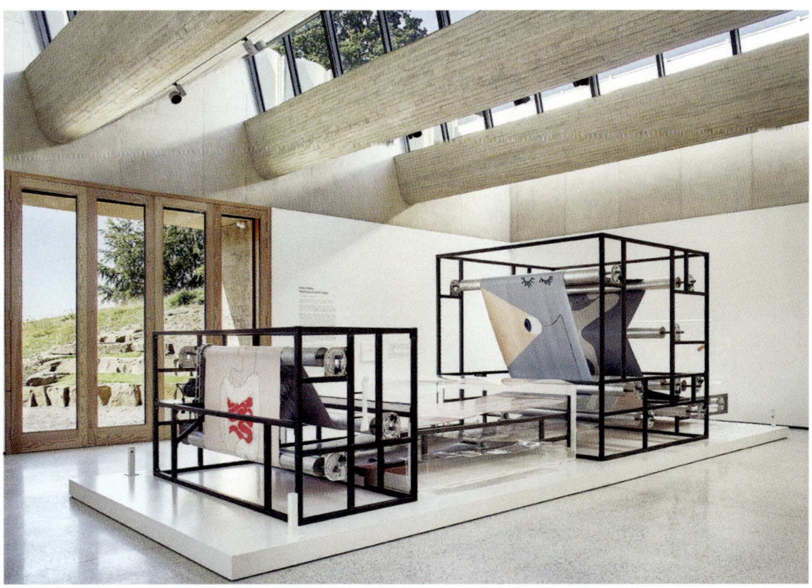

Slacker 2019 – Yorkshire Sculpture Park. Photo: Mark Reeves

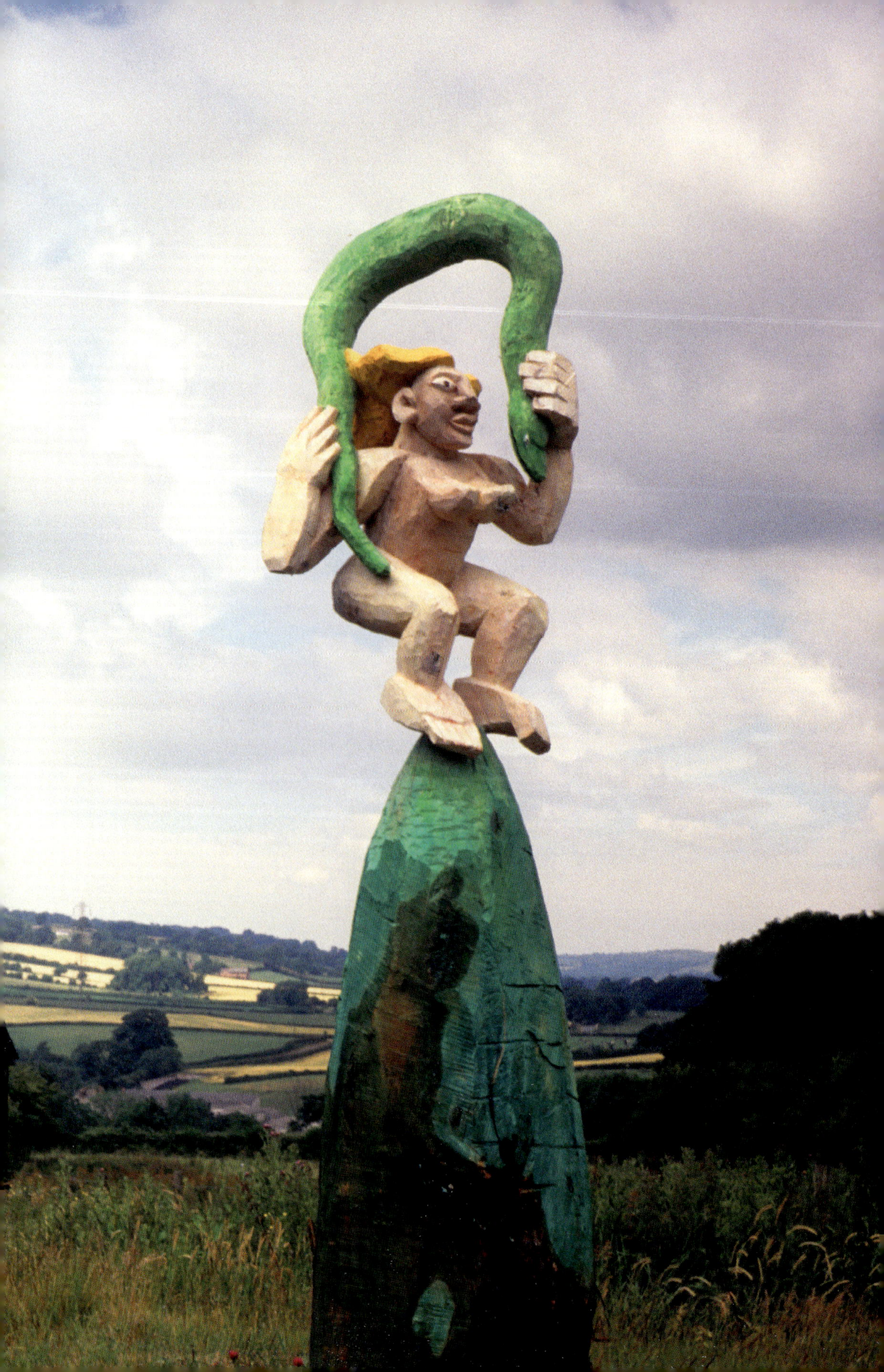

CHRISTINE KOWAL POST

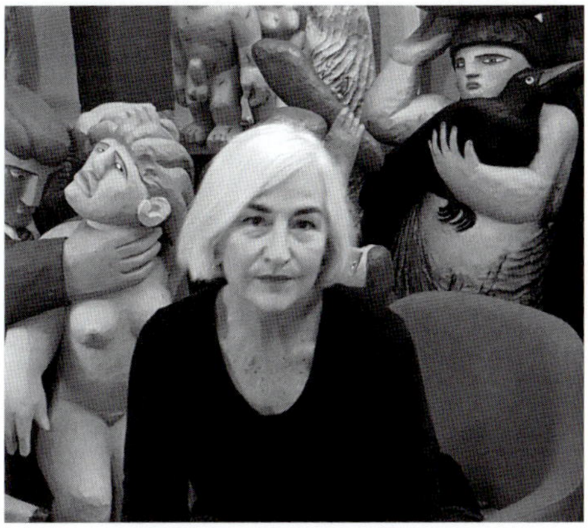

Born in Nigeria to parents of British and Polish origins, Christine Kowal Post was inspired by the African woodcarvers she saw as a child. On returning to the UK she studied Fine Art and Italian at University College of Wales, Aberystwyth (1970-74) and Accademia delle Belle Arti, Florence (1972–73). Kowal Post had her first studio in Liverpool and has also worked in Treuddyn, North Wales and the Netherlands. Since 1997, she has been living and working in East Sussex. In 2005, Kowal Post was elected to the Royal Cambrian Academy and in 2014 elected to Royal Society of Sculptors.

IN HER OWN WORDS

I was born in Nigeria and, for the first ten years of my life, I had this window onto another culture which was enthralling. I absorbed all of that generosity and wealth of culture, but I was an outsider who didn't understand and wasn't integrated into the host cultures of Ghana or Nigeria, or my parents' cultures of Poland and UK. West Africa is home to some of the best woodcarvers in the world and I grew up surrounded by woodcarvings because my mother loved and appreciated them and passed this admiration on to me, and although I couldn't fully experience their meaning, I recognised their profound power.

In West Africa I also saw woodcarvers working with very rudimentary tools made out of bits of old car. That taught me that it's not the tools that matter, it's what you do with them. I recognised there was a function in these carvings – a mask is part of a costume which in turn is part of a dance, or perhaps it's a figure which has a symbolic or ritual purpose. I was awestruck. Not only that, the carvers had special status, but it could be dangerous because you could be harmed for having those powers.

My parents recognised my creativity but wanted me to be able to support myself and did not encourage me to study art. As a result, I went to university to read English

Left: *Skipping Eve*, 1989.

but changed my courses so that I was studying the History of Art and Italian which led to a year in Florence. Renaissance art couldn't be further removed from tribal art but it showed the great flowering of humanism in European culture, of a growing interest in the intellect and the individual. Later, I came to understand the negative aspects of that humanism with regard to the elevation of humans beyond the animal world.

At this time, I read *The Female Eunuch* by Germaine Greer whose feminist ideas had a great influence on me. I have witnessed shocking discrimination against women but I soon came to realize that women were not always more sympathetic, encouraging or helpful than men in the world of art. When I started carving in the early 1980s it was Neo-Expressionism that was popular, and I was very fortunate to discover woodcut printmaking through the artist Max Blond, who also showed me that it was possible to be a practising artist. This contact with wood and chisel led onto carving three dimensionally and I went on to teach myself how to carve. It was important that I had a life-partner who was encouraging and supportive, and I moved into artist studios in Liverpool, which was a hugely creative period for me.

I feel a strong affinity with many of the early 20th century Expressionist carvers such as Jacob Epstein, Erich Heckel, Ernst Ludwig Kirchner, Hermann Scherer, as well as Ossip Zadkine, but also the Renaissance church carvers Tilman Riemanschneider and Wit Stoss. I have also found inspiration in European folk art, as well as the sculptures of countless anonymous traditional carvers of West Africa.

My favourite timber for carving is lime-wood which is native to European forests and has been used for carving for centuries. Its qualities of creaminess and softness make it easy to carve, and it lends itself to being painted because it is so light with no visible grain. Wood is clean and smells good. I like subtracting the wood from the figure within the log, making something with the simplest of tools that, when finished, has meaning and content. The whole thing is labour intensive and it does feel as if you've given life to something which then goes out into the world. Memes, not genes.

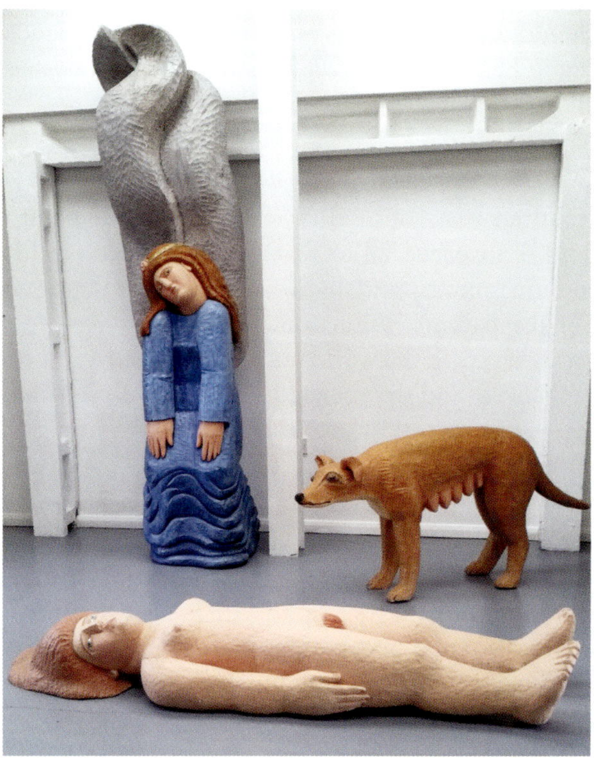

They think they are Fallen Angels, 2009–10

Amazons, 2000–16.

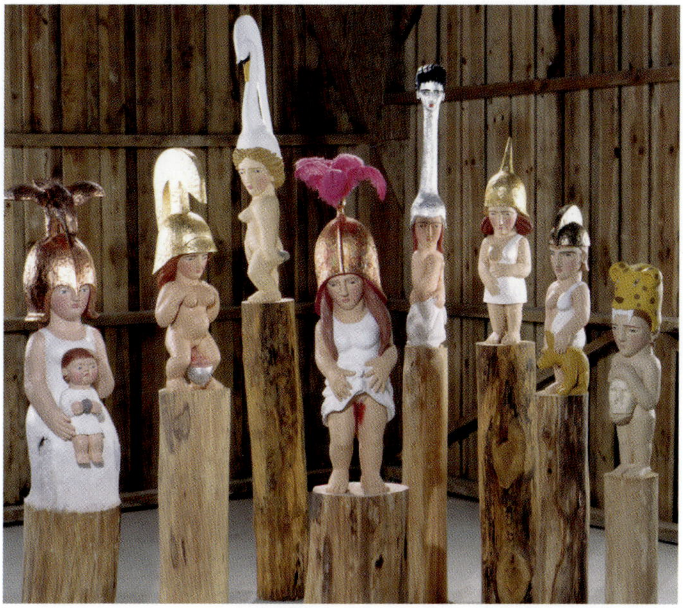

The female body is usually the starting point for me. The art history I studied was full of images of women seen through the eyes of men. That injustice and imbalance has meant that it has been difficult to make a living as a woman artist. You only have to look at the collections of the major public galleries to see the gender difference. But I believe it's cultural, so I hope it can and will change. I'm cautiously optimistic.

This desire to create new images of women resulted in my first solo exhibition *Strong Women* (1985–91) showing exuberant pieces with titles like *It's Great to be a Woman*. This was followed by my exhibition *Bad Women* (1993–95) with rather more sober studies of women who were often misogynistically represented in history, such as sirens or temptresses. In the *Corporeal Insults* (1995–2002) exhibition I explored the fragility of our bodily existence.

Many of my figures could be described as Amazons, the title of my exhibitions in Rheine and Beckum, Germany (2000–16). Amazons were thought to be mythological warrior women, but recent excavations in Ukraine (the historical area where Herodotus described them living) have unearthed the graves of women buried with their spears and horses, and it's not difficult for women today to imagine warrior women existed. We can identify with them. We know women can be tough and strong. Sometimes my pieces parody the stereotype of those other images made by men of draped 'nudes'. I love playing around with those images, because they have endless permutations and meanings. But none are definitive statements. I'm not saying women are like this or that. My Amazons may be tough and strong but they are pulled in other directions as a result of their biology. They menstruate, bear children, and can be vulnerable under these pressures, so in the *Amazons* I'm exploring ideas about gender, patriarchy, the place of women in society, violence and who wages war.

Recent work explores our attempts to control nature. My installation *Wolfpack* (2019) exhibited in Venice, is about our connectedness with dogs who, when they get the opportunity to be with other dogs, revert to pack behaviour inherited from their wild ancestors.

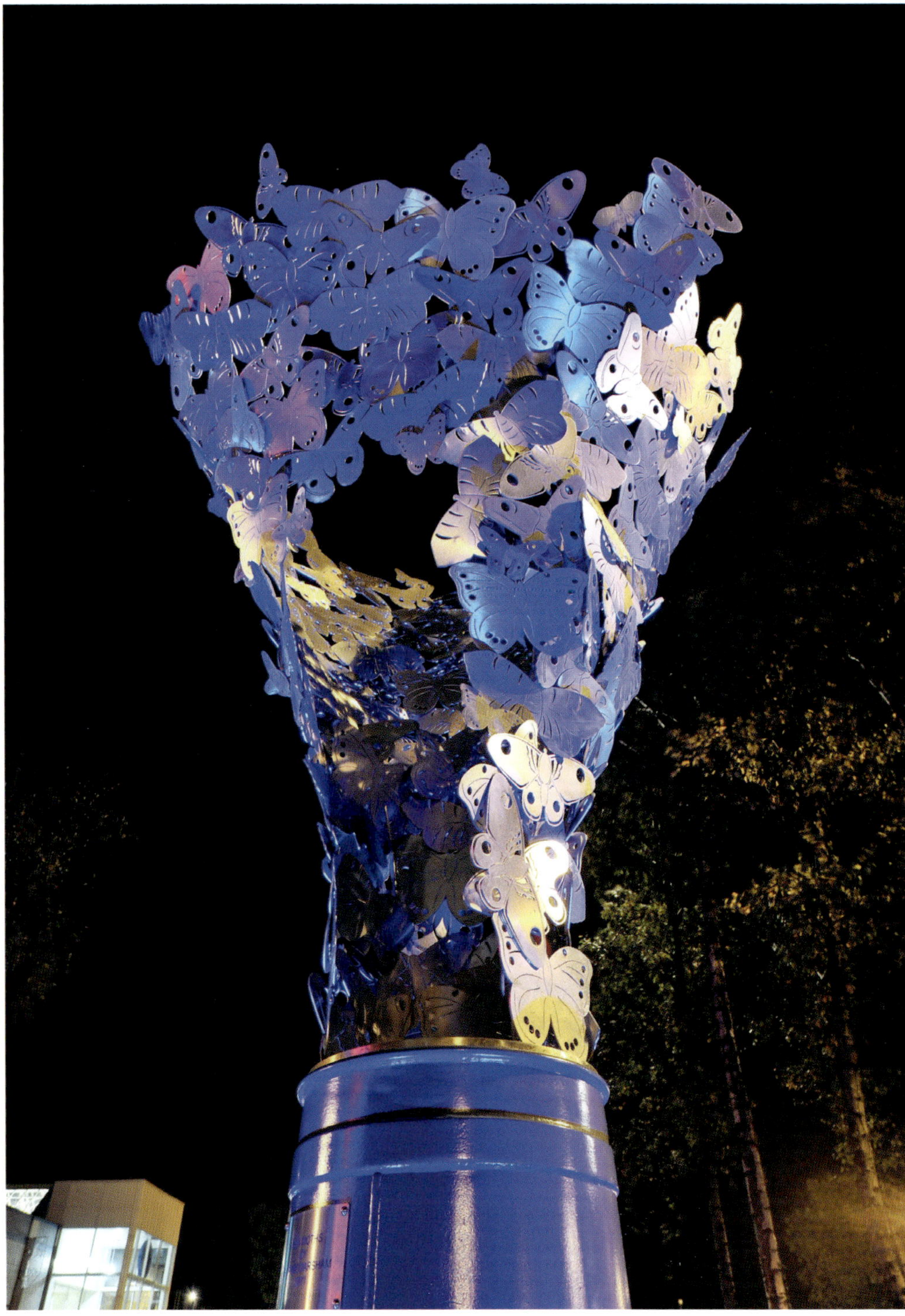

Silk Moths, 2011 Leigh, Manchester.

SOPHIE MARSHAM

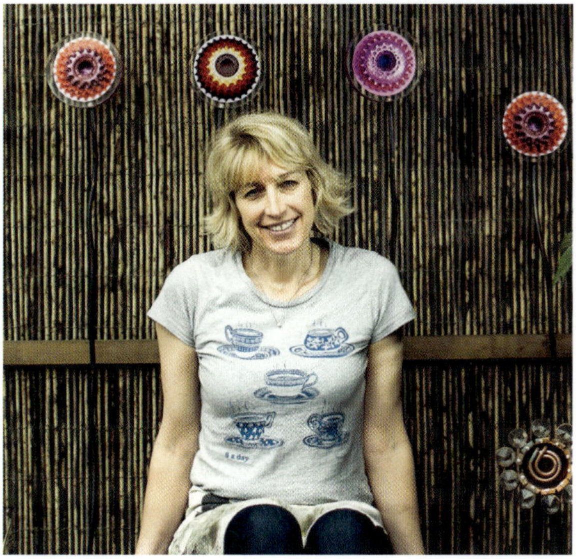

Sophie Marsham is a London-based sculptor who works with stainless steel, copper, bronze and found objects. At the Chelsea School of Art in London, Sophie trained as a public artist and therefore much of her work is designed and made for installation in buildings or public spaces.

HOW DID YOU COME TO MAKE SCULPTURE?

I became a sculptor after studying a degree in Public Art and Design at the Chelsea School of Art in London from 1988 to 1993, and specialized in sculpture.

WHO WERE YOUR INFLUENCES AND OR ROLE MODELS?

I was influenced by Elisabeth Frink and Barbara Hepworth amongst others, as I was inspired by the fact that they worked in bronze and stone, both very challenging materials.

WHO ENCOURAGED YOU?

I worked for five years before art school and was massively encouraged by the sculptor, Gerry Judah and the American jeweller, John Henry Whitmire, as I had worked for both of them prior to studying.

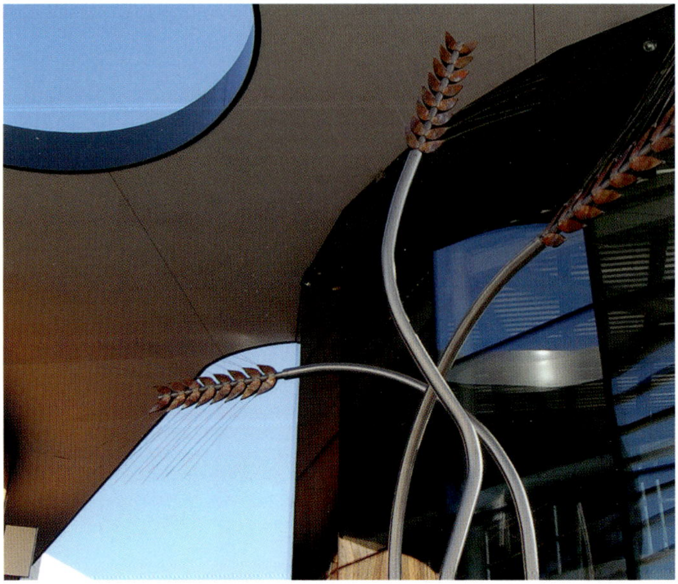

Barley 2006
at Cheltenham

DO YOU USE THE HUMAN FIGURE IN YOUR WORK?

I sometimes use the human figure in my work, but usually it is quite abstracted.

DO YOU USE FOUND OBJECTS?

I often use found objects such as spring mattresses, antique pen nibs, copper plates, cutlery and stainless-steel medical tools. I have worked with reclaimed objects since art school.

IS THE SCALE IMPORTANT?

The scale of the work is very important and I love to vary the scale from tiny hand-held pieces to works of over six metres, such as my piece *Barley* [above], which was made for a shopping centre in Cheltenham, UK.

MULTIMEDIA OR ONE MEDIUM?

I tend to work with a variety of mediums depending on the site. The work is usually permanent but not always. Permanent pieces can be seen in Cheltenham, Leigh in Greater Manchester, Kilburn in London, the Ritz Carlton in Grand Cayman and Pawleys Island in South Carolina.

IS THERE A PARTICULAR THEME OR THEMES WHICH ARE CENTRAL TO YOUR WORK?

My sculptures are mostly inspired by nature, such as my piece *Silk Moths*. I am fascinated with observing natural objects in their environment and always aware of beautifully repeated patterns found in nature, such as a bird's feather or petals of a flower. It is often that the smallest objects have been created with the most thought and precision. I use this as a starting point, when designing new pieces.

DO YOU LIKE TO DO COMMISSIONED WORK OR NOT?

I generally work to commission which I prefer, especially if the work is site-specific as I always enjoy the challenge of designing sculptures that will enhance a particular space.

TELL US HOW YOU HAVE DEVELOPED AS AN ARTIST.

Having started with jewellery, which I found limiting as too small and intricate, the scale grew enormously and having worked with steel for the first eleven years, I am now working with much more of a variety of materials, such as resin and bronze but still keeping the core ideas.

WHERE IS YOUR SCULPTURE EXHIBITED?

I exhibit in various sculpture gardens around the UK, most notably the Hannah Peschar Sculpture Garden and the Lemon Street Gallery in Cornwall. Smaller scale work is sometimes exhibited at the Mall Galleries in London.

TELL US ABOUT YOUR FAVOURITE SCULPTURES – YOUR OWN OR BY SOMEONE ELSE.

My favourite sculptors working today are Cornelia Parker, Kendra Haste and Ann Carrington. They all work in various metals, often on a large scale and make beautiful, thought-provoking work from often quite utilitarian objects.

WHAT'S NEXT?

I'm currently designing a new large-scale Public Art commission for Battersea in London and making new pieces for the Hannah Peschar Sculpture Garden for the coming season.

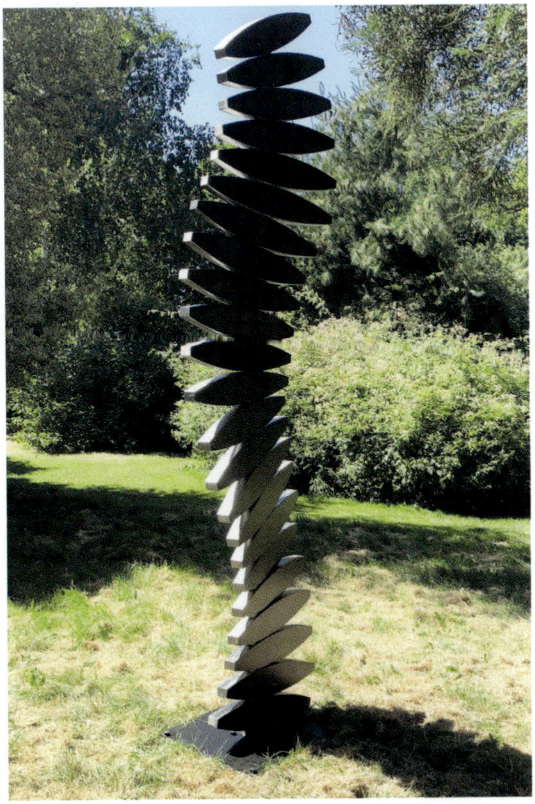

Stacked Form Burghley Sculpture Garden 2018

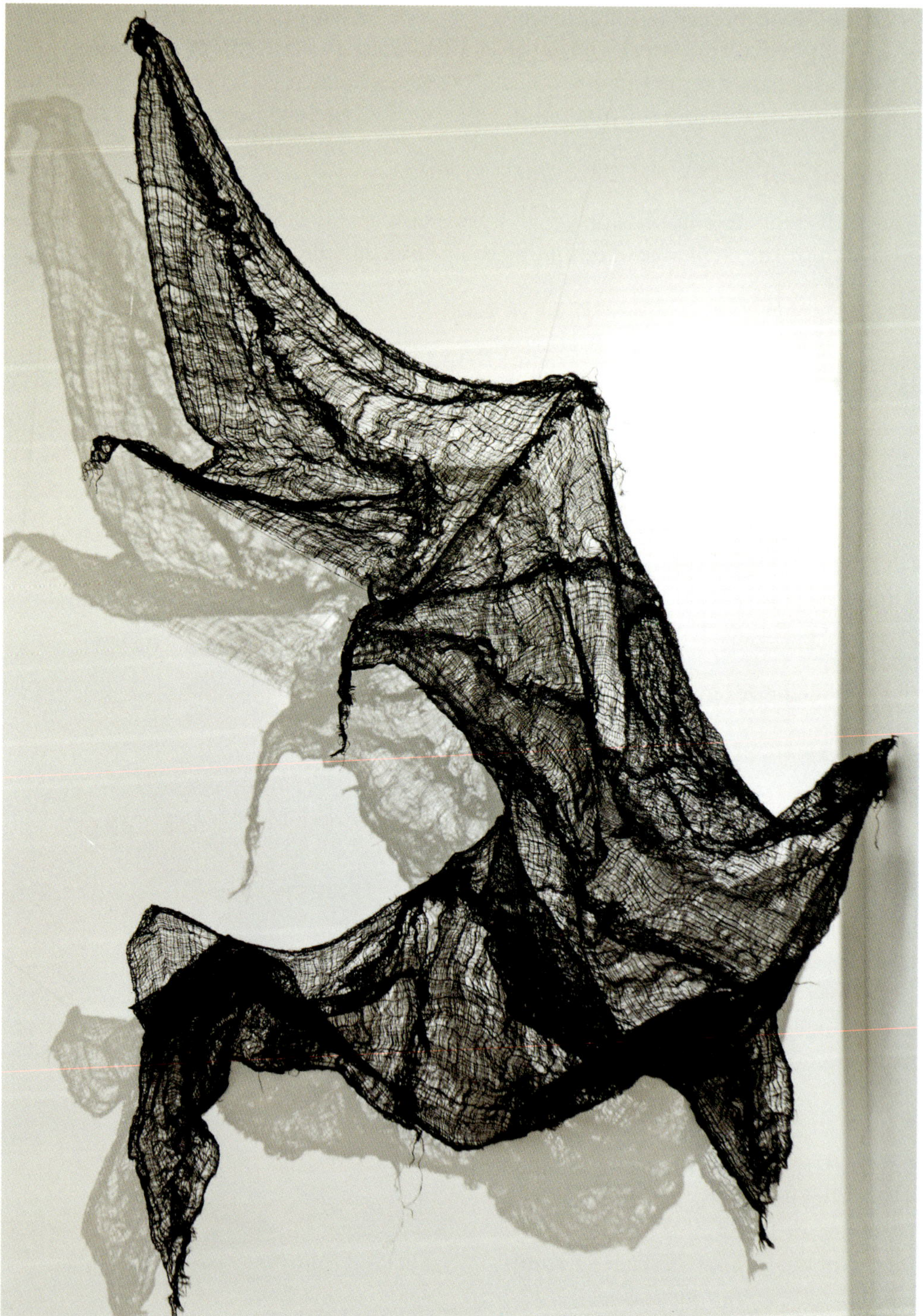

Never Hurry the Sunrise 2013

NNENNA OKORE

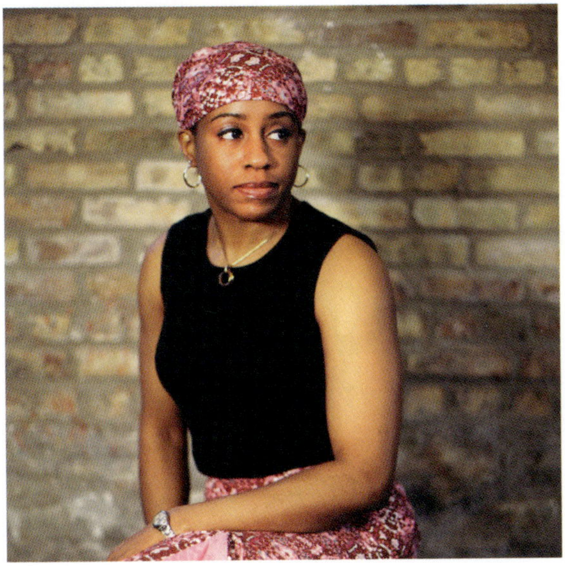

Nnenna Okore was born in Australia but at the age of 4 she moved to Nigeria with her parents who were academics. She received the First Prize for the African Child Art Competition, organized by UNESCO in 1993 and in 1995 won the UNIFEM Women's Empowerment Art Competition, which included trips to Dakar, Senegal, and Beijing, China, to represent African youth in the Women's World Conferences. She earned her B.A. degree in Painting from the University of Nigeria, Nsukka (First Class Honors) in 1999, where she received guidance from Ghanaian artist El Anatsui, who helped her broaden her scope beyond painting and begin to think in terms of creating three dimensional objects and more experimental art. Okore travelled to USA in 2002 and subsequently received her MA and MFA at the University of Iowa.

A participant in over 100 solo and group exhibitions, her works have been shown at the Museum of Art and Design, New York, Peabody Essex Museum, Salem, Tang Museum of Art, Skidmore College, New York, Museum of Contemporary African Diasporic Art, New York, Spelman Museum of Fine Art, Atlanta, Museu Afro Brasil, São Paulo, Brazil, Memphis Brooks Museum of Art, Memphis and Samuel Dorsky Museum of Art, New York and October Gallery, London.

Okore is Professor in the Art Department at North Park University, Chicago, where she teaches Three-Dimensional Design, Sculptural Practices and Drawing, among other subjects.

Cycles and Cyclones 2017 © Nnenna Okore, Courtesy Daimler Art Collection, Stuttgart/Berlin

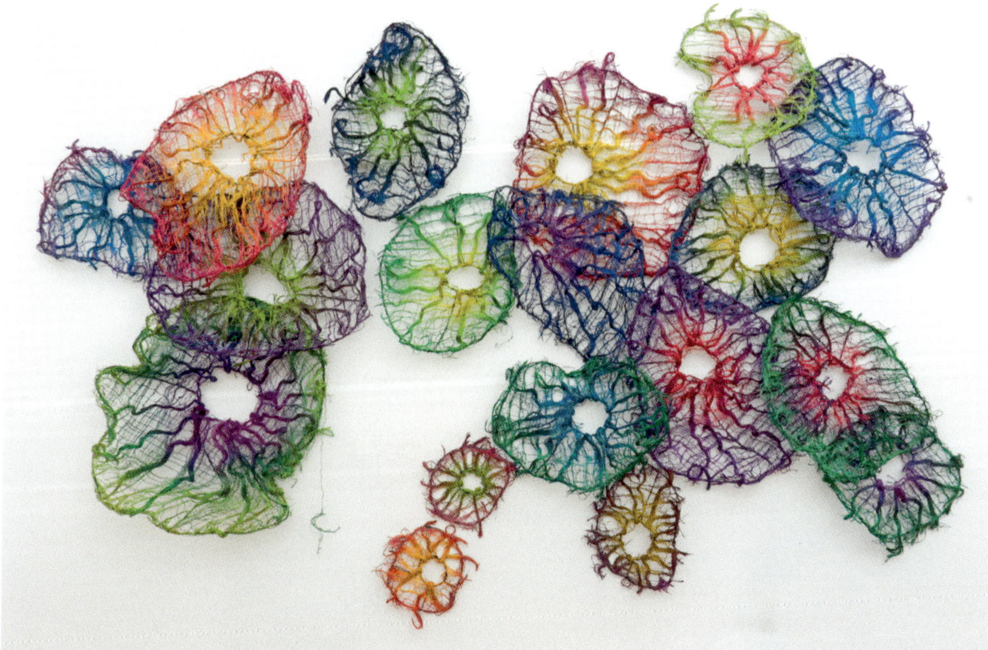

IN HER OWN WORDS

When I create, I am lost in the world of schisms, earthiness and abstraction. My works meander, dance and cascade delicately through space, bearing the traces of branches, vines, roots, veins, textile and shrivelled skin. Biomorphic and ethereal formations reveal alluring entanglements of grace and flow. Deep within its core, my works reflect the transient and innate qualities of life and death.

Holland Cotter said of my work in the New York Times: "One extraordinary paper piece, dyed pink and brown, seems to burst from the gallery wall like a giant dried and withered rose. Like all of Ms. Okore's best work, this is a tough, unlovely image, about when recycling passes into disintegration."

Having grown up in south-eastern Nigeria, my aesthetics and visual perceptions are shaped by my environmental encounters. Spending time outdoors, navigating the dusty terrains and observing cycles of growth and metamorphosis in nature, shaped the memories of my childhood years. Tree barks, dried grass, crawling vines and numerous intricate and tactile surfaces within the surrounding area invited numerous sensory perceptions. I am also drawn to the shapes of irregular shrubbery and undulating landscapes because of their ephemeral and ever-changing nature.

Over the years, I have employed in my work man-made, organic and fibrous materials sourced from my surroundings. Materials like sticks, paper, clay, burlap, hessian and rope. In recent times, I have especially been enamoured by jute fabric due to its reducible and de-constructible property. I mostly tease out and fray the fibres until they are nearly diminished and depleted. At this point, the fabric goes through multiple stages of tattering, sewing, dying, starching and stiffening with acrylic gel mediums. When the fabric becomes extremely gossamer, it is supported with thin wire structures that lend it strength and form. The balance between the ethereal and firmness embodied within these dainty forms become strikingly sublime.

My creative process is labour-intensive, repetitive, enduring and demanding. It will sometimes take months of slow transformation to arrive at the finished state. I engage deeply and spiritually with my materials – listening to them, hearing their voices and following their lead. I am often surprised by the intricate tactility that results from the processes of amassment, layering and interweaving of multiple units.

Through my explorations, I strive to understand the relationships between old and new, birth and death, age and decay, fragility and potency, materiality and ephemerality. I have also been employing time-based elements, light, shadow and other spatial attributes in my installations. Part of my quest is to marry the work, space and time, in order to extend the viewers' experience of the physical space. I seek to blur the boundaries between the viewer and the work, so that they may have a deep sensory experience that is grounded in the moment.

Drawing inspiration from great artists, such as Magdalena Abakanowicz, Ursula von Rydingsvard, Ann Hamilton, Eva Hesse and Kara Walker, I strive to push the boundaries and scale of my material and compositions.

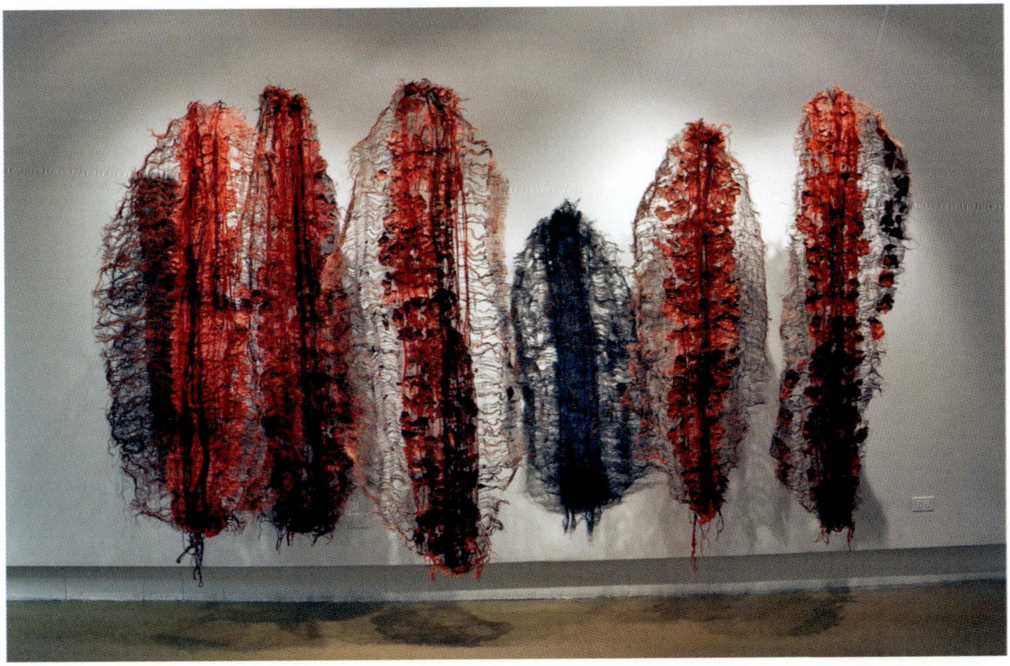

Emissaries 2009

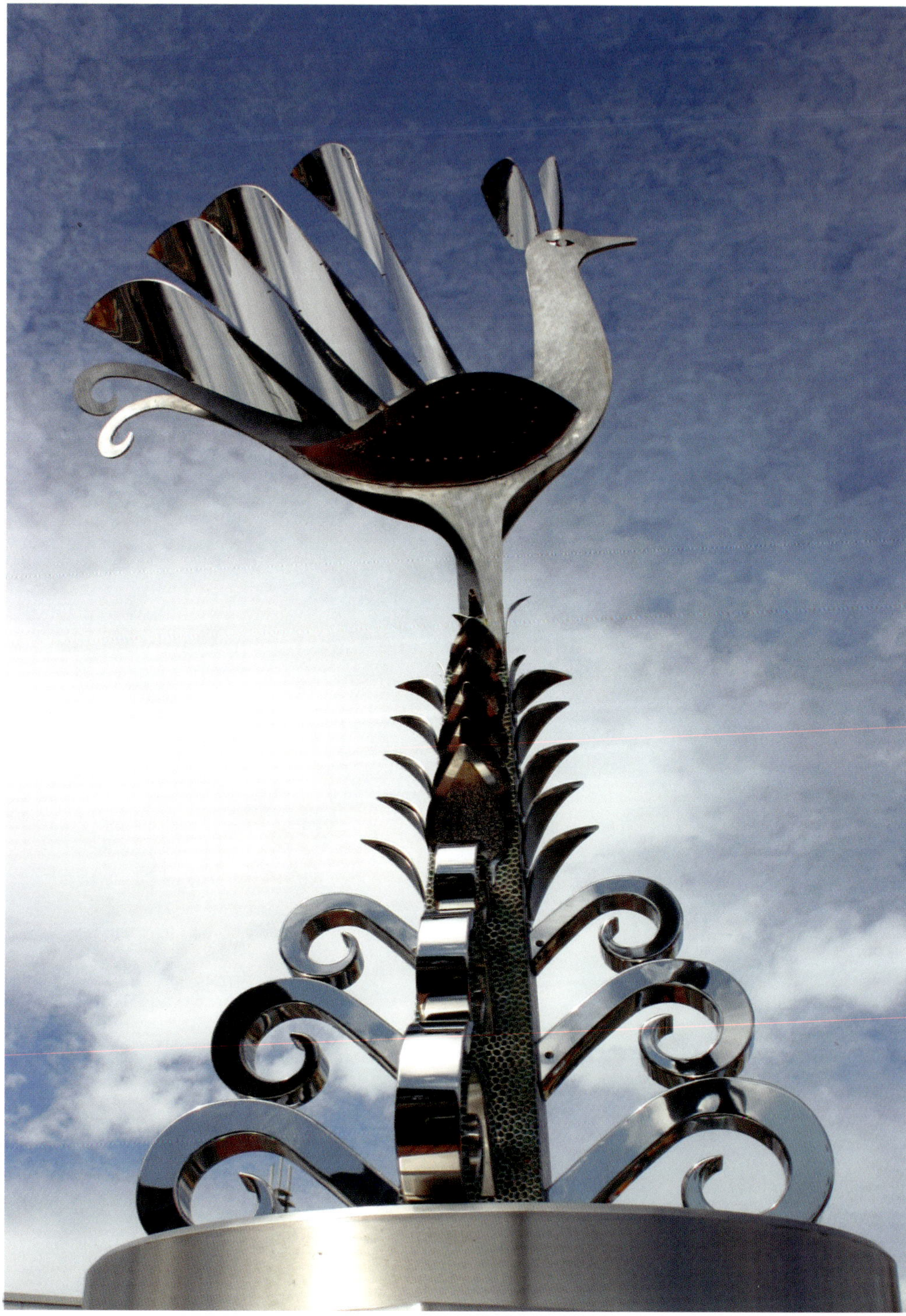

Peacock – Sandwell and Dudley Railway Station, West Midlands 2005

ANURADHA PATEL

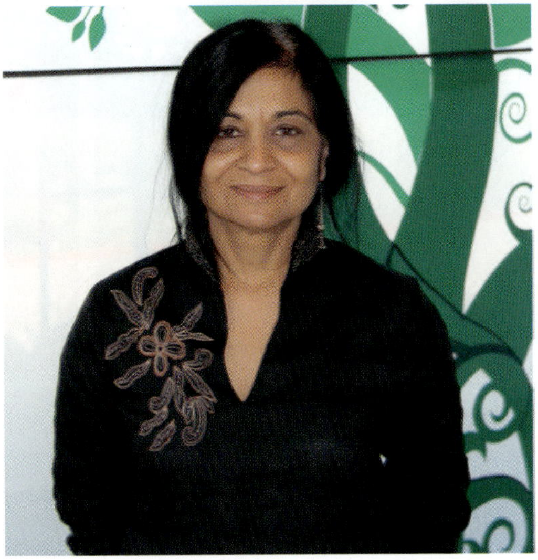

Anuradha Patel, known as Anu, was born in Gujarat, India. At a very early age she moved to Uganda, East Africa and then moved to England in 1972. She studied Fine Art at Lanchester Polytechnic in the early 80s and spent time living in Australia from 2007 where she has established a practice in public art and studio-based work. Her many public commissions include: Birmingham New Street Station, *Tree Sculpture* for forecourt commissioned by Network Rail, Reservoir Northern Gateway, public art project, Melbourne, Australia, *Light In Winter* City of Melbourne, Federation Square, Hobson's Bay Public Art Trail, *Indian Summer,* Tooting, London, *Decorative Seat* commissioned by Channel 4, ArtWork for Burleys Flyover, Belgrave Road, Leicester, *Vahana* Sculpture, *Transition Of Riches* Exhibition. Birmingham Museum Art Gallery.

IN HER OWN WORDS

I am an Indian artist, born in Gujarat, India. When I was a child, my family moved to Uganda, East Africa. Here I spent my childhood.

My strong memories are that of spending most of my time in an outdoor environment in a near-perfect climate, exploring details of plant forms and the natural world. I first worked with clay in the riverbank behind the school.

I studied Fine Art in England in the early 80s and have continued my practice as an artist in a variety of media. In recent years, I have also established a practice in Australia in public art and studio-based work.

Memorial Sculpture – Grand Central Station, Birmingham 2018

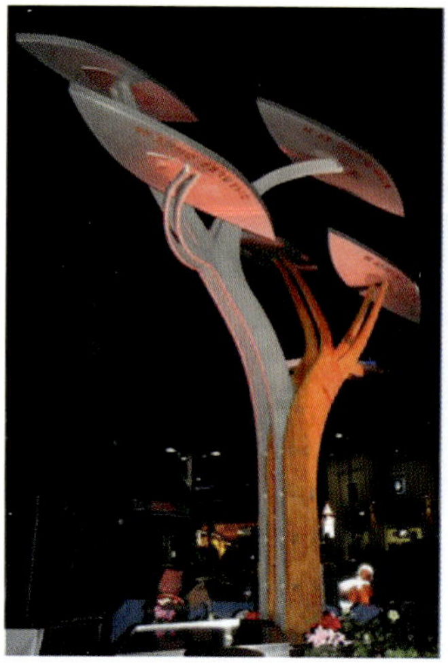

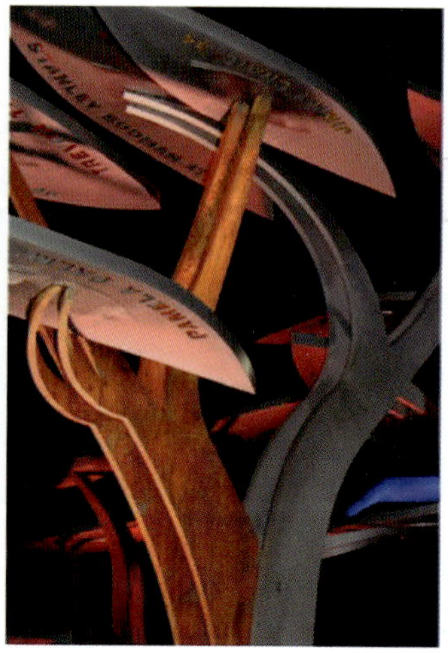

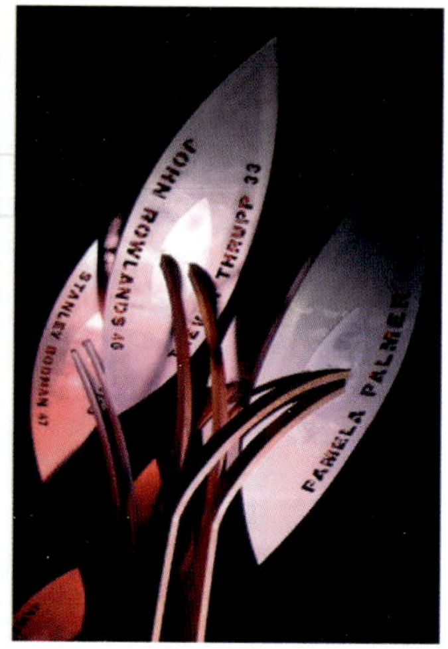

Much of my life has been in transit. This has challenged and inspired my work. I gain inspiration from the world that surrounds me, being in awe of the natural order and the defiance of nature and the silent intelligence with which it continues to survive and grow. The Indian Folk Art tradition has been a source of inspiration too with its decorative and stylistic use of form, line and pattern.

There is an autobiographical element to my work, often in the form of visual diaries. The images are an emotional expression of situations, events and experiences. Drawing is an integral part of my work and is further explored in the form of paper cutting, a traditional technique widely practised in India and in many other parts of the world.

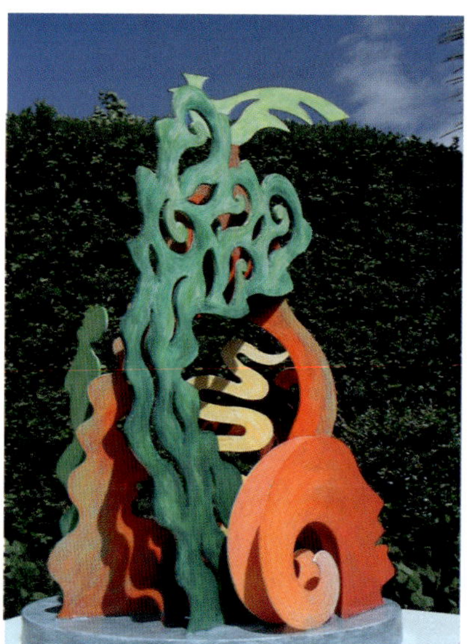

Secret Garden, private collection, 2004

As an artist/designer, my primary experience over the last thirty years has been in the field of public art design and studio-based work. The artworks are made largely in metal, using industrial processes such as laser cutting. This process enables me to transfer directly my studio practice of paper cutting into intricately cut designs in metal.

I work as a freelance artist/designer. Over the years I have had a variety of work opportunities. These include teaching art and design, artist's residencies and workshops, exhibitions and public art commissions. These have all informed and expanded my knowledge of materials, methods and application. I am very much open to using new materials and techniques as and when appropriate.

Most of my projects in recent years have been public art commissions. These have often involved working within the community in collaboration with local residents, schools, and other design professionals. The commissions take the form of sculpture as well as functional design and are usually site-specific. I work in a variety of materials. The use of material is often determined by the concept and the nature of the location/site.

Themes for artworks are often based on the geographical aspects and history of the locality.

As a sculptor, I also work in ceramics and metals. Currently I am working on a series of ceramic sculptures on the theme of organic rock formations, mountains and tree forms. I make work in phases where a series of works are produced at a time, based on a certain theme.

I enjoy working paradoxically, taking a spontaneous and organic approach when working with ceramics and painting and in contrast, with the precision and engineering required for programming laser-cut art and larger constructed artworks. The processes used for making the artworks are very varied.

A lot of my work is made by steel fabricators. Methods include laser cutting, rolling, welding both steel plates and sections. The work ranges from two to three dimensions. I generally provide detailed designs, either in the form of computer-generated drawings, or as maquettes.

Within public art projects, often methods and materials used in wider building construction are explored and adapted.

I have worked on schemes which include natural stones, glass set in aggregates and integrated lighting systems.

Colour is a very important aspect of my work, both natural and synthetic, applied colour.

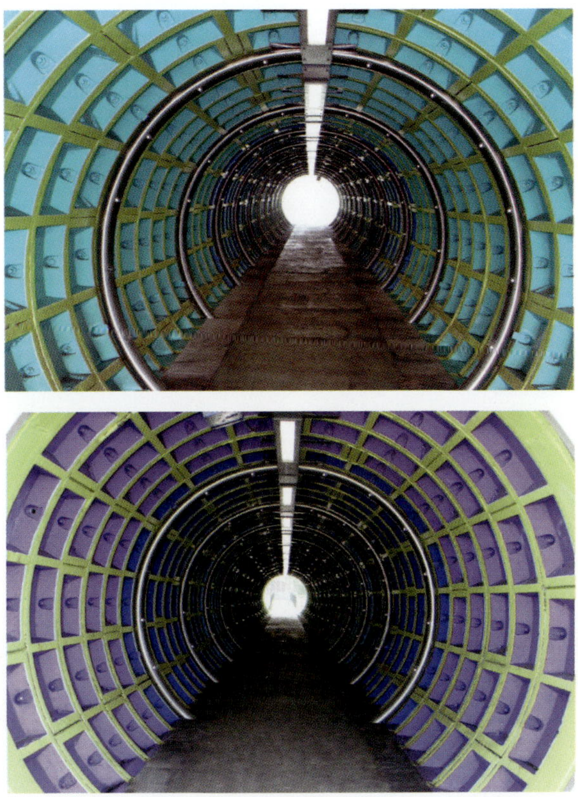

Right: *A13 Artscape* – Charlton Crescent Subway, London Borough of Barking and Dagenham 2002

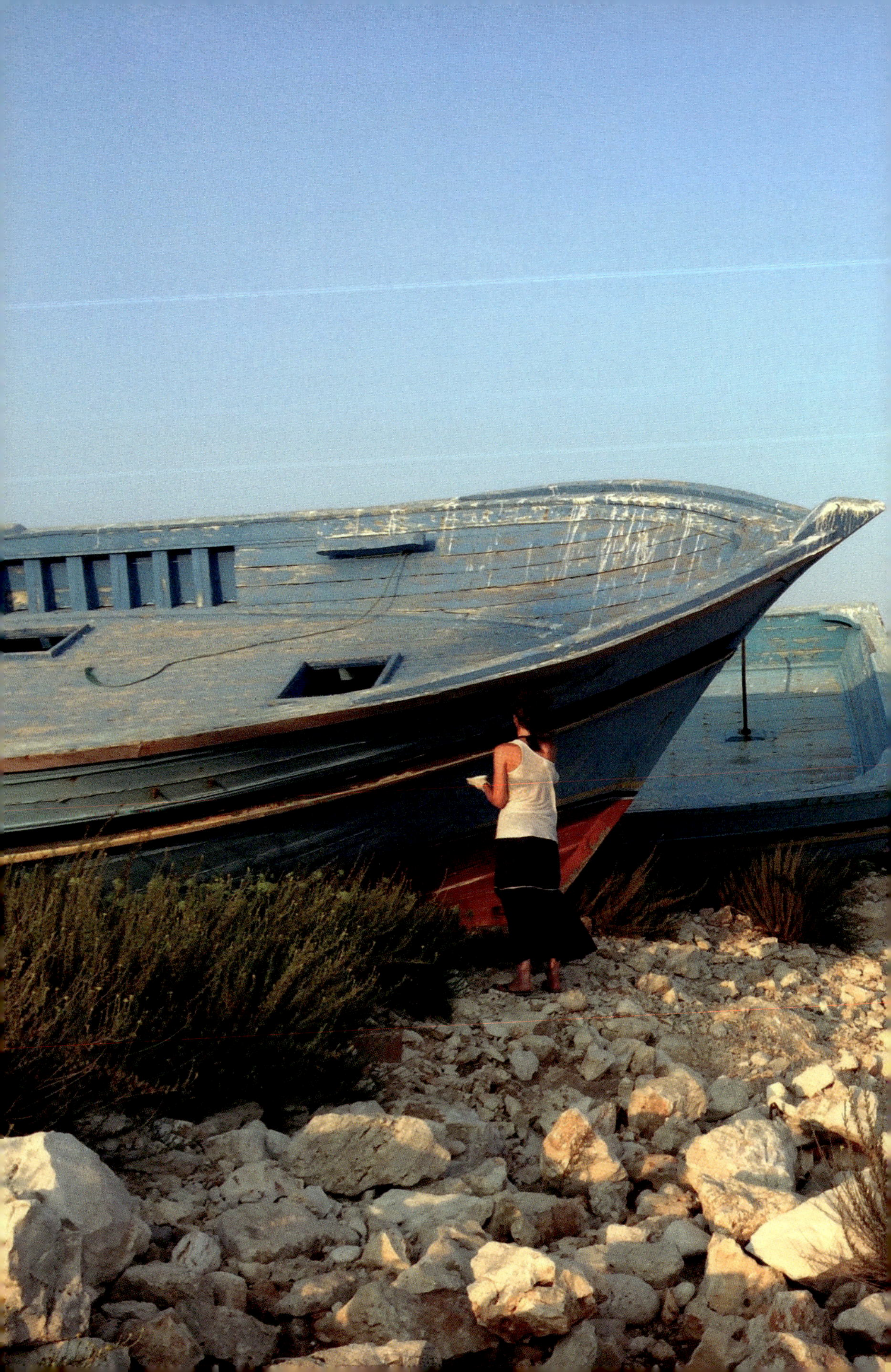

MAYA RAMSAY

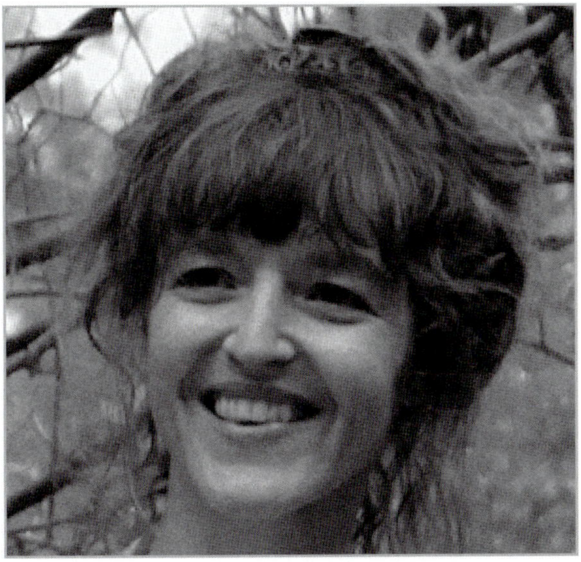

Maya Ramsay graduated from Chelsea School of Art, Fine Art B.A. (1998) and Central Saint Martin's School of Art, Fine Art M.A. (2009). In 2012, her project *Station X: documenting the derelict buildings of Bletchley Park,* featured on Radio 4's *Today* programme and was exhibited at MK Gallery and in Alan Turing's hut at Bletchley Park Museum. Ramsay's first solo exhibition *Wall Talk* won the London Group Solo Show Award in 2014 and was shortlisted for the 2014 Artraker Award for Conflict. Her project *Wall of Sound*, rubbings from the wood-chip wallpaper in Jimi Hendrix's London home, won EMERGENCY 2016 and was presented at the opening of Hendrix House and as part of London Jazz Festival. She was awarded Arts Council England funding for her project *Countless* (2016–18), working with the unidentified graves and shipwrecked boats of migrants who died at sea whilst trying to reach Europe. *Countless* was first exhibited in a solo show at Aspex Gallery in 2017. Ramsay's sculpture *Leave or Remain* won the Artlyst prize in 2019 and her short film *Leave or Remain* was a prize winner at the 2019 Swedenborg Film Festival. Her works on migrant deaths at sea were displayed at The Hague in 2019 and she curated the highly acclaimed *Sink Without Trace* exhibition on migrant deaths at sea at P21 Gallery, London in 2019.

HOW DID YOU COME TO MAKE SCULPTURE?

I come from a family of painters and focused on painting until my Foundation course at Chelsea College of Art, where experimenting with different disciplines was obligatory.

Left: Maya Ramsay at work on the *Countless* project with shipwrecked migrant boats, Sicily, 2018

Leave or Remain, remains of a shipwrecked migrant boat, 2018

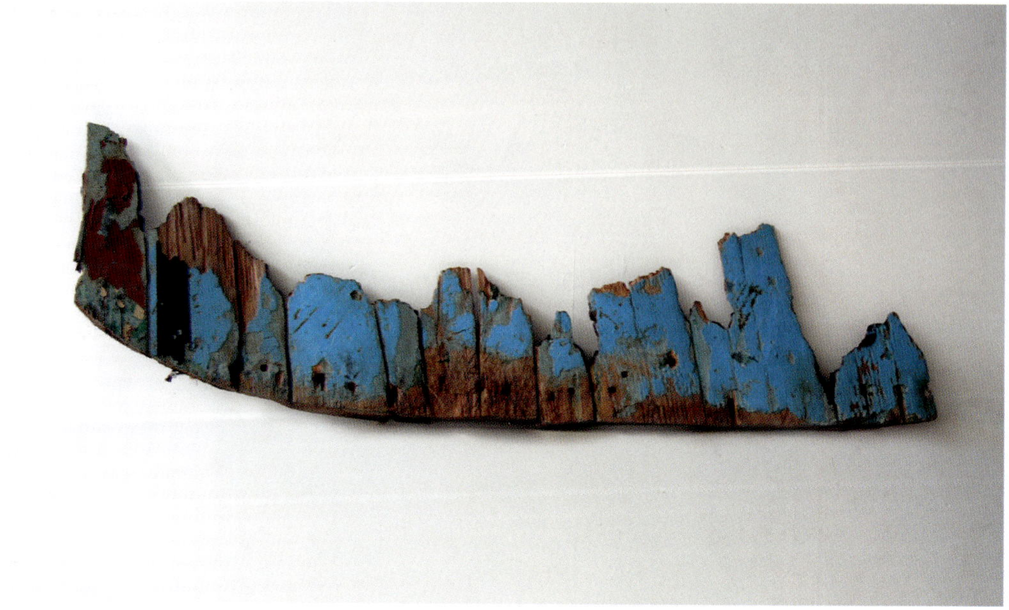

I made sculptural works using found materials from a scrap yard next to the college and became hooked.

WHO WERE YOUR INFLUENCES AND OR ROLE MODELS?

As a student I was influenced by Eva Hesse, Anya Gallaccio and Rachel Whiteread, amongst others.

WHO ENCOURAGED YOU?

I was encouraged by my family and some of my tutors at art school.

DID YOU HAVE ANY FORMAL TRAINING?

I studied a B.A. in Fine Art at Chelsea College of Art and an M.A. in Fine Art at Central Saint Martin's School of Art. None of my studies involved formal training in sculpture.

DO YOU USE THE HUMAN FIGURE IN YOUR WORK?

No.

DO YOU USE FOUND OBJECTS?

All of my works are based on found objects. I work with historically and politically important sites, employing a variety of processes to capture visual histories that would otherwise be lost or unseen. These processes include lifting surfaces from the sites and re-presenting found objects.

DO YOU USE THE NATURAL WORLD?

I often work in derelict buildings and on sites where the natural world has taken over. My works incorporate found natural materials and involve the natural process of decay. In 1999, I used lichens to make a series of works on environmental pollution and I made works with carbonised cobwebs in the derelict buildings at Bletchley Park in 2012.

FREE-STANDING OR ATTACHED?

Both.

IS THE SCALE IMPORTANT?

Yes.

IS THE ENVIRONMENT IMPORTANT?

My works are made on site, often in harsh and sometimes dangerous environments.

EPHEMERAL OR LONG-LASTING?

Long-lasting.

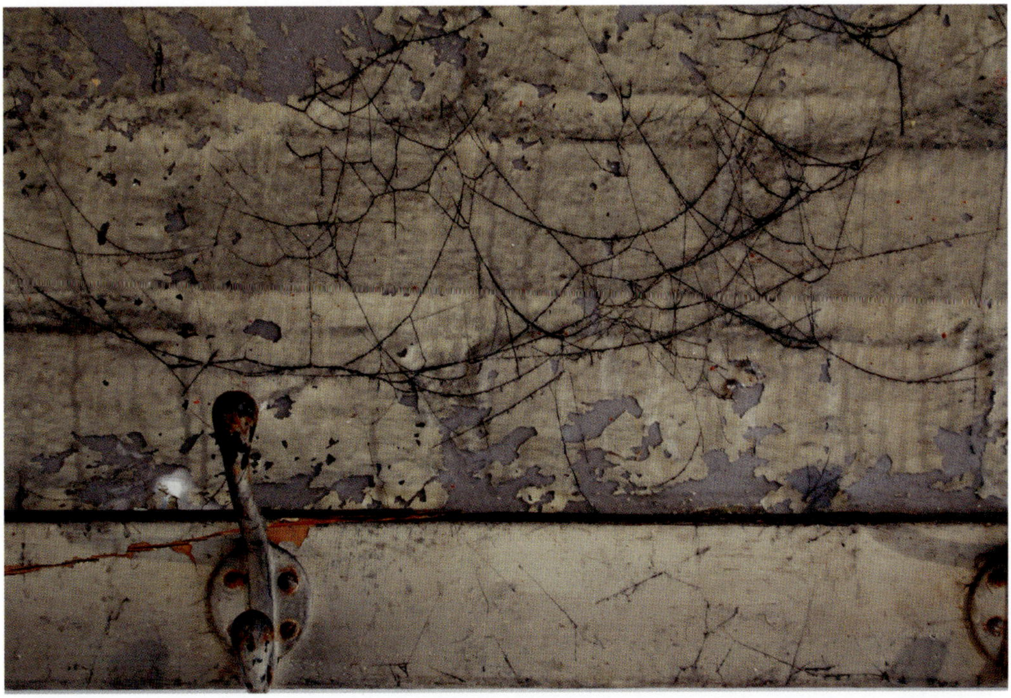

Intercept Operator (detail), surface lifted from Bletchley Park wall with carbonised cobwebs and Code-breaker's coat-rack, 2012

Untitled, nails and rope from a shipwrecked migrant boat, 2017

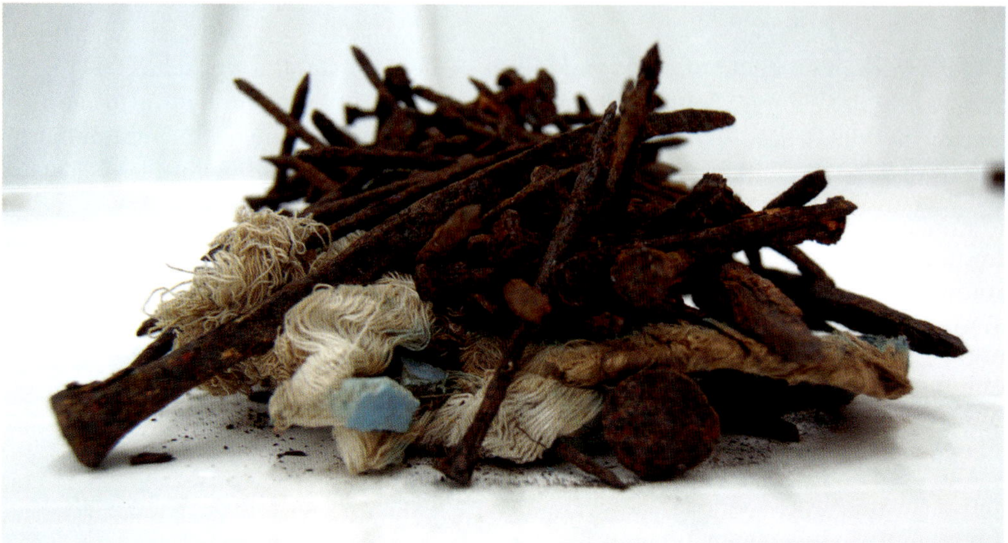

MULTIMEDIA OR ONE MEDIUM?

Multimedia.

IS THERE A PARTICULAR THEME OR THEMES WHICH ARE CENTRAL TO YOUR WORK?

My projects range from working with the derelict buildings of Bletchley Park where the Code-breakers worked in World War II, to the wood-chip wallpaper in Jimi Hendrix's London home, to the unidentified graves and shipwrecked boats of migrants who died at sea whilst trying to reach Europe. For the past ten years I have worked predominantly with sites that have a historical relationship to conflict and for the past three years I have focused on the subject of migrant deaths at sea.

HOW DO YOU GET YOUR IDEAS FOR AN ARTWORK?

I conduct thorough research on my subjects before making the work. The ideas for works are gradually formed through the research.

DO YOU LIKE TO DO COMMISSIONED WORK OR NOT?

My projects are usually self-initiated.

TELL US HOW YOU HAVE DEVELOPED AS AN ARTIST.

I developed a technique for being able to lift surfaces from buildings when I was a BA student and continued to work with this process for the next twenty years. In the last five years my practice has expanded to include film, found objects, frottage and photography.

WHERE IS YOUR SCULPTURE EXHIBITED?

My work has been exhibited in the UK, Germany, Holland and Italy.

IS IT MORE DIFFICULT FOR WOMEN ARTISTS TO MAKE A LIVING THAN MEN?

It was definitely more difficult for female artists historically, perhaps that has changed or at least is in the process of changing.

TELL US ABOUT YOUR FAVOURITE SCULPTURES – YOUR OWN OR BY SOMEONE ELSE.

My sculpture *Leave or Remain* (2018) is a found object, the remains of a burnt shipwrecked migrant boat. It is at once an object of immense sadness but also has an innate beauty. This dichotomy is disturbing and fascinating.

Intercept Operator (2012) is a surface lifted from a wall of a building where the Code-breakers worked during World War II at Bletchley Park. The building had lain derelict for many decades and spiders had completely covered the walls of one corridor in a myriad of cobwebs. Following a fire in the building the cobwebs had carbonised onto the walls. The cobwebs are captured in this work alongside the Code-breaker's coat hooks.

WHAT'S NEXT?

I am returning to the subject of the climate emergency in my work, the most important subject of our times.

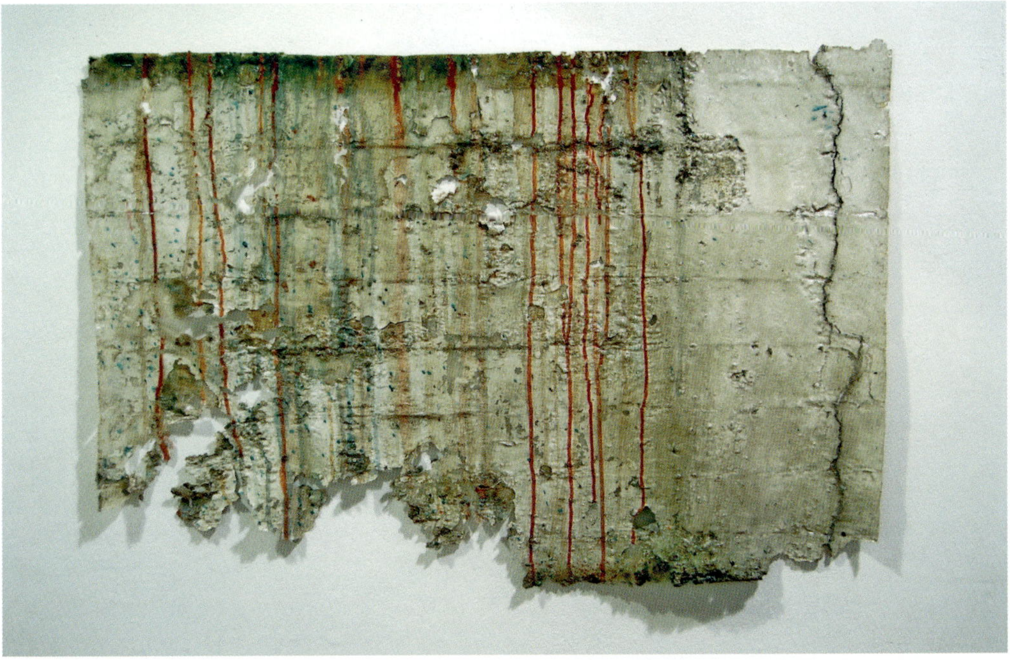

Bloodletting, surface lifted from wall, 2011

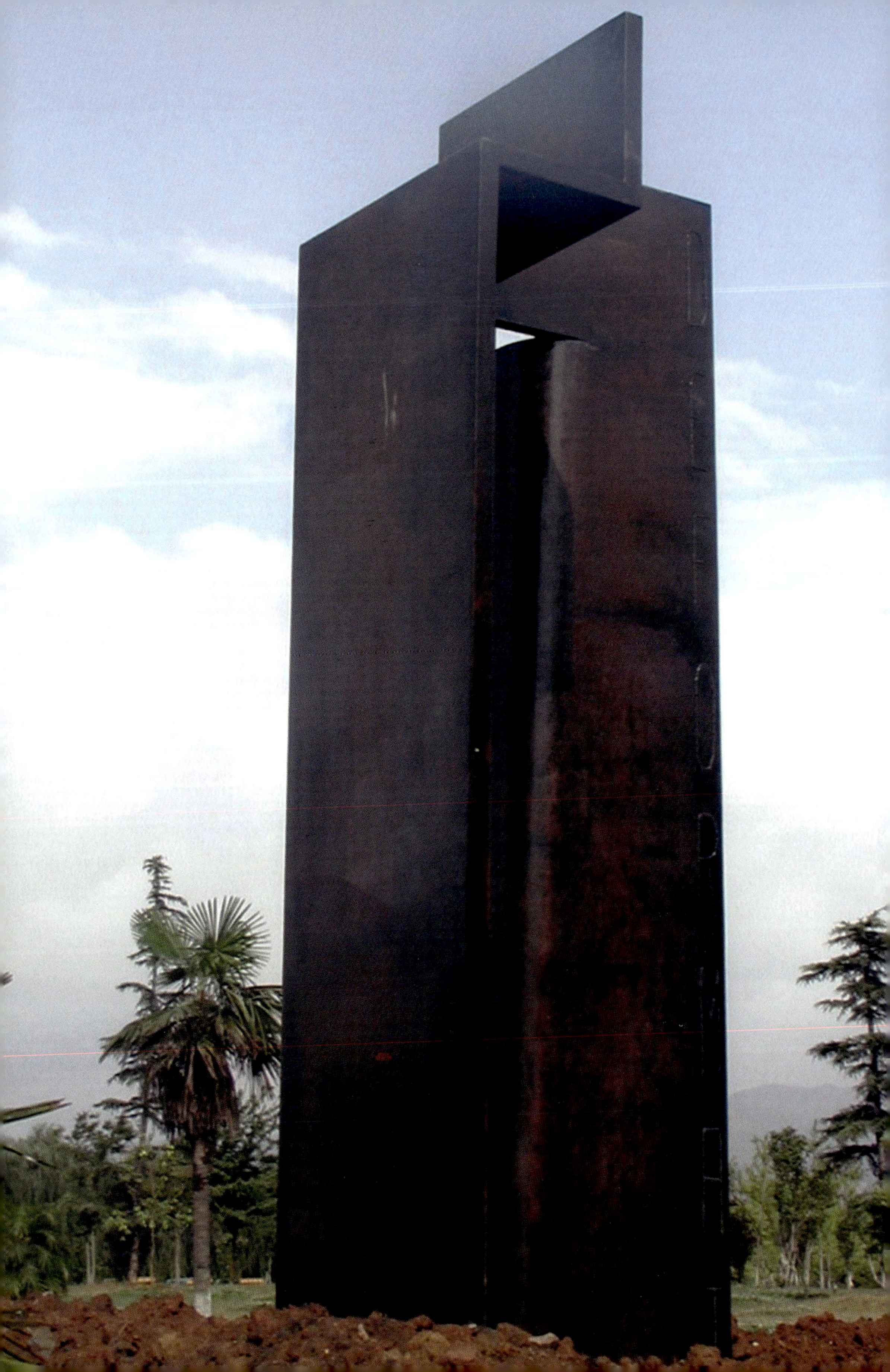

MARIANNE REIM

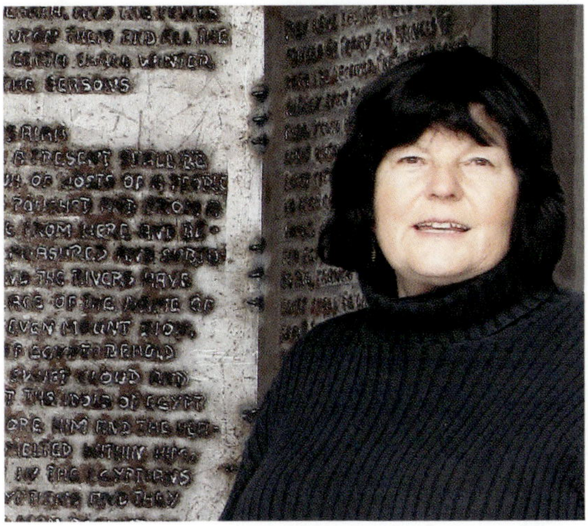

Marianne Reim was born and raised in Germany and migrated to Canada when she was 22. She attained a B.A. Degree in Art and Art History at McMaster University in Hamilton, and began to work as an artist and sculptor. She now lives in St. Catherine's in Ontario, Canada. Her work has been exhibited globally in nineteen countries across six continents. The recipient of several grants and the winner of numerous awards, her work can be found in private collections, in the government of Ontario Art Collection Archives, and in the public collections of art galleries and sculpture parks all over the world. Her travels in Africa, Tanzania and Namibia, interacting with Bushmen and the Massai culture, led to an exhibition at the Nafasi Art Space in Tanzania, where she was an Artist in Residence.

IN HER OWN WORDS

I was born and raised in Germany and emigrated to Canada when I was 22. After completing my B.A. in Art and Art History at McMaster University in Hamilton, I began my career as an artist working in steel and stone, exploring concepts of humanism as expressed through language and a variety of materials.

Since 1994, I have been working on a series of sculpted books titled *Das Buch* cut from steel and sometimes stone. They currently number sixty-eight different books. They are personal interpretations of my history within a larger cultural history. These books contain steel pages which can be turned and read, and they are bound. The

Left: *Plastic Deformation*, 2005 Daguan Park, Kunming, China

Das Buch XVII, 1997

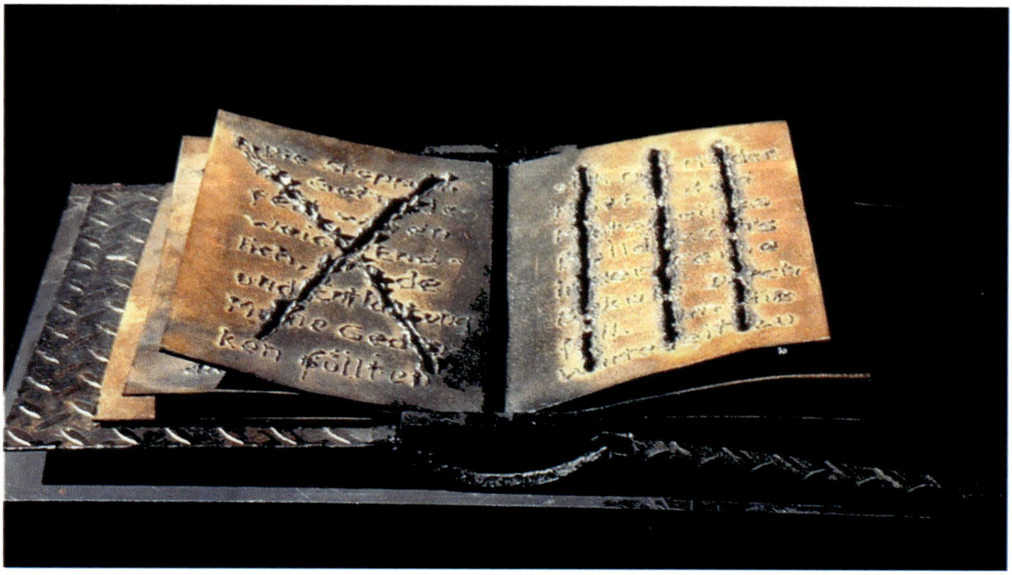

antithesis of paperbacks, these books are constructed through a process of cutting, burning and welding into the sheets of steel. In this manner, I am able to inscribe a universal language through form and line.

The content of the books emerge from my own memories: for example *Das Buch* 10 was inspired by a visit to the Berlin Wall. *Das Buch* 18 contains a diary-like entry, another one in Latin reflecting my interest in the universality of language. Although the books follow a chronology representing key moments in my life, they are created in the style of relics so that the personal is transcended and they become a kind of metaphor for all human history contained within a "Book of Life".

Shirley Madill writes of these sculptured books in *A Negotiation of Memories*: "Marianne Reim's art is a spiritual visual poesis. Experiencing her work is like traveling through a mysterious world of hidden messages and inscriptions that are to be decoded like sacred archaeological finds where we might discover the true meaning to our existence. Through a synthesis of text and image, she offers verbal/visual messages that have symbolic reference to history and life experience."

In 2013, my installation *Burnt Offering* took on the challenge of welding the complete English translation of the ISAIAH Dead Sea Scrolls onto large plates of steel. My installation consisted of almost ninety enormous plates of steel joined together in the form of open pages. The viewer experienced walking among the steel pages within the gallery space, in order to read the texts there.

My new body of work is inspired by found material and my interest in scientific attempts to explain and define human origins and global migration patterns and how they impact on our notion of cultural identity.

I have been exploring my origins according to my mitochondrial sequence, which one can receive through DNA analysis. I discovered my ancestry left East Africa some 50,000 years ago. In 2015 and 2017, I travelled to Africa, Tanzania and Namibia, a journey that included explorations of archaeological sites, interacting with Bushmen and the Maasai culture.

I completed the journey with an exhibition at the Nafasi Art Space in Dar es Salaam in Tanzania, where I was invited to participate as one of the Artists in Residence. Nafasi is one of the leading visual arts platforms in Tanzania and they believe in the potential of art to create positive social change.

The specific forms of my work float on the surface of a well of memory. I create discreet objects, objects in series and installations. My preferred material is steel, and/or stone. In my constructions the material wears its identity through rough-cut-edges, visible welds and an undisguised slabness. I may combine it with glass, photographs and miscellaneous findings by cutting, burning and welding – experience and emotion are melded into steel.

In 2018, my work was part of the *Reviving Humanity* Memorial exhibition in Sharm el Sheikh in Egypt. In 2019, I had an exhibition titled *Symbols and Metaphors* at the Haegeumgang Theme Museum, Geoje, South Korea.

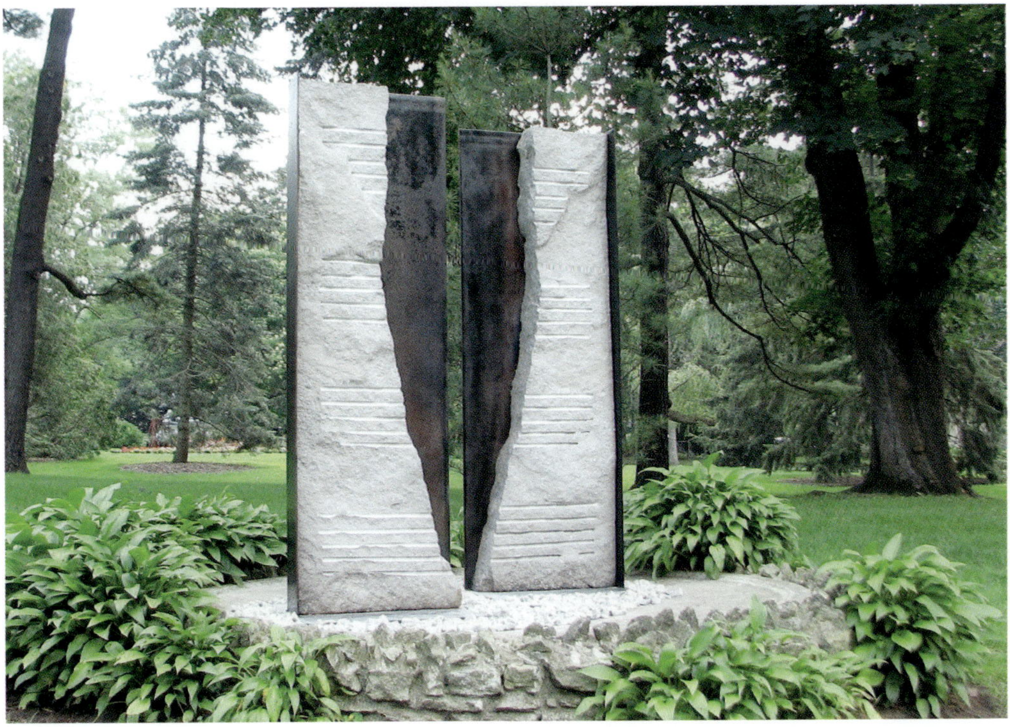

Hearing the Song, 2002 Glenhyrst Sculpture Park, Ontario

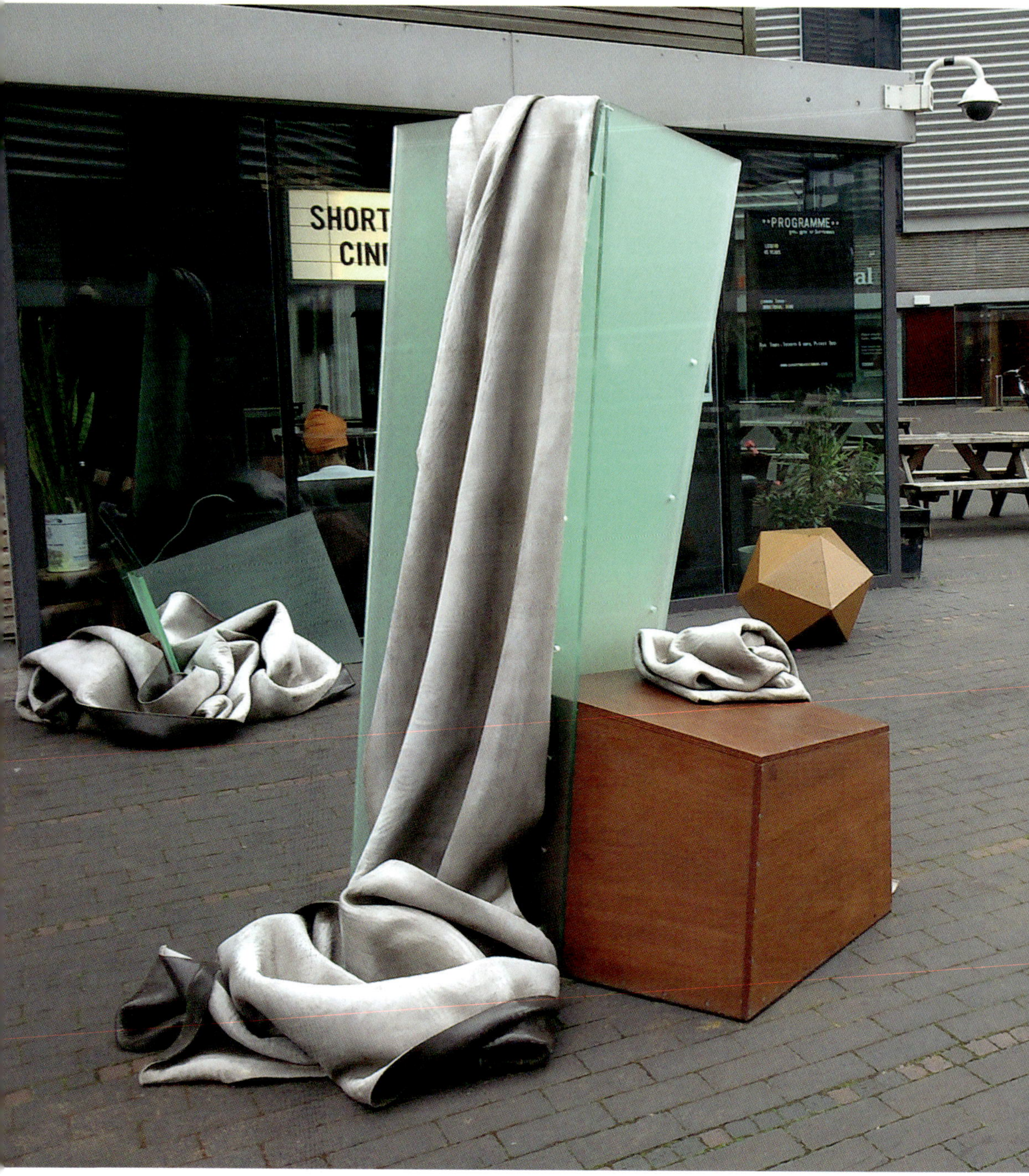

Loss of object and bondage to it Fig. 2, 2015 – Bermondsey Square

FRANCES RICHARDSON

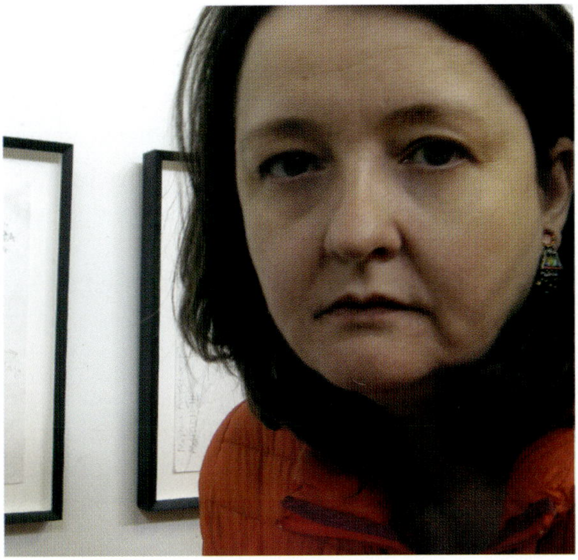

Frances Richardson was born in 1965, Leeds, UK and received her M.A. in Fine Art Sculpture from the Royal College of Art, London in 2006. Previous to this, she studied for a B.A. (Hons) Fine Art at Norwich School of Art and Design, Norwich. She exhibits both nationally and internationally and her solo exhibitions include: *Not even nothing can be free of ghosts,* Cross Lane Projects, Kendal, Cumbria and Standpoint Gallery, London 2018, *In Times Of Brutal Instability*, Chiara Williams Contemporary Art, London Art Fair 2018, *Loss of object and bondage to it* Fig.2, Bermondsey Square Sculpture Commission, Vitrine Gallery, London 2015, and *Ideas In The Making: Drawing Structure*, Trinity Contemporary, London 2011.

In 2017, Richardson was awarded the Mark Tanner Sculpture Award and Chiara Williams Contemporary Art Solo Award and was nominated for the Max Mara Art Prize for Women 2015–17 in collaboration with Whitechapel Gallery.

IN HER OWN WORDS

I've always been interested in making things. My parents encouraged me to observe things, to understand how things are formed and made. They took me to museums and art galleries including Barbara Hepworth's studio in St Ives and historic sites like the cairns in Scotland. As geologists, they were always pointing out features in the landscape that would give clues to the structures and material of the ground below. At home I made my own clothes. At school I took wood- and metal-working classes along with technical drawing. But I didn't really think of making things as "sculpture" until on a Foundation Course at Jacob Kramer Leeds College of Art. At that time there was an exhibition of Anthony Caro's sculptures at the Leeds City Art Gallery – it kind of set something off. In the catalogue text by Tim Hilton I marked just one sentence, a quote from Caro's essay, 'Some Thoughts After Visiting Florence…': "Art thrives on the discrepancies between its territory and the real world, and it exploits the tensions between these frontiers".

After the Foundation Course, I graduated from Norwich School of Art in Fine Art Sculpture B.A. (Hons), then thanks to a Commonwealth Foundation Fellowship I travelled to Nigeria and spent a year there, being trained as a Yoruba carver under Master Carver Segun Faleye. I was fortunate to be admitted into another culture, but there was no point in just copying it. You have to learn to sing your own song. The main thing I learnt was how to be myself.

Commenting on this, Derek Horton wrote: "This unique experience is manifest, not in the form or style of the work, but in her sensitivity to materials, her concentrated attention to symbolism and her understanding of the unifying interrelationship of manufacture, nature and philosophy." – review of the exhibition *Not even nothing can be free of ghosts,* Corridor8.

I make large works that operate within specific architectural spaces, and also small works, hand-held size. I like works to be explicit, so you can see the material and how it has been made and at the same time to transcend this, to activate a cognitive embodied understanding, a feeling. I want the object to play on the boundary of the real and the imagined.

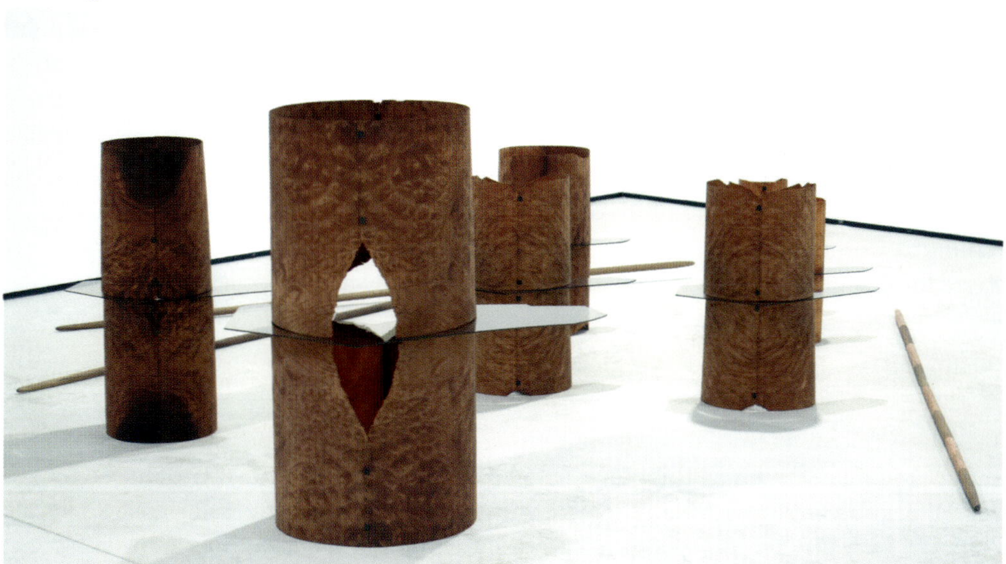

Not all temporary objects can be avoided 2018

i-Beam to walk through, 2011

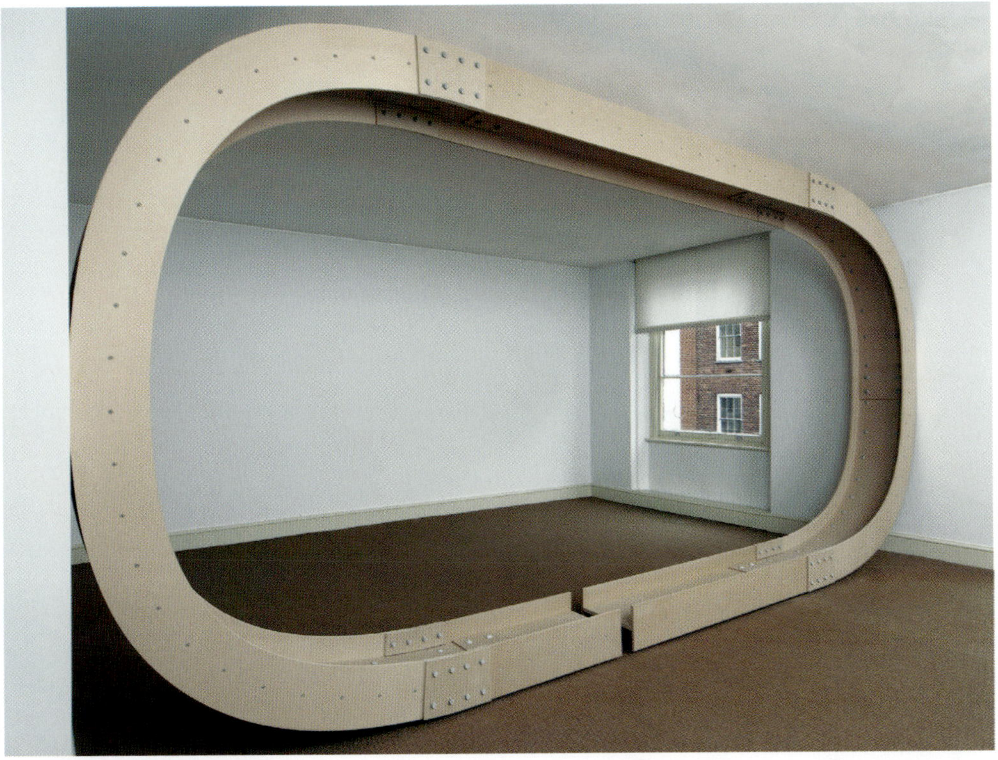

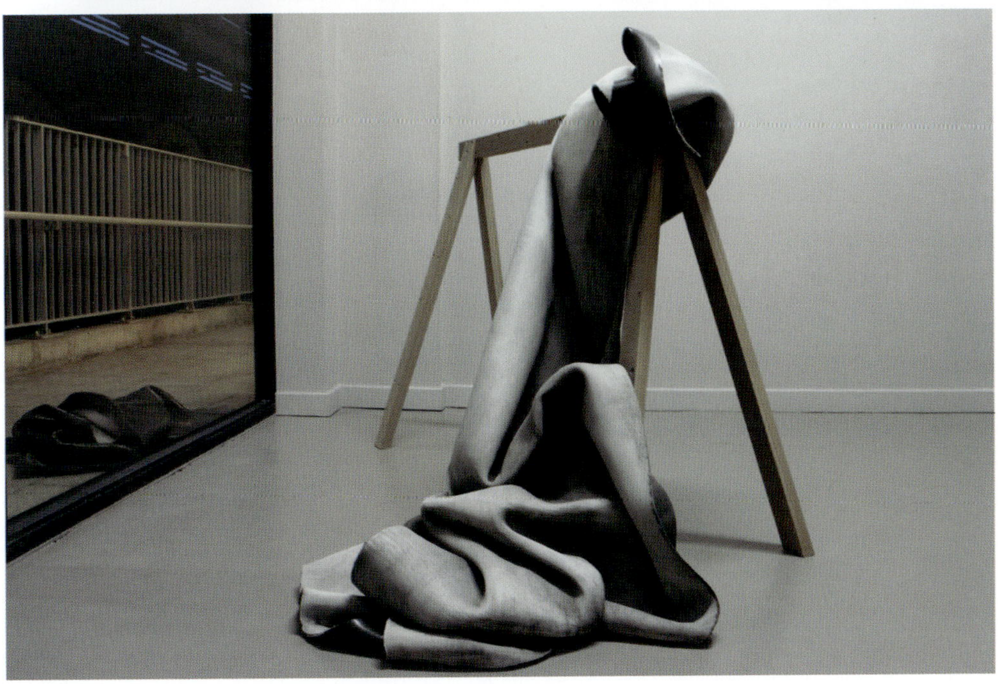

Loss of object and bondage to it 2014 – Lubomorov-Easton, Deptford. Photo: Nancy Elser

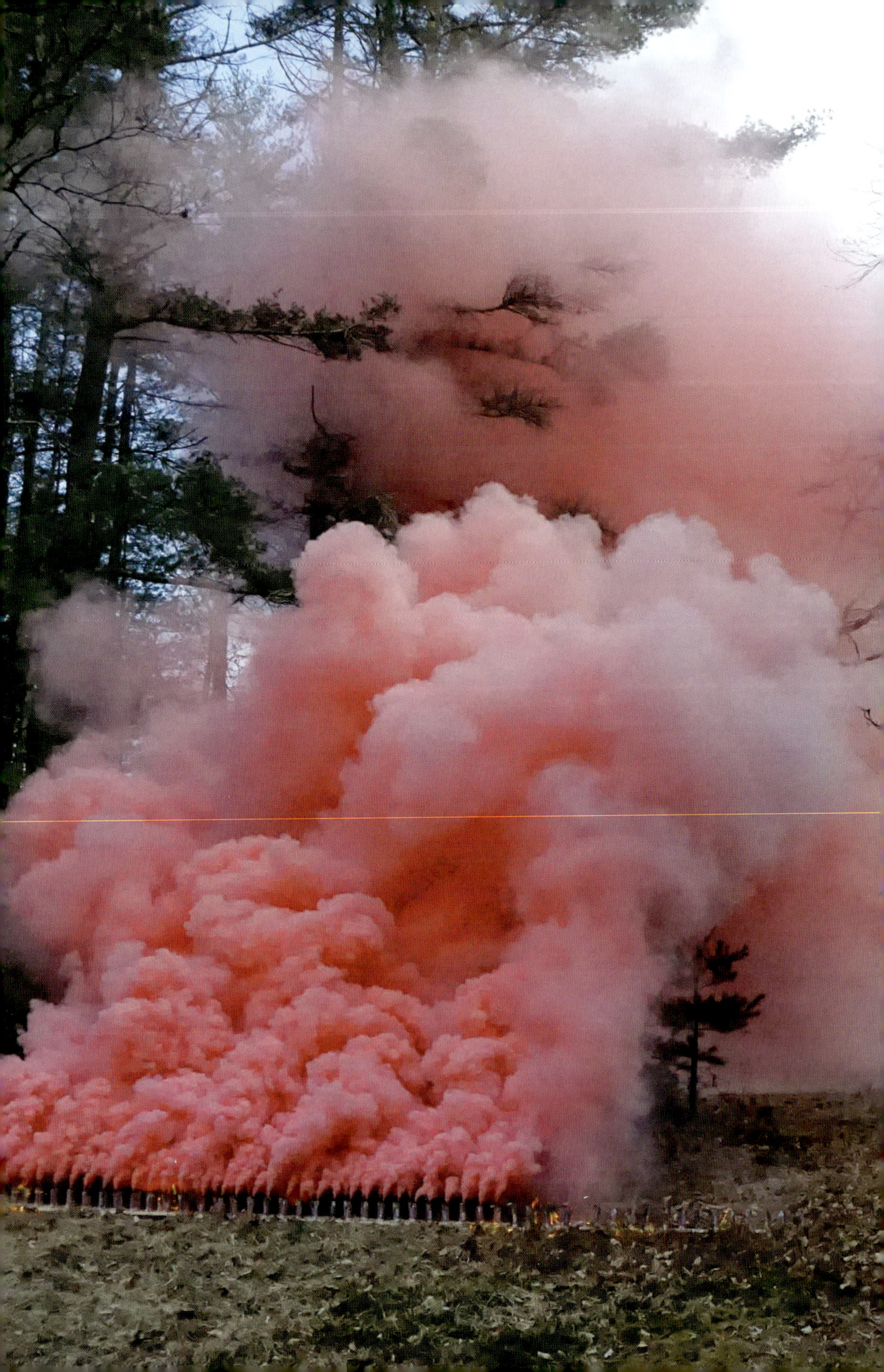

RAPHAELE SHIRLEY

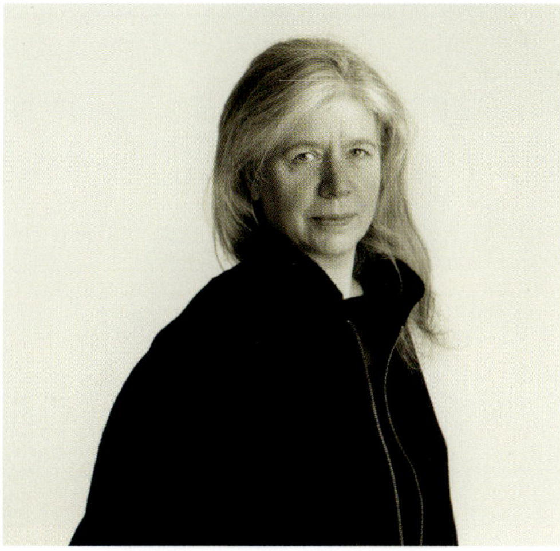

Raphaele Shirley is a French/American visual artist working in NYC. Employing diverse mediums such as neon, LED, laser, water mist, sound, and occasional pyrotechnics, as well as traditional materials, she creates sculptures and site-specific environments which play on tensions between ephemerality and permanence. Her many solo exhibitions include: *12.6 Lyrae* The Chimney, New York (2016), *0910 Light Shots*, Chelsea Art Museum, New York (2010); *Arctic Lights*, Dorfman Projects, New York (2010); *Jewels of Kvinesdal*, Kvinesdal, Norway (2009); *Sunken City Episode II* Emily Harvey Foundation, New York (2008), *Video Art in the Age of the Internet,* Chelsea Art Museum (2007).

Her work has been featured in group exhibitions including: The KAI Art Center opening in Tallinn, Estonia (2019); *Chance Ecologics,* Queens Museum, New York (2016); *Magnetic North: Artists of the Arctic Circle*, UBS Art Gallery, New York (2014); *Sandnes* 2160, Museum of Moving Image, New York (2013); *Cyland Festival*, The State Hermitage Museum, St. Petersburg, Russia (2008); *Drift,* National Center for Contemporary Art, Moscow, Russia (2008) and at several biennales including: *Erased Walls,* Mediations Biennale, Berlin, Germany (2010); 12th International Media Art Biennale, National Museum, Wroclaw, Poland (2008).

She has also been a founding member of projects including The New York International Fringe Festival (1997–2000) and [Pam] Perpetual Art Machine (2005–2010). She has been the recipient of grants from the Norwegian Arts Council (2009–2010). In 2016 she was a one-year resident with her collaborative project *3by3by3* at HarvestWorks in New York.

Left: *100 Pink Smoke Flares* 2016. Above: Portrait by David Heald

e-media-c 2018 at Hunter College's Black Box Theater in New York. Photo: Michael Lisnet

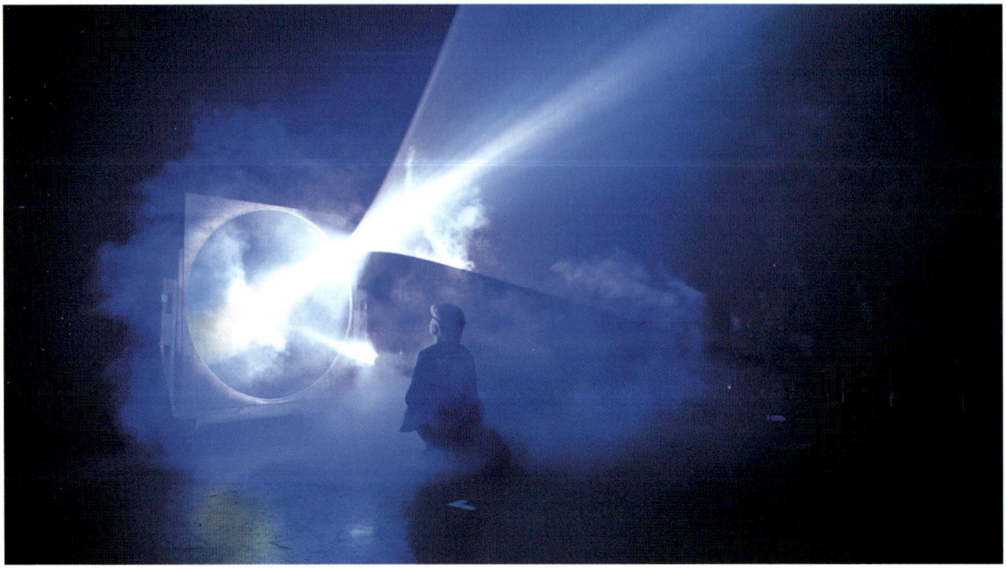

IN HER OWN WORDS

In the south of France, in my mid-teens, I became friends with a group of sculptors working with René Coutelle, himself a former student of August Rodin. This group was passionate about pre-Renaissance art and literature. Learning granite and marble stone-carving and clay-sculpting from them, I also spent many hours in the museums of London, Paris, Munich, in Italy and in Greece, studying these periods in art history.

I discovered the sculptor Camille Claudel, who became my first role model. I studied her work and life, inspired by her incredible resilience in an environment where men were the creators and women mainly the subject/object (model). Her work pierces through commonality and imitation to reach levels of incredible tenderness and the sublime, this, despite the crushing creative force and manners of Auguste Rodin, her mentor and lover, and in a general climate of disbelief and lack of support from her peers.

Fuelled by this inspiring artist and the teachings of Coutelle's apprentices, I pursued formal training, through elective courses, in traditional drawing, painting, photography and sculpture in my late teens/early twenties, in Europe, where I lived until 1993. I trained extensively in figure drawing. Finally, after graduation from high school in France, I entered the Beaux-Arts d'Aix-en-Provence. An invitation to work on cultural projects brought me to New York in1993.

In New York, I maintained my practice while securing a small live/work studio at 537 Broadway in the Fluxus building, home of the former Grommet Factory founded by George Maciunas, now the Emily Harvey Foundation. I expanded my practice to theatre in order to continue working at a larger scale, and to meet new colleagues, creating sets, props, costumes and video design with directors Karin Coonrod (Arden Party) and Aaron Beall (Founding director of New York International Fringe Festival).

I was greatly influenced by Retrospectives at the Museum of Modern Art of Bruce Nauman (1993) and Jasper Johns (1996), opening my mind to conceptual sculpture as well as crossovers between sculpture and painting. I learned from the Fluxus artists' happenings and found-object-based work, intermedia practices with Elaine Summers and inclusion of the element of chance following John Cage. Rachel Whiteread became my new role model and I studied artists such as Frank Stella, Sol LeWitt, Robert Smithson, Nancy Holt, Lynda Benglis, Louise Bourgeois, Agnes Denes and Roman Signer.

After securing a position as a studio assistant to Nam June Paik (1997–2002), working with technology upturned my art practice even further. In particular, the science of light became a central interest and part of my artistic language, while helping to build Paik's laser works *Jacob's Ladder*, *Olympic Park Waterscreen* and *Three Elements*, and many of Paik's CRT-based works.

In 2001, renting a studio in Williamsburg, New York, I returned to regular studio practice, no longer solely a traditionally trained artist, but with the influence of theatre, art collectives, multimedia, public art installations as part of my repertoire.

Here I started a series of rule-based studies of collected styrofoam packaging. I chose these subjects as a neutral starting point to sort through all the possibilities in art I had discovered since arriving in New York. The concept in this research was to reveal the potentials of the objects without staging them, creating a taxonomy of forms and ideas. In my approach, I was seeking indeterminate scale and meaning; the objects

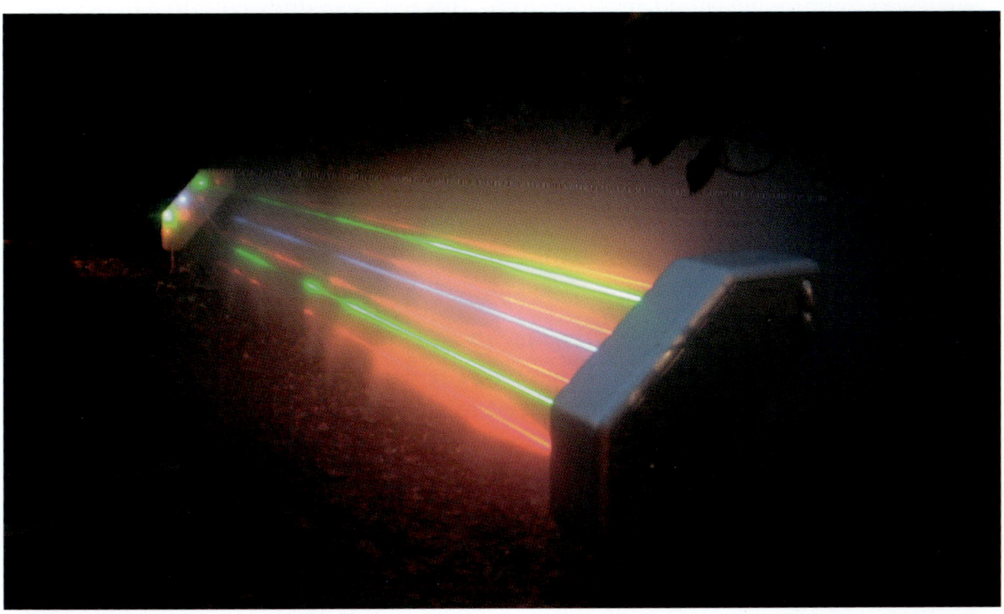

Shooting Stair 2019.

12.6 Lyrae 2016. Photo courtesy of The Chimney

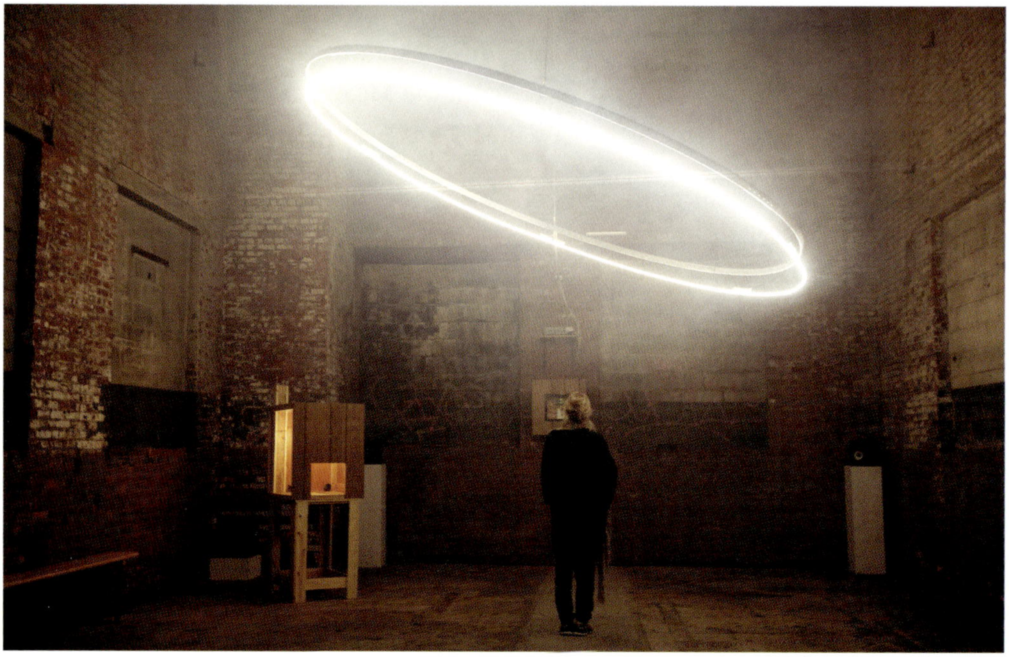

presented could suggest miniatures, models, hand-sized to monumental, the context determined by the viewer. The body of work became a photographic series, stand-alone sculptures and site-specific installations. Eventually, I cast some of the styrofoam pieces in bronze (*Home*, 2007), latex, wax and plaster (*Atlantis*, 2007) and created an immersive sculpture, *Elevation-in-Time*, 2007. This ten-year study culminated in a series of installations/exhibitions called *Sunken City* (Emily Harvey Foundation, 2008) and finally the commission *Jewels of Kvinesdal* (Utsikten Center, Norway, 2009). Here the environment became an integral part of the work, as it included a 60-foot L-shaped light beam, integrating the fjord's weather fluctuations as an active participant to the piece.

At this point of completion, marking a new juncture, I considered eliminating the "object" to work only with light and atmosphere, taking as a departure point minimalism and the painting *The Creation of the Universe and the Expulsion of Paradise* by Giovanni di Paolo (1445) which had captured my attention.

I began the series *Light Shots*, *Arctic Lights* and *100 Pink Smoke Flares*, integrating space and the environment as a key element. The *Arctic Light* series made during two sailboat residencies in Svalbard, Norway, were abstract sculptures, sketched in space using "light-brushes" and a zodiac-boat, expanding from 10-foot shapes to encompass the entire bay. The sculptures float in space, exploring concepts freed from physical restrictions, time-lapse photographs becoming the final artwork.

Throughout my practice ideas come to me as a "flash", at night or upon viewing other artist's work or inspiring spaces. The ideas sit in my mind for several weeks, or months, until settling into a certitude to be realized. Many ideas are monumental in scale, involving compound technologies: sound, light, atmosphere (natural or generated). In order to realize their full potential, I have become interested in performance, investigating new dimensions in ephemeral sculpture. I include live or recorded compositions to mark transiency, drawing the audience into an installation, creating an impression of immersion, underlining a work's evolution in time. Composers/musicians I have worked with include Algis Kizys, Laura Ortman, Vinnie Signorelli (*12.6 Lyrae,* 2016*)*, David Watson, Kevin Shea, Peter Zummo (*13 Trees,* 2016, */e-media-c,* 2018), Rhys Chatham (*3by3by3,* 2013), Shirish Korde *(Questions for the Moon,* 2016*)*.

To challenge my practice further since 2014, I have begun creating non-ephemeral wall-hung sculptures, exploring limits between painting and sculpture, light and form, searching for notions of the "Infinite" and site-specificity while employing minimal and finite means. The works are inspired by themes of cosmology, representation of divinity in pre-renaissance painting and world religions.

I'm currently working on multimedia installations for public spaces and new wall-hung sculptures which break from the limit of the circle, employing an array of technologies or no technology, simply raw materials.

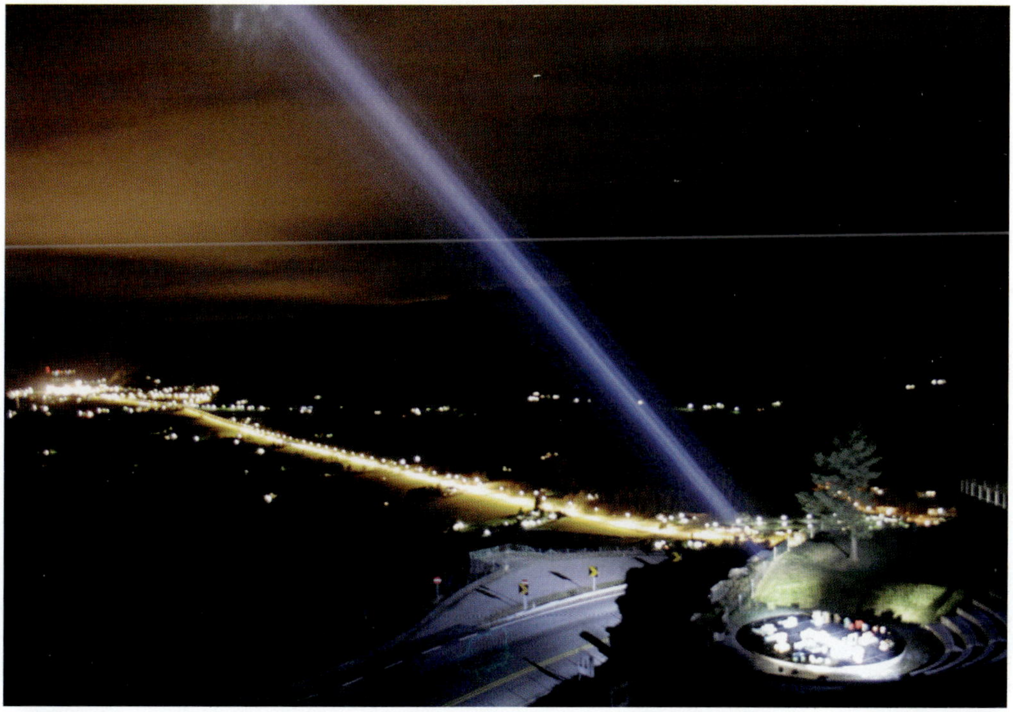

Jewels of Kvinesdal – Utsikten Center, Norway, 2009

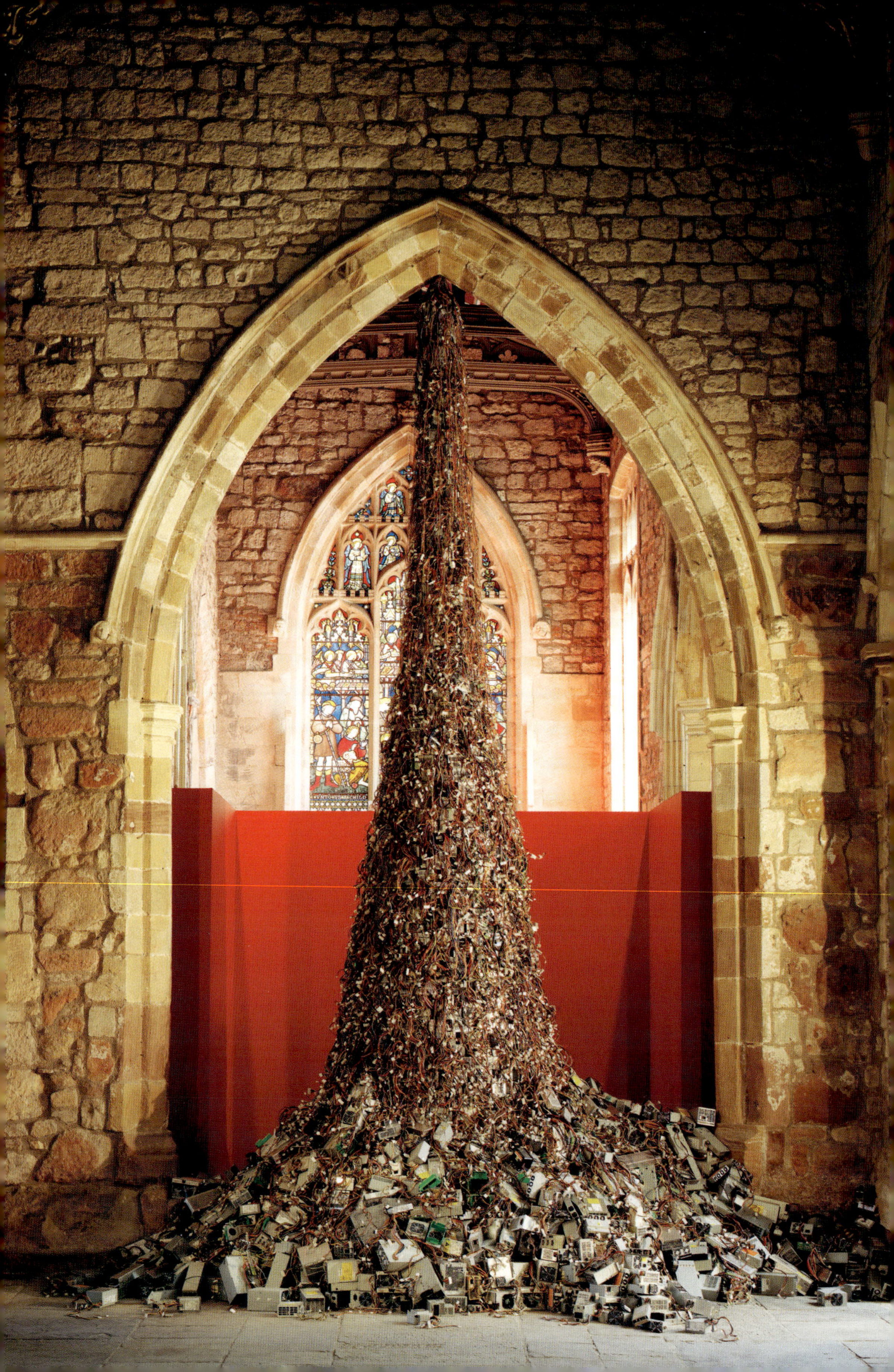

SUSAN STOCKWELL

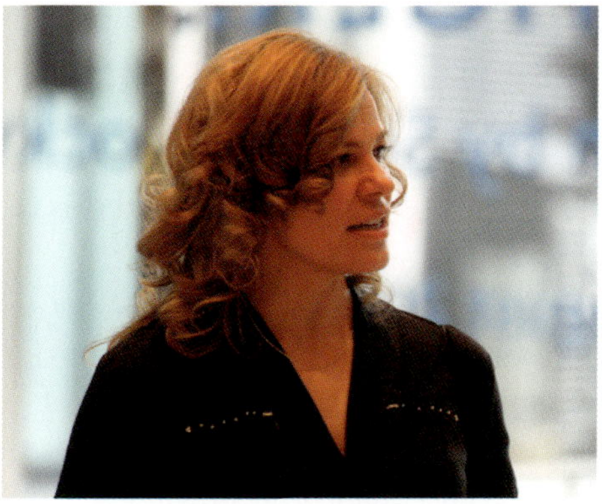

Susan Stockwell was born in Manchester, England and attained her B.A. in Fine Art from Sheffield Hallam University (1988) and her M.A. from the Royal College of Art (1993). She now teaches Fine Art part-time at the University of East London.

Stockwell also develops work through participatory art practice and has worked with a range of groups including Prison inmates, Cuban refugees and Afghanistan and Iraq veteran soldiers in rehabilitation. The project, *Piece Makers* was in collaboration with The National Army Museum London (2012–16). In 2013, she made *Sail Away,* an interactive installation in Tate Modern's Turbine Hall for the Hyperlink Festival. In 2014–15 she was Artist in Residence at the Royal Shakespeare Company in Stratford-upon-Avon where she made new work for the exhibition *Sea-Markings* (2015).

Stockwell has exhibited extensively around the world, including at Tate Modern, and the Victoria & Albert Museum, London, The National Museum of China, Beijing, The Katonah Museum of Art and the Children's Museum of Art in New York, the Art League of Houston, USA and Manchester City Art Gallery.

Her work is in public and private collections including: The V&A Museum, The Tropenmuseum, Amsterdam NL, the London Transport Museum, Bedfordshire University, UK, Black Rock Investments and Yale Centre for British Art, USA.

susanstockwell.co.uk

IN HER OWN WORDS

My work draws from my background, growing up in a Northern English urban culture in what I call a "make do and mend" socialist household where everything was recycled and my mother made our clothes, a skill I inherited and have used in my work. My father was a historian who worked in education and strongly believed in creativity and doing something worthwhile with your life. He read the *Chronicles of Narnia* to

Left: *Flood* 2010 St. Mary's Church, York. Photo: Shannon Tofts

his whole school for an hour each day, with the conviction that the development of a creative imagination was a vital part of education.

I make sculpture, installation, collage, film and drawings. I am best known for my large-scale, site-specific installations and sculptures installed in galleries, museums and public spaces. The work arises out of my interest in the political forces that have come to shape our world from colonialism to the social movements of the 19th and 20th century. This has led me to research international trade and cultural mapping and I have made artwork in response. I have also linked this research to the politics of feminism and the body.

An example of this is *Territory Dress*, 2018 [below] a commission for the Tropenmuseum in Amsterdam, concerned with claiming female territory and our colonial past and its contemporary significance. Maps of the Dutch colonies are fashioned into the shape of a regal dress with frills and folds made of paper and cloth maps. Small model money boats and maps of significant territories are concealed inside the neck, womb and train of the dress, which creates a kind of movement, as if passing through time, pulling the weight of a brutal past whilst the hollow of the stomach questions the origins of bodily and national proprietary. As a legacy for the work I made a film, *Territory Dress,* 2019, which explores the sculpture and juxtaposes it with archival film of past seafaring imagery.

My carefully sourced materials are often organized into monumental shapes like stacks and cascades or smaller quilts, dresses and maps. The use of large quantities of material invokes notions of mass production, collective history and memory. Three examples of installations where I have sourced pre-used materials that hint at this sense of collective history are *Sail Painting*, *Flood* and *Sail Away*.

Sail Painting at the RSC was a large-scale site-specific installation that hung in the public atrium in front of the theatre and was made as a result of

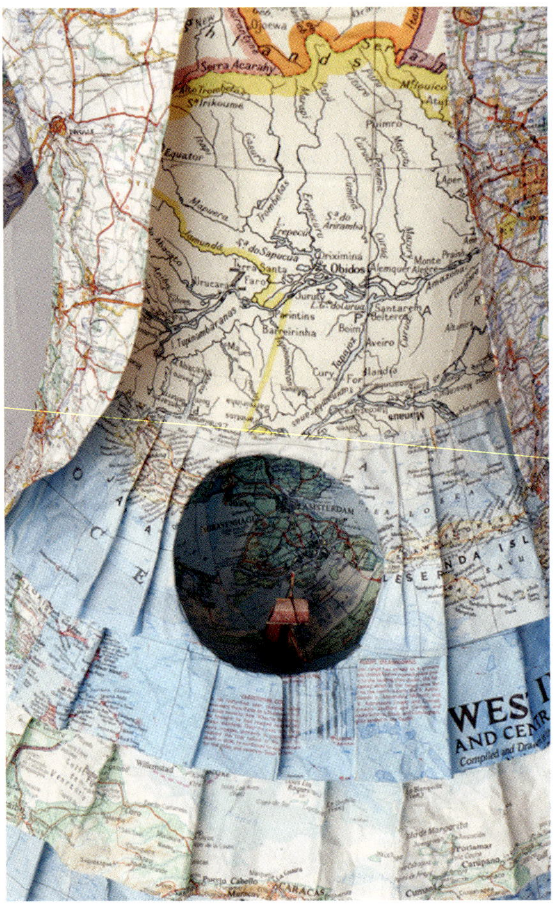

Territory Dress 2018 detail Photo: Tropenmuseum, Amsterdam.

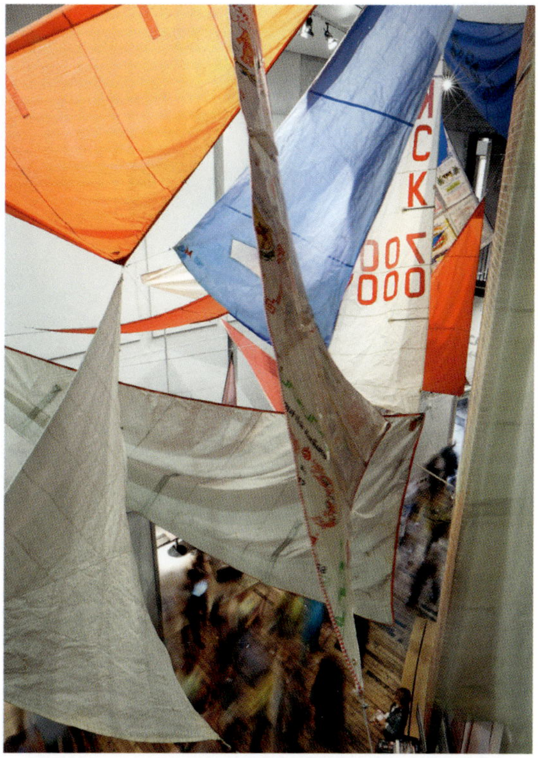

Sail Painting 2015, RSC. Photo: Jeff Leyshon

a year long residency there (2014–15). It consisted of thirty-two appropriated and handcrafted sails (made from old plastic food sacks), which hung at angles in the three-storey atrium. Seen from different vantage points the viewer felt they could be walking inside a three-dimensional abstract painting.

Flood (York 2010) was made from four tons of recycled computer components that cascaded eight metres down from the ceiling in to the altar area of St Mary's, a de-consecrated 13th century church in York. Addressing questions of climate vulnerability and outmoded systems of ecology management, the computers were dissected and their innards exposed, revealing the underbelly of the machines we depend on yet take for granted – an autopsy of our consumer society. Bob Clark describes this work in *The Guardian*, "Stockwell, while playing with themes of consumer waste, refers to the "toxic exquisiteness" of her hi-tech raw materials, hinting at the double-edged fascination her best work generates."

For the large-scale installations, the materials I use are often borrowed from industry and returned to the sponsor to be recycled. In the 90s, I made a body of work from industrial scale toilet tissue sponsored by Kimberly-Clark, and another body of work from 2010 onwards made from computer components, where the materials were temporarily borrowed from the recycling chain. I chose these everyday 'commodity' materials because they contain 'stains of existence' and act as ready-made signifiers, which I sculpt in ways that delicately reveal their obscured politics, environmental harm and hidden beauty.

Sail Away consists of many small boats made from old paper currency, tickets and maps that form a large-scale snaking flotilla. It was initially exhibited in Tate Modern's Turbine Hall as part of the Hyperlink Festival 2013. It explores the idea of 'connections' in travel, trade, mapping and personal and social histories. The boats are beautiful, delicate and playful. In mythology, boats are symbolic of the transition from the material to the spiritual world and are carriers for our dreams as well as vessels for our adventures, escape and journeying. By combining boats and money these dream

Sail Away 2013, Turbine Hall, Tate Modern (Hyperlink Festival)

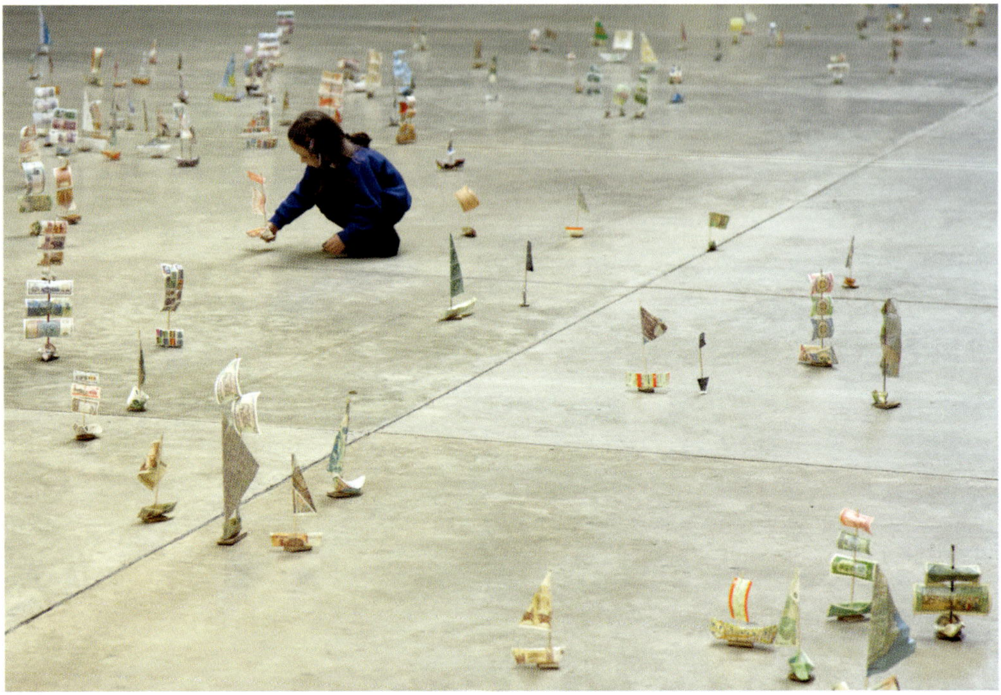

carriers gain other, deeper meanings. As part of the festival, eight hundred people made and contributed their own boats to the flotilla, transforming it into a huge collaboration. A stop-frame film shows the flotilla as it multiplies and contracts.

The installation *B-side Ecology* (2008) at the Hong's Foundation for Education and Culture in Taipei addresses issues of waste and recycling. A tidal wave of electronic materials was laid out on the gallery floor and formed onto blocks, raising questions about our throwaway attitudes to consumer products and our increasing use and unsafe disposal of plastics and rare earth materials. This was my first computer component installation, inspired by living in Taiwan, the home of the electronics industry. I became fascinated by this material's potential, inherent beauty, political content, architectural structure and map-like design. The curator and architect Grace Chung describes the work's gently revealing nature: "Accumulation, transformation, detritus, debris, everyday materials are all recurrent themes in Stockwell's work. Meticulously handcrafted, the benign sublime beauty in the work belies the devastating effects of our culture and our role in shaping it. Look more closely, and one is confronted by a cultural urgency of global proportions. Political and cultural colonisation, globalized waste and consumption are reconfigured by Stockwell's work into a new festering eco-system of meaning that slowly seeps like the rising ocean level." (exhibition text at the Hong's Foundation).

These works employ the material culture of everyday domestic and manufacturing products, such as toilet paper, recycled computer components, maps and paper currency and I transform these seemingly banal products into compelling artworks. In seeking to reconnect an object's past, its related history and materiality with contemporary issues, my practice underscores these materials' urgent interconnection to collective memories, desires and ecological shortfalls; aspects that evoke, expose and challenge features of social, racial and gender inequality and injustice.

My influences, inspirations and role models are many, from my parents, partner, artists and life experiences. As I get older, I become more confident and demanding of myself with more rigorous questions about the way we live.

I am currently Artist in Residence at Pinsent Mason's law firm in the City of London, which involves exhibiting my work in the public spaces and offices and making a participatory quilt with staff contributions. The quilt contains people's reflections on our current times, referencing subjects like climate change, community and the human impact of the COVID-19 global pandemic.

A solo exhibition, *Hidden Histories, Untold Stories* is also forthcoming at Warrington Museum and Art Gallery, where I will be showing artwork that re-frames and re-imagines their collection.

Taipei Stack and *Freefall* 2008 at the Hong's Foundation, Taipei

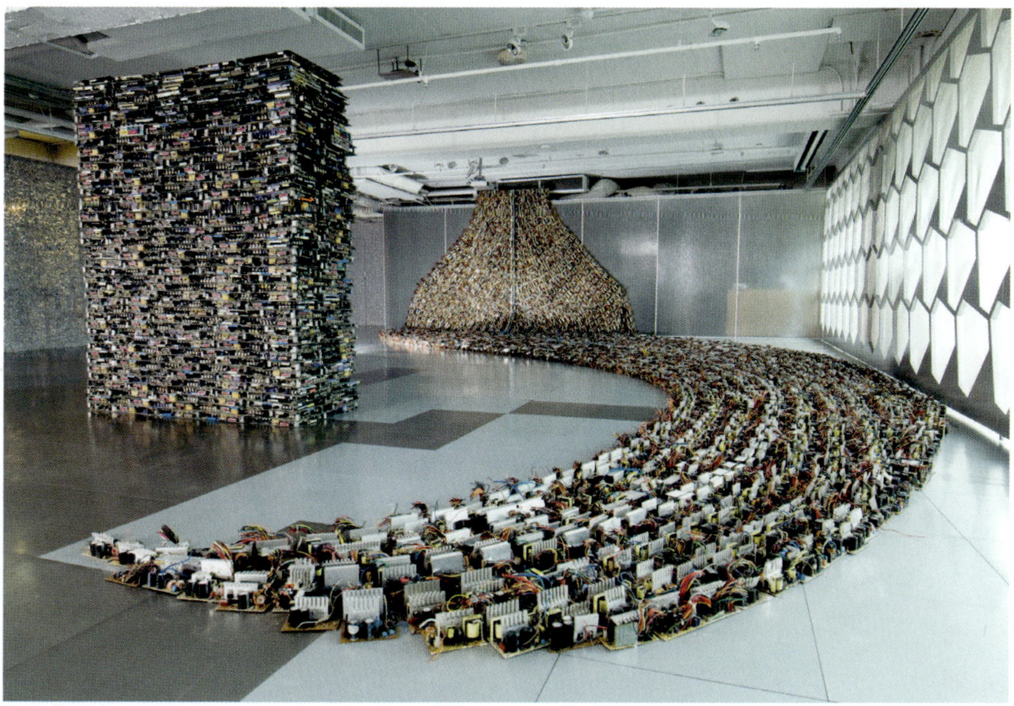

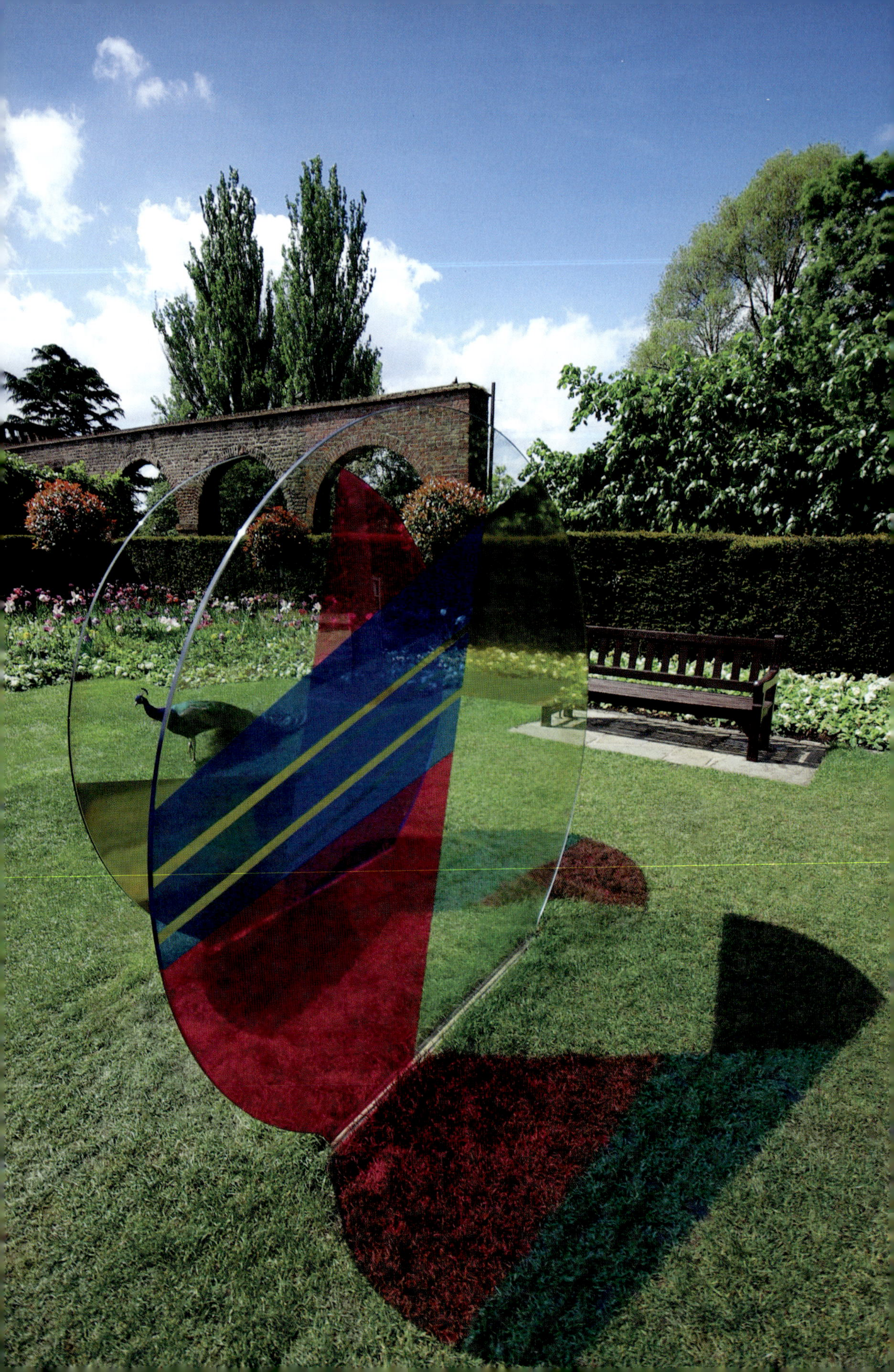

SINTA TANTRA

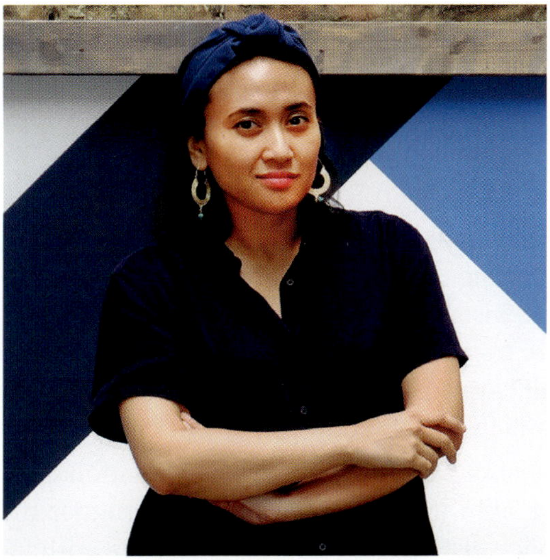

A British artist of Balinese descent, Sinta Tantra was born in New York in 1979. She studied at the Slade School of Fine Art, University College London 1999–2003 and at the Royal Academy Schools London 2004–06. In 2017 she was the first recipient of the Bridget Riley Drawing Fellowship at The British School at Rome. Tantra currently lives in between London and Bali.

Highly regarded for her site-specific murals and installations in the public realm, commissions include; Karachi Biennale (2019), Sharjah Islamic Art Festival (2019), Honor Hills, Seoul commissioned by Hyundai (2019), Facebook HQ London (2018), Lee Tung Avenue, Hong Kong (2018), Folkestone Triennial UK (2017), Newnham College, Cambridge University (2016), Songdo South Korea (2015), Royal British Society of Sculptors (2013), Liverpool Biennial UK (2012), Southbank Centre (2007).

Solo shows include: *Modern Times* (Kristin Hjellegjerde Gallery, London 2020), *Your Private Sky* (Kristin Hjellegjerde Gallery, London 2018), *A House in Bali* (ISA Art Advisory, Jakarta 2017), *Flatland: A Romance of Many Dimensions* (Pearl Lam Gallery, Hong Kong 2016) and *Fantastic Chromatic* (Kristin Hjellegjerde Gallery, London 2015). International group shows include: *On the Nature of Botanical Gardens,* (Framer Framed, Amsterdam 2020), *Strangers in Town* (Kristin Hjellegjerde Gallery, Berlin 2019), *Woven & Illuminated,* (Kristin Hjellegjerde Gallery, Berlin 2019), *Voyage to Indonesia,* The World Bank, Washington (2018); *Tetap Terang / Always Bright,* ISA Jakarta 2018; *High Noon*, Accademia Belle Arti di Rome, Rome (2017), *Quotidian,*

Left: The Eccentricity of Zero – Holland Park, London, 2013 commissioned by RSS

Pearl Lam Gallery, Shanghai (2017). Awards include: British Council's International Development Award (2014) and The Pyramid Deutsche Bank Award (2006).

IN HER OWN WORDS

Graphic shapes, bold lines, and at times tropical motifs, wrap around architectural spaces such as buildings, bridges, public squares and parks. As an artist, I'm interested in colour and form occupying the liminal space between two-and three-dimensions. I am drawn to working on an architectural scale, creating works that question the decorative, functional and social role of art, turning the white cube space inside out.

Drawing is always the starting point for my practice, exploring the slippage between the two and the three-dimensional world – the clarity of line, its distortion, the push and pull. My paintings, installations and sculptures are designed on the computer first and like blueprints, are transferred to the surface or site and then executed. Once lines are marked, colours are systematically added, layer by layer. I consider my process as something physical and sculptural: 'built' rather than 'emerged', 'cut' rather than 'blended'.

I have close-knit teams both in my studios in London and Indonesia. The way I work is perhaps more akin to that of an architect/designer than a traditional artist. This 'blueprint' approach gives me the flexibility to work with fabricators from all over the world. From sculpture foundries in England to sign painters in Pakistan, my initial drawings become a universal language to realize my final projects.

I take inspiration from a wide range of sources from classic Hollywood movies with Marilyn Monroe, Audrey Hepburn and Charlie Chaplin to modernist artists like Eileen Grey, Sonia Delaunay, Annie Albers and visionaries such as Buckminster Fuller and

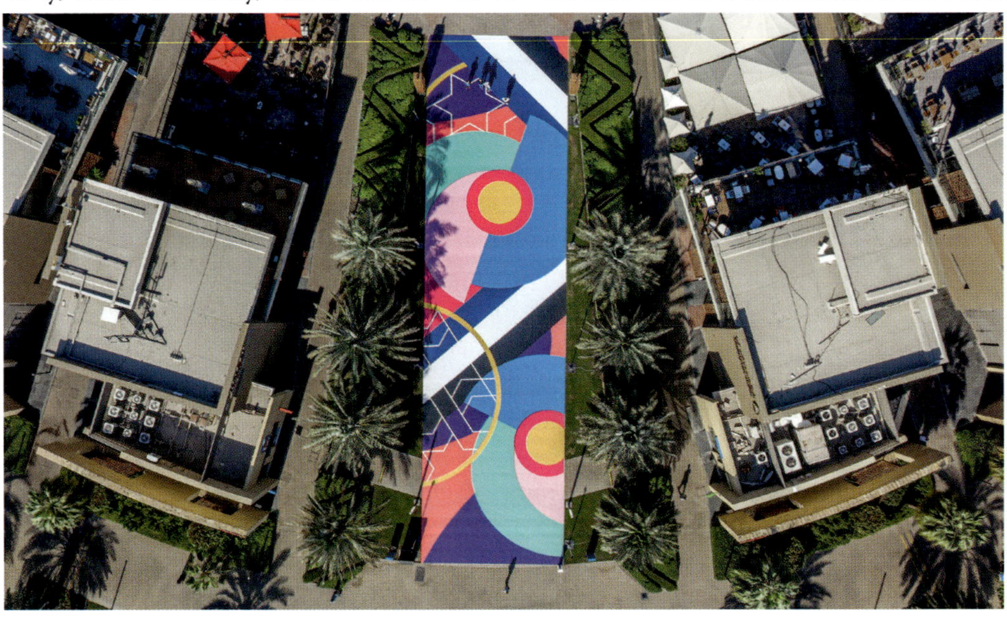

Horizon to Horizon, 2019 commissioned Sharjah Islamic Arts Festival

A Beautiful Sunset Mistaken For a Dawn, 2012 commissioned by Canary Wharf Group, London

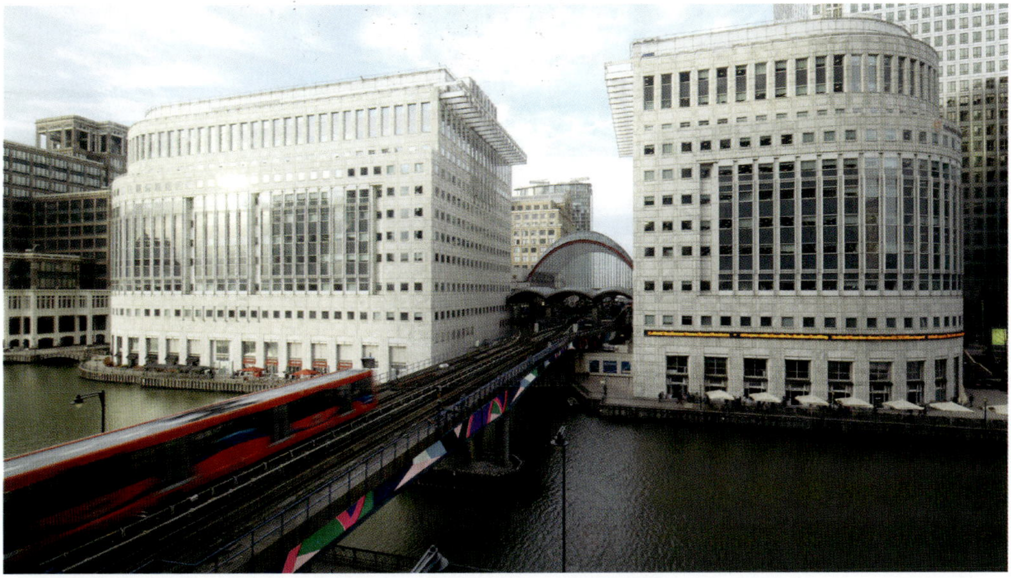

Walter Gropius. You could say I have a fondness for old-fashioned glamour combined with something utopian. What I like most about these people are their interdisciplinary ways of working and their relentless drive to push boundaries between art and life.

These days, I spend a lot of my time in Bali, where most of my family continue to live. While I regularly show and exhibit in Europe, Asia, and more recently, the Middle East, Bali has always been a significant influence on my art, giving me a sense of who I am and my origins. Daily activities in the village are still centred around religious ceremonies where activities such as dance, music and art are frequently performed. The island's position on the equator gives a unique and beautiful light on its natural surroundings and I try to capture these bold colours into my work.

Two generations ago, my Balinese grandparents would have been able to carve and weave and this is something I want to continue with my art. In some of my more recent pieces, I have pushed myself to work beyond digital technology and work with Balinese craftsmen to make traditional woven tapestries and textiles. I have also been experimenting with wood-carving and stone-carving as a means of creating new art. In this way, I am somehow piecing together parts of my identity, merging together the past with the present and then back again.

As I continue to grow as an artist, I have adapted in ways that I could not have known or foreseen. Quite often, the sites that I'm working on are immensely large and physically challenging. Over the years, I've developed good communication skills, especially working in non-English speaking countries, looking at the bigger picture to make the process more collaborative. In a male-dominated practice such as sculpture, especially where female Asian artists are few and far between, I hope my work can set a positive change for a younger generation of artists to emerge.

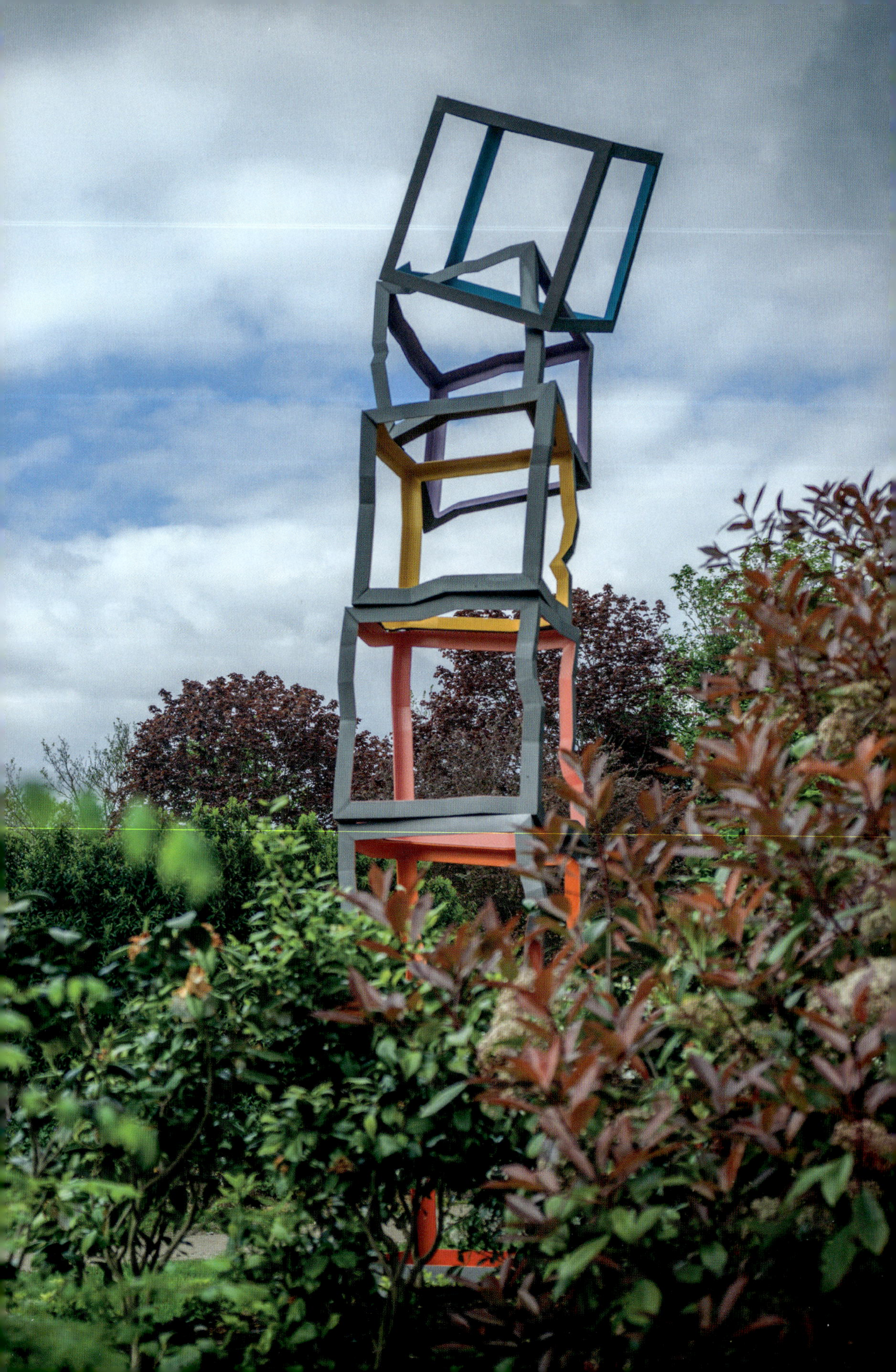

ALMUTH TEBBENHOFF

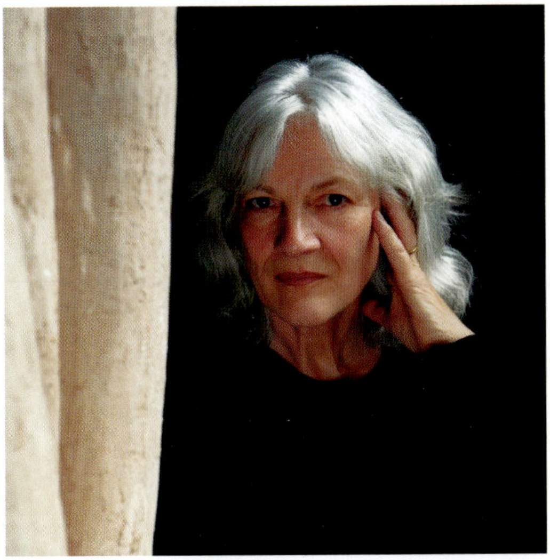

Almuth Tebbenhoff was born on a farm in Germany in 1949. She studied ceramics at Sir John Cass School of Art, London in 1972 and drawing classes and lectures at the Royal College of Art by invitation from Sir Eduardo Paolozzi. She has been commissioned by the Cass Sculpture Foundation, St George's Hospital, Richard Rogers building in Chiswick, University of Leicester and her work is available at the Saatchi Gallery and Pangolin, London. Awards include: NOA Competition, London Group Sculpture Prize, Arts Council England, grant for sculpture installation at Cafe Gallery, Southwark Park, London and the Pollock-Krasner Foundation, New York.

HOW DID YOU COME TO MAKE SCULPTURE?

From primary school (in Northern Germany) onwards I had wanted to be an artist. I painted and drew when and wherever I could. One day I saw a young woman throwing pots on a wheel and I loved that and thought about being a potter. However, I didn't get on with any of this until I was 23, when I enrolled on a ceramics course in London.

WHO WERE YOUR INFLUENCES AND OR ROLE MODELS?

I started my art career in ceramics in 1972, and I admired Lucie Rie, Hans Coper, Gordon Baldwin and some bold American ceramic artists. As it was the 70s, I discovered Edward Kienholz, Jackson Pollock and Rauschenberg, and lots of other powerful expressionists. At the same time I was blown away by Georgia O'Keefe.

Left: *Sunset Stack* 2019. Photo: Steve Russell. Above Portrait photo: Genevieve Stevenson

Later on I discovered Agnes Martin and also James Turrell, who's been a big hero for me. On the other end of the scale is Louise Bourgeois, whose work I admire. There are many extraordinary artists blazing the way.

WHO ENCOURAGED YOU?

In 1977 I met Eduardo Paolozzi, who was very helpful. He invited me to attend drawing classes, use the library and come to his lectures at the Royal College of Art, as well as encouraging me to use the facilities there, meet other students and generally broaden my horizon. He had seen some of my work in an exhibition, and something about it had impressed him, yet he thought I was too un-slick.

DID YOU HAVE ANY FORMAL TRAINING?

I didn't do a foundation course in art. I had to make money to live as I had left Germany at the age of 17 and arrived in the UK without any contacts or money to study. By the time I was 23, I could spare enough time to do a three-day-a-week course at the Sir John Cass School of Arts in Aldgate.

Flow 2018 at the Salisbury Museum. Photo: Steve Russell

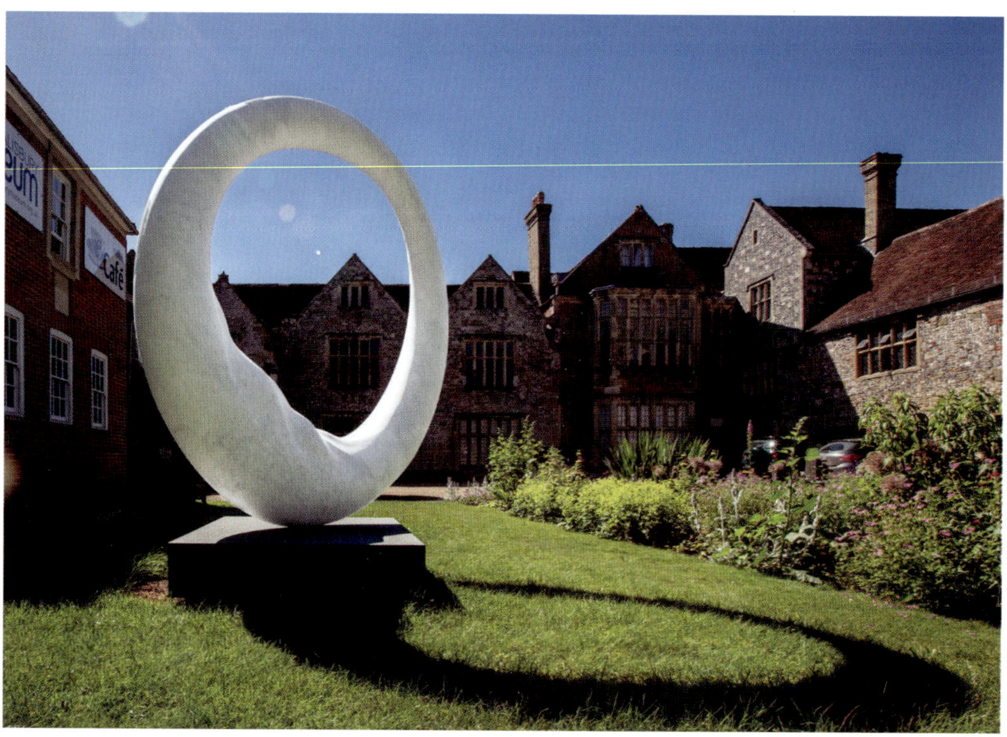

DO YOU USE THE HUMAN FIGURE IN YOUR WORK?

From 1975 to 1983, as a form of training, I set myself the task of making one figurative piece every day. I would get friends to model, or if there weren't any, I'd open a newspaper and attempt to work from photos. I made tiny figures and heads as well as life-sized and larger. I needed to know the structure of the human figure.

DO YOU USE FOUND OBJECTS?

For a short time (a couple of years at most), I used all sorts of things in collages, including found objects which I strung, glued, pegged and nailed together.

DO YOU USE THE NATURAL WORLD?

The natural world is my main inspiration now. It probably always was, but I had to work my way through all sorts of 'isms' and styles to find my voice.

FREE-STANDING OR ATTACHED?

I work on free-standing pieces as well as wall-based ones. In the late 80s, after a course in metal fabrication at South Thames College, I began working with steel, and I developed ideas using angle-iron, which I welded into geometric illusions of objects in space. At that stage I was influenced by minimalism and I loved the clean lines and uncluttered spaces. All that work was wall-based and I gradually developed free-standing pieces from these ideas.

IS THE SCALE IMPORTANT?

Scale is very important and ideas change dramatically on different scales. I am currently working on the largest piece in steel I have made and, at 6.7 m high, *The Stack* is quite overbearing in the studio. But then, by the time it is sited in the open grounds of a private sculpture park it will be dwarfed by the surrounding trees and it will look right. At this same time I am working on small ceramic pieces the size of small matchboxes for light relief. Each sculpture has an optimum size, and experience teaches me what that is.

IS THE ENVIRONMENT IMPORTANT?

Yes, very.

EPHEMERAL OR LONG-LASTING?

I work mostly with long-lasting materials, often quite slowly, because materials like marble cannot be rushed. I love that as it gives me time to think and feel, and I work until something looks right. Then again sometimes I make very fast and ephemeral pieces (such as a floor piece of marble dust). They can be just as good and satisfying, but get swept up shortly afterwards. I draw a lot with fast gestures in black ink on paper.

Vortex 2018. Photo: Steve Russell

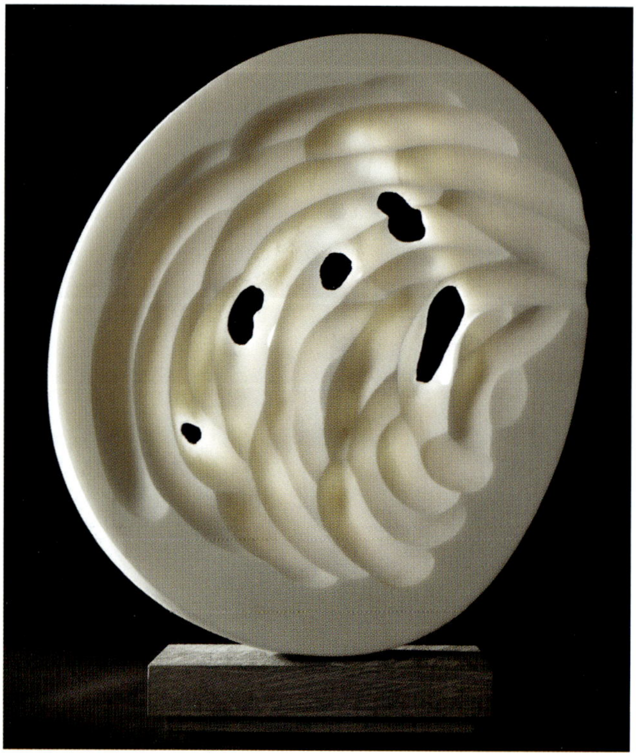

MULTIMEDIA OR ONE MEDIUM?

I tend to stick to one material at a time. I've never managed yet to combine marble with steel, but recently I stuck a ceramic shape into a steel sculpture and it worked.

IS THERE A PARTICULAR THEME OR THEMES WHICH ARE CENTRAL TO YOUR WORK?

I think the central theme would have to be light or space or nothingness. If I work with marble I dig deeply into the stone to bring light into this dense material, and if I work with steel I make empty cages for the sky.

HOW DO YOU GET YOUR IDEAS FOR AN ARTWORK?

Ideas flow into me from nowhere. Mostly first thing in the morning when I wake up. I sometimes "receive" fully-formed ideas for sculptures. Or when I squidge clay about, my hands just find shapes which I develop intuitively.

DO YOU LIKE TO DO COMMISSIONED WORK OR NOT?

I like to work to commission if I am given a free hand to make something for a particular space. I don't carry out someone else's ideas.

TELL US HOW YOU HAVE DEVELOPED AS AN ARTIST.

I have been single-minded about my art. Invariably, there have been some mistakes over the years, but I'm learning from the failures, and these end up teaching me more than anything else. I always hoped that deep down there were a few masterpieces that only I could make, and so I set about getting to them. I generally just said yes to everything that crossed my path unless it was illegal, and life just pushed me into the direction I'm going in.

WHERE IS YOUR SCULPTURE EXHIBITED?

I recently showed my latest marble sculpture *Flow* outside the Salisbury Museum. I work with different galleries, and I often show with The London Group, of which I am a member.

IS IT MORE DIFFICULT FOR WOMEN ARTISTS TO MAKE A LIVING THAN MEN?

I believe it is getting better now, but when I started exhibiting my sculptures in the late 70s early 80s, men invariably topped the lists and very few women came through. It was very frustrating and also humiliating, and #Metoo doesn't begin to describe that misery.

TELL US ABOUT YOUR FAVOURITE SCULPTURES – YOUR OWN OR BY SOMEONE ELSE.

I loved being in James Turrell's *Deer Shelter* in the Yorkshire Sculpture Park. I enjoyed Richard Serra's massive steel pieces in the Gagosian Gallery in London. Chillida's fork-like sculpture sticking out into the sea springs to mind, Anselm Kiefer's *Lead Library* and Ai Wei Wei's *Tree*, because I had that same idea a long time ago and didn't have the support to make it.

WHAT'S NEXT?

I am working on an installation of small clay pieces on large stone islands. I love Rembrandt's landscape drawings because they remind me of my home in North Germany. Flat windswept land with wide horizons and small towns dotted around. I want to capture that feel of open space and the huddle of small communities.

Empty Spheres III c.2013 Photo: Steve Russell

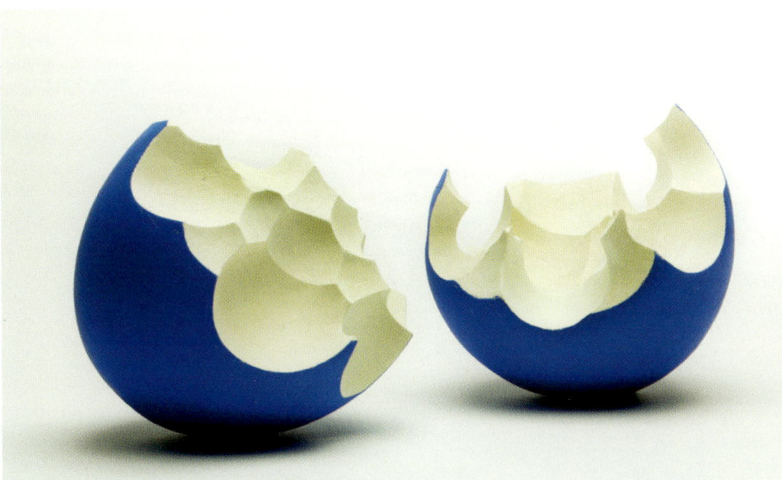

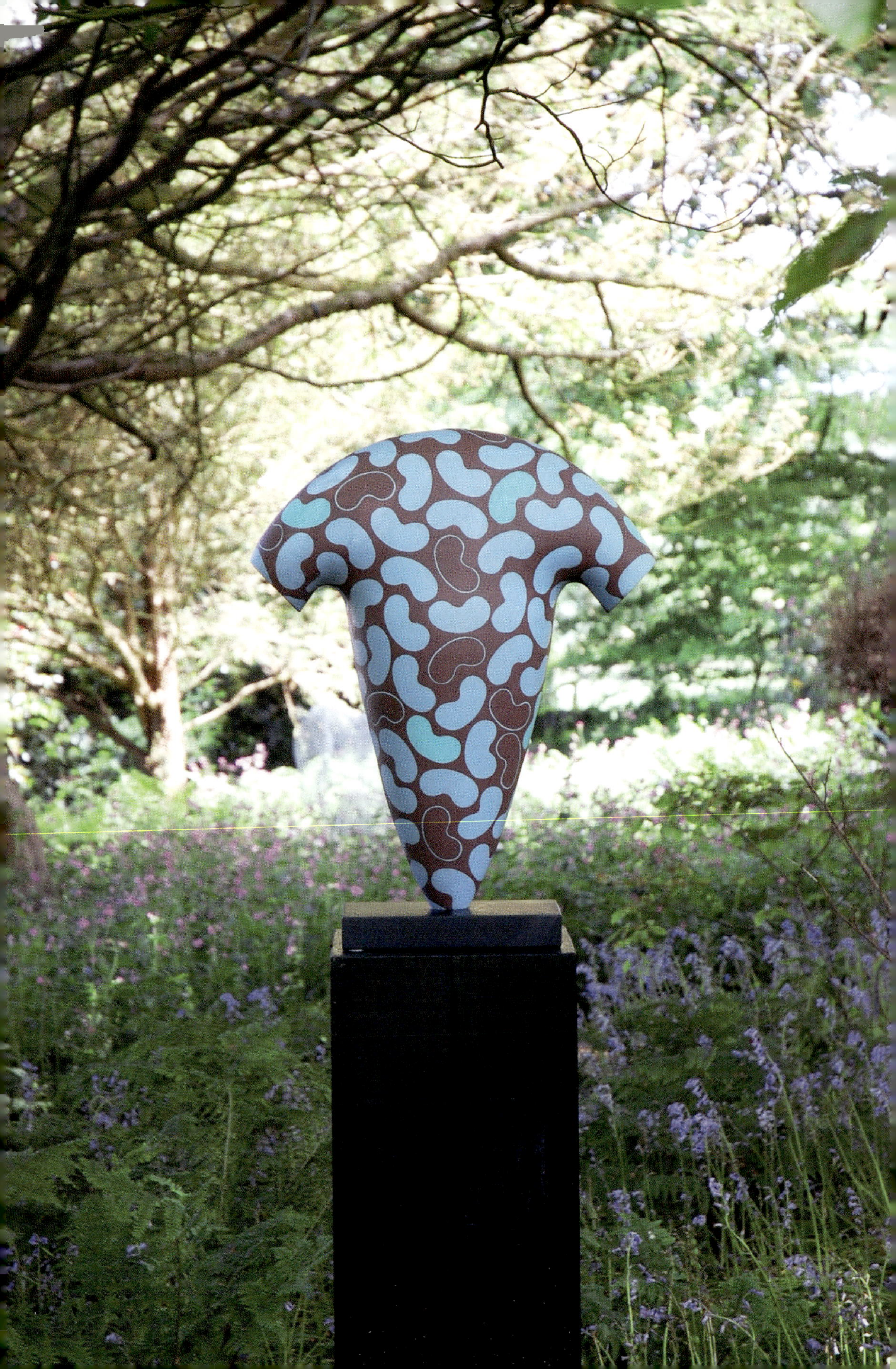

PATRICIA VOLK

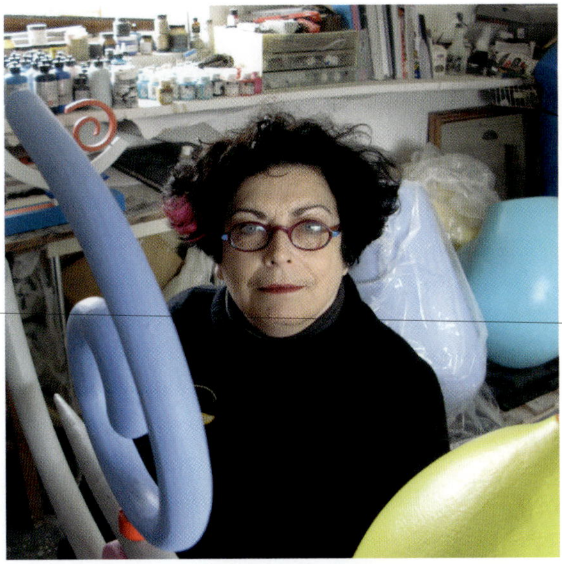

Born in Belfast, Northern Ireland, she ascribes her need to create something "well made" to her father who was a builder. She studied at Middlesex Polytechnic, then at Bath, and now has a studio in Wiltshire. Her work has been widely exhibited, including at the Beukenhof-Phoenix Gallery in Belgium, Chichester Cathedral and the Royal West of England Academy. It has also been acquired for the collections of Swindon Museum & Art Gallery, Lord Carrington, Anthony Horowitz OBE, Simon Relph CBE, the British Consul (Ivory Coast) and Mary Portas. She was Regional Winner of the ING "Discerning Eye" prize in 2007 and was shortlisted for the Brian Mercer Residency.

One of her pieces was also selected as a Southern Arts prize. In 2017 she was invited by the Designer Crafts Foundation to go to Israel as a guest sculptor. Her commissions include *Water Deities, Audience and Muse* and in 2019 her specially commissioned work appeared on television as part of the prestigious "ITV Creates Project".

She is represented in the UK by the Hannah Peschar Gallery and Cavaliero Finn.

IN HER OWN WORDS

As a sculptor I love working with the directness of clay, using all the techniques, coiling and slab building, making one-off pieces, which are fired then finished with acrylic paint. Classical sculpture was always highly coloured but we have this erroneous idea that they were all white and sterile-looking. My obsession as an artist is with catching a

Left: *Claim* 2013

Deities at Hannah Peschar Sculpture Garden 2000

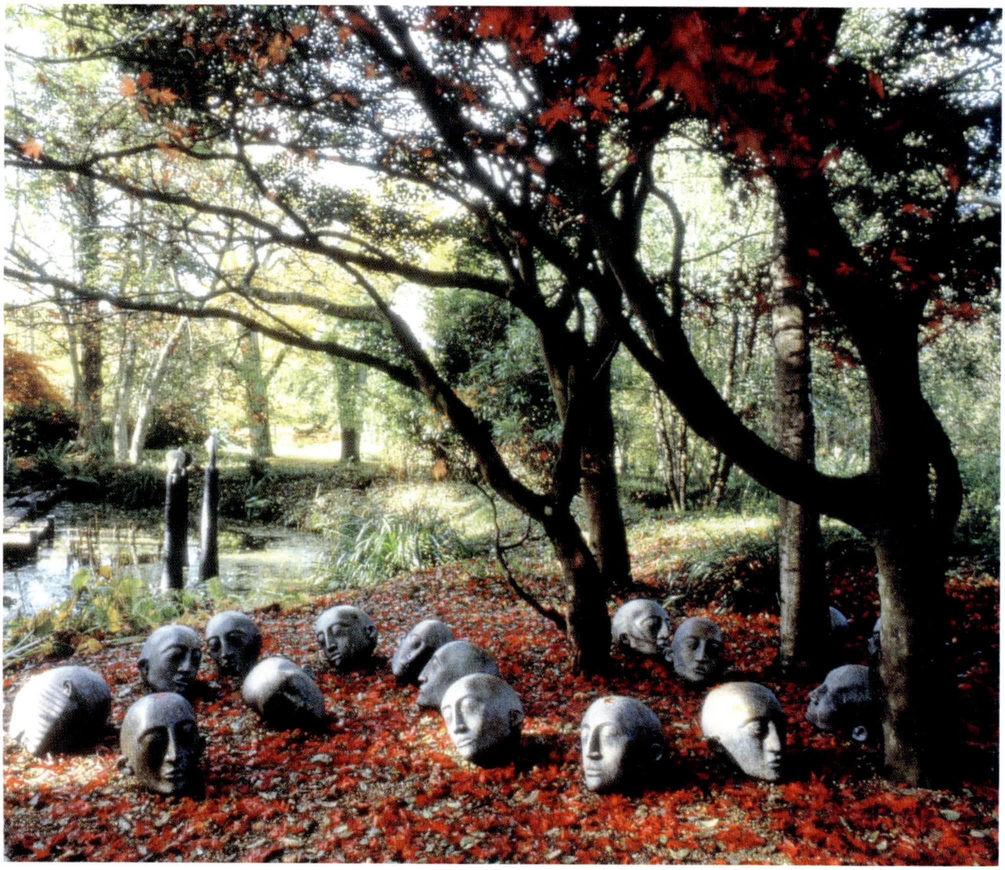

very simple form or line, then enhancing it with colour. Sometimes these stand alone, or are in combinations that I hope suggest opposites such as strength and fragility, stability and precariousness – very much reflecting the relationships we have as human beings. But also rest and activity, grace and motion – always attempting to give an inert object a lively, almost living, presence and a sense of strong individual character. But it's all in the eye of the beholder, to me. I never want to be too prescriptive or restrictive to the viewer's imagination.

There was a time when figurative semi-symbolic heads were an obsession of mine, but they were inevitably interpreted as a kind of person or an attribute of a person, whereas an abstract form needn't be that – it can simply be a juxtaposition of colours, or a pleasing or discordant form or combination of the two that has drama, but avoids having a specific meaning. In fact it defies that. And that was incredibly liberating to me.

The sculptor Jun Kaneko says that conceptual ideas just grow out of doing the work and I subscribe to that, absolutely. I start with no preconceived ideas, no drawings,

Crowd 2009.

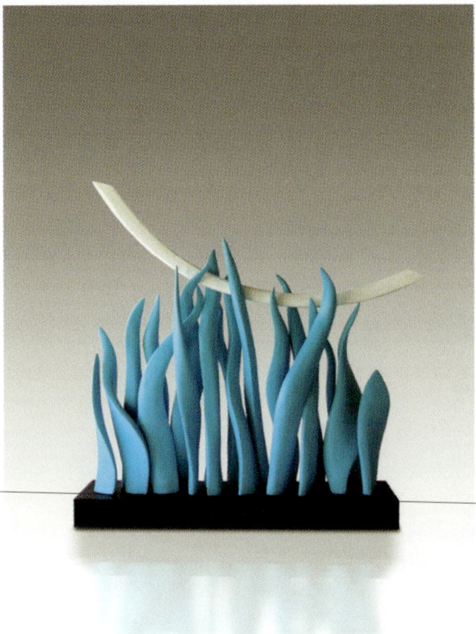

and only a vague idea in my head, if that. I see the work is largely a symbiosis between me as a maker and the material. I find if I start with a hard and fast concept it gets in the way, and is also in danger of being illustrational: that's fine for some people, but it's not how my mind works, or what I find exciting.

The thing I always come back to is the simplicity of line – a curve that might be so right that it takes your breath away, something that's almost like a musical note in the air. Just trying to get a physical object that is more than just a solid object, that has an emotional impact or uplift or a grace or beauty, and sometimes you don't even know why.

What excites me, I discovered, is the abstraction rather than trying to create a piece that represents or illustrates an idea you have beforehand. Really, working in clay is like play, and, being dyslexic, I have trouble expressing ideas in words, so I chose a medium where words aren't necessary. Or, you could say, it chose me.

You just put one colour against the other in a way that is satisfying or dynamic. It's purely visual and non-intellectual. If there is a deeper meaning I like to think that is brought by the viewer. I don't like to limit their experience by giving a sculpture a set explanation or description, if I can help it – if I do, I keep it as loose as possible, just a hint or pointer. Sometimes (only sometimes!) I know what is going on in my head, but more often I let my hands do the "thinking". That doesn't mean it's easy – far from it, because I take a very long time to consider the exact colours and weigh them up. Some might watch my activity and indecision and quite honestly think it's the total obsessiveness of a mad person. But that's OK! I'm an artist. And nobody said this was an exact science. It's nothing if not completely subjective and completely immersive.

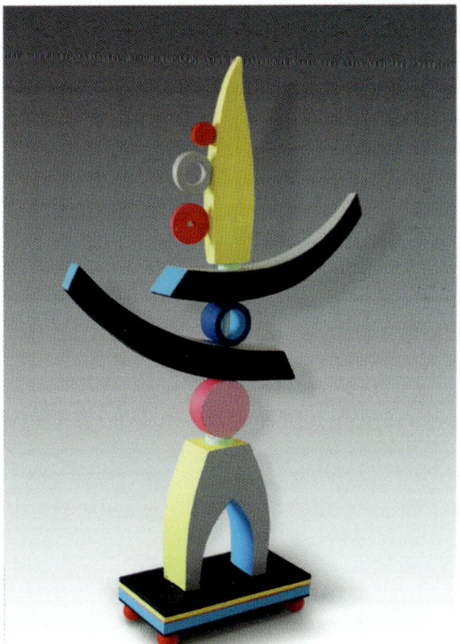

Pharos 2016

There are so many influences, sometimes imagining a beautiful line, or using as a starting point, a curve I've used in the past. I like the thought that the pieces look light, and float – a

Totem Deities 2002

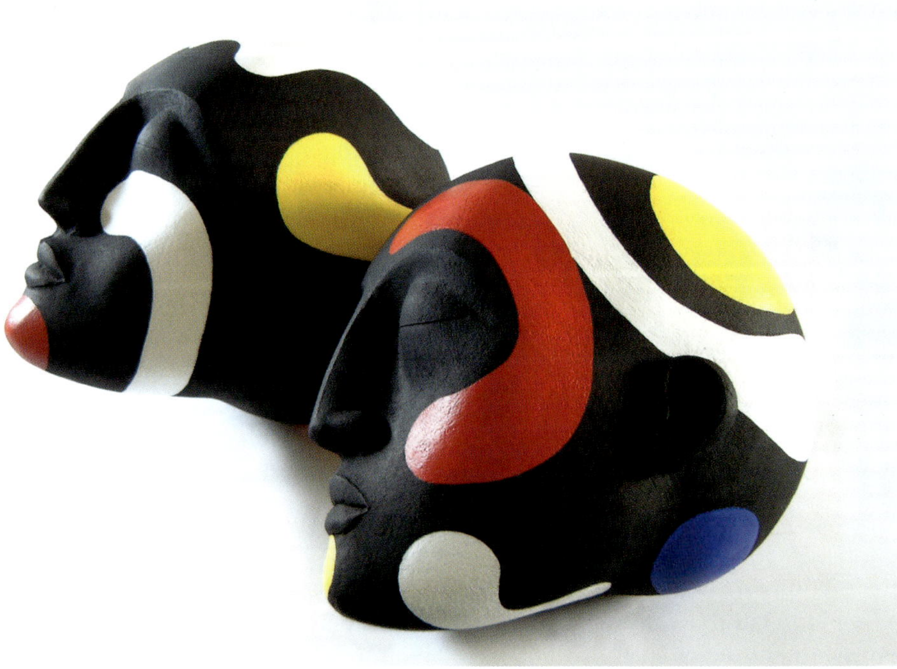

contradiction to the obvious physical weight of clay. I like the idea of uplift. I'm adamant they should be viewed at eye level, by walking around and looking at them from different angles. The surface texture can work to make the flatness of colour more nuanced and less machine-manufactured looking, adding a natural edginess on a vivid unnatural blue, for instance. I always work on a series of pieces at the same time because of the nature of the material (you cannot rush it), but the finished product is defined by the time it is modelled, which can be affected by all sorts of things: weather, temperature, my mood and so on. If you pushed me to say, I would like the combination of non-figurative form and colour combination to set off a series of ideas in the viewer's mind – tranquillity, elegance, power, sadness, rest, action, conflict, a sense of movement… all these things triggering human emotions of some kind.

I think a sculptor can have craft and imagination and be creative, but there are also craftspeople who are superb at what they do, but do not have the creative level of input. There are artists who are highly creative who do not have craft skills – they can literally phone somebody to make what they want, and that's fine – in that case, the craftsman is at the service of an artist. It's all about understanding your individual role and not being arrogant, not having a pretence to intellectual depth if it isn't genuine or honest. It's no good calling a piece *Baudelaire* just so that it sounds super-important. That is nonsense. It's the finished artwork that defines itself and either has quality or it doesn't.

Modigliani and Giacometti influenced me a lot when I was doing heads, as did the sculptors of the Renaissance. I think now there are an awful lot of abstract painters who are having a huge impact on me, simply because of the pared-down nature of their work, and sometimes it takes my breath away. The Agnes Martin exhibition at Tate Modern blew me away, and the stillness and rigour of her work was incredibly inspiring. I love Jun Kaneko. Enormous big things with spots on them, so they really appeal to me. I understand them and make a connection, although I could never begin to analyse that connection in words. It's a soul-to-soul connection, if anything. As if art bypasses the conscious mind completely.

I clearly remember the very first drawing I did when I was in junior school, and a teacher calling another teacher in to show her what I'd done, and I felt enormously proud. It caused such a lot of interest from the teachers, and in a way I may be trying to recapture that feeling of well-being and pleasure. In myself, and in others.

One of my dreams is to do a series of shapes like the ribs of an animal, so that you would have them in a line in a room, and you would look through them, and each one would curve this way then that way, until you see a big wall-piece at the end. But I haven't quite worked that out yet!

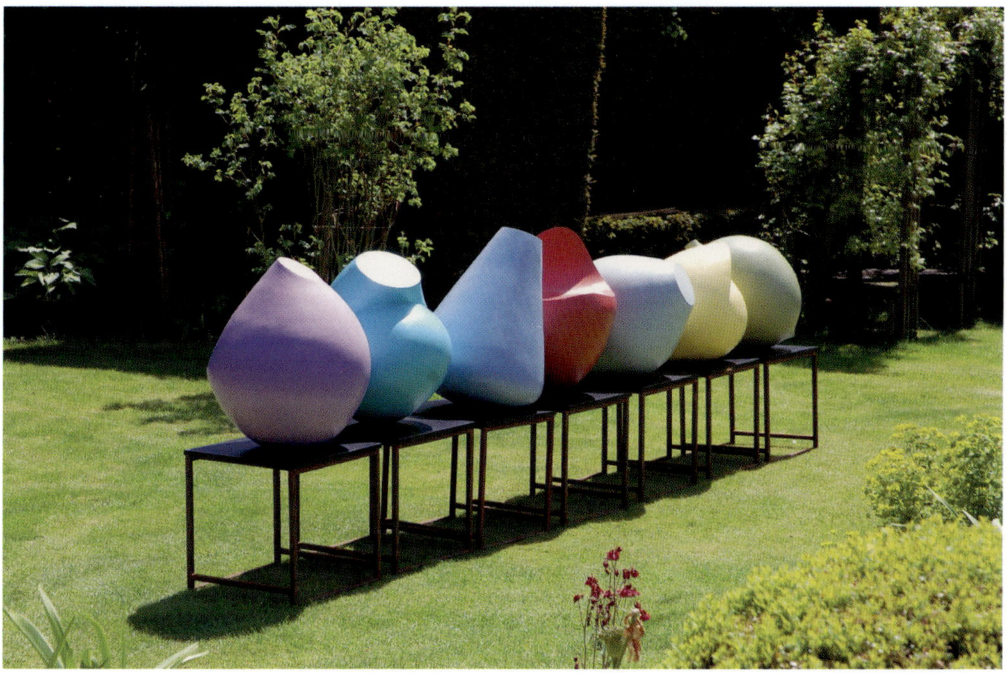

Individuals 2011

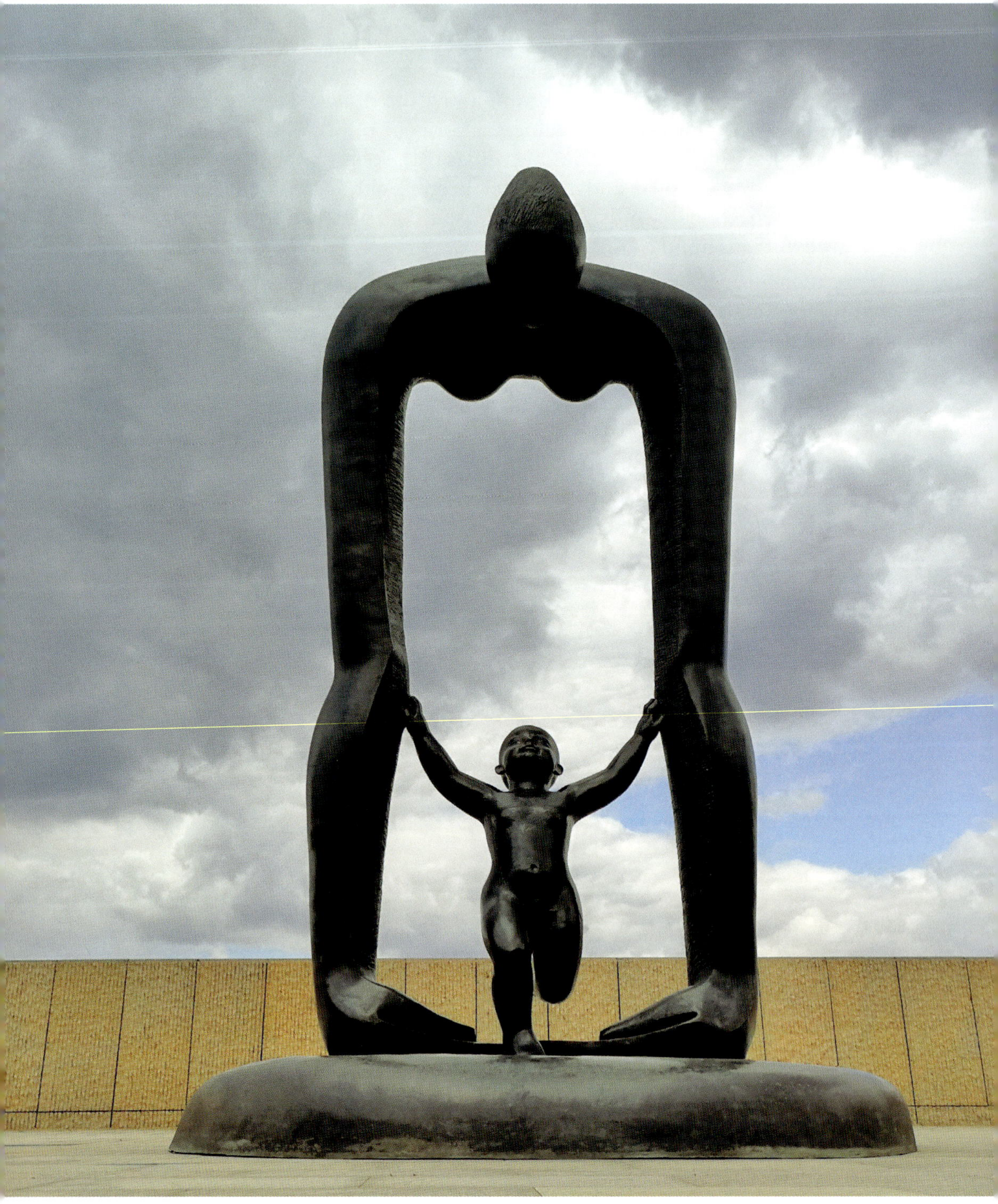

The Gate of Life 2001, Changchun World Sculpture Park (China)

ZHANG YAXI

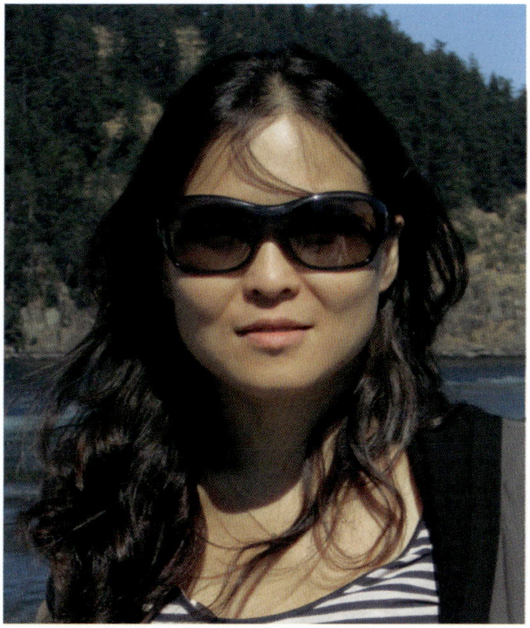

Contemporary Chinese sculptor Zhang Yaxi lives and works as a professional sculptor in Chongqing (formerly within Sichuan province), China. She has created monumental sculptures up to seven metres in height, and her sculpture has been exhibited in several international sculpture symposia and national sculpture exhibitions as well as being commissioned for public and corporate spaces. *The Gate of Life*, a monumental urban sculpture in bronze, was created during the China Changchun International Sculpture Symposium 2001. *Pregnant* was a monumental snow sculpture created on a frozen lake in Harbin, China. *Honorable Hero – General Ba* is a monumental work created during the 4th International Sculpture Symposium of Vietnam in December of 2003.

Her award-winning *Mother and Child* is a monumental sculpture for the city of Golmud in Qinghai Province, and she collaborated on the Tennis Terracotta Warrior series for the ATP/Tennis Master Cup Shanghai 2007 with fellow sculptors Laury Dizengremel and Shen Xiaonan.

HOW DID YOU COME TO MAKE SCULPTURE?

As a teenager, I studied in the high school affiliated to the Sichuan Fine Arts Institute in Chongqing. At that time, I thought the most fashionable thing was to learn Western-style oil painting and sculpture. Back in the 1980s, very few women studied sculpture in China, so I chose to become a sculptor as a challenge.

WHO WERE YOUR INFLUENCES AND OR ROLE MODELS?

My father, a ceramic artist, was the first to influence me, and later Michelangelo and Rodin.

WHO ENCOURAGED YOU?

No one encouraged me to learn sculpture. They thought it was hopeless for women to study sculpture.

DID YOU HAVE ANY FORMAL TRAINING?

Yes, I studied sculpture in the sculpture department of the Sichuan Fine Arts Institute for five years (B.A.), and later I went to the sculpture department of the Central Academy of Fine Arts in Beijing for one year (Post-Graduate).

DO YOU USE THE HUMAN FIGURE IN YOUR WORK?

My work often uses the human body either traditionally or in stylized ways.

DO YOU USE FOUND OBJECTS?

I have sometimes done so. I love experimentation.

DO YOU USE THE NATURAL WORLD?

I often use landscapes, textures and animals as my inspirations.

FREE-STANDING OR ATTACHED?

It all depends on the specific context, I have created sculptures either way. One of my specialities is relief, but many of my very large public works are free-standing, though of course always secured into the ground.

IS THE SCALE IMPORTANT?

Model sketches known as maquettes are very important as preliminaries to larger artworks; they can quickly and easily express one's ideas, especially when one is commissioned to create large public sculptures.

Mother and Child 2007 – Golmud, Qinghai, China

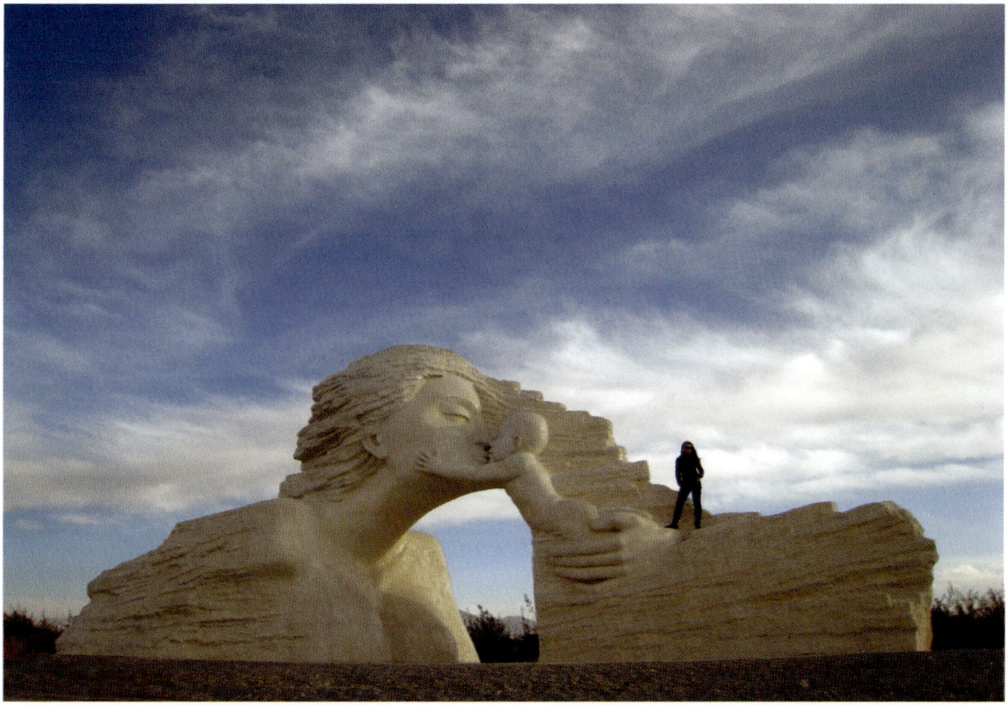

IS THE ENVIRONMENT IMPORTANT?

The location is an essential ingredient in the mix of creating sculpture. All sculpture is art within space, so must take the environment into very careful consideration.

EPHEMERAL OR LONG-LASTING?

I hope my work can be preserved for a long time. It is the continuation of my life.

MULTIMEDIA OR ONE MEDIUM?

My sculptures are made of stone, bronze, steel, cement and other materials including fibres.

IS THERE A PARTICULAR THEME OR THEMES WHICH ARE CENTRAL TO YOUR WORK?

Yes, as a female artist, I prefer the themes of life, mother and child, and samsara (the cycle of death and rebirth to which life in the material world is bound). Many works are made around these themes.

HOW DO YOU GET YOUR IDEAS FOR AN ARTWORK?

Nature, fine art in history, unexpected events in life, and so on.

Couple 2010 – Boryoung City, Korea

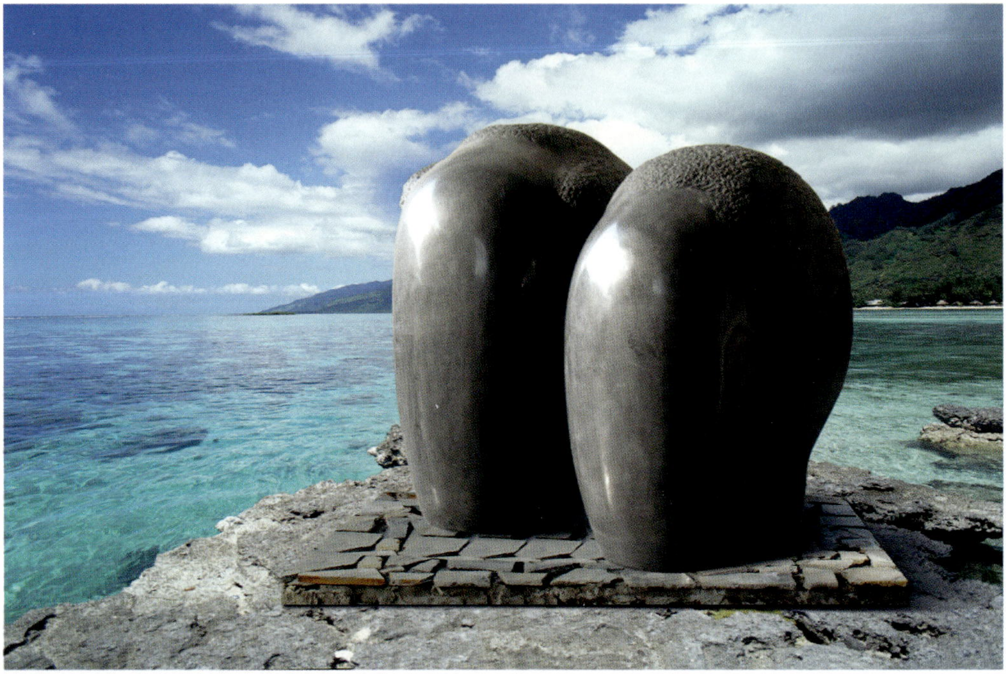

DO YOU LIKE TO DO COMMISSIONED WORK OR NOT?

I do. I like to undertake commissioned work, and I think most of the sculptures that great sculptors have done in the past were commissioned pieces. It is a dance in chains, more challenging than simply making one's own works.

TELL US HOW YOU HAVE DEVELOPED AS AN ARTIST.

I believe learning is a lifelong thing, as we can always improve various aspects of our abilities. Learning the approaches to fine art in all kinds of different cultures, keeping an open mind, are paramount. The development of the world today, and studying new materials and technology is also very important. At the same time, as an artist I always try to keep a childlike innocence, endowed with imagination and creativity, but of course the most important element still is hard work. I believe the old Chinese saying that "God rewards those who work hard".

WHERE IS YOUR SCULPTURE EXHIBITED?

In many public and corporate places throughout China and the world. I have also participated in sculpture exhibitions/symposia in China, South Korea, India, Vietnam, Taiwan and other countries.

IS IT MORE DIFFICULT FOR WOMEN ARTISTS TO MAKE A LIVING THAN MEN?

Yes, it is more difficult for all female sculptors than it is for men. Female artists may have to work twice as hard and sacrifice more to succeed than male artists. Female artists who have the courage and confidence face this reality. Only by using their own artistic language to express their unique visual experience and psychological experience can they achieve the same status as male artists.

TELL US ABOUT YOUR FAVOURITE SCULPTURES – YOUR OWN OR BY SOMEONE ELSE.

As a sculptor, I like a lot of sculptures, especially the excellent bronze wares, jade wares and Buddhist sculptures of ancient China, as well as Indian, Egyptian, African and Western classical sculptures, and many contemporary sculptures. It is impossible to pinpoint favourites.

WHAT'S NEXT?

In the future, I hope to make more works highlighting the traditional and contemporary, East and West, individuals and groups.

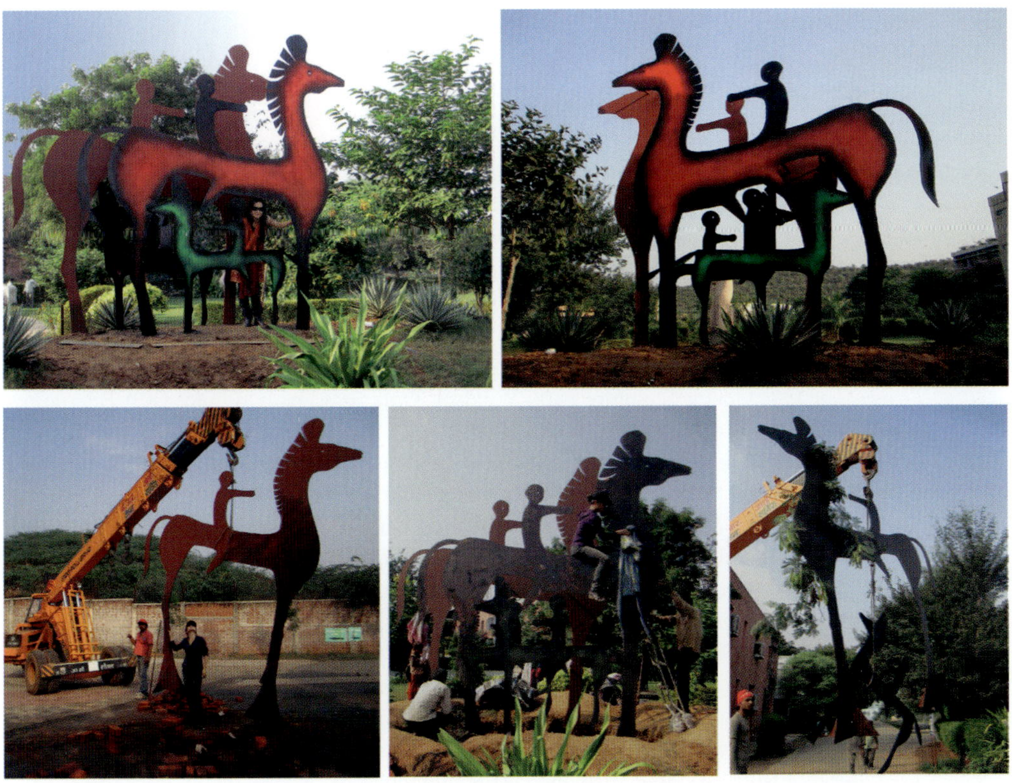

Horses 2010 – Gwalior, India and installation of the artwork

IMAGES

p. 3 *The Offering* Malvina Hoffman 1919. Photo: CC0

p.4 *Millicent Fawcett - Courage Calls* Gillian Wearing 2018 – Parliament Square. Photo: Garry Knight. CC0

p.10 *The Mist* Anna Golubkina 1899 decorative vase in the Russian Museum. Photo: CC0

p.12 *Hon* Niki de Saint Phalle 1966 – Moderna Museet, Sweden. Photo: CC0

p.13 *Colonial Dress* Susan Stockwell 2010 Photo: Colin Hampden-White courtesy of the artist.

p.14. *dock* Phyllida Barlow, Tate Britain, 2014 Photo: © Tate. Courtesy Hauser & Wirth.

p.15 *The Dinner Party* detail Judy Chicago 1979 © Judy Chicago. Photo: CC0

p.18 *Family Group* Janis Ridley. © Janis Ridley Photo courtesy of the artist

p.20-21 *The Sleeping Faun* Harriet Hosmer 1870, Cleveland Museum of Art Photo: CC0; *The Clasped Hands of Elizabeth and Robert Browning* Harriet Hosmer 1853, Metropolitan Museum of Art. Photo: CC0

p. 22-23 *The Death of Cleopatra* Edmonia Lewis 1876 – Smithsonian American Art Museum Photo: CC0 Hiawatha by Edmonia Lewis 1868 – Metropolitan Museum of Art. Photo: CC0

p. 24-25 *Sakuntala/Vertumnus and Pomona* 1905 – Musée Rodin, Paris. Photo: CC0/ADAGP; Camille Claudel in her studio with Jessie Lipscomb. c.1887 Photo: CC0

p.26-27 *Young Girl* Florence Wyle 1938 Photo: CC0; Partial view of *Queen Elizabeth Way Monument* by Frances Loring,1939 Photo: CC0 Photo of the artists by Gilbert A. Milne, 1950, Archives of Ontario.

p.28-29 *Figure For Landscape* 1960 – Getty Museum, Los Angeles. Photo: Cheryl Robson; Portrait of the artist © Bowness, Figure Archaean 1959 – Oxford. Photo: CC0 © Barbara Hepworth © Bowness

p.30-31 *Maman* 1999, Collection Guggenheim Museum, Bilbao, Spain © The Easton Foundation Photo: Didier Descouens; Portrait photo: Louise Bourgeois 1996 © Chris Felver

p.32-33 *Untitled* (S.037, S.031, S.053) c. 1955–72 De Young Museum, San Francisco Photo: Alexandra Courtis; Portrait photo by Xavier Lanier, 1969 © 2020; *Andrea* 1968, Ghirardelli Square, San Francisco. Photo: Nick Amoscato; © The Estate of Ruth Asawa / Artists Rights Society / DACS 2020 Courtesy The Estate of Ruth Asawa and David Zwirner

p.34-35 *Big Bellies* © Alina Szapocznikow 1968, KMM/The Netherlands Photo: Gerardus CC0 *Woman with child* © Alina Szapocznikow 1949 Warsaw. Photo: CC0. Courtesy of Hauser & Wirth

p.36-37 *Pumpkin* 1994, Naoshima Island, Japan. Photo: Ciakpicz CC0; *Narcissus Garden*, 1966/2009, Instituto Inhotim, Brazil, 2009 Photo: Stephanie Torres CC0. © Yayoi Kusama and Victoria Miro

p.38-39 *Dancing Nana* (yellow) 1995 Musée des Beaux Arts, Lille. Photo: Jean-Philippe Granger CC0 *The Footballers* 1993, the Olympic Museum, Lausanne Photo: Saliko CC0 © Niki de Saint Phalle Charitable Art Foundation / ADAGP, Paris and DACS, London 2020

p.40-41 *Flying Men* 1982,Odette Sculpture Park, Windsor, Ontario, Canada. Photo: CC0 *Paternoster,* Paternoster Square 1975 © The Elisabeth Frink Estate and Archive. All Rights Reserved, DACS

p.42-43 *Addendum* 1967, Tate, 1979 Photo: © Tate; *Hang Up* 1966, Art Institute of Chicago. Photo: Mark B. Schlemmer, Jeu de Parme, Paris 1993 © Eva Hesse Estate Courtesy Hauser & Wirth

p.44 *The Dinner Party* 1979 installation view © Judy Chicago. Gift of the Elizabeth A. Sackler Center for Feminist Art, Brooklyn Museum, NY. Photo: Donald Woodman/ ARS, NY/DACS, London 2020

p.46-47 *A.C.Q. (1)* © Senga Nengudi 2016-17 –Viva Arte Viva, Venice Biennale 2017 Courtesy Thomas Erben Gallery, New York; *Nuki Nuki: Across 118th St* by Senga Nengudi c. 1981/2013, Installation view, Henry Moore Institute, Leeds, 2018–19 Courtesy the Henry Moore Foundation Photo: John McKenzie

p.48-49 *The Serpent Fountain* 2017,Villa Medici, Rome. Photo: Jean-Pierre Dalbéra; © Annette Messager / ADAGP, Paris and DACS, London 2020

p.50-51 *The Wounded Star* 1992, Barcelona. Photo: CC0; *Glowing Core* 2015, La Llotja de Palma, Mallorca Photo: CC0 © Rebecca Horn /ADAGP, Paris and DACS, London 2020

James 2018 © Caroline Brisset

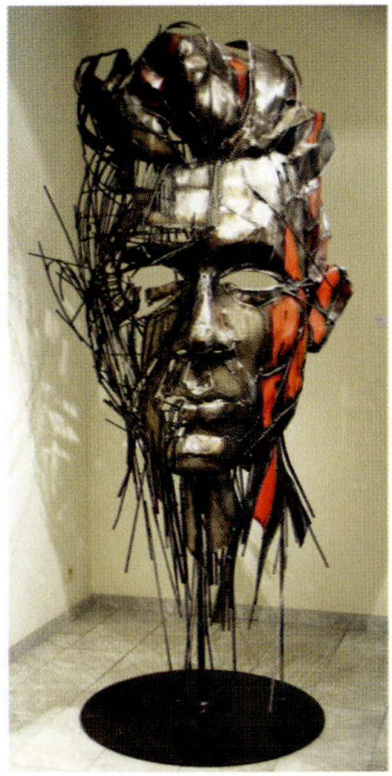

p.52-53 *untitled: upturned house 2* by Phyllida Barlow – Installation view – The Tate Modern, 2012 Photo: © Tate ; Portrait photo: Ruth Clark © Phyllida Barlow courtesy the artist/ Hauser & Wirth. *Rig* by Phyllida Barlow – Installation view, Hauser & Wirth, London 2011

p.54-56 *Hot Spot III* 2009 © Mona Hatoum. Courtesy the artist & MdbK Leipzig Photo: dotgain.info; *Impenetrable* 2009 – Installation view at Mathaf: Arab Museum of Modern Art, Doha © Mona Hatoum. Courtesy Mathaf: Arab Museum of Modern Art Photo: Markus Elblaus

p.58-59 *Cold Dark Matter: An Exploded View* © Cornelia Parker 1991. Collection: Tate. Photo: Hugo Glendinning. Courtesy the artist/Frith Street Gallery, London. Blown-up garden shed and contents, wire, light bulb. Installation view, Chisenhale Gallery, London.With thanks to the British Army; *Embryo Firearms* © Cornelia Parker 1995. Photo: Edward Woodman. Courtesy the artist/ Frith Street Gallery, London. Colt 45 guns in the earliest stage of production, Edition of 2. Special thanks to Colt Firearms Manufacturing, CT, USA

p.60-61 *Shibboleth* by Doris Salcedo 2007 – Tate Modern, London. Photo: David Levene www.davidlevene.co.uk ©Doris Salcedo

p. 62-63 *SITUATION Absolute Beach Man Rubble* © Sarah Lucas 2013 – Whitechapel Gallery, London. Photo: Stephen White; *Cigarette Tits (Idealized Smokers Chest II)* © Sarah Lucas c. 1999. Photo: Andrew Russeth, The Female Gaze at Cheim and Read, New York. Portrait: Sarah Lucas, *Fighting Fire with Fire*, 1996. Courtesy Sadie Coles HQ, London.

p. 64-65 *Holocaust Memorial* 1995-2000 – Jugendplatz Vienna Photo: CC0; *House* 1993, Mile End, East London Photo: CC0 © Rachel Whiteread. All rights reserved, DACS 2020

p.66-67 *The Light Pours Out of Me* Anya Gallaccio c. 2012 – Jupiter Artland, Wilkieston, West Lothian Photo: Jim Barton; *Orford Ness* Anya Gallaccio c. 2014 SNAP/Aldeburgh Festival Photo:Amanda Slater. © Anya Gallaccio. Courtesy the artist/Thomas Dane Gallery/Blum & Poe, Los Angeles//New York/Tokyo.

p.68-69 *Crawling* 2000. Photo: Jonty Wild Courtesy Yorkshire Sculpture Park; *Pink Lady Hare and Big Brown Dog* 1999. Photo: Tania Dolvers © Sophie Ryder; Portrait Photo: Gabriel Kenny-Ryder

p.70 *A Day in the Woods* © Caroline Kampfraath 2015 Courtesy of the artist

p.72–p.207 All photographs supplied courtesy of the individual artists, unless otherwise credited.

p.203 *James* 2018 © Caroline Brisset. Arthema Gallery, Brussels. Courtesy of the artist

p.204 *Mam'selle V* 2015 Musical Sculpture © Vivienne Lowe. Courtesy of the artist

p.206 *OLAUDAH EQUIANO* – African, slave, author, abolitionist 2006 © Christy Symington MRSS/ DACS 2020 Photo: Sylvain Deleu, Parliamentary Art Collection UK 2019

p.207 *The Thicket Inside* 2017 © Laura Ellen Bacon. Courtesy of the artist. Hignell Gallery.

Front cover: *The Scallop* © Maggi Hambling, 2003, Aldeburgh CC0; *Sakuntala* 1905, Camille Claudel, © Musée Rodin, Paris; *Figure For Landscape* 1960, © Barbara Hepworth © Bowness Photo: Cheryl Robson; *Cold Dark Matter: An Exploded View* © Cornelia Parker 1991 Collection: Tate. Photo: Hugo Glendinning; *Maman* 1999, Louise Bourgeois 1999, Guggenheim Museum, Spain CC0 © The Easton Foundation Photo: Didier Descouens; *Nana Mosaïque Noire,* 1999, Graubünden, Chur, Switzerland © Niki de Saint Phalle. Back cover: *The Wave* © Lucy Glendinning 2009, Blackpool. Photo credit: Sean Conboy.

Mam'selle V 2015 Musical Sculpture © Vivienne Lowe

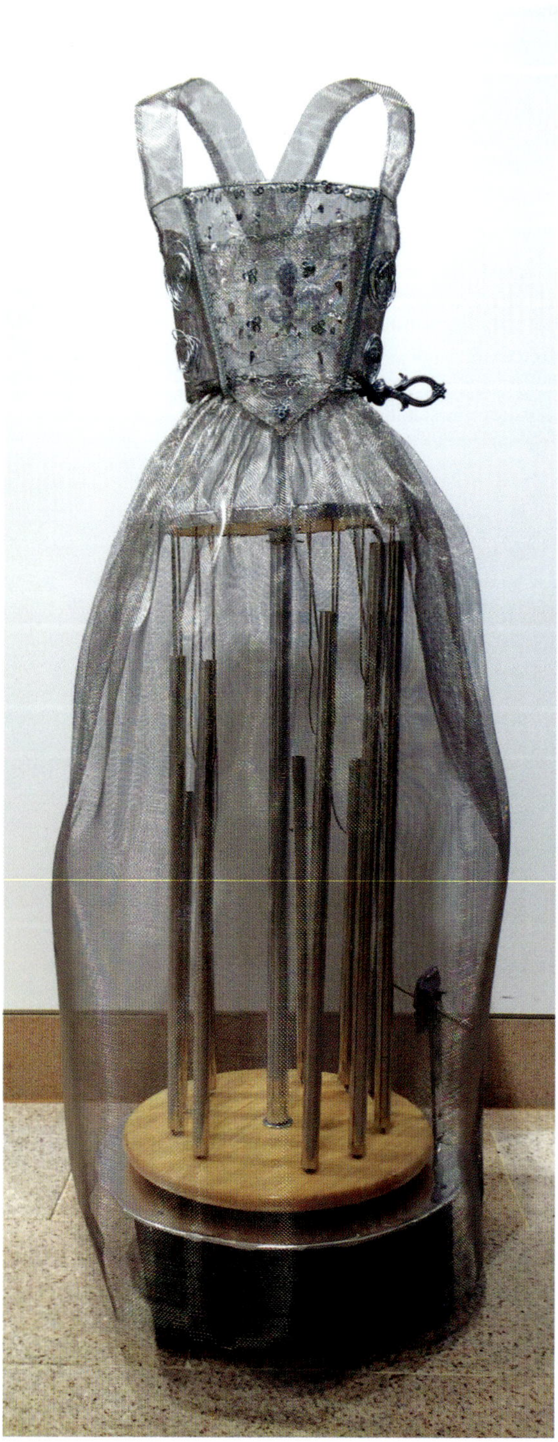

INDEX

OLAUDAH EQUIANO 2006 © Christy Symington Photo: Sylvain Deleu

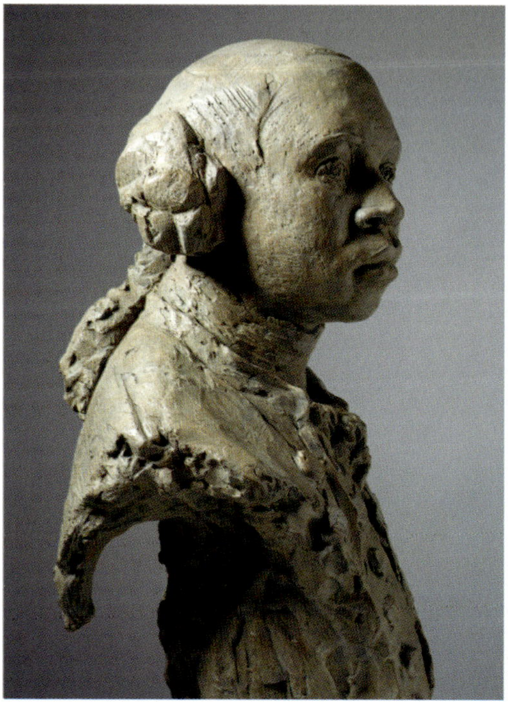

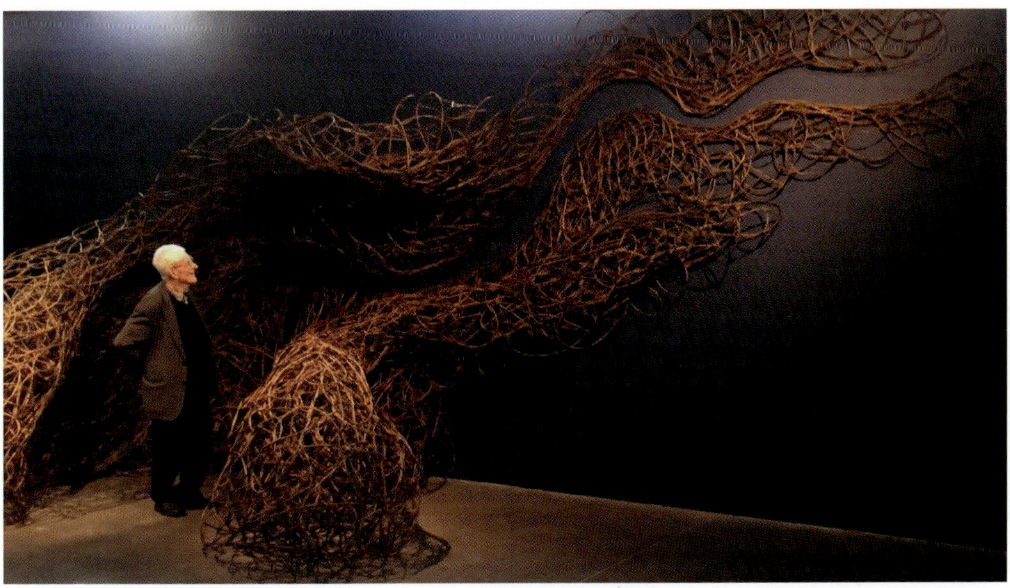

The Thicket Inside 2017 © Laura Ellen Bacon

FOR MORE GREAT BOOKS GO TO

www.supernovabooks.co.uk

Other books in this series:

50 Women in the Blues

50 Women in Film

50 Women in Theatre

and for fiction and drama by women

www.aurorametro.com